MANPOWER A
OF THE ᴇᴍᴘɪʀᴇ
IN THE TWO WORLD WARS

MANPOWER AND THE ARMIES OF THE BRITISH EMPIRE IN THE TWO WORLD WARS

EDITED BY
DOUGLAS E. DELANEY,
MARK FROST, AND
ANDREW L. BROWN

CORNELL UNIVERSITY PRESS
Ithaca and London

First published 2021 by Cornell University Press

Library of Congress Cataloging-in-Publication Data

Names: Delaney, Douglas E. (Douglas Edward), 1964– editor. | Frost, Mark (Mark Richard), 1974–editor. | Brown, Andrew L. (Andrew Lawrence), 1968– editor.
Title: Manpower and the armies of the British Empire in the two world wars / edited by Douglas E. Delaney, Mark Frost, and Andrew L. Brown.
Description: Ithaca, New York : Cornell University Press, 2021. | Includes bibliographical references and index.
Identifiers: LCCN 2020039600 (print) | LCCN 2020039601 (ebook) | ISBN 9781501755835 (hardcover) | ISBN 9781501755842 (paperback) | ISBN 9781501755859 (epub) | ISBN 9781501755866 (pdf)
Subjects: LCSH: Great Britain. Army–Colonial forces– History–20th century. | Great Britain. Army–History—World War, 1914 -1918. | Great Britain. Army—History–World War, 1939–1945. | World War, 1914–1918–Manpower–Great Britain. | World War, 1939–1945–Manpower–Great Britain. | Commonwealth countries–Armed Forces–History–20th century.
Classification: LCC UA668 .M36 2021 (print) | LCC UA668 (ebook) | DDC 940.4 / 1241–dc23
LC record available at https:/ / lccn.loc.gov / 2020039600
LC ebook record available at https:/ / lccn.loc.gov / 2020039601

In memory of Private James Hewitt, 13th Battalion,
Canadian Expeditionary Force

CONTENTS

Conclusion: The Many Dimensions
of Mobilizing Military Manpower
DOUGLAS E. DELANEY AND
ANDREW L. BROWN   214

ACKNOWLEDGMENTS

This collection would not have been possible without the support of the Social Sciences and Humanities Research Council of Canada (SSHRC) and the Canada Research Chair (CRC) in War Studies at the Royal Military College of Canada (RMC), for which we are grateful. SSHRC and CRC funding allowed us to exchange ideas in person and really workshop the book when we went over each other's drafts. We are also are grateful for the assistance of several people at RMC, including Suzanne Robertson, who made all the administrative arrangements, Jaya Surapaneni, who finalized all the travel claims, and Kevin Brushett, chair of the Department of History, who helped us knock down so many administrative obstacles.

For the collection itself, we wish to thank our contributors for their chapters and their patience with us as editors. At Cornell University Press, Emily Andrew and Alexis Siemon were wonderful—meticulous, patient, encouraging, and kind. We also owe thanks to the anonymous reviewers, whose insightful comments helped improve the final product, and to Caroline Vary-O'Neal, who formatted the manuscript.

The following institutions have kindly given permission to reproduce material to which they own the copyright: the Trustees of the Imperial War Museum; the Trustees of the Liddell Hart Centre for Military Archives; Library and Archives Canada; Archives New Zealand; and Tameside Local Studies and Archives Centre. Documents quoted from the UK National Archives and Parliamentary Papers are Crown Copyright.

Finally, this book is dedicated to Private James Hewitt, 13th Battalion, Canadian Expeditionary Force (CEF). Born in Tunbridge Wells, Kent, in 1889, Hewitt, an unmarried fireman, emigrated to Canada, joined the CEF in September 1915, and died on 13 June 1916, during the 1st Canadian Division counterattack at Mont Sorrel. His name is emblazoned on the Menin Gate in Ypres, Belgium, along with 54,606 other British, Canadian, Australian, South African, Indian, and British West Indian soldiers who have no known grave.

ABBREVIATIONS

2NZEF	2nd New Zealand Expeditionary Force
AAG	assistant adjutant-general
ACF	Active Citizen Forces
AFP	African Film Productions
AFV	armoured fighting vehicle
AG	adjutant-general
AIF	Australian Imperial Force
AJHR	*Appendices to the Journals of the House of Representatives*
AMS	Army Medical Services
ANC	African National Congress
AN&MEF	Australian Naval and Military Expeditionary Force
ANZ	Archives New Zealand
ANZAC	Australian and New Zealand Army Corps
AOH	Australian Official History
Arty.	Artillery
ATC	Australian Training Centre
ATS	Auxiliary Territorial Service
AWM	Australian War Memorial
AWOL	Absent Without Leave
BC	British Columbia
BCATP	British Commonwealth Air Training Plan
BEF	British Expeditionary Force
BL	British Library
BNAF	British North African Force
BOI	Bureau of Information
Bty	Battery
CAB	cabinet
CC	Cape Corps
CCORI	Central Council for the Organisation of Recruiting in Ireland
CCS	Casualty Clearing Station
CEF	Canadian Expeditionary Force

CFAD	Cape Fortress Air Defence
CGA	Canadian Garrison Artillery
CGS	chief of the general staff
CIGS	chief of the imperial general staff
CIM	Censor Indian Mail
CIM	Controller of Industrial Manpower
CO	commanding officer
COTT	Central Organisation of Technical Training
CSM	company sergeant-major
CWAC	Canadian Women's Army Corps
DAG	deputy adjutant-general
DIA	Department of Internal Affairs
DNS	Director of National Service
DVA	Department of Veterans Affairs
FFI	free from infection
GOC	general officer commanding
GOCRA	general officer commanding Royal Artillery
GOI	British government in India
HMSO	Her/His Majesty's Stationery Office
HQ OMFC	Headquarters Overseas Military Forces of Canada
IMC	Indian and Malay Corps
INC	Indian National Congress
IOR	India Records Office
IRA	Irish Republican Army
IRFU	Irish Rugby Football Union
IST	Imperial Service Troops
IWM	Imperial War Museum
LAC	Library and Archives Canada
LHCMA	Liddell Hart Centre for Military Archives
LSIC	Labour Supply Investigation Committee
MAC	Motor Ambulance Convoy
MD	Military Department
MLA	Member of the Legislative Assembly
MOA	Mass Observation Archive
MO	Medical Officer
MP	Member of Parliament
NAA	National Archives of Australia
NAI	National Archives of India
NASA	National Archives of South Africa
NCO	noncommissioned officer

NEAS	Non-European Army Services
NFA	Natal Field Artillery
NLA	National Library of Australia
NLI	National Library of Ireland
NLNZ	National Library of New Zealand
NMC	Native Military Corps
NRMA	National Resources Mobilization Act
NS	Nova Scotia
NSS	National Selective Service
NV	National Volunteers
OCB	Officer Cadet Battalion
OCTU	Officer Cadet Training Unit
ON	Ontario
ONS	Organization for National Security
OR	other ranks
OTC	Officer Training Corps
PDC	Physical Development Centre
PEI	Prince Edward Island
PJBD	Permanent Joint Board on Defene
PIN	Ministry of Pensions and National Insurance
PT	physical training
Q	Quarter-Master Services
R	Rupee
RA	Royal Artillery
RAF	Royal Air Force
RAMC	Royal Army Medical Corps
RASC	Royal Army Service Corps
RCAF	Royal Canadian Air Force
RCGA	Royal Canadian Garrison Artillery
RCN	Royal Canadian Navy
RGA	Royal Garrison Artillery
RMLI	Royal Marine Light Infantry
RMT	reserve motor transport
RMO	Regimental Medical Officer
RN	Royal Navy
RO	recruiting officer
RSM	regimental sergeant-major
SAAF	South African Air Force
SAEC	South African Engineer Corps
SANDFA	South African National Defence Force Archives, Pretoria

SANDF, DOC	South African National Defence Force, Documentation Centre
SANF	South African Naval Force
SAP	South African Police
SAR&H	South African Railways and Harbours
SAWAS	South African Women's Auxiliary Services
SIW	Self-Inflicted Wounds
SMC	Secretary of the Militia Council
TA	Territorial Army
TF	Territorial Force
TNA	The National Archives (Kew)
UDF	Union Defence Force
UWH	Union War History
UVF	Ulster Volunteer Force
VC	Victoria Cross
VCO	viceroy's-commissioned officers
VD	venereal disease
WA	War Archives
WMA	War Measures Act
WO	War Office
WOSB	War Office Selection Board
WVF	World Veterans Federation

MANPOWER AND THE ARMIES
OF THE BRITISH EMPIRE
IN THE TWO WORLD WARS

Introduction
Britain and the Military Manpower Problems
of the Empire, 1900–1945

DOUGLAS E. DELANEY AND MARK FROST

Manpower was the central military problem of the British Empire and Commonwealth during the first half of the twentieth century. British military planners of the Edwardian era wrestled with it, again and again. In almost every war scenario they contemplated, in almost every military emergency they imagined, they bumped into continental armies that were both big and well organized—Russians on the North-West Frontier of India, Germans in France or in Holland or in both. These prospects unnerved the senior soldiers of a small country with a relatively small population. The great powers of the continent counted their war establishments in millions, while the British regular army could barely scrape together 120,000 troops for expeditionary operations, as a War Office memorandum from 1903 noted: "The population of the United Kingdom is 41,606,220; that of Germany 57,000,000. England, however, only prepares in peace for active service abroad of three Army Corps and three cavalry brigades—a total force of about 120,000 men. . . . Germany, on the other hand, has available for defence an army of over 3,000,000."[1] And the Russians, with a population double that of Germany, had a standing army twice the size. Britain alone could never match those military forces. Some adroit diplomacy could help, and it did, a little. The Anglo-Japanese alliance of 1902 and the solidification of the *entente cordiale* with France and Russia (1904–1907) reduced the number of potential adversaries, but the possibility of a confrontation with a first-class continental land power—Germany—still remained. Building a bigger army based on peacetime conscription was a political impossibility in Britain; five compulsory service bills were defeated in Parliament between 1908 and 1914.

But Britain did have an empire of more than 390 million people who could be tapped for manpower. As early as 1901, War Office planners recorded their hopes for colonial forces in the future:

> No one who has studied the military needs of the Empire, and followed the course of the present [South African] war, can have failed to notice the vital importance of [colonial contingents] in the future of a thoroughly sound system of Imperial defence. . . . The day may come—there is no reason why it should not come—when 10,000 of such troops may be ready in Australia, 10,000 in South Africa and 10,000 in Canada. . . . Could India be made strong enough not only to look after herself, but to be a radiating centre of force, instead of, as now, an anxiety to the Empire, most Imperial problems would be solved. England would be . . . free to send help (when she could safely do so) to the Mediterranean, or Egypt or elsewhere.[2]

Indeed, as studies from the 2010s have shown, British military authorities put a lot of effort into forging colonial forces that were capable of working with the British Army in time of war.[3]

It paid off—and well beyond 10,000-man contingents. (See table 0.1.) Between 1914 and 1918, Britain, India, and the dominions mobilized a combined total of nearly 8.5 million men and women for their armed forces. By 1916, there was a sixty-division British Expeditionary Force (BEF) in France and Belgium, to which the dominions contributed ten-plus well-equipped and British Army–compatible infantry divisions and a cavalry brigade, while the Indian Army fielded two cavalry divisions. By 1918, there were seven Indian divisions and two Australian and New Zealand Army Corps (ANZAC) mounted divisions in the Middle East, and this was on top of sixteen British divisions in the Middle East, Africa, and Salonika. Efforts to create compatible armies that were capable of expansion in time of crisis paid dividends during the Second World War as well. India alone raised eighteen divisions over the course of the war (plus two training divisions) from the largest all-volunteer army ever assembled: more than 2 million Indians being recruited between 1939 and 1945. Canada put three infantry divisions, two armored divisions, and two independent armored brigades into the field, and the dominion also raised another three divisions for home defense. Australia assembled four infantry divisions and one armored division for the 2nd Australian Imperial

Table 0.1   Mobilization of military manpower, United Kingdom, dominions, India

COUNTRY	TOTAL POPULATION[a]	ARMED SERVICES[b]	ARMY
1914–1918			
United Kingdom	45,370,530	5,704,416	5,052,856
Canada	7,449,262[c]	628,964[d]	619,636
New Zealand	1,008,468	128,525	127,986
Australia	4,455,005	416,809	412,584
South Africa	5,973,394	136,070[e]	136,070
India	315,086,372	1,440,437[f]	1,440,437
1939–1945			
United Kingdom	47,762,000[g]	5,521,000	3,788,000
Canada	11,506,655	1,051,600[h]	730,625
New Zealand	1,639,000	224,000[i]	160,000
Australia	7,137,000	993,000	727,200
South Africa	10,522,000	345,000	291,031
India	388,998,000[j]	2,125,503	2,065,554

Sources: Douglas E. Delaney, *The Imperial Army Project: Britain and the Land Forces of the Dominions and India, 1902–1945* (Oxford: Oxford University Press, 2017), 103, 239; War Office, *Statistics of the Military Effort of the British Empire during the Great War, 1914–1920* (London: HMSO, 1922), 740, 756–79; Randal Gray and Christopher Argyle, eds., *Chronicle of the First World War*, vol. 2: *1917–1921* (Oxford: Facts on File, 1991), 288; G. W. L. Nicholson, *Canadian Expeditionary Force, 1914–1919* (Montreal-Kingston: McGill-Queen's University Press, 2015), 535; Arthur Jose, *The Official History of Australia in the War of 1914–1918*, vol. 9: *The Royal Australian Navy* (Sydney: Angus & Robertson, 1941), appendix 2, 472, appendix 5, 475; Henry Newbolt, *History of the Great War*, vol. 5: *Naval Operations* (London: Longman's, 1931) appendix J, 433; Government of Canada, *The Canada Year Book, 1914* (Ottawa: King's Printer, 1915), 74–76; Commonwealth Bureau of Census and Statistics, *Official Year Book of the Commonwealth of Australia, No. 12, 1919* (Melbourne: Government Printer, 1919), 1019–29; New Zealand Department of Statistics, *The New Zealand Official Year Book, 1919* (Wellington: Government Printer, 1920), 254–62.

[a]Population figures are official estimates for the years closest to 1914 and 1939.
[b]The figures provide estimates for the gross number who served during the wars.
[c]Includes Newfoundland and Labrador (population 242,619).
[d]Not including an additional 11,922 personnel from Newfoundland and Labrador who were mobilized during the war.
[e]Does not include 82,769 "black" laborers and 1,925 "coloured" troops.
[f]Approximately 2,300 Indian personnel served with the Indian Royal Marine (IRM).
[g]Estimated population actually in the country (resident population) in June 1939. This estimate excludes members of the armed forces serving overseas and merchant seamen at sea.
[h]Including women and those mobilized under the National Resources Mobilization Act.
[i]Includes transfers of servicemen between arms and men who enlisted more than once.
[j]Not including Burma.

Force (2 AIF), plus another two armored cavalry divisions and eight infantry divisions (not completely manned) for the militia and home defense; two of those infantry divisions saw active service in the New Guinea campaign. New Zealand sent one infantry division to the Mediterranean and a two-brigade division to the Pacific, where it worked under American command until its disbandment in October 1944. The South Africans sent two infantry divisions to the Western Desert and later sent an armored division to Italy.

This was extraordinary, in the truest sense of the word. There was nothing ordinary about Britain or its empire raising big armies in war. If there was a British way in warfare, it was to use the Royal Navy for control of sea lanes of communication, ally with continental powers that could field mass armies, finance those allies when necessary, and send relatively small expeditionary forces as a sign of Britain's commitment to the coalition.[4] The rest of the time, the British Army was engaged in imperial policing, the Indian Army was focused on internal security and small-scale frontier wars, and the dominions were barely interested in military affairs. So when time came to mobilize mass armies for the First World War it was largely an ad hoc affair. Britain, India, and the dominions may have agreed on standard building blocks for army expansion—common organizations, equipment, and staff procedures—but no infrastructure or legislation was in place to raise imperial armies, keep them fighting in wartime, and demobilize them efficiently when peace came. Raising armies was an exceedingly complex business. It was more than counting people, putting them into uniform, and assigning them to units and formations, as military and political authorities across the empire learned between 1914 and 1918. It demanded measures and processes for recruitment and selection in voluntary military systems and equally efficient measures and processes for registration and assignment in armies built on conscription. It demanded training establishments capable of transforming factory workers and farmers into riflemen, in addition to providing the officers, staffs, and commanders to lead them in battle. It demanded policies and welfare measures, such as mail delivery and leave, to maintain morale. It demanded balance between the needs of the other armed services (navies and air forces), industry, and agriculture. And it demanded often-overlooked medical services to mend soldiers when wounded, as well as programs and pensions to look after them when their fighting time was done.

This was why, in 1920, the Committee of Imperial Defence established a standing interdepartmental subcommittee to look at how to manage manpower if it ever became necessary to raise mass armies again. The Sub-Committee on Man-Power deliberated only intermittently throughout the interwar period, but it did manage to sketch principles for national registration, national service (conscription), a schedule of industries and occupations of national importance that should be exempted conscription if it came to that, and a Ministry of National Service to manage it all. Britain, India, and the dominions also committed to maintaining military compatibility, which had been so crucial to raising and fighting imperial armies during the First World War, and all the respective general staffs stayed in close contact to make sure of it.[5] The imperial mobilization of the Second World War did not happen without some difficulty, but it was far less a seat-of-the-pants affair than the mobilization that had taken place a generation earlier.

This volume brings together a diverse group of distinguished scholars for a transnational examination of army mobilization in the British Empire and Commonwealth during the era of the two world wars. It does so by looking specifically at Britain, India, Canada, Australia, New Zealand, and South Africa. While not the whole empire by any stretch, these six constituencies accounted for the majority of combat troops mobilized. During the First World War, for example, they accounted for 99 percent of 2,580,000 British Empire fighting troops deployed in October 1918.[6] They provided the great bulk of military manpower during the Second World War as well.

The inspiration for this undertaking originally came to us through the work of two esteemed colleagues: one a Canadian who writes on African military history, the other a New Zealander who writes on his country's military past.[7] We were struck by how different were the manpower problems in each of their studies. Tim Stapleton's essay on "The Africanization of British Imperial Forces in the East African Campaign" is a fascinating examination of how, in 1917, the crushing manpower demands of the Western Front forced British military authorities to rely almost exclusively on African troops for the fight against German forces in East Africa.[8] New Zealand's military manpower problems, on the other hand, had nothing to do with shortages. As John Crawford tells us, New Zealand, which had been conscripting for overseas service since 1916, had a reinforcement problem—*too many* reinforcements, to be precise, and this caused domestic problems for the government of William Massey, who had to convince his public that the dominion was not contributing disproportionately to the imperial war effort.[9] Stapleton and Crawford reminded us that First World War manpower problems were not simply issues of never enough men or finding enough men or even of moving men from one theater to another. Decisions taken for one theater of war or part of the empire affected other theaters of war or parts of the empire. What the Stapleton and Crawford essays really did was suggest how rich and varied the study of military manpower could be, especially within the British Empire system. And that led us to the current volume. It is not a definitive and exhaustive study—military manpower in the British Empire is too complex an issue to be captured in any one volume—but this collection does comprise new transnational perspectives on the subject.

To date, no book has been written on the manpower of the British Empire and Commonwealth before, during, and after war. There are some useful compilations of raw statistical data that encapsulate empire-wide figures, especially for the First World War.[10] Most manpower studies, however, have been completed for national armies, in a somewhat "siloed" approach, and usually for a single war. For the United Kingdom, Keith Grieves has examined British responses to the competing manpower demands of the armed services and industry, while Peter Simkins has looked exclusively at the project of generating "new army" divisions.[11] The British Civil Series of histories for the Second World War includes a volume called *Manpower Problems* by Major-General A. J. K. Piggot, but, at only ninety pages, it is highly selective as to topics examined.[12] The official history, *Manpower* by H. M. D. Parker, details the work of the Ministry of Labour and National Service, but while it remains the standard work, its concern is exclusively British.[13] Jeremy Crang has produced a fascinating social and organizational history of the army at home, 1939–1945, and Allan Allport examines how that army responded to the citizen soldiers who filled its ranks.[14] These British war histories and compilations, while useful for understanding how the United Kingdom generated military forces, do not analyze the contributions of India or the dominions and how they related to British military forces.

Indian and dominion military histories have been equally stove-piped. In Canada, manpower and conscription have garnered much attention, particularly the latter because it has been such a divisive issue. In 1977, J. L. Granatstein and J. M. Hitsman published *Broken Promises*, a book dedicated to the issue of compulsory military service during both world wars. Richard Holt has examined the organizations, structures, and polices that were created "on the fly" to handle Canada's complex manpower issues during the First World War, while Daniel Byers's *Zombie Army* has done the same for the army of the Second World War.[15] For the Australian Army, manpower and conscription have been examined in two volumes of the official history series on the Second World War.[16] These issues have also been explored in army institutional histories by Jeffrey Grey and Albert Palazzo, as well as in the social history studies of Joan Beaumont.[17] In New Zealand, Paul Baker and John Crawford have written useful studies on the dominion's manpower issues during the First World War, while W. G. Stevens's 1958 publication, *Problems of 2 NZEF*, remains the enduring source for the Second World War.[18] Ian van der Waag and H. J. Martin and Neil Orpen have captured the South African mobilization experience during the two world wars.[19] And there have been a number of excellent institutional studies on the expansion of the Indian Army during the same period. These include works by Kaushik Roy, Daniel Marston, David Omissi, S. N. Prasad, and George Morton-Jack.[20] The present volume seeks to build on this body of dominion and Indian scholarship and connect it more closely to the military manpower history of Great Britain.

The literature on the postwar care and compensation of veterans is not nearly so well developed as that of operational military history, but it is growing. To date, Julie Anderson, Deborah Cohen, Jeffrey Reznick, Marina Larsson, and Alison Parr have completed excellent national studies of disabled veterans in Britain, Australia, and New Zealand, respectively.[21] Historian Jessica Meyer and clinicians Edgar Jones and Simon Wessely have critically reviewed the experiences of psychologically scarred British veterans from both world wars.[22] Serge Durflinger has written a captivating examination of Canada's war-blinded.[23] And authors Terry Copp and Mark Humphries have compiled a unique collection of primary sources reflecting the diversity of British Commonwealth experience with battle exhaustion, but a truly transnational study of postwar veteran experience still awaits an author.[24]

There are only three transnational studies that deal with manpower: F. W. Perry's *The Commonwealth Armies* (1988), Roger Broad's *Volunteers and Pressed Men* (2016), and Steve Marti's *For Home and Empire* (2019).[25] Both Perry and Broad deal with the raising of armies in Britain, India, and the dominions during the two world wars, but theirs are largely studies of government policy, neither dealing directly with the experience of soldiers themselves, let alone the postwar care of ex-servicemen and women and their families. Marti's unique and illuminating focus on voluntary mobilization in three dominions—Canada, Australia, and New Zealand—places voluntary enlistments for the armed services on par with community volunteerism and offers insights into social divisions based on class, gender, race, ethnicity, and indigeneity. Demobilization and after-war care for veterans was beyond the scope of Marti's work, as it was for Perry and Broad. The current collection is the first "follow through" of before-war, during-war, and after-war manpower issues from an imperial, or transnational, perspective. How did the British Empire and Commonwealth mobilize manpower for their armies during the two world wars? And how did they care for veterans, both able-bodied and disabled, when the fighting was over?

Answering these questions requires a multinational and multifaceted approach, one that places the distinct narratives of individual nations in a comparative perspective. The nations of the British Empire tackled similar manpower challenges in two world wars, but they did not always tackle those challenges in the same way. Take the issue of conscription during the First World War, for example. The empire badly needed more men for its armies in 1917, but getting them was no simple matter. Home fronts affected the manning of armies everywhere, although rarely in the same way. The United Kingdom was already conscripting young men for its military forces in 1917 (except in Ireland), and so was New Zealand because the domestic political situation in both countries was fairly stable and the populations were firmly behind the war effort. This was not the case across the empire. The Australian government failed twice in plebiscites to conscript men for overseas service, largely as a result of opposition from organized labor and the Irish Catholic followers of Archbishop Daniel Mannix. The results of Australia's failure to impose conscription manifested themselves most acutely in October 1918, when the Australian Corps had to be sidelined, permanently as it turned out, for lack of reinforcements. For its part, the Canadian government imposed compulsory military service despite the opposition of French-speaking Canadians and farmers and after having fought a very nasty and divisive election campaign in December 1917. Conscription allowed the Canadian Corps to fight on at full strength until the last day of the war, but the issue led to several deadly riots at home and left ethnic cleavages that lasted decades. In India, conscription was out of the question, the "mutiny" of 1857 never being far from the minds of military planners in the subcontinent. The bottom line is that each jurisdiction handled conscription differently. And yet, in spite of divergent approaches to recruitment and selection, all the armies of the empire adhered to fairly standard training systems for both officers and other ranks, which in turn fostered interoperability. These matters were difficult to understand then, and they remain difficult to understand nearly a century later. This volume digs deeply into a variety of military manpower issues and experiences, exposes and explains the complexities, and thereby provides a fuller understanding of how the British Empire and Commonwealth mobilized during challenging times.

We examine three aspects of military manpower: (1) recruitment, conscription, and selection; (2) the training, employment, and experience of the soldiers themselves; and (3) demobilization and veterans' care. We also offer findings and observations based on these lines of inquiry. Jean Bou explores the first of these topics with his examination of the expansion of the Australian Imperial Force (AIF) during the First World War and the various organizational and political problems associated with creating, expanding, and maintaining it (chapter 1). Richard S. Grayson reflects on appeals to Irish identity during the First World War and considers how both nationalists and unionists viewed enlistment in the British Army as a way of furthering their competing political goals (chapter 2). Men enlisted for a variety of reasons. Kent Fedorowich and Charles Booth, using the city of Bristol as a case study, examine the experience of thousands of British-born migrants who joined dominion armies or returned to enlist in British regiments during the First World War (chapter 5). Daniel Byers investigates the complexities of governing and administering a country mobilized for total war (chapter 11). He looks at how Canadian prime minister W. L. Mackenzie King and his government fought the Second World War on a scale that no one had previously imagined possible and thus had to overcome some early and predictable inefficiencies. Kaushik Roy scrutinizes manpower mobilization for the Indian Army during the two world wars, looking at which communities Indian military authorities targeted for recruitment and why (chapter 6). Ian van der Waag demonstrates how political and racial divisions in South Africa undermined the union's Second World War effort (chapter 12), and Ian McGibbon explores the difficulties New Zealand faced, despite conscription, in meeting its overseas and home-defense commitments between 1939 and 1945 (chapter 13). Paul Bartrop examines how the Australian government, desperate for manpower, converted "enemy aliens" into soldiers in the 8th Employment Company in 1942 (chapter 9).

The question of training, employment, and experience of troops features prominently in four chapters. Roger Sarty uses the example of the Canadian Garrison Artillery during the First World War to demonstrate the importance of a relatively small nucleus of expertise to the massive expansion of the Canadian Expeditionary Force (CEF), the artillery arm in particular (chapter 4). Gary Sheffield presents a comparative treatment of British army officers in the two world wars, examining recruitment, training, and battlefield performance, with particular emphasis on officer-man relations (chapter 7). Emma Newlands looks at what manpower meant for the individual person in her examination of civilian-to-soldier transitions in the British Army of the Second World War (chapter 10). And Jonathan Fennell analyses the mobilization of British and Commonwealth manpower during the Second World War, what the war meant to the soldiers who fought it, and how soldiers' expectations affected armies in the field. He argues that, in many ways, the conflict was a contested, divisive experience and a far cry from a "People's War" (chapter 8).

How did armies conserve manpower during war and care for the sick and disabled in the peace that followed? Jessica Meyer considers how manpower conservation influenced the work of the Royal Army Medical Corps (RAMC) in the areas of recruitment, treatment, and rehabilitation during the First World War (chapter 3). She also looks at how the British state cared for veterans and managed the reintegration of demobilized soldiers into the workforce. Meghan Fitzpatrick documents how Britain and the dominions met the needs of a new generation of veterans in the decade that followed the Second World War. Comparing British and dominion pensions and care systems, she explores the sensitive problems of measuring disability and quantifying human suffering. She also considers the unprecedented education and training opportunities available to veterans, some of whom took advantage of them, some of whom did not (chapter 14).

Military manpower is a matter of national policy and grand strategy. The following chapters remind us that it is also a human matter. Managing manpower affects the most vital assets of any nation: people. As Sir Ronald Adam, the adjutant-general of the British Army from 1941 to 1946, later wrote, "Men and women remain the most important assets of an Army."[26]

CHAPTER 1

The Government That Could Not Say No and Australia's Military Effort, 1914–1918

Jean Bou

When war broke out in 1914, the Commonwealth of Australia was a nation barely more than a dozen years old, the federation of the Australian colonies having occurred only in 1901. From a population of fewer than 5 million people, the country eventually sent 330,000 men overseas, where they fought at Gallipoli, in the Sinai-Palestine campaign, and on the Western Front. For a young country, this was an enormous undertaking and one that dwarfed anything that had been undertaken to that point. Unsurprisingly, perhaps, there were significant difficulties. This chapter outlines the raising and expansion of the Australian Imperial Force (AIF) as well as some of the policy choices that accompanied that process. It describes how the government's ardent commitment to the empire and the war led, in combination with what might be best described as naivety and an underdeveloped administrative and military capacity, to a number of systemic problems and profoundly divisive politics. To that end, this chapter examines how the AIF was created, how and when it was expanded, and how these steps combined with poor decision-making to cause problems in administration, training, command, and finding enough men. Finally, it considers the link between the 1914–1916 decisions to expand the force and the government's unsuccessful efforts in 1916 and 1917 to introduce conscription for overseas service via plebiscite—efforts that split the ruling Labor Party and fractured the country politically and along sectarian lines.

Creating and Expanding an Expeditionary Force

The military forces inherited from the six separate Australian colonies by the new Commonwealth of Australia in March 1901 were a mixed bag. Apart from a small cadre of instructors, administrators, and fortress gunners, all the troops and officers were part-time soldiers of various kinds. Some were unpaid volunteers, although most were actually paid to don a uniform. But their part-time character, the variability of colonial resources, and the policy choices of their half-interested colonial governments meant that equipment was insufficient or antiquated, and military competence generally low. Postfederation reforms, begun by the first and only general officer commanding (GOC) of the Commonwealth Military Forces, Major-General Sir Edward Hutton, and continued by other Australian and British officers, were beset with difficulties and achieved only modest success. In light of this, and driven in large part by growing anxieties about Japan, a more radical idea was gaining traction by the end of the decade, and, in 1911–1912, what is generally known as the Universal Training era began.

Although there were a variety of exemptions, mostly for those who lived too far away from a town where they could parade, this compulsory scheme aimed to make all able-bodied males part-time militiamen, beginning with cadets in their teens and ending when they passed out of the ranks after fourteen years' service, aged twenty-six. The defense budget and the forces expanded dramatically under the compulsory training scheme, but the system was hamstrung by the myriad complications of part-time service and an underdeveloped military system, which was still in its infancy in 1914.[1] Moreover, the provisions of the Defence Act forbade sending these men overseas unless they volunteered for active service. The result was that, when war came, a separate expeditionary force had to be created, which left the militia to continue at home, where it withered on the vine as military resources went to the fighting forces overseas.

As war erupted in August 1914, the need for expeditionary forces demanded the government's attention. The first operational requirement was capturing German New Guinea, and to do that the Australian Naval and Military Expeditionary Force (AN&MEF) was hastily raised and sent northward, where, after a few skirmishes, it ejected the Germans that September and expanded Australia's modest Pacific empire.[2] This effort was soon overshadowed by the creation of the AIF, which was to be dispatched to the main theaters of war. In early August, the outgoing government of Joseph Cook, then in "caretaker mode" due to a looming federal election and seemingly spurred by inaccurate reports that Canada had promised 30,000 troops, offered a 20,000-man force to London. In the heat of an election campaign, the Labor opposition leader, Andrew Fisher, did not hesitate to commit the nation, famously, to its "last man and last shilling," and, upon winning the election in September, his government soon offered more troops. The AIF's first contingent, made up of a complete infantry division and a light horse brigade, left Australia on 1 November after a hurried period of raising and equipping the units. More was soon on offer. A fourth infantry brigade and two more light horse brigades were raised by the end of 1914, to be followed by two more infantry brigades early in 1915. These latest infantry brigades helped establish in Egypt the 2nd Australian Division, which soon went to Gallipoli, where it joined the 1st Australian Division and the New Zealand and Australian Division.

The end of the Gallipoli campaign in late 1915 brought about the greatest period of the AIF's expansion. The 3rd Division was raised in Australia and then sailed direct to England, where it trained thoroughly, the only Australian division in the war to do so *before* commencing operations. It was committed to the Western Front in late 1916, although its first major action was at Messines in mid-1917. Meanwhile, in Egypt, each of the relatively experienced units of the 1st and 2nd Divisions was each divided in two during the early months of 1916 to create a cadre for expansion. By blending these with the nearly 40,000 reinforcements that had accumulated in Egypt during 1915, the old divisions were brought up to strength and two new divisions, the 4th and 5th, were added to the order of battle. Three light horse brigades were paired with the New Zealand Mounted Rifles Brigade to create the Australian and New Zealand Mounted Division, which was to continue fighting in the Middle East until the end of the war. Later expansions of the mounted arm in 1917–1918 meant that the AIF finished the war with five light horse brigades, which together made up the better part of two mounted divisions in Palestine (the Australian Mounted Division, created in 1917 from the Imperial Mounted Division, being the other).[3]

There were other expansions. The Australian government proposed a sixth infantry division in May 1916, but the War Office initially declined it because no one was sure, not least the Australians, if the Commonwealth could generate sufficient recruiting to sustain it. The government kept trying, however, and, at British urging, the 6th Division was raised in England in early 1917. But a lack of reinforcements from Australia and high casualty rates on the western front led to its being picked clean of manpower and eventually disbanded before it had a chance to see any action.[4] Still, other Australian combat units and supporting elements contributed to the British Empire's war effort. These ranged from battalions of camel-borne mounted infantry in Palestine, several squadrons of the Australian Flying Corps, siege

Table 1.1   Units of the expeditionary forces into which Australian troops were chiefly organized, 1914–1918

Army Corps Troops	2 × corps mounted regiments 2 × corps cyclist battalions 3 × army field artillery brigades Army field artillery subsections Army corps engineers Army wireless telegraph section engineers Entrenching battalion Topographical section Provost corps
Mounted Divisions	5 × light horse brigades 5 × machine-gun squadrons Field squadron engineers 2 × field troops engineers Signals squadron 5 × signal troops Mounted divisional train 2 × depot units of supply 5 × mobile veterinary sections
Infantry Divisions	15 × infantry brigades 5 × pioneer battalions 5 × machine-gun battalions (20 companies) 10 × field artillery brigades 5 × divisional ammunition columns 35 × trench mortar batteries 15 × field engineer companies 5 × divisional signals companies Wireless signals section 5 × divisional trains (20 companies) 5 × field bakeries 5 × field butcheries 25 × depot units of supply Motor ambulance workshop 5 × mobile veterinary sections 15 × field ambulances 5 × sanitary sections 5 × infantry base depots
Miscellaneous Units	Siege artillery brigade (2 batteries) 4 × service flying squadrons 4 × training flying squadrons Aeroplane squadron (half-flight) for Mesopotamia Mining corps (3 companies) 3 × tunneling companies Electrical and mechanical mining and boring company Naval bridging train Divisional ammunition park 5 × divisional supply columns (mechanical transport) Reserve park Armored motor car section Railway supply detachment 3 × light railway operating companies 3 × broad gauge railway operating companies 2 × remount units Remount section 2 × veterinary sections

Table 1.1   (continued)

Veterinary hospital
Wireless signal squadron for Mesopotamia
10 × companies Imperial Camel Corps (2 × battalions and half of a third)
Camel brigade field ambulance
Cavalry divisional signal squadron for Mesopotamia
4 × general hospitals
3 × casualty clearing stations
3 × auxiliary hospitals
2 × stationary hospitals
Dermatological hospital
Salvage corps
Army ordnance corps
Ordnance company (Inspector Ordnance Machinery section)
2 × hospital ships
Dental services
Nursing services
Other administrative, training and departmental units
Naval and Military Expeditionary Force for service in New Guinea

Source: Official yearbook of the Commonwealth of Australia, no. 12 (1919): 1020–21; modified drawing on Ross Mallet, "First AIF Order of Battle 1914–18," accessed 4 November 2014, http://www.aif.adfa.edu.au:8888/.

Note: Includes the AN&MEF and units sent to Mesopotamia. Not all units existed at once due to disbandments and amalgamations during the war.

artillery batteries, mining companies, and remount units and hospitals (see table 1.1). Many of these support units were designed to meet imperial needs and did not directly support the AIF's combat formations.

Hence, as the war reached its costliest stages in 1917–1918, the AIF comprised five infantry divisions, the better part of two mounted divisions, a range of army and corps troops, and a host of miscellaneous units that were involved in or supporting the fighting in variety of ways. It was a remarkable demonstration of Australia's commitment to the war and to supporting the British Empire. That enthusiasm came at considerable cost, however. In the first instance, the young and war-inexperienced country encountered numerous problems of creating, expanding, and maintaining a large military. A further complication was that Australia's politicians, as well as the government agencies under their control, proved to be rather poor at managing some of these problems, which exacerbated them and helped bring about a political crisis that still rates as the most divisive and bitter in Australian history.

A Multitude of Growing Pains

Raising, expanding, and sustaining the AIF was a demanding enterprise, and problems were frequent, particularly in the war's earlier years. Some difficulties, such as how to administer the mass of manpower and resources deployed overseas, were, after a poor start, overcome, while others could never fully be conquered. This section examines three key personnel-related problems: training (with some observations of the related matter of administration), command of the force, and finding sufficient manpower.

Training the Australian Imperial Force

Despite the large military establishment that had grown in Australia by 1914, the country possessed little in the way of a military training organization. The only standing full-time institution, the Royal Military College at Duntroon, had been established in 1911 to provide permanent instructors and staff officers for the expanding militia, but when the war broke out, it had not yet produced its first junior officers, even as its first classes graduated early to bolster the AIF. Almost all other training before the war was conducted within units, leading to highly variable results. When the first contingent left Australia, it continued this practice. In broad terms, this worked reasonably well in Egypt in 1914 and early 1915, although the lack of training time meant that Australia's earliest formations were badly underprepared for their first battles.[5] This in-unit-training policy failed once the Gallipoli campaign got under way. As minimally trained reinforcements began arriving in Egypt, the units in which they might have completed their training were busy fighting, and the AIF had little to no administrative or training system in place either to manage them or prepare them for service at the front. Measures to redress this training shortcoming were slow to come because the man in charge of the entire contingent, Major-General William Bridges, was also commanding the 1st Australian Division in action at Gallipoli. He had little time to attend to the demands of the whole force, and, anxious that force administration not lead to his having to give up his field command, was not inclined to do so in any event. After trying and failing to get the British Army to take responsibility for the AIF's "tail" in Egypt, Bridges established an intermediate base in Egypt, but he did not do much to support the officer whom he sent to command it, Colonel Victor Sellheim. Eventually, Britain's War Office stepped in and appointed a British regular, Major-General James Spens, to oversee the training of the Australians and New Zealanders in Egypt.

Spens greatly improved the training arrangements, but it was months before his system produced useful material, and properly trained reinforcements did not make it to Gallipoli until late in the campaign. Even then, the system remained underdeveloped and scandalously ad hoc; and indeed the appointment of Spens can be seen as one example of the many extemporizations that characterized both the AIF and wider British imperial armies through 1915. Spens brought a few experienced British Army instructors, but they were spread thin, and the Australian instructors whom commanding officers sent to Spens from the front tended to be poor performers, rather than the energetic and competent men the situation demanded. Finally, as the year went on, the mass of volunteers arriving in Egypt started to overwhelm the training battalions there. Most of these units eventually contained between 2,000 and 4,000 men, often under the command of junior and relatively inexperienced officers.[6] Not surprisingly, training standards slipped or were almost nonexistent, and major disciplinary problems festered.

The doubling of the AIF's divisions in Egypt in 1916, a measure that soaked up the excess manpower in the bloated training battalions, restored some semblance of balance and order to the force, but it also brought about new problems. While the AIF had seen considerable combat at Gallipoli, the notion that it was now experienced should be treated with caution. Older or less capable officers had been weeded out, and competent ones were starting to take the reins, but the AIF's training before Gallipoli had been incomplete, meaning the force's underpinnings were not particularly strong. Training had been impossible in the cramped conditions at the Anzac Cove beachhead, and even if it had been possible, there was no training program to execute.[7] In broad terms, the Australians at Gallipoli had endured, but there is little to suggest that there was much systemic learning and adaptation going on, and certainly no worthwhile local training programs.

Splitting up somewhat haggard units to create cadres for the army's expansion did spread the AIF's experience in early-1916, but it also greatly diluted it. Rather than provide balanced and strong cadres, some unit commanders took the low road and used the opportunity to get rid of their malcontents or duds. Worse, in the quest to find enough officers for every level of command, some unsuitable men received too-hasty promotion. Often, there was not enough equipment to go around, with the result that many men had yet to even hold a rifle on parade. Moreover, this expansion necessitated updating the AIF's organization to meet the demands of the western front by adopting the same establishments as the British Territorial and New Armies. Suddenly there were machine-gun companies, cyclist units, pioneer battalions, and all the other new capabilities that the AIF now had to incorporate. The more technical the demands, the harder it was to train new units. Getting the artillery prepared had been difficult in 1914–1915, and it was still a severe challenge for the new formations in 1916, particularly when one of the two new corps that they were arranged in (I Anzac and II Anzac) had to take much of its artillery back to allow an earlier-than-anticipated deployment to France. The costly failure of the 5th Division during the diversionary battle of Fromelles in mid-July 1916 had numerous contributing factors, but it undoubtedly owed much to the commitment of an underprepared division to battle.[8]

The AIF divisions that went to France in 1916 were, thanks to the demands of expansion and rebuilding in that year, in many ways neophyte formations, even though the war was nearly two years old, and many members of the force had been in uniform since August 1914. The situation was different for each division because of the strength (or otherwise) of their commanders, their previous experience, and how they were introduced to battle on the western front. But, in many ways, the AIF of 1916 was entirely comparable to, and in some cases worse than, the many British New Army formations that arrived in Belgium and France that year. Like the rest of the British imperial army around them, the Australians would improve and, by 1918, they were among the British Expeditionary Force's (BEF's) best troops. That process of British (hence Australian) learning and adaptation, encapsulated in the now-common but inadequate term of "learning curve" (or latterly the more gentrified "learning process"), has been well explored.[9] But for the purpose of considering manpower management, and to build on our discussion of the AIF's earlier experiences, it is worth noting how the AIF's training system changed after 1916.

The shift of the bulk of the AIF to France that year saw a similar relocation of its main administrative and training establishments to England (a modest capacity was maintained in Egypt to support the troops staying in that theater). While still in Egypt, the system that Spens had created was formalized into the Australian Training Centre (ATC), which was an explicit attempt by the AIF's GOC, the British Indian Army officer Lieutenant-General Sir William Birdwood, to bring the AIF's training system fully under its own control (Birdwood eventually took over after Bridges's death in 1915, see below for more details).[10] The British commander-in-chief in Egypt, General Sir Archibald Murray, then made an attempt to gain control of the ATC for himself, but lost out in April, when the AIF's administration and training establishments moved. The intermediate base now became the AIF administrative headquarters in London (on Horseferry Road with branches across the city), while the training depots and units were installed in camps around Salisbury Plain. Here the training units were under Australian command, and, following the practice already established in Egypt, each training battalion was directly linked to a formation at the front so as to become its depot unit. The AIF also created its own field artillery and machine-gun training establishments. Despite their organizational independence, these units taught soldiers according to British syllabi, and all other specialist training was run by British Army schools across the country. Hence, while the AIF developed its own administrative and training structures, it, like the AIF's fighting formations, remained intimately linked with the British Army, its organizations, and its resources. Economy and imperial compatibility recommended that this be so.

The provisions for making this arrangement work shifted from time to time and for reasons that were not always strictly practical. Later in 1916, as Victor Sellheim was eased out of commanding the AIF administrative headquarters, the training establishments were also separated from this command. They were given their own head, initially Brigadier-General Sir Newton Moore, who reported directly to Birdwood for matters of administration and policy, and to the British Army's Southern Command for training. Moore was replaced in 1917 by Major-General James McCay, whose dispatch to England highlighted the difficulties of managing a prominent senior officer. With a background in politics, McCay had been Australia's minister for defence in 1904–1905. A prominent citizen-soldier from before the war, he had commanded a brigade at Gallipoli before receiving command of the 5th Division in the expansion of 1916. His tenure as a division commander had not been successful—he was the commander at Fromelles—and he was likely the

FIGURE 1.1. Australia experienced challenges recruiting enough men for the AIF as it expanded from 1916 onward. These newly enlisted AIF troops undergo a kit inspection on the rifle range, Enoggera, Brisbane, 1918. Image source: Australian War Memorial, H11605.

most unpopular senior officer in the AIF due to his difficult personality, his inability to get on with his staff, and his patchiness as a field commander. Ill health provided a pretext for his removal from division command, but there was a hint that the Labor government preferred that he not come home to possibly cause difficulties through his political connections. He was not liked there, either. So the government, over Birdwood's objections, gave McCay the training establishments in England instead. The hardest work had been done, and he did a competent job of further reorganization in 1917, but he remained a difficult man. He irritated one commander of the AIF administrative headquarters in London, Brigadier-General Thomas Griffiths, so much that he asked to be sent back to France.[11] Not surprisingly, rumors that McCay might replace Birdwood, when the latter moved up to army command in 1918, caused widespread alarm among Australian senior officers.

The Difficulty of Finding Commanders

While considerations of manpower usually revolve around examinations of the make-up of a force, the matter of command is also important. Even though this topic is usually treated differently, it is examined here because finding commanders was a significant manpower issue (or at the risk of anachronism, a human-resource issue) due to the AIF's origins and expansion.

As the shuffling of McCay indicates, the question of command in the AIF required considerable attention. At the most senior levels, it brought up some profound matters of personnel and mismanagement, and it raised questions about who was competent, who was agreeable to the force and the politicians, and who should command the Australian force. As noted above, Bridges, an Australian regular officer with extensive administrative but little command experience, was the AIF's first commander. As the inspector-general in 1914, he had proposed that a British officer, Edward Hutton, who had been Australia's GOC just after federation, would make a suitable commander of the entire AIF. But the government rejected the proposal and opted instead for Bridges, who was also GOC 1st Australian Division, an appointment he cherished so much that he consciously avoided anything that might interfere with his field command, including, as noted above, such important matters as the force's administration and training system. Once he had created the aforementioned administrative and training organization, he flatly refused to deal directly with the man he appointed to run it, and would do so only through the British commander in Egypt, Lieutenant-General Sir John Maxwell. While at Gallipoli, Bridges communicated with Sellheim only via his British corps commander, Birdwood. It was a decidedly peculiar approach for the commander of a national contingent. After Bridge's death in May 1915, Birdwood filled in temporarily as acting GOC AIF, but the government opted to send another Australian permanent officer, Colonel J. Gordon Legge (then serving as the Australian chief of the general staff), as a proper replacement as the AIF commander and GOC 1st Australian Division. Bridges had been respected in the AIF, if not widely liked due to his brusque manner, but few people thought fondly of Legge, who was seen as "political and quarrelsome."[12] He soon so annoyed those around him that the Mediterranean Expeditionary Force commander, General Sir Ian Hamilton, asked Lord Kitchener, the secretary of state for war, if Legge's appointment might be reversed. Australian brigade commanders were further aggrieved that this distasteful man had been brought from Australia and promoted (two ranks) over their heads.

They did not have to wait long. Legge, like Bridges, focused on his division, to the exclusion of his other AIF responsibilities. It took little more than a month for Birdwood to transfer him to Egypt, where he took command of the then-forming 2nd Australian Division. Legge was still in overall charge of the AIF, but Birdwood worked adroitly to have him relieved of those responsibilities as well. Since his temporary command of the AIF, Birdwood had kept up a correspondence with the minister for defense, George Foster Pearce, and the governor-general of Australia, Sir Ronald Munro-Ferguson. He gained their confidence, and it was not long before Birdwood suggested that he should take over the AIF. Pearce, Munro-Ferguson, and other notables in Melbourne agreed, and Legge was relegated to divisional command only (a role in which he was unsuccessful) and eventually sent home to Australia to resume his appointment as chief of the general staff.[13]

In appointing Birdwood to replace Legge, the Australian government was in part facing the reality that the command and administrative abilities of senior Australian officers were lacking. The AIF's expansion in 1916 meant that at least a lieutenant-general was required to lead it, but making senior Australian officers into major-generals or lieutenant-generals at that stage of the war proved tricky—of the three Australians appointed to divisional command in 1916, two were removed by early 1917.[14] Turning to Birdwood made sense in 1915 and 1916, although, as the war progressed, the nationalist urge reemerged and, by late 1917, there were Australians capable of doing the job. Thus it was that, in 1918, the Australian John Monash succeeded Birdwood to command the Australian Corps. Although there were frank discussions about whether Birdwood should continue in administrative command of the force, the debate was cut short by the armistice that November.

Finding Men for the Australian Imperial Force

Finding suitable senior officers was a challenge, but not an insurmountable one. What did prove increasingly difficult as the war went on was finding enough men for them to command and lead in battle. In total, 416,812 enlisted in the AIF during the war.[15] Of these 83,000 did not proceed overseas, either for medical reasons, desertion, some other sort of unsuitability, or because the war ended before their embarkation.[16] The numbers of men recruited were not evenly spread across the war. Men enthusiastically joined in 1914, and the rush of volunteers continued in 1915, particularly midyear, when the Gallipoli fighting demonstrated the seriousness of the endeavor. That July, recruiting figures hit their peak, with 36,575 men signing up, followed by another 25,714 in August and 16,571 in September. These monthly figures were never reached again, and, for the remainder of 1915, the average slipped to about 10,000 per month. The AIF's relocation to France in 1916 brought another spike in enlistments, with 76,741 men signing up between January and May, but thereafter the trend was decisively downward.[17] A final surge occurred in September–October 1916, when 20,845 men joined up, a figure usually attributed to men preempting the looming conscription plebiscite by opting to volunteer rather than be called up.[18] That December, the monthly intake slipped below 5,000, and even that figure was never exceeded again. The following September, the monthly total had plummeted to fewer than 3,000—and that number would only be exceeded on two more occasions. The last modest spike came in May 1918, when 4,888 men enlisted, probably in response to the sense of crisis that came with the German spring offensives of that year (see table 1.2).[19]

How many reinforcement men the AIF needed was never clear during the war. Various figures were advanced, and the topic became politically charged in the tense atmosphere that accompanied the two conscription plebiscites of 1916 and 1917. In 1915, as the casualties of Gallipoli accumulated, the British Army Council urged the Australian government to enlist and dispatch 9,500 men per month just to keep the existing formations of the AIF up to strength. In 1915, that target was technically achievable, but the expansion of the force from two to five infantry divisions, not to mention the coming casualties on the western front, meant that manpower became an enduring problem. Following the 1916 battle of the Somme, the British advised that an immediate special draft of 20,000 men, and a further 16,500 for each of the next three months (making for nearly 70,000 men), would be required to avoid the necessity of taking men out of the 3rd Division, which was then training in Britain.[20] But meeting that sort of figure was highly improbable; in the last

Table 1.2   Total Australian enlistments, 1914–1918

YEAR	NUMBER
1914	52,561
1915	165,912
1916	124,355
1917	45,101
1918	28,883
Total	**416,812**

Source: Ernest Scott, *Official History of Australia in the War of 1914–1918*, vol. 11, *Australia during the War* (Sydney: Angus and Robertson, 1941), 871–72.

quarter of the year, fewer than 30,000 men enlisted. In the lead up to the first conscription plebiscite in 1916, Labor prime minister William "Billy" Hughes, who had succeeded Fisher in October 1915, made much of the War Office figures and cited the 16,500-men-per-month figure as part of his argument in favor of the "yes" vote. By mid-1917, however, the demand seemed to have lessened somewhat, and, in May, the Army Council concluded that 4,000 men per month should suffice.[21] With a second conscription plebiscite on the horizon, the Australian government kept this figure to itself and publicly contended that 7,000 recruits would be needed each month to keep the extant forces in the field.

The second plebiscite, held in December 1917, failed, too, which meant that volunteerism was the only method left to sustain the AIF. How many men could be enlisted remained a hot topic, and in 1918, in an attempt to defuse the political tensions, the chief justice of Australia, Sir Samuel Griffith, was appointed to determine how many men were actually required. He concluded that an average of 8,233 enlistments per month was necessary. Unfortunately, as there was nowhere near that number of men coming forward (the monthly average for 1918 was 2,625 enlistments), authorities settled on the more modest, but still unlikely, target of 5,400 per month.[22]

Curiously, despite the reliance on volunteerism, the nation's recruiting apparatus remained relatively rudimentary. Nothing too elaborate had been required in 1914 or early 1915, while men were still thronging to the colors, but by mid-1915, concerned Commonwealth parliamentarians organized a Federal War Committee. It worked with similar state-based committees to encourage men to enlist. This was soon enhanced by the creation in each military district of a central executive that oversaw local recruiting committees, which formed in towns and districts all across the country. These local committees, drawing in part on the results of the July 1915 war census, drew up lists of men who were "eligible" and then conducted targeted canvassing that urged them to sign up.[23] This new enterprise helped keep recruiting reasonably high until about mid-1916, when the possibility of conscription began to loom. In anticipation of a "yes" vote, the government began calling men into the militia for training in late 1916, which had the effect of diminishing the role of the local recruiting committees somewhat.

With the defeat of the conscription proposal in October 1916, however, recruiting dropped precipitously. The appointment of a director-general of recruiting and the revamping of state and local committees failed to arrest the decline. By this time, the political tensions in the wider community seriously affected the recruiting system. The people involved in recruiting committees were closely identified with the "yes" campaign and often publicly criticized in the tense lead-up to the second plebiscite in December 1917. For many of them, the second "no" vote was too disheartening, and they resigned from their committees, eviscerating them in the process. The final reform in 1918 was the appointment of a Commonwealth minister for recruiting, but diminished enthusiasm and the ruptures over conscription meant that little could be done to reverse the trend of declining enlistments.[24]

Did the Australian Imperial Force Over-Expand?

The problem of recruiting enough men to support the AIF as it expanded from 1916 onward raises the question as to whether the AIF was too large a force for the country to sustain. A few studies suggest that this was indeed the case.[25] As outlined above, the AIF underwent a remarkable expansion in early 1916, and it made several sputtering attempts at further expansion afterward. In both 1916 and 1917, the AIF failed to raise a sixth infantry division. Indeed, the Australian government, either out of enthusiasm, its own political reasons, or perhaps a keenness to display its imperial loyalty, took nearly every opportunity offered to increase the size of the nation's contingent. The politics of the conscription debates and plebiscites were complex, and a detailed examination of these is beyond the scope of this chapter. It will instead conclude by focusing on the decision-making, or lack thereof, regarding the size of the AIF and how that may have affected the decision to pursue conscription.[26]

By mid-1917, the AIF's fighting elements comprised five infantry divisions, the better part of two mounted divisions, ten companies of camel-mounted infantry, an Australian Flying Corps, plus a range of support and ancillary troops (see table 1.1).[27] To this end, Australia sent roughly 330,000 men overseas from a total (white) adult male population of 2.47 million men, a very significant 13.48 percent of the nation's manpower.[28]

A comparison with Canada and New Zealand is instructive. Ottawa committed about the same proportion of its male population to the war, but did so from a cohort that contained nearly a million more men (its male population being approximately 3.4 million), meaning that it devoted nearly 460,000 men to the war.[29] However, when doing so, it chose to support a notably smaller force in the field than the AIF, with the Canadian Expeditionary Force's (CEF) fighting core limited to four infantry divisions and just two mounted regiments (which together with a British cavalry regiment constituted a Canadian cavalry brigade). A fifth division was raised but stayed in Britain as a depot to keep the other divisions up to strength; it was disbanded in 1918. Limiting the Canadian commitment in this way brought several benefits. The CEF was, for example, never forced to reduce the number of battalions it fielded as were the BEF and the AIF. The Canadians were also able to develop their expertise in specialist areas, such as heavy artillery and counterbattery fire, in ways the AIF could not. Moreover, its relatively sound manpower situation meant that it was also able to provide greater support services to the frontline troops and maintain units that were larger than the imperial norm. Canadian machine-gun battalions, for example, were much larger than British ones, and each Canadian division had three engineer battalions, as opposed to three companies in the wider BEF.[30] This did require the introduction of conscription (at a high political and social cost in Canada), but the Canadian Military Service Act became law only in the autumn of 1917, and the first Canadian conscripts did not get to France until mid-1918.

New Zealand also introduced conscription during the war, but did so earlier, in 1916, which enabled the dominion to make use of almost 20 percent of its manpower, enlisting 112,000 men from a total male population of 580,000.[31] Like Canada, however, it also limited the combat formations it sent to war, largely restricting the New Zealand Expeditionary Force (NZEF) to a division of three infantry brigades (a fourth brigade was briefly raised, but did not see action), its artillery and divisional troops, and a single mounted brigade in Palestine.[32] Britain attempted to get further New Zealand contributions from time to time, but the dominion's minister for defense, Sir James Allen, resisted and remained focused on maintaining the extant formations. Like the CEF, the NZEF did not need to reduce the number of battalions in their brigades later in the war, and, unlike the AIF's formations, the New Zealand Division finished the war virtually at full strength, with reserves of trained men in England and more still training in New Zealand.[33]

AIF expansion in early 1916 was based on the manpower that had accumulated in Egypt or was on its way from Australia, but little or no thought appears to have been given to how such a force might be maintained. Charles Bean's official history suggests that there was an expectation of 12,000 men arriving per month, but for how long military authorities thought it would continue is not stated.[34] The new divisions were built during a period of enthusiastic recruiting, but even then it should have been evident that such inflows were unsustainable, as the British decision to resort to conscription ought to have made clear. Indeed, the matter of conscription had already been raised in Australia and the first political battle lines drawn in the latter part of 1915.[35] The decisions taken about expanding the force meant that the government and the AIF were left with just two options for the future: reduce the AIF or introduce conscription. The former course was considered from time to time but never enacted. In 1916, the disbandment of the 3rd Division was contemplated in the War Office (as it was again in 1917) but opposed by Birdwood, and the breaking up of some of the light horse in Egypt was also discussed in that same year.[36] Similarly, a 1918 attempt to convert one of the divisions to a depot division was aborted in the pressures and panic of the German spring offensives. A process of reducing brigades from four to three battalions started in 1918 (it had not been completed by the war's end), but, on the whole, the AIF proved remarkably resistant to the idea that it should be made smaller. Each time such a proposal came up, rather than return to a simple assessment of what could be sustained, AIF authorities harped on esprit de corps and the disquiet that disbandments would cause. Why the force resisted so strongly is unclear. Disbandments would upset men and deprive officers of cherished appointments, but this seems insufficient justification for maintaining an unsustainably large field force. Birdwood's ambition could have played a role, and he tried (unsuccessfully) on a few occasions to gain command of a new Australasian or dominion army. Certainly, reducing the AIF would not have helped in this regard.[37] Similarly, he might have seen any diminution of the AIF as doing the same to his standing.

Whatever the reason behind the AIF's failures to grapple with the problem, there was no compensating control emanating from the Australian government either. Neither the hands-off minister for defense, Pearce, nor the prime minister, Hughes, made any notable effort to consider the AIF's force structures themselves or to push the AIF rationalize itself. More broadly, there was no effort to appraise the overall manpower situation and draw any conclusions about what the home economy needed, how many men could be spared, and what could be realistically channeled to the AIF. The closest attempt at anything like this was the aforementioned 1915 war census, which was intended only to discover how many men were theoretically suitable for the military.[38] Rather than manage what was on hand, the government instead resolved instead to introduce conscription as a way of sustaining what it had enthusiastically, but rather carelessly, created. The difficulties of doing so were considerable. Hughes knew the matter would be highly contentious, both within his ruling Labor Party and with the electorate in general. This was reflected in his decision to seek a mandate via plebiscite rather than parliamentary vote—only a plebiscite would have yielded the required legitimacy.[39] As the war went on, Hughes perhaps had little political choice. Something of a firebrand, he built his reputation in part on tub-thumping exhortations for a total war effort and excoriated British politicians for their supposed timidity and unwillingness to do what needed to be done. For Hughes to admit that the expanded AIF could not be sustained might have exposed him politically both at home and in Britain. Conscription probably had to be considered at some point, but so did a judicious reduction or restructuring of the AIF. Hughes and his government chose only the former and painted themselves into a corner in the process.[40] In the end, they committed the government (in all its shifting forms in 1916–1917) and the country to what proved to be one of the most heated and divisive periods in Australian history.

Chapter 2

Irish Identities in the British Army during the First World War

Richard S. Grayson

Irish identities in the British Army during the First World War must be placed within the context of centuries-long traditions closely related to both national politics and mobilization. As Thomas Bartlett and Keith Jeffery have pointed out, due to the conflicted nature of Irish history with both state and informal "armies" playing major roles at key moments, there should be no surprise if "an Irish military tradition turns out to be central to the Irish historical experience and a key element in modern Irish identity."[1] The trope of "Irish" soldiers was that they were brave and valuable as shock troops, but also lacking in discipline and unreliable. Such thinking had roots in longstanding English views of the Irish as a people, which had solidified in the late eighteenth century but had deeper forebears.[2] For instance, there were medieval tellings of the deeds of Cú Chulainn and others who exhibited "reckless daring, spectacular ferocity and indomitable courage," while also displaying the "simple-mindedness, guilelessness and even witlessness" that had been attributed to Celts by Romans.[3] Ideas of the Irish as a martial race certainly survived into the First World War. In February 1916, the Irish Parliamentary Party leader, John Redmond, wrote of "the Irish people" having "been endowed in a distinguished degree with a genuine military spirit, a natural genius and gift for war which produces born soldiers and commanders."[4] Meanwhile, two separate traditions created ideas that would inform service in the First World War: one was a Protestant military narrative of service in times of crisis, the other a story of service for foreign nations in an "Irish Brigade," most notably for France against Britain at Fontenoy in 1745.[5]

All this had a significant impact on recruitment of the manpower of Ireland in the nineteenth century. At Waterloo in 1815, around 30 percent of Wellington's 28,000 men, including of course Wellington himself, were Irish.[6] Irishmen constituted over 42 percent of the British Army by 1830, a time when Ireland's share of the United Kingdom population was around one-third. Indeed, there were more men from Ireland than from England in the army. Even as the Irish population fell from the Great Famine onward, and even as Irish numbers in the British Army fell with it, Ireland still contributed more than its share of the population.[7] Economics played a role in this. By 1901, Ireland was still contributing disproportionately (13.5 percent of the army from 12 percent of the population) because army life proved popular for unemployed young men, especially those from towns and cities. That said, one in three Irish recruits in the Edwardian era were rural laborers, a reflection of the effects of rural poverty.[8] By the outbreak of the war, around one-third of Irishmen in the British Army were Catholic (compared with about three-quarters of the population), while Protestants dominated the officer class. Geographically, Dublin dominated prewar recruitment, providing around 30 percent of recruits from only 11 percent of the population.[9]

Irish involvement in the British Army formally manifested itself in the Irish infantry regiments. These had centuries-long antecedents, but the infantry units that went into action in the First World War were organizationally the product of the 1881 Childers Reforms, which restructured the infantry regiments of the British Army, including eight Irish regiments: Connaught Rangers, Royal Dublin Fusiliers, Royal Inniskilling Fusiliers, Royal Irish Fusiliers, Royal Irish Regiment, Royal Irish Rifles, Royal Munster Fusiliers, and The Prince of Wales's Leinster Regiment (Royal Canadians). They were joined by the Irish Guards in 1900.[10] Irish cavalry units had longer lineages: the 6th Inniskilling Dragoons since 1751, the 4th (Royal Irish) Dragoon Guards since 1788, and the 5th (Royal Irish) Lancers and the 8th (The King's Royal Irish) Hussars since 1861. The North Irish Horse and South Irish Horse came into being in 1908 after being formed as "Imperial Yeomanry" in 1902.[11] Of course, Irishmen had also joined non-Irish units of the British Army and would continue to do so, but they had ample opportunity to engage with Irish identities through the Irish regiments.

Mobilizing Irishmen in 1914–1918

Keith Jeffery has argued that Irish recruitment can be understood through three models of recruitment relating to the wider British Empire. One is "metropolitan," in which recruitment took place by making largely similar appeals to those made in the rest of the United Kingdom. Another is "dominion," in which the political goals of those in Ireland aligned to those of the United Kingdom in the same way as did goals of Canada, Australia, New Zealand, Newfoundland, and South Africa. The third is "colonial," in which Irish troops were essentially treated as human resources and mercenaries.[12] None of these models alone explains all of Irish recruitment, not least because, in John Morrissey's words, the involvement of Irishmen in the British military and their "incorporation . . . into the British colonial project was both a partial integration and not without contradictions and ambiguities."[13] But each of them describes significant aspects of Irish recruitment between 1914 and 1918.

During the First World War around 210,000 Irishmen served in the British forces, first in Irish regiments and later in Irish divisions. The first Irishmen to mobilize were those already serving in the regular army, as well as those who had signed up prewar as reservists (whether Army Reserve or Special Reserve). As war broke out, these latter men were summoned to their units, and in August 1914 there were 58,000 Irishmen mobilized—21,000 regular troops, 30,000 reserve other ranks, 5,000 naval ratings, and close to 2,000 officers.[14] At the time, each of the Irish infantry regiments had one battalion in India (or elsewhere outside the United Kingdom) and one based at "home" (often England). The first Irish battalion to be deployed in France was the 1st Irish Guards on 13 August, followed the next day by the second battalions of the Royal Munster Fusiliers, Connaught Rangers, Royal Irish Regiment, and Royal Irish Rifles. Of the eighteen regular Irish infantry battalions, all except three were on the Western Front by the end of 1914.[15] These regular battalions played their part in all the major battles of the Western Front in 1914–1915, yet none of those battles is ever seen as having any particularly Irish dimension. Some of that is because the Irish battalions played their part alongside others from throughout the United Kingdom and the British Empire and never as part of any specifically "Irish Division" (nor even a brigade).

As those regulars fought, three divisions with a specifically Irish character were being formed at home from volunteers. This story of Ireland's recruitment to the British Army is intimately connected with national politics and is dominated by the political nature of volunteering for the 16th (Irish) Division, a largely Catholic formation, and the 36th (Ulster) Division, an almost exclusively Protestant formation. However, the 16th Division did not begin as a political formation, nor did the 10th (Irish) Division, which was nonpolitical in nature. The initial raising of the 10th Division was a prominent early attempt to mobilize Irishmen linked to rugby, eventually as D Company of the 7th Royal Dublin Fusiliers. As the "Dublin Pals," this unit adopted the "Pals" name common in the north of England but which was not otherwise used in Ireland. Their origins were in a call on the second day of the war by Francis Henry Browning, president of the Irish Rugby Football Union (IRFU), for the formation of IRFU volunteers, initially for home defense. They drilled in the evenings after work from 24 August. In early September, when they numbered around 250, the commanding officer of the 7th Dublins offered to take them on as a company in his battalion. At the same time, newspapers appealed to "Young Men of Dublin" to join the "Dublin 'Pals' Battalion," offering them the chance to serve in a unit with their friends.[16] These appeals made the Dublin Pals unusually middle class for an infantry battalion, while also being a clear example of men enlisting along with friends from a sense of "collective sacrifice" and belonging.[17] The 7th Dublins became part of the 10th (Irish) Division, the first Irish division, formed on 21 August 1914.[18] This arose from a decision to establish new divisions in six of the army's eight regional commands, and the designation of the division as "Irish" was more a reflection of military organization than politics. At least in its recruiting, the 10th Division fitted Jeffery's "metropolitan" model.

By the end of August, though, the war secretary, "Lord Kitchener [was] very disappointed at the slowness with which the Irish Division in the New Army [was] filling up."[19] Perhaps it suffered from not making overt appeals to sectarian sentiments—as the 16th and 36th Divisions would later do—but men from paramilitary groups still joined it. Indeed, if one was keen to enlist as early as possible, then the battalions of the 10th Division offered a chance to do that close to home, with the result that groups of Ulster Volunteer Force (UVF) members chose to join the 10th rather than await the formation of a specifically unionist division. If one was desperate to serve king and country, why wait for the unionist leadership to form a division for the UVF? Some 220 men of the UVF from Tyrone and another forty from Belfast, for example, joined the 10th rather than await the formation of a specifically unionist division.[20] Such influxes were not enough to fill the division, however. In fact, by 5 September, it was the only one of the initial six "K1" divisions not to have filled its infantry battalions. This meant that, in the next few weeks, recruits from England were drafted in. Even so, the division was probably 70 percent Irish (or of Irish descent) when initially completed.[21]

As the 10th Division was forming, recruitment received a strange boost from two opposing camps closely connected to national politics. Had Home

Rule been implemented in 1914, the unionist UVF and members of the nationalist Irish Volunteers might have fought each other in an Irish civil war. Instead, their competing political goals led men from both sides to enlist in the British Army in a way that illustrates Jeffery's "dominion" recruiting model at least for Irish nationalists who linked their own political interests to the British war effort. From the war's outbreak, discussions had taken place between the War Office and the unionist leader, Sir Edward Carson, with the secretary of state for war, Lord Kitchener, wanting to recruit the UVF (which numbered 90,000) into the wider army and Carson wanting the UVF to join en masse. By early-September, though, Carson was satisfied. He had received sufficient assurances that the unionist identity of the UVF would be maintained to authorize mass enlistment for UVF men.[22] Early recruitment was enthusiastic: the 107th (Belfast) Brigade was full within a week, although as Timothy Bowman points out, because urban areas had higher enlistment rates than rural ones, and because the influx took place at a time of peak recruiting across the United Kingdom, expectations were artificially raised about likely overall numbers. As it turned out, recruiting in other parts of Ulster was slower, and the division was not quite full by the end of 1914.[23] Its artillery even had to be recruited in London.

In spite of the UVF not actually constituting the entirety of the 36th Division, the idea that the UVF had moved into the 36th as a bloc took a strong hold in the collective memory of the war, particularly in Ulster. That view is not without its problems, as some recent scholarship has demonstrated. Some UVF members had already joined the 10th Division, while others had already been called to the colors as reservists, who would serve alongside former Irish Volunteers in regular units such as the 2nd Royal Irish Rifles.[24] A local study of West Belfast suggests that perhaps one-third of UVF members did not serve in the 36th (Ulster) Division at all, and Bowman suggests that "barely a majority" of 31,000 UVF enlistees overall joined the 36th.[25] Those facts notwithstanding, the 36th Division was, and still is, seen as "an unambiguously unionist and Protestant formation," which "exemplified on a grand scale the 'pals' battalions of some other divisions."[26] Such recruitment efforts point once more to Jeffery's "metropolitan" model.

Meanwhile, the political dimension of recruiting was increased as nationalists were directed to the 16th (Irish) Division, which took on the idea of being an "Irish Brigade" as at Fontenoy. Formed on 11 September 1914 as part of the second wave of "K'" divisions (like the 36th), it did not initially have a political connection. However, with royal assent to Home Rule coming in mid-September 1914, the Irish Parliamentary Party leader, John Redmond, encouraged members of the Irish Volunteers to enlist. He had previously offered their services to the British government for home defense. However, with the formation of the 36th Division, unionist recruitment was visibly outstripping that of nationalists, and Home Rule, though passed, was not to be implemented during the war. Nationalists had to be seen to be doing their part, in case any chance of Home Rule slipped away and demonstrations of loyalty to the wider United Kingdom might prove decisive for long-term political goals. On 20 September, speaking at Woodenbridge, County Wicklow, Redmond said to assembled East Wicklow Irish Volunteers that they had a "two-fold duty" to defend Ireland and to take up arms "wherever the firing line extends in defense of the right of freedom and religion in this war."[27] Redmond's call had not been authorized by the Provisional Committee of the Volunteers, which condemned him and expelled his supporters from the committee. This resulted in a split within the organization. The vast majority of members (93 percent) stayed with Redmond and joined a new organization, the National Volunteers (NV). From these ranks came men who joined the 16th (Irish) Division, first in the 47th Brigade, which was cleared for them. They joined just as the UVF had done, in groups, with, for example, men from Belfast being concentrated in the 6th Connaught Rangers and the 7th Leinsters.[28] That they did so was all the more remarkable given a decades-long campaign by nationalists to dissuade Irishmen from joining the British Army.[29] By the end of February 1915, the battalions of the 47th Brigade were largely full (some over-strength), but battalions in the division's other two brigades were not; so some men, mostly NV, were spread throughout the division.[30] This meant that the 16th (Irish) Division as a whole was more nationalist politically than when first established.

Although political recruiting dominated much of the high-profile activity to secure volunteers in Ireland, there were also broad efforts to recruit men into *any* kind of unit rather than a specific one—a circumstance that illustrates both Jeffery's "metropolitan" model and his "colonial" one. This continued well after calls from Carson and Redmond had ceased to dominate recruitment. The UK-wide Parliamentary Recruiting Committee initially appealed for men to fight for King and Country, the latter meaning the whole of the United Kingdom, subsuming any concept of Ireland into the wider nation (a further example of Jeffery's "metropolitan" model). Often, recruiters in Ireland simply adopted the same "coaxing, wheedling and cajoling" methods used in Britain, with language adapted to an Irish context. This exploited men's concerns about sexual and familial relationships and was especially apparent in textual newspaper advertisements. Irish men did not want to be unappealing to women or embarrassing to their families, just as English men did not want to be unappealing to women or embarrassing to their families.[31]

There were also Irish-specific recruiting efforts. In early 1915, a specifically Irish body was established: the Central Council for the Organisation of Recruiting in Ireland (CCORI). In October 1915, that was replaced by the Department of Recruiting for Ireland and then the Irish Recruiting Council from May 1918.[32] These bodies had a significant impact on the nature of recruiting in Ireland. A study of 203 posters held at Trinity College in Dublin shows that, while no 1914 poster referred to Ireland, by 1915 (the peak of Irish-specific posters) 96 percent of posters mentioned "Ireland" or "Irish." Irish-specific posters made up more than 80 percent of all posters circulated in Ireland over the course of the war.[33] Nuala Johnson argues that four themes dominated Irish recruiting posters: protection of the Irish countryside, theological justifications (with reference to German violence against Catholic targets in Belgium), ideas of Irish heroism and spirit, and gender roles (including presentations of the female figure of Erin, and the protection of her and other women).[34]

Particular types of identities of Irishmen appeared in recruitment posters. One identity was simply that they were "Irish"—serving in Irish regiments surrounded by other Irishmen and Irish symbols (figure 2.1a).[35] Another was that they exhibited specific fighting qualities as embodied by Michael O'Leary, a Victoria Cross (VC) winner in the Irish Guards. He appeared in a poster with his cap rakishly pushed back and was said to be worth ten Germans (figure 2.1b).[36] He had won the VC at Cuinchy in February 1915 when he "killed five Germans who were holding the first barricade, after which he attacked a second barricade, about 60 yards further on, which he captured, after killing three of the enemy and making prisoners of two more."[37] Such fighting qualities were central to portrayals of Irishmen at specific moments in the war, when images of the Irish as a martial race made regular appearances. Tom Kettle, a former nationalist Member of Parliament (MP) and an officer in the 9th Royal Dublin Fusiliers in the 16th Division, wrote of Irish soldiers as exhibiting the same "instantaneity" exhibited by "Irish football forwards."[38] The Times's military correspondent Charles Repington wrote about the Irish as the British Army's "finest missile troops."[39] Irish soldiers were seen in similar ways to soldiers from the dominions, and perhaps also to black French colonial troops.[40]

What was the effect of these recruiting messages and the accompanying impact of mobilization linked to Irish politics? Throughout the war, Ireland's voluntary recruiting was, like that of Britain, most intense in August 1914. Later peaks (though never higher than in that month) came in late 1915, after the Easter Rising in 1916, in early 1917, and in early 1918. The campaign against the threat to introduce conscription in Ireland in the spring of 1918

FIGURES 2.1A AND 2.1B. Recruiting agencies used posters like these to appeal to the Irish community. Image source: Library of Congress, Prints & Photographs Division, LC-USZC4-10979 and LC-USZC4-11356.

initially caused a slowing of recruitment, but it then rose later in the year. Such peaks were often a response to specific recruiting campaigns as, for example, in a push for Royal Flying Corps and then Royal Air Force recruits in the summer of 1918.[41]

There is much debate over the extent to which recruiting was successful in Ireland, who enlisted, and why they did so. This debate is directly related to considerations of Irish identities in the British Army because it addresses how far men who enlisted were influenced by emotional connections to a particular community. For more than two decades, the most discussed interpretation has been David Fitzpatrick's article "The Logic of Collective Sacrifice: Ireland and the British Army, 1914–1918." Its starting point is that enlistment in wartime "cannot easily be explained in terms of rational action." This, he said, was because the risk of death outweighed any financial gain (even for the unemployed), while other forms of "adventure" would be available without such high probability of harm. Fitzpatrick pointed instead to "the influence of group affiliations and collective pressures" to explain Ireland's recruitment in the First World War.[42] Drawing comparisons with the rest of the United Kingdom for 1914–1915 (after which point Great Britain had conscription and Ireland did not), Fitzpatrick reached two broad conclusions. First, "the relationship between enlistment and insecurity of employment was inverse rather than direct." In other words, men did not have to be unemployed or underemployed to be more likely to enlist. Second, there was a relatively broad reluctance of industrial workers to enlist compared with Britain. In Ireland, there was no particular reluctance or enthusiasm in specific industries.[43] He also pointed to broadly similar enlistment rates among Protestants and Catholics, which suggests that religion was not a major determinant. What really drove Irishmen to enlist, Fitzpatrick argued, were family traditions and membership in paramilitary groups or fraternities. Specifically in Ulster, membership of the UVF or the NV had a significant impact on propensity to enlist.[44] The pattern of recruits from Ireland being less "underemployed" than those from Britain was observed in recent work on militias and supports Fitzpatrick's case.[45]

Subsequent research, however, has challenged some of Fitzpatrick's findings on the "underemployed." For example, in West Belfast, while the enthusiasm of UVF and NV enlistment was broadly in line with Fitzpatrick's thesis, some UVF members enlisted more rapidly than others due to their unemployment. Their membership of the UVF was perhaps a factor, but the final nudge came from the need for work.[46] Meanwhile, a study of the 10th Division, while accepting Fitzpatrick's broad arguments for Ireland as a whole, found evidence for economic motivators in some parts of the division, particularly among unskilled workers.[47] Timothy Bowman's work on the UVF argues that recruiting for the 36th Division was uneven in Ulster and that there were pronounced difficulties in rural areas.[48] This has led to criticism of Fitzpatrick's work for not fully recognizing the significance of the rural-urban divide in Ireland, with Ireland's rural enlistment being much lower than Britain's.[49] Some of this debate can never be resolved, of course, because ultimately, what was in the minds of men as they enlisted cannot be known: if someone was an unemployed member of the UVF, what was most important to him— work, belonging, or some other factor—cannot be reconstructed from surviving records. On balance, however, new scholarship suggests that "the logic of collective sacrifice" was not the only influence on recruitment.

Yet in parts of Britain, recruiters felt that attaching a specific and collective Irish identity to battalions was worthwhile, in much the same way that it was worthwhile for Indian and South African authorities to form units based on ethnicity or territory, as Kaushik Roy and Ian van der Waag demonstrate in chapters 6 and 12. The "London Irish Volunteers," for example, who had been formed in 1859, eventually became part of the Territorial Force formed in 1908 as the 1/18th (County of London) Battalion (London Irish Rifles), London Regiment. At the outbreak of the war in 1914, another battalion was raised, the 2/18th.[50] Famously, it was a soldier of the 1/18th Battalion who kicked a football across No Man's Land at Loos in September 1915.[51] Liverpool recruited the 1/8th (Irish) Battalion, King's (Liverpool) Regiment in a similar manner, with the 2/8th raised in October 1914.[52] But it was in Tyneside where the biggest efforts were made. The region had no "Irish" unit prior to the war, but from November 1914 to January 1915, the 24th to 27th Battalions of the Northumberland Fusiliers were labeled as the 1st to 4th Tyneside Irish.[53] The first hint of such change came in early September 1914, when the *Newcastle Evening Chronicle* carried a proposal from Irish-connected local worthies, who cited the example of Pals battalions and said: "The number of Irishmen resident in this district is a large one, and although great numbers of our countrymen have already joined, we believe it is possible to get the necessary number of men who, no doubt, would prefer to enlist in such a regiment of distinctive character in which all would be comrades and friends."[54] A poster that proclaimed "God Save our King and country!" urged "all eligible Irishmen . . . to fight for the great principles of freedom and the rights of small nations, and against military tyranny and despotism."[55] Other appeals claimed: "The greatest fighting men of our time are Irishmen."[56] Initially aiming for one battalion, the Tyneside Irish eventually numbered four battalions, which meant that they could constitute their own brigade (the 103rd) in the 34th Division.[57] While we can never be sure how "Irish" all those who enlisted were, and many would have been at least second generation, the Tyneside Irish certainly stand out as the most successful initiative to recruit from any diasporic community in Britain.

Identities in Service

Ireland's identity as a participant in the war is today grouped in terms of three key battles: Gallipoli in 1915, the Somme in 1916 (especially July and September), and Messines in June 1917, with Gallipoli arguably the poor relation. During the war itself, all three battles were much discussed in newspapers and in Irish homes, and they helped give rise to expressions of different Irish identities, but so too was the role of Irish soldiers in the context of the German spring offensive of 1918, an event that does not now loom large in Ireland's popular memory of the war. Both during the war and since, the role of regulars, specifically as "Irish" soldiers, on the Western Front in 1914 and 1915, has gained far less attention. Instead, it is overshadowed by narratives of later great battles in which the roles played by the three volunteer divisions are highlighted, even though many regulars also took part. If I can be allowed to drift briefly into anecdote for illustrative purposes, my own family story serves as an example of myth muddling memory. Growing up in England in the 1970s and 1980s, I often heard stories of the family "home" in Lurgan, County Armagh. "Uncle Jimmy"—my grandmother's brother, Sergeant 5073 James Powell—was often mentioned as killed during the war and the story passed on was that he had died "on the Somme" in 1916.[58] Only much later, in 1987, when I visited the Western Front, did I establish that he had actually been killed at Hooge (Belgium) in September 1915, while serving in a regular battalion, the 2nd Royal Irish Rifles, which was a unit in the 3rd Division. This made me suspicious about assertions that two other great-uncles had served "on the Somme," although many years later it became clear that they had done so, both with the 36th (Ulster) Division. More widely, concentration of memory around the first day of the Somme can still be seen in the murals painted on Northern Irish houses and in the name of the organization that commemorates the First World War: "The Somme Association."[59]

Gallipoli was the first occasion on which Irishmen were widely seen as going into battle as units of Irishmen. These units started fighting at Cape Helles in late April 1915 as part of the initial landings on the peninsula. In the 29th Division, the 1st Dublins and 1st Munsters were together in the 86th Brigade, while the 1st Inniskillings were in the 87th Brigade. It was a bloody affair, hard to describe in any terms as a success, except that the landing had been made and a beachhead established. As news gradually reached Ireland, the Dublin *Evening Mail* described "A TERRIBLE DEATH-ROLL" in the 1st Dublins. However, newspaper coverage also suggested that there were especially Irish martial qualities on display at Helles, with reports of the Dublins and Munsters being "selected to lead the way in the landing of the Expeditionary Force on the Gallipoli Peninsula" and talk of "The Dash of the Irish."[60] Yet Helles did not come to occupy the central place in Irish memory of Gallipoli. That soon went to the 10th (Irish) Division landings in Suvla Bay in August 1915, not least because of newspapers' interest in the Dublin Pals. One objective captured by the 7th Dublins on 7 August was Hill 53, which became known as "Dublin Hill," a common expression of identity with soldiers naming their wartime locations after places at home. The idea that the Pals' sporting skills gave them special characteristics appeared in an officer's comment on how the men advanced—"with a dash for all the world like a wild forward rush at Lansdowne Road [football stadium in Dublin]."[61] After the withdrawal from Gallipoli in January 1916, there was much discussion of Irish soldiery having been let down by poor leadership. In August 1916, the *Freeman's Journal* published a poem that was unusual for its outright criticism of "dullard generals" who "lost / The gorgeous East, won at such cost / By the Irish at Gallipoli."[62] Such attitudes informed coverage of the initial report of the Dardanelles Commission in March 1917, which the *Freeman's Journal* headlined as "Where Irish Troops Were Sacrificed by Blunders."[63] So it was no surprise that the rebel song *The Foggy Dew*, written in 1919, drew comparisons between the Easter Rising and Gallipoli: "'Twas far better to die 'neath an Irish sky / Than at Suvla or Sud el Bar."[64]

Similar narratives of Irish valor appeared in coverage of the 16th Division's capture of Guillemont and Ginchy on the Somme in September 1916. Nationalist newspapers carried stories celebrating the "valour" and "great dash and gallantry" of the 16th Division. The *Freeman's Journal*, which described the division as "The Irish Brigade" (traditions dating back to Fontenoy) reported that it "has more than fulfilled the high expectations of the Nationalists of Ireland, and its deeds are worthy of the great tradition its title recalls."[65] Such views of the "dash" of the Irish appeared both in *The Times* and in the official history of the Leinster Regiment.[66] However, one account from an officer of the 7th Leinsters, J. H. M. "Max" Staniforth, stressed "there was none of the 'wild, cheering rush' one imagines. We stopped outside the parapet to straighten the line, and then moved forward at an ordinary walk."[67] Staniforth's view of the 16th Division was akin to the narrative attached to the Ulster Division earlier on the Somme.

At the Somme on 1 July 1916, there was an opportunity to link contemporary military service to unionist identities, and some did so. The date coincided with the anniversary of King William III's defeat of King James II at the Battle of the Boyne in 1690. That is now marked on 12 July due to calendar changes, but the date in 1690 was actually 1 July. The 36th Division's war diary noted that, "No date could have been more auspiciously chosen for the day on which the Ulster Division was to prove its value as a fighting force." It added, "The cries of 'No surrender, boys' . . . showed how well the men appreciated the historical associations of the day and the example they were called on to follow."[68] Similar sentiments appeared in the war diary of the 9th Inniskillings.[69] Some of this confused two events since the expression 'No Surrender' derives from the siege of Derry, though it is widely used generally in Ulster as an expression of unionist identity.

Three points relative to identity emerge from 1 July 1916. One is that those who wrote the records were aware of the coincidence, even if such historical awareness and expression were not widely spread among men who were understandably more concerned about the pressing matters of advancing and survival. As one veteran wrote on the fiftieth anniversary of the battle, "Nothing was further from my mind than the Boyne on the Somme."[70] Second, those who wrote about the characteristics of the soldiers of the Ulster Division focused not on the "dash" seen at Gallipoli, but on discipline.[71] The 9th Inniskillings' war diary noted that "the discipline maintained by all was magnificent[,] the advance being carried out as if it was a parade movement."[72] The commanding officer, Ambrose Ricardo, later recalled that there was "no fuss, no shouting, no running; everything orderly, solid and thorough, just like the men themselves."[73] Third, commemoration of the Ulster Division on 1 July 1916 became a central element of unionist identity even before the war's end.[74] As Gillian McIntosh argues, the story of the Somme was central to the creation of interwar unionism, with unionist writers pointing out the contrasts between the activities of loyal Ulstermen on the Somme in 1916 and the Easter Rising in Dublin in the same year.[75]

A different narrative surrounds the June 1917 battle of Messines, during which the 16th and 36th Divisions fought in positions alongside each other. Both then and since, commentary has focused not on the fighting qualities of the soldiers but on commonalities of men from different traditions. The Island of Ireland Peace Park, opened on the site of the battle in 1998, has become a key location for commemorations focusing on reconciliation between Britain and Ireland and between communities in Ireland.[76] Irish president Mary McAleese set the tone at the park's inauguration: "The men of the 36th Ulster Division and the 16th Irish Division died here. They came from every corner of Ireland. Among them were Protestants, Catholics, Unionists and Nationalists, their differences transcended by a common commitment not to flag but to freedom. Today we seek to put their memory at the service of another common cause."[77] During the battle there were reports of a "friendly rivalry" between the two divisions: "There was a race between the South and North Irish as to whether a green flag or an orange should be planted first above the ruins of Wytschaete. I do not know which won, but both flags flew there when the crest had been gained."[78] Perhaps that competition undermines notions of commonality but another correspondent noted how "Dublin men were going into the barrage, touching shoulders with their comrades of an Orange Lodge in North Ulster."[79] Years later, veterans of the two divisions recalled fighting side by side.[80]

More problematic was post-battle coverage of the death of Major Willie Redmond, the Nationalist MP for East Clare and brother of John Redmond, who was serving in the 6th Royal Irish Regiment in the 16th Division.[81] Wounded at Messines, he was collected on the battlefield by 36th Division stretcher-bearers and died at an aid post after being giving the last rites by a 36th Division chaplain. His death attracted massive newspaper coverage.[82] The nationalist press saw hope of Irish unity, with the *Freeman's Journal* writing that "the prospect of a union with the men of Ulster today is brighter than it has been" because Redmond "gave his life for a united Ireland."[83] This, of course, was the hope of nationalist leaders.[84]

But in reality, prospects of unity between north and south remained remote. Indeed, although Irish battalions managed to maintain an Irish identity as long as they existed, the composition of the two divisions had changed significantly since 1914, which meant that many in the division were English conscripts by the time of the Messines battle.[85] Meanwhile, the idea that men of divergent unionist and nationalist opinions reconciled on the battlefield is difficult to sustain because the chances of meeting someone from the other division during the battle were limited.[86] More widely, it can be difficult to know exactly how the men of the 16th and 36th Divisions really got on as there are so few accounts from the ranks. The commander of the 6th Connaughts, Rowland Feilding, cited a joke about "fraternising with the enemy" when his unit played the 9th Royal Irish Fusiliers at football in April 1917, and there were certainly some tensions.[87] While men may have collaborated in the shared tasks of fighting and surviving, and while they may have enjoyed good relations on an individual level, the joke about fraternizing with "the enemy" hinted at an underlying sense of difference that was not extinguished by being far away from Ireland.[88]

There was one other major event that occasioned discussion of the nature of Irish soldiers: the German spring offensive of March 1918.[89] As the onslaught opened, the 16th Division came under ferocious German attack and, as was the case all along the British section of the front, was forced to withdraw. Its withdrawal was neither markedly more rapid nor more extensive than elsewhere, but that did not stop Field Marshal Sir Douglas Haig from commenting in his diary: "Our 16th (Irish) Division which was on the right of VII Corps and lost Ronssoy village, is said not to be so full of fight as the others." In the post-war typescript version of his diary, he added, "In fact, certain Irish units did very badly and gave way immediately the Enemy showed."[90] Haig's view of Irish soldiers being slack in defensive roles spoke to wider perceptions of them as being reckless in matters of trench life (such as failing to take adequate cover and being untidy) and generally ill-disciplined.[91] The division was even accused—perhaps not seriously—of being full of Sinn Féin supporters. However, when the Chief of the Imperial General Staff, Field Marshal Sir Henry Wilson, later investigated, he found no evidence for the accusation. Indeed, he pointed out that the division's ranks were one-third non-Irish and his verdict influenced the British official history of the war: the division was "tired, undertrained and holding poor positions" but still "fought bravely but unavailingly on that terrible day against a numerous, determined and skilful enemy."[92]

Until this point in the war, there had never been any serious question over whether Irish regiments were a liability on the battlefield. Indeed, maintaining their Irish identity had been policy, as it had been for Scottish and Welsh regiments. In January 1917, General Headquarters in France decreed that Irish, Scottish, and Welsh soldiers should not be transferred to regiments other than those of their own "nationality." This was part of an effort to maintain local links in units as a boost to morale, but that did not mean maintaining Irish divisions for the whole war. By mid-1918, the 16th Division had lost most of its Irish battalions, while the 10th Division had lost all of theirs. Only the 36th Division maintained its identity to the end of the war. However, there remained a focus on keeping regular Irish battalions in the field (though not in "Irish" divisions), so those units first deployed saw the war through to the end did so because they were boosted by transfers from volunteer battalions.[93]

The persistence of Irish identities after the war was surprising, despite competing loyalties. Two examples of British veterans who became members of the Irish Republican Army (IRA) during the post-war phase of the Irish Revolution illustrate the point. Emmet Dalton was a senior figure in the IRA and a confidante of Michael Collins after serving as a British officer from 1915 to 1919. He was lauded as an IRA hero in later years, yet during the 1966 commemorations of the Easter Rising, he urged that those who had fought in the British Army should be commemorated properly. Michael McCabe fought in the rising, then joined the British Army, and later served in the anti-Treaty IRA before reenlisting in the British Army during the 1930s and serving through the Second World War. Yet when he died in 1975, his death certificate issued by the Republic of Ireland did not refer to his Republican service but rather described him as a "Retired British Soldier." At his end, the identity of an Irishman serving in the British Army defined his life.[94]

CHAPTER 3

Conserving British Manpower during and after the First World War

JESSICA MEYER

In the *Royal Army Medical Corps Training Manual* (1911), which was used by the Royal Army Medical Corps (RAMC) throughout the First World War, the corps is described as being "maintained firstly with a view to the prevention of disease and secondly for the care and treatment of the sick and wounded." The manual goes on to note that "while these are the objects with which [the corps officer] is maintained, the interests of the Army require something even more," namely "a general knowledge of military science, especially as regards the administration of an army in the field."[1] In this chapter, it is argued that general knowledge of military science could and did incorporate an appreciation of, and support for, military priorities through the provision of medical care. In other words, the practice of both preventative medicine and curative medicine by the RAMC during the First World War was dictated not only by medical priorities relating to the care and healing of patients, but also by military priorities, principally the need to conserve military manpower. These two priorities were both complementary and competitive. The synergies and tensions between them shaped the work of the RAMC throughout the war.

This chapter explores how the military priority of manpower conservation affected the nature and wartime work of the RAMC in three areas—recruitment, treatment, and rehabilitation. It considers first how matters of manpower conservation shaped RAMC work in terms of general military recruitment and how the policies of recruitment affected the corps itself. It then examines how the work of the RAMC, particularly as it pertained to manpower conservation, affected how soldiers viewed the corps. It concludes by considering how tensions between the army's medical priorities continued to play out in Britain's postwar policies on pensions and the rehabilitation of disabled ex-servicemen. In doing so, it argues that the military prioritization of manpower conservation created a complex, sometimes problematic, legacy for the RAMC as a branch of the armed services and for the provision of medical care under the auspices of the state.

Recruitment

The importance of manpower conservation to military effectiveness, and its influence on the work of the RAMC in particular, was evident from the very beginning of the war, especially where it concerned the medical inspections of new recruits. As historian Jay Winter notes: "The medical examination of recruits was an essential part of the attempt by all combatant nations to find and to train millions of men of sufficient physical fitness to sustain their battle plans. . . . By the end of the war, the question had arisen in acute form as to how to distinguish between men who were fit enough to fight and men whose presence in uniform or at the Front would do them and their comrades no good at all."[2] Winter goes on to argue that the British military faced two problems when it came to the effective recruiting of the most suitable manpower: "On the one hand, medical examinations revealed that a significant proportion of the British working class had grown up and had lived in conditions which made them unable to fight under any definition of fitness. Even the most threadbare net could not fail to catch the disabilities of tens of thousands of men who presented themselves for military service. But, on the other hand, military and medical definitions of fitness were sufficiently imprecise as to ensure that many British men wound up in the army who should never have been there in the first place."[3] At the heart of this conundrum lay the work of the Army Medical Services (AMS) examining officers. Before the war, these men identified potential medical deficiencies on the basis of a "careful and unhurried examination."[4] From August 1914, however, they were conducting markedly hurried examinations. The pressures of mass industrialized warfare, with its insatiable appetite for manpower, reduced the time available for medical inspections to five minutes per doctor per recruit. Each recruit was seen by four different doctors—one to take measurements, one to assess general condition, one to test nerves and sensory responses, and one to test chest, abdomen, and mental condition—in a system comparable to a factory production line. Some 10 percent of recruits were rejected on grounds of poor physical fitness, which Winter describes as "the strategic cost of poverty."[5] Nonetheless, the hectic tempo of mass mobilization meant that a large number of men suffering from illnesses and impairments wound up classified as fit for service.[6] Their presence in the military had implications for manpower conservation, since such men with undiagnosed chronic illness, such as tuberculosis or heart defects, were more likely to become part of the wastage statistics or require increased medical investment to make them effective as soldiers. While it remains unclear exactly how many men actually did pass medical examinations with such impairments undetected, the inclusion of "aggravation" as a diagnostic category in the system of awards for military pensions indicates official awareness of the potentiality.[7]

It is worth noting that, when the production-line system of medical examinations was instituted at the start of the war, responsibility for assessments shifted from the War Office to Local Government Boards (civilian), as part of an overhaul of the Ministry of National Service. Winter argues that this was, in part, a political decision to quell growing labor unrest stemming from fears that conscription under the Military Service Act of January 1916 would result in a pronounced militarization of society.[8] It also demonstrated the ways in which the AMS faced their own problems in relation to mobilizing sufficient manpower for the armed services, as the shift from military to civilian authority addressed tensions over the needs of the military, industry, and civil society in relation to the supply of manpower for total war. For the medical profession, as for industry and for commerce,[9] there were concerns about recruitment and conscription practices. Over-recruiting could be as problematic as under-recruiting. As Winter points out, the recruitment of physicians to the war effort meant that between 1915 and 1918 "there was very little medical care to be had at all in many rural and urban areas of Britain."[10] He goes on to suggest that "the fact that there was no crisis in the provision of medical care in wartime Britain was in part . . . a reflection of the efficiency of the medical community's organisation for war service. . . . The history of the medical profession in wartime is largely a history of an exercise in self-government, safe from the interference of the recruiting machine of the War Office and later of the Ministry of National Service."[11] Ian Whitehead, while he agrees that "on the whole a successful balance was struck between the military and civilian demands on the nation's doctors," also notes that the slowness and caution of the government's approach to the coordinated mobilization of doctors, particularly after conscription was introduced, meant that "murmurings about the Army's allegedly extravagant demands for doctors were never entirely silenced."[12] Recruitment of medical officers was thus a balancing act between the demands of the military and the needs of the civilian population, and these were competing demands that could never fully be reconciled.

It was not only the recruitment of doctors to military service that caused tensions. The recruitment of men to the ranks of the corps risked reducing the army's combatant manpower by placing physically fit men in noncombatant roles. The establishment of the RAMC as a formal, and ultimately royal, army corps during the second half of the nineteenth century had coincided with the rise of the international humanitarian movement, which, from its inception, worked to define medical care in the context of war as a noncombatant activity.[13] Thus, even when the officers and men of the medical services did carry arms, they did so on "the basic principle . . . that arms were only to be used by RAMC [personnel], whether officers or soldiers, in defense of their patients."[14] Although they served on the battlefield, RAMC personnel were not combatants. That affected the types of men military authorities sent to the corps. Ultimately, because medical service personnel were not supposed to fight, military authorities diverted to the corps men who were short of stature, men who were physically unfit, and men who were overaged.[15]

That had not always been the case. Initially, according to the official historian of the medical services during the war, "the recruiting of personnel for the Army Medical Services did not differ in its general aspect from the recruiting of the army generally."[16] Reserves and territorials filled in behind regulars, and new recruits joined the corps to take their places. Under the prewar plans to send a six-division expeditionary force to the continent in the event of a European war, orderly posts in home hospitals vacated by RAMC personnel, who were the first to be deployed with field ambulances, field hospitals, and base hospitals, were to be filled by men from the Territorial Force RAMC, the Home Hospital Reserves of the St. John Ambulance Brigade, and St. Andrew's Ambulance Station. According to the *Official History*, in the early days of the war, these plans were carried out successfully.[17] However, the dramatically expanding expeditionary force soon began to draw in the reserves as well. In 1914 alone, three new cavalry field ambulances, each comprising ten officers and 224 other ranks, were sent to France. And in 1915 "Territorial Force divisions went overseas with their own field ambulances [three per division], second line field ambulances being formed to replace those first line field ambulances which had been allotted to regular army divisions." Complicating matters further, "the divisions of the new armies . . . were accompanied by three field ambulances each, mobilized, with one or two exceptions, from the various training centres and depots of the R.A.M.C. which had been formed to meet the expansion of the corps."[18] In all, fifty-seven British divisions (regular, territorial, and New Army) deployed to the western front between 1914 and 1917. In these circumstances, the trained reserves of the AMS were quickly depleted.

It was not simply the creation of the New Army and Territorial divisions that increased demand on medical manpower. Changing procedures for evacuation resulted in the 1914 creation of a new type of medical unit, the Motor Ambulance Convoy (MAC), which was staffed by three medical officers (MOs) and fourteen RAMC other ranks who worked with 120 Royal Army Service Corps (RASC) drivers and mechanics.[19] Over the course of the war, the MAC evolved into a headquarters and three sections, staffed by two officers, one warrant officer, three non-commissioned officers (NCOs), and twenty-four other ranks from the RAMC, plus six officers, two warrant officers, eight NCOs, and 168 other ranks from the RASC. While the MAC was always numerically dominated by RASC personnel, it was classed as a military medical unit and commanded by an RAMC officer of field rank (major or lieutenant-colonel).[20] This, combined with the necessity of liaison between the two corps to make the system function, demanded that the RAMC commit men to its organization and management. Other units, such as mobile laboratories and the increasingly important specialist sanitary squads, placed further demands on the regular military medical services for noncommissioned manpower, for which prewar planning had not accommodated.[21]

As a result, during the first three months of the war, active recruiting for the RAMC occurred without restriction, alongside the mobilization of reservists. In total, 26,336 men voluntarily enlisted with the corps in this period.[22] The RAMC demand for men enabled those such as George Swindell, at just over five feet and two inches in height, to fulfil their active wish to enlist. Swindell recalled signing up with a friend:

> I was five feet two and one eight [sic] inches, Jimmy was five feet, eleven and a half inches, the recruiting officer, grabbed Jimmy by the arm, come along you are just the size we want, but looking at me with a look of pity and scorn, in a rather loud tone remarked we want men here, go away and grow. . . . I gave up hope, and was just leaving the Office, when the Sergeant came and called me back, the Officer had just had an order from the War Office, 20,000 men required at once for the Royal Army Medical Corps, height not less than five feet, three inches, so in I went, in the seventh heaven of delight.[23]

And soon after the recruiting MO allowed him to stand on his tiptoes for the height measurement, he was in. J. B. Bennett, another recruit of questionable physical ability, tried to enlist in the East Surrey Rifles:

[I] failed the sight test (Astigmastism), having been caught out on the blind side of the hexagonal test chart despite memorising the visible faces. I had pocketed my normal spectacles. I appealed and obtained a second test without success. . . . Nothing daunted, I pursued my endeavours at recruiting centres in London for four wearying days and failed similar tests with the addition of height. In a last effort I went to the local Drill Hall following a recruiting "tip off" on Sat. 9th. September and succeeded with the 3rd East Anglian Field Ambulance, with which I served throughout the war, having evaded the sight test. The N.C.O. left me to answer a 'phone call in an adjoining room and forgetfully asked me if I had read the sight testing panel. My affirmative was accepted and so I passed the test that I never had.[24]

Recruiting MOs turned many a blind eye to meet manpower demands for noncombatant units such as the RAMC, just as they did for "teeth" units.[25] Whatever manpower savings were garnered by having men like Swindell and Bennett fill ranks in noncombatant units in the RAMC, the unrelenting reinforcement demands of the frontline units pinched recruiting for the RAMC even further. As the British official medical services historian notes, "Owing to the demands for men as reinforcements to the combatant ranks, the recruiting for the Royal Army Medical Corps was restricted not only in numbers but also in categories as the war went on, and had to be supplemented in hospital services to a great extent by women."[26] In the early years of the war, recruitment to the corps was episodic, with periods of unrestricted enlistment being followed by months of no enlistment at all. After May 1915, though, general recruiting for the corps ceased altogether, with the exception of a brief period between 24 October and 4 November 1915, during which time 8,639 recruits were taken into the RAMC.[27] After January 1916, reinforcement of the corps was governed by the Military Services Act, with the War Cabinet assuming direct control of the allocation of manpower.[28] Even then, "men allotted to [the RAMC] . . . were chiefly men of a category of fitness lower than that required for combatant units."[29]

As a result of these limitations, the nature of the men who served with the RAMC changed from the start of the war. While the corps had initially attracted white-collar workers, "men whose occupation in civil life was that of clerks, school masters[,] . . . students of all descriptions,"[30] as well as clergymen who were officially discouraged by the Church of England hierarchy from enlisting in the combat arms,[31] the closing of direct recruitment to the RAMC in 1916, in response to the military's on-going requirements for combatant servicemen, meant that the option of going straight into the RAMC was no longer available to enlisting soldiers. Instead, emphasis was increasingly placed on redirecting to the RAMC conscripted men with "special qualifications such as dispensers, laboratory attendants, nurses, masseurs, mental and operating room attendants, sanitary inspectors, splint makers, electro mechanics, and men holding first aid and nursing certificates."[32] Military hospitals, quite logically, drew most of their staff through national service from the civilian personnel of asylums and infirmaries.[33]

Nor was it only the civilian occupations of RAMC men that changed after 1915. The overall fitness of enlistees dropped steadily and systematically as well. Whereas men such as Swindell and Bennett may have volunteered on a wave of war enthusiasm and taken advantage of doctors' willingness to turn blind eyes to their physical shortcomings, from mid-1915 it became actual policy to enlist men who would previously have been deemed unfit: "provision was made for the employment in hospitals at home of men of the regular and territorial force, who were permanently unfit for service abroad, in order to release men of the R.A.M.C. for medical units overseas."[34] These could include both soldiers temporarily in the process of recuperating from illness and injury and those whose medical impairments permanently unfitted them for frontline service but were not so severe as to warrant a full discharge from the armed forces.

At the same time, an order was issued to replace men who had been "combed out" of new drafts and noncombatant units, including those of the RAMC. These were men, aged nineteen to thirty-nine, who were encouraged to enlist in combat battalions. Thus, the RAMC was left with men aged seventeen to nineteen and forty to fifty to fill the ranks of the corps—men whose health and age would previously have been considered less than suitable for *any* form of military service. That fit men were "combed out" of RAMC units can be seen in the regular announcements of transfers to combatant units in the pages of the *'Southern' Cross*, the journal of the 1st Southern General Hospital, Birmingham.[35] Indeed, the unofficial history of the hospital clearly illustrated the ways in which the RAMC sought to fill its ranks, both at home and overseas, in the face of wider military demands for combatant manpower: "At first, the Unit was increased in size by direct enlistment, and their numbers gradually became more until they reached the maximum at the end of 1915. From that time onwards all the men fit for General Service were drafted to other Units for service overseas, and others, unfit, were drafted in to replace them [in the hospital]."[36] Recycling of injured men and men unfit for combat service to fill gaps left by "comb-outs" had a knock-on effect on the overall health and fitness of the corps. As Ward Muir, an orderly serving at the 3rd London General Hospital, Wandsworth, noted in 1916, "As far as

FIGURE 3.1.   The army's demand for manpower drove the RAMC's wartime medical practices. Medical evacuation and treatment practices sought to improve manpower efficiency and prevent unnecessary wastage. Preventive medicine—such as measures to avoid trench foot and disease— reduced casualties from poor hygiene. Image source: © Imperial War Museum, Q1220.

our unit was concerned it had already . . . been combed out five times; and this in spite of the fact that . . . our Colonel declined to look at any recruit who was not either over age or had been rejected for active service. The unit was thus made up even then, of elderly men and of 'crocks.'"[37] The enlistment of RAMC other ranks in the later years of the war, therefore, reflected the army's steady demand for fit men who could fight. The RAMC largely had to make do with the leftovers of manpower selection.

Treatment

While recycling was one way the RAMC conserved manpower, a more significant manner of doing so was through the prevention of disease and the efficient treatment of wounds. Efforts to treat the wounded centered initially on the rapid evacuation of wounded men to base (theater) and home hospitals for treatment (see Figure 3.1).[38] As the war progressed, however, the focus shifted to treatment nearer the point of injury.[39] Most histories of British medical evacuations emphasize the linear nature of the casualty evacuation process, which stretched more or less unbroken from no man's land to convalescent hospitals in the United Kingdom. Yet, by 1916, as Mark Harrison has demonstrated, the system of evacuation had evolved to provide numerous points of exit, either to command (rehabilitation) or convalescent depots, for men whose wounds and illness could be treated successfully farther forward. At each point, men discharged from medical treatment would undergo physical retraining at military convalescent depots before returning to their fighting units. For men who made it all the way to base or even home convalescence in Blighty, but whose injuries were not so serious as to require discharge from military service, a period in a convalescent depot ensured that they received a reintroduction to military life plus some physical training, all of which was required after a potentially prolonged period in hospital blues, the somewhat infantilizing uniform worn by men while in medical institutions.[40] At this stage, they would also receive a medical evaluation that might result in being reallocated to military duties away from the front line, perhaps as stretcher bearers or hospital orderlies with the RAMC.

The processes of medical evacuation and treatment were thus designed to enhance manpower efficiency and prevent unnecessary wastage, imperatives that also underpinned the practice of preventive medicine in the armed forces. Regular inspections by regimental officers for conditions such as trench foot and scabies, for example, were designed to prevent casualties due to carelessness and poor hygiene. As Harrison has argued, "When soldiers had been imbued with notions of cleanliness in the past, these had been inculcated through orders and regulations, often on pain of punishment. This was still the case in 1914–18 but soldiers were increasingly taught the virtue of hygiene as a form of civic responsibility."[41] A soldier could let down his mates or his unit by getting sick and having to be evacuated. He could also let them down by passing on whatever had afflicted him. Mobilizing a mass army of citizen soldiers forced political authorities to make concessions, such as the right to refuse vaccination on the grounds of conscience. The army, however, "was rather uncomfortable with such egalitarian ideas and tended to revert to more familiar disciplinary and punitive regimes" to ensure compliance. This often cast RAMC medical officers, particularly regimental medical officers (RMOs), in the role of medical policeman, investigating men's conditions, not impartially but often cynically, in an effort to prevent malingering.[42] Unsurprisingly, this element of military medical practice resulted in RMOs being viewed with suspicion by ordinary soldiers, as reflected in Wilfred Owen's satirical portrayal in "The Dead-Beat":

We sent him down at last, out of the way.
Unwounded;—stout lad, too, before that strafe.
Malingering? Stretcher-bearers winked, "Not half!"
Next day I heard the Doc's well-whiskied laugh: "
That scum you sent last night soon died. Hooray!"[43]

Max Plowman was even more damning of medical callousness in his postwar memoir, *A Subaltern on the Somme in 1916* (1927):

I find [Brown] lying on the ground, breathing heavily and apparently un-conscious. . . . This is a case for the doctor. After searching for some time, I find him at mess in the Headquarters dug-out; so I send down a message. He comes up, evidently annoyed at being disturbed, so I apologize as we go to the boy together. The doctor bends over him a moment, and then, rising, shouts with astonishing fury: "You damned young scrimshanker, get up! What the devil do you fancy you're playing at? Think you can swing the lead on me? Get up, or I'll have you in the guard room."

He pushes the boy with his foot, but the lad does not stir.

"Don't you think he is ill?"

"Ill? There is nothing the matter with him at all. Just 'wind up,' the bloody young coward. Leave him there if he doesn't get up, and don't call me again. I don't waste my time over these damned scrimshankers."

He turns and goes back to the dug-out.

This strikes me as callous brutality, and for a moment I am at a loss to know what to do. The men around come to the rescue. They pick the boy up, assuring me they will look after him. As they carry him off, I hear them murmuring, "Brute." "Swine."[44]

Medical officers themselves could struggle with these demands of military services, as Whitehead points out, "no amount of training or experience made it any easier for Medical Officers to accept these limitations on their sense of duty to the sick, wounded and dying."[45]

Medical policing as an element of manpower conservation could also be counterproductive. Skepticism of conditions such as shell shock and other invisible injuries and illnesses sometimes led to leaving men in combat roles when they actually posed a danger to their comrades, either through failure to perform appropriately or through the spread of infection. One effective solution was treatment of conditions near the front line. This was certainly true of shell shock, which was first treated in specialist units formed from converted casualty clearing stations (CCS) in November 1916. From 1917, commanding officers were given greater discretion to determine whether a shell-shocked soldier should be removed from his company.[46] This method was also used for the treatment of certain physical injuries, which were moved no further back than the clearing station. While improvements in abdominal surgery at CCSs saved lives, these units also became static sites of care for the effective treatment of infections. These positive developments almost certainly improved the army's rates of rehabilitation and retention. As Harrison points out, "67 per cent of casualties wounded in the theater were being returned to duty without need for evacuation to the UK. The saving in manpower which accompanied the evolution of forward treatment is incalculable and represents a major departure from pre-war thinking among senior commanders."[47] There can be little question that forward treatment by the RAMC played a vital role in maintaining military manpower.

Rehabilitation

Not all men could be recycled or retained, however. Even with improvements in preventative, curative, and rehabilitative medicine, many men who survived illness and injury did so with impairments that not only rendered them unsuitable for military service, but which were also life-changing on return to civilian life. Increasingly, the British government had to acknowledge this impact both at a personal level and in relation to the management of economic manpower in civil society. The foundation of the Ministry of Pensions in 1916, which signaled the statutory right to a disability pension, was part of the wider range of welfare reforms put in place to support and encourage mass mobilization.[48] Although often represented as parsimonious in practice, particularly after the government spending cuts associated with the Geddes Axe of 1922, the right to a disability pension (with allowances for dependents), treatment, and, in the most extreme cases, constant medical attention reflected the ways in which the war had shaped popular attitudes toward state responsibility for men whose service and sacrifice it demanded in wartime.[49] Again, the discourse around shell shock is instructive. Debates in parliament over the status of so-called service patients in mental asylums pointed to the exceptionality of men whose conditions were caused by their service in war.[50] While never as openly debated, similar considerations shaped the pension ministry's treatment of men suffering a range of impairments, from malaria to gunshot wounds. Appropriate war service was at the heart of entitlement to pension for impairment or injury.

Also important to the ministry's approach to pensions was conservation of manpower for industry and the economy. Policy, as Joanna Bourke has shown, was shaped by industrial approaches to disablement and labor management.[51] In both its propaganda and its practice, the ministry employed the language of economic independence and personal self-reliance in conveying its responsibilities toward pension claimants. John Galsworthy, who would become the editor of *Reveille*, a quarterly journal in support of disabled ex-servicemen, wrote in the introduction to the reports of the Second Inter-Allied Conference on the After-Care of Disabled Men, "we shall so recreate and fortify the rest of [the disabled ex-serviceman] that he shall leave hospital ready for a new career. Then we shall teach him how to tread the road of it, so that he fits again into the national life, becomes once more a workman with pride in his work, a stake in the country and the consciousness that, handicapped though he may be, he runs the race level with his fellows."[52] Achieving these aims required not only the provision of rehabilitative care and vocational training, but also financial support in the form of pensions—but at a level that discouraged reliance on the state. Pensioners were not merely encouraged, but expected, to undergo training in suitable vocations (which might not always be the same as their chosen career) as part of their medical rehabilitation, and applicants were inspected and re-inspected, sometimes over many years. The rationale was that improvements in their physical condition should result in lower pension payments, which, in turn, would encourage the disabled veteran to earn his own living.

While many pensioners believed such ministry attitudes and policies bordered on abuse, most accommodated themselves to the ministry's aim of boosting industrial manpower by returning veterans to economic activity. Indeed, a number articulated their desire for work as a rejection of the need for a pension. E. C. Booker, for example, told the ministry, "I am trying to make myself and my family self-supporting and thereby independent of any pension," while J. L. Campbell-White claimed, "If I could get a decent job, I should not trouble about a Pension."[53] The importance of financial independence to notions of mature masculinity and the need to conserve and expand economic manpower for the good of British society thus remained central tenets of government and veteran responses to war disability.

Conclusion

Manpower conservation and the provision of medical care were related elements of military and government policy, both during the mobilization for the First World War and in the decades that followed. Between 1914 and 1918, the army's demand for manpower was the driving force behind medical practice, whether diagnostic, curative, or preventative. In the war's aftermath, the economic need for industrial manpower was just as important in shaping medical practice in relation to disabled veterans. Historian Fiona Reid argues that "men . . . came out of the trenches with the firm belief that because they had gone to war they deserved good state-funded medical and social care, not just during the conflict but afterwards too."[54] This may be true, but the assertion also needs to be nuanced to reflect the influence manpower considerations had on attitudes toward state-provided medical care. The preeminence of manpower conservation may have originated with army and state policy arising from the military imperatives of war, but old attitudes were effectively transmitted to British servicemen during and after the war. Even when practices aimed at getting men back to the front or the factory were challenged as shoddy or cruel, they nonetheless continued to influence the way men understood their health and its relationship to their social and economic place in society.

In examining the centrality of manpower both to the work of the military medical services during war and to state-funded medical care after war, we can thus understand men's attitudes toward their entitlement to medical care for service-related injury or impairment. They generally accepted that the manpower needs of the army and industry ultimately regulated levels of care and compensation. Such attitudes would endure and eventually go on to shape the foundations and formation of the welfare state in Britain after another world war.

CHAPTER 4

The Canadian Garrison Artillery Goes to War, 1914–1918

ROGER SARTY

The little-known garrison artillery branch of the Canadian Militia played a unique part in mobilization for the First World War. Legislation limited the militia to home defense, a role in which the garrison artillery had a leading part for the protection of sea ports and which it fulfilled throughout the war. At the same time, the units met the unexpected need for "siege" batteries of heavy howitzers for the Canadian Expeditionary Force (CEF), the organization created in August 1914 to raise contingents for overseas service. The militia garrison artillery units showed extraordinary initiative, continually and successfully pressing headquarters in Ottawa to raise additional siege batteries, while delivering all the qualified personnel needed, and still more men to complete other types of artillery units that required personnel trained to work with heavy equipment. By contrast, most units of the militia, lacking the resources to recruit and train men in large numbers, became dormant as the government scrambled to find the means to recruit overseas reinforcements. These efforts were of limited success until the imposition of compulsory service in the last year of the war. All the while, the militia garrison artillery units at home delivered formed units and trained reinforcements for overseas service, even as they met new enemy naval threats to Canada's key ports, which became more vital than ever for the shipment of North American war supplies to Britain and Europe.[1]

Strikingly, the officers on the rolls of the militia garrison artillery units that mobilized in 1914 succeeded in leadership roles throughout the whole of the war, especially in the units that served in combat on the Western Front. This was important evidence of the robustness of the peacetime organization. The officers were community leaders in cities that, not coincidentally, had been stations for the British Army artillery in Canada during the eighteenth and nineteenth centuries and became the home stations of the Canadian artillery; these were "artillery towns" in which the militia units were important institutions. Garrison gunners also benefited from an identity as an elite group of technicians especially suited for warfare in the industrial age. They were a nucleus of technical expertise that was crucial to mobilizing and training the powerful artillery brigades of the CEF. They were also pioneers of new techniques for long-range and indirect fire that proved so vital to success on the Western Front.

Garrison artillery, which included fixed fortress guns and heavy mobile armament, has an important place in Canadian history. During both the French and British regimes, defense of the vast and thinly populated territory had depended upon fortifications and heavy guns. The Canadian volunteer militia, established in 1855, the legal beginning of the modern Canadian Armed Forces, featured many garrison as well as field batteries of artillery. So, too, did the militias of the Maritime colonies, which were integrated into the Canadian militia after confederation by the federal Militia Act of 1868.[2] The first units of the Canadian regular army, known as the permanent force, were batteries established in 1871 to take over the fortifications at Kingston, Ontario, and Quebec City from the departing British Army garrisons. Within each battery was a section responsible for the fixed fortress armaments and another for field guns. By the late nineteenth century, the distinction between garrison and field artillery became more pronounced with the rapid progress of technology, particularly in naval warfare. In the British Empire, coastal artillery led the development of long-range fire, designing the sophisticated mountings and fire-control equipment needed to engage fast-moving steam warships whose guns could bombard ports from ranges of ten kilometers and more. Canada, following the British Army, divided the artillery into two distinct branches, garrison and field, with the permanent force garrison units being designated the Royal Canadian Garrison Artillery (RCGA), and the militia units the Canadian Garrison Artillery (CGA).

But the most important prewar development for the garrison branch was the 1905–1906 transfer to the Canadian Department of Militia and Defence of the recently modernized British coastal artillery fortifications that protected the Royal Navy dockyards at Halifax, Nova Scotia (NS) and Victoria-Esquimalt, British Columbia (BC). Numbers 1 and 2 Companies of the RCGA moved from Quebec City to take over the Halifax establishment, while three new companies were organized—3 and 4 at Quebec City, and 5 at Esquimalt (see table 4.1). Some specialists from the departing Royal Garrison Artillery (RGA) companies transferred to the Canadian service, where their expertise with modern armament was urgently needed. The total strength of the RCGA thus rose to some 600 officers and men, or about one-fifth of the permanent force. New Canadian permanent force Royal Schools of Artillery at Esquimalt, and especially Halifax, were valuable assets in training both permanent force and active militia personnel. And particularly important for the purposes of this volume, during the First World War, these training establishments, together with the existing schools at Quebec City and Kingston, would train officers and other ranks for service overseas in heavy and siege artillery.

In 1914 the militia garrison artillery included four coastal defense regiments to support the permanent force at Canada's defended ports. In addition, there were two heavy brigades and an independent heavy battery in the eastern part of the country to provide mobile batteries for field divisions.

As the British warned of approaching war, Canadian garrison gunners were deployed in defense of ports on both coasts. At Halifax, headquarters of the peacetime army's 6th Division, the administrative area for the Maritime provinces, the militia gunners had exercised for decades with British regulars and then the Canadian permanent force garrison, so arrangements there were mostly complete. But knowledge that German fast light cruisers were in the western Atlantic during early August 1914 prompted authorities to authorize the 3rd Regiment to place four 4.7-inch guns on mobile carriages in improvised coastal defense emplacements on Partridge Island at the entrance to the port of

Table 4.1   Peacetime organization of the Canadian Garrison Artillery, 1914

Coastal defense, Royal Canadian Garrison Artillery (permanent force)	1 and 2 Companies, Halifax 4 Company, Quebec 5 Company, Victoria-Esquimalt
Coastal defense, Canadian Garrison Artillery (active militia)	1 (Halifax) Regiment, 4 companies 5 (British Columbia) Regiment, Victoria-Esquimalt, 3 companies 6 (Quebec and Lévis) Regiment, 3 companies 3 (New Brunswick) Regiment, Saint John, NB, 3 companies
Heavy artillery, RCGA (permanent force)	3 Company, Quebec
Heavy artillery, CGA (active militia)	Montreal Heavy Brigade, 2 batteries Prince Edward Island Heavy Brigade, 2 batteries Cobourg Heavy Battery

Saint John. The guns were of limited value for coastal defense, as the wheeled carriages, even when improved with local equipment, could not traverse quickly enough to track a fast ship. They did bolster the morale of the population, however. More important, they were good for training for field work, and the regiment used the coastal battery garrison to train new recruits to prepare them for overseas drafts through the whole course of the war.

On the west coast, the permanent force and militia garrison at Victoria-Esquimalt on Vancouver Island also mobilized on well-laid plans, but the absence of fixed defenses at the mainland ports caused a panic in the province, until a British and allied Japanese cruiser could rush to the scene. The Cobourg Heavy Battery loaded its four new sixty-pounder guns for a transcontinental rail trip to establish an emergency coastal battery at Vancouver for a few weeks.

The most pressing requirement was to strengthen the coastal artillery garrison at Halifax to maintain readiness around the clock for a long war. Rear-Admiral R. S. Hornby, Royal Navy (RN), commander of the Royal Navy cruiser force that took up station at Halifax to protect heavy shipping traffic to Britain, insisted there could be no relaxation of the army's defenses. The frequent fogs off Halifax made the prospect of a surprise attack on the port something to be taken seriously, but the tiny Canadian navy had no destroyers or submarines available for extended seaward defense, and the Royal Navy could not spare vessels from European waters. The army garrison, as a result, carried an unusually large responsibility for the security of Hornby's main operating base. To help ease the pressure on the two permanent force companies (331 personnel) and the 1st (Halifax) Regiment (282 personnel), militia headquarters had the Saint John regiment and the Prince Edward Island (PEI) brigade each send a detachment of seventy-five personnel to the Halifax forts early in March 1915.[3] Later that month, at the request of the British government, detachments from the militia garrison artillery helped the RCGA at Halifax raise a new unit of 100 personnel (No. 6 Company, RCGA) to mount and operate coastal artillery at St. Lucia in the British West Indies. Thus it seemed that the Canadian regular units would not have a chance to serve in Europe. This was fine with Major-General Sam Hughes, the minister of militia and defense, who held professional soldiers in contempt and believed that citizen volunteers had superior fighting qualities.

Some professional garrison gunners did go overseas with the CEF, but as individuals. In fact, most of the garrison artillerymen in the first two contingents had already trained in permanent force or militia service. In late August 1914, men who volunteered for overseas service proceeded to Camp Valcartier (outside Quebec City), where they were sorted into new units of the CEF. The first overseas contingent comprised the 1st Canadian Division and reinforcement units. Included in that order of battle was No. 1 Heavy Battery, whose 219 personnel included seventy-four trained gunners, mainly from the Montreal Heavy Brigade, commanded by Major F. C. Magee from the 3rd (New Brunswick) Regiment.[4] An additional sixty-eight trained gunners, mostly from the 3rd Regiment, with another 100 personnel recruited by that unit, served in the Divisional Ammunition Column.[5] The men had to be physically strong because garrison artillery work was a physical business. The standard for garrison artillery soldiers was five feet eight inches in height and 150 pounds in weight, traits that made garrison gunners useful for delivering and heaving heavy artillery ammunition to frontline batteries.

Soon after the first contingent sailed to England in October 1914, mobilization began for the second contingent, comprising the bulk of the 2nd Canadian Division. It was a prolonged enterprise that continued through the winter of 1914–1915. No. 2 Heavy Battery, which concentrated for training at Halifax, drew its personnel, seven officers and 211 of other ranks, from all the heavy brigades and coastal defense regiments in eastern Canada. Of the eight officers, seven were experienced members of the militia units, as were forty-seven soldiers of other ranks.[6] At the same time, 6th Division at Halifax raised the headquarters and No. 1 Section of the 2nd Divisional Ammunition Column, which was recruited largely by the 3rd Regiment in Saint John and concentrated in Fredericton. The officer commanding the whole column, Lieutenant-Colonel William H. Harrison, and seven of the remaining nineteen officers also came from the 3rd Regiment, as did more than seventy of the other ranks from the trained garrison on Partridge Island; fifty other personnel with no prior service had been recruited by the regiment in New Brunswick.[7] The heavy batteries and divisional ammunition columns landed in France with the 1st and 2nd Divisions in February and September 1915, respectively. The ammunition columns were integral to the Canadian divisional field artillery establishments, but the heavy batteries were assigned to British formations, as the British were grouping heavy batteries to meet the urgent need for concentrated firepower. Only the 1st Heavy Battery had modern armament, including four sixty-pounder guns; 2nd Heavy Battery, like many British batteries, operated older 4.7-inch guns until they were replaced by sixty-pounders in early 1917.[8]

When the second overseas contingent had sailed for England in May–June 1915, militia headquarters authorized the organization of a "heavy battery depot" to supply reinforcing drafts to the heavy batteries and ammunition columns that had gone overseas. The raising of that unit reveals a good deal about the administration and politics of Canada's wartime citizen army and the workings of the artillery community. The original authorization for the unit, dated 3 June 1915, instructed 4th Division headquarters in Montreal to have the Montreal Heavy Brigade select the commanding officer and recruit two-fifths of the personnel, including a subaltern and sixty-four soldiers from the other ranks. The PEI Heavy Brigade was to provide another two-fifths of the personnel (two officers and sixty-four soldiers), and the Cobourg Heavy Battery the remaining fifth (a subaltern and thirty-six soldiers). The 6th Division was to find accommodation for the composite unit in Halifax and provide access to the training facilities there.[9] None of the Montreal brigade's battery commanders was "available," but Lieutenant-Colonel Frederick Minden Cole, a former commanding officer who had already applied for an overseas command, agreed to step down in rank to major in order to accept the appointment.[10]

Raising units locally made some sense, but it could also be a tricky business. On 19 June 1915, Major-General R. W. Rutherford, the permanent force gunner who commanded 6th Division, received two unusual telegrams from Charlottetown about the organization of the new unit. One was from a newspaper editor and the other from Donald Nicholson, the federal member of Parliament for the area, each saying that the visiting militia minister had asked them to find out who had authorized Captain W. B. Prowse of the PEI Heavy Brigade to advertise that he was raising a full heavy battery as a dedicated island unit. Hughes had given no such authority.[11] The minister's idiosyncratic method of communicating, in this case through two separate third parties, neither with any link to the military, was just one of the ways in which he frustrated senior officers. Rutherford replied that he had followed headquarters' orders in assigning Lieutenant-Colonel A. G. Peake, officer commanding the PEI Brigade, not Captain Prowse, to raise personnel for two-fifths of the new heavy battery depot. Evidently satisfied that the military staff had not defied ministerial authority, Hughes was happy to accede to the enthusiasm he found on the island. At his instruction, on 28 June 1915, the 6th Division issued orders for the PEI Heavy Brigade to raise its own unit, designated No. 2 Heavy Battery Depot "to be raised and officered exclusively from the Province of Prince Edward Island."[12] Lieutenant-Colonel Peake took command of the new unit, with Captain Prowse as the second in command.

Even before this decision, Lieutenant-Colonel Beverley Armstrong, commanding the 3rd Regiment at Saint John and a prominent local lawyer, protested that the Montreal, Cobourg, and PEI garrison artillery had each been allowed to raise units that represented them at the front, while his own regiment had been afforded no such recognition.[13] A total of 534 serving and former noncommissioned officers and soldiers of more junior ranks from the unit had already joined the CEF, including all branches of the service, but "no unit that has as yet gone has been identified with our corps."[14] Headquarters, in a Solomon-like decision, promptly assigned the 3rd Regiment to raise the part of Minden Cole's unit, now designated No. 1 Heavy Battery Depot, which had originally been allocated to the PEI brigade.[15] This the 3rd Regiment did, drawing on the experienced personnel in the unit's coastal defense battery on Partridge Island (near Saint John) and bringing in new recruits to replace them.

The expansion of the garrison artillery overseas began inauspiciously with a July 1915 War Office message appealing for a supply of trained garrison artillery personnel. They were needed for the "siege" howitzers, six-inch caliber and larger, that Britain was producing in an emergency effort to counter Germany's strong arsenal of high-angle-fire weapons: "The [Army] council are aware that there are in Canada several well-trained batteries of Coast Artillery, the personnel of which . . . might be of great assistance in manning the new Siege Batteries now in course of formation."[16] The militia council in Ottawa thought the request "impracticable" "in view of the fact that a company of garrison artillery has already been provided for St. Lucia, and that Canadian harbours on the Atlantic are threatened with a new form attack."[17] The danger came from German submarines, then launching a successful offensive against Allied shipping in the western approaches to the British Isles. Intelligence (false as it turned out) that U-boats were heading to North American waters brought a warning to the Canadian government from Vice-Admiral Sir George Patey, recently appointed commander-in-chief of the British cruiser forces based at Halifax and Bermuda, that his ships were vulnerable to torpedo attack and of no use against submarines. Renewed appeals to the Admiralty for destroyers, effective anti-submarine ships, were in vain. More than ever, the security of Canadian ports depended on the army. At Halifax the vestigial Royal Canadian Navy installed an anti-submarine net, covered by army searchlights and quick-fire batteries, and at Saint John improvements began at the improvised battery on Partridge Island.

An 18 August 1915 cable from Hughes, then in England, relayed that "fully fifteen hundred" gunners were needed, which implied that the British were after something other than one or two of the permanent force coastal artillery companies. Things clarified when Hughes returned early in September 1915 and a cable arrived at the same time from the chief of the imperial general staff reminding Hughes that he had "promised to take up question of furnishing some garrison artillery units," whose personnel could help man the new siege batteries.[18] Hughes approved the staff's recommendation that three siege batteries should be mobilized from militia artillery by converting the two new heavy battery depots at Halifax and Charlottetown and by

FIGURE 4.1. Canadian Corps heavy artillery in action, East of Arras, September 1918. Back in Canada, the Canadian Garrison artillery played an important role in raising personnel for CEF artillery units by drawing on the strong support of local communities. Image source: National Library of Scotland. License CC BY 4.0, https://creativecommons.org/licenses/by/4.0/.

organizing a third battery in Montreal. The batteries were to be placed at the disposal of the War Office, separate from the newly formed Canadian Corps in France. For the third battery, headquarters took up an offer by Lieutenant-Colonel Richard Costigan, officer commanding the 6th Field Brigade in Montreal, to raise an overseas field brigade: Would he be willing to raise a siege battery instead? Costigan agreed and nominated one of his battery commanders, Major E. G. M. Cape, an engineer and head of a prominent construction firm, to command it.[19]

Major-General Sir Willoughby Gwaktin, the capable British officer who had served as Canada's chief of the general staff since 1913, had already notified the War Office that Canada could offer two or three batteries. These units, he cabled, would comprise "partially trained artillerymen but without present knowledge of heavy ordnance: Gunners excellent type, very intelligent. Some permanent force will be included. Will you accept?" The War Office responded that all were needed, and "if practical more to follow." Gwatkin, who resisted Hughes's prejudice against the permanent force and willingness to keep excessive militia forces on home duty in response to local political pressures, sent a minute to the staff with evident relief: "The ground is clear. Will you please proceed."[20]

Word traveled quickly, and Lieutenant-Colonel Armstrong in Saint John renewed his bid to raise New Brunswick's own siege battery. He had, he explained, been in touch with Major L. W. Barker, one of the 3rd Regiment's best prewar battery commanders, who was anxious to take a battery overseas. There were twelve other officers who had asked to go, as had several qualified noncommissioned officers with the coastal defenses on Partridge Island.[21] "We are now coming to the time of year when it is easiest to obtain recruits," Armstrong wrote. "In my capacity as Recruiting Officer I have constantly to combat two objections with the best class of recruits. One is that they do not want to be quartered for the winter in their home town and the other is that they prefer artillery."[22] Headquarters approved the raising of No. 4 Battery at Saint John on 9 October 1915.[23]

Gwatkin did everything possible to expedite the organization of the four batteries. His determination to "stiffen" militia units with permanent force specialists was strengthened by two letters from Brigadier-General H. C. Thacker, a senior RCGA officer who was about to assume command of the 1st Division artillery in France. The British, Thacker wrote, had stripped their coastal defenses of all but essential regular army RGA specialists to mobilize heavy and siege batteries.[24] In making his "plea for the R.C.G.A. (with special reference to those at Halifax)," he noted that, with the expansion of the CEF during 1915, all the other permanent force combat units were finally "at or on their way to the front, and I think it will be a *very bad* thing for the future of the R.C.G.A. if they were not strongly represented there."[25] No sooner had Gwatkin received these letters when he got an urgent personal note from Minden Cole complaining that his and Cape's requests for a few specialist permanent force noncommissioned officers for Nos. 1 and 3 Batteries had been rejected by the chain of command. An annoyed Gwatkin directed the adjutant-general to make sure the battery commanders got the people they needed, adding, "The Officer Commanding R.C.A. appears to be making difficulties which I hope you will disregard."[26] Gwatkin got things done. He went further and ordered the coastal division commanders to release every RCGA gunner who wanted to go overseas and could be spared. The returns came back that sixty soldiers beyond those needed to complete the militia batteries were available. Headquarters attached all these as supernumeraries to No. 2 Siege Battery when it embarked for overseas on 27 November 1915.[27] No. 1 Battery sailed on 22 November and No. 3 Battery on 18 December.[28] Again, Gwatkin got things done.

The War Office was "glad to take as many siege Batteries as can be raised," so the Canadians continued to raise them.[29] Temporary overcrowding at artillery camps in Britain delayed the sailing of No. 4 Battery until the spring of 1916, but other batteries soon followed. The appeal from the War Office resulted in the raising of four additional batteries in Canada. Headquarters initially estimated that only two could be raised in a timely fashion,[30] but had not counted on the enthusiasm of the garrison artillery community, which really was remarkable. On 12 April, headquarters approved conversion of the Charlottetown depot into an overseas siege battery and pressed for haste. Lieutenant-Colonel Peake, commander of the PEI Heavy Brigade, explained that winter conditions had all but prevented recruiting, but that prospects were good now that the roads were opening. Peake, it will be recalled, had raised No. 2 Battery. He had taken the unit to England and, although occupying only a major's appointment, refused to take down his militia rank as a lieutenant-colonel. Early in 1916, he relinquished command over the issue and returned to Canada. In April, militia headquarters approved Peake for command of the new PEI battery, he having agreed to step down in rank.[31] The organization of another new battery began on 13 April, when headquarters accepted an offer from McGill University's principal, Sir William Peterson, to raise a siege battery. Peterson had established McGill's Officer Training Corps in 1912, the first in the country, and he personally headed the military instruction committee. The siege battery proposal may have originally come from professor of psychology and one-time officer in the PEI Heavy Brigade, Captain W. D. Tait, whom Peterson nominated to command the battery. Tait had been on active service at Halifax since the beginning of the war, serving in the 6th Division's section that mobilized units in the Maritime provinces; Captain Cyrus MacMillan, second in command, was also a professor at the university and a former member of the PEI Heavy Brigade; and, like Tait, he had served in Halifax since the outbreak of war. Peterson urged haste in organizing the McGill battery, as the students and faculty would disperse at the upcoming end of term. Headquarters obliged and accepted Tait's recommendation that fifty of the recruits immediately move to Halifax for training.[32]

Mobilization of the third and fourth new batteries was the result of initiatives from the garrison gunners in the Maritimes. On 13 April, the 6th Division sent word that the 3rd Regiment at Saint John had already raised "practically a whole [additional] siege battery." The staff in Ottawa appeared to have forgotten that, in October 1915, they had authorized the regiment to recruit both No. 4 Battery and additional personnel as reinforcements, which the regiment had done with its usual energy. Headquarters immediately approved the mobilization of 3rd Regiment personnel as a second Saint John siege battery for early dispatch overseas.[33] Selected for command was Major L. T. Allen, commander of the 3rd Regiment coastal artillery detachment at Halifax, an appointment he had lobbied to escape. He had warned Lieutenant-Colonel Armstrong about the unrest among the gunners at Halifax at not being allowed to go overseas, a feeling only heightened by a newspaper article criticizing the lack of patriotism in men who remained on home service. Allen had proposed that experienced troops from the coastal defense garrisons should be permitted to go overseas as new recruits were trained to replace them, which was now beginning to happen. He was allowed to bring personnel from the Halifax detachment with him, and they were replaced from the 3rd Regiment's coastal defense battery at Saint John.[34]

Lieutenant-Colonel S. A. Heward, the artillery commander of the Halifax garrison, made a strong appeal for the RCGA to raise its own overseas battery. Of immediate importance, some forty-three members of the permanent force artillery in the fortress would soon complete their engagements, and most seemed determined to leave and join other overseas units. On 20 April 1916, headquarters authorized the establishment of the new siege battery, provided that sufficient personnel remained in Halifax to keep the coastal defenses fully efficient. The RCGA had already started to recruit and train replacements. Heward, reverting to the rank of major, took command of the new battery.[35] In March 1916, militia headquarters authorized the 1st (Halifax) Regiment to raise units for the artillery of the 4th Division, which was then still mobilizing. The coastal gunners raised the headquarters and ammunition column of the 14th Field Brigade (138 personnel), and No. 2 Section (174 personnel) of the 4th Divisional Ammunition Column, which, after field training in the militia's large artillery camp at Petawawa, Ontario, sailed in September 1916.[36]

The siege batteries began to move to France in the spring of 1916, under new numbers assigned by the British on the Royal Artillery's order of battle (see table 4.2). What had been Nos. 1 and 2 Batteries, now 97 and 98, supported British corps from the opening of the battle of the Somme. The former No. 3 Battery (now 107) supported the Canadian Corps, which was still in Ypres area, and moved with the corps when it joined the Somme battle for the attack on Courcelette in September.[37] The former No. 4 Battery, now 131, had already entered action on the Somme in August. The British had organized a fifth Canadian battery, the 165th, from the surplus personnel who had come from Canada with the first four batteries, supplemented with reinforcements from Montreal. This battery, together with Major L. T. Allen's battery from Saint John (raised as No. 7 Battery, and now 167), joined the British artil-

Table 4.2   Canadian siege battery designations, 1915–1918

UNITS RAISED IN CANADA	DESIGNATION IN BRITISH ORDER OF BATTLE	REDESIGNATION IN CANADIAN ORDER OF BATTLE
1 Overseas Battery (Bty.) Siege Artillery (Arty.) 23 Sept. 1915; Montreal/Saint John/ Cobourg	97 (Cdn.) Siege Bty. 24 Feb. 1916 9.2-inch howitzers	1 Cdn. Siege Bty. 29 Jan. 1917
2 Overseas Bty. Siege Arty. 23 Sept. 1915; Prince Edward Island	98 (Cdn.) Siege Bty. 24 Feb. 1916 6-inch howitzers	2 Cdn. Siege Bty. 29 Jan. 1917
3 Overseas Bty. Siege Arty. 23 Sept. 1915; Montreal	107 (Cdn.) Siege Bty. 24 Feb. 1916 6-inch howitzers	3 Cdn. Siege Bty. 29 Jan. 1917
4 Overseas Bty. Siege Arty. 9 Oct. 1915; Saint John	131 (Cdn.) Siege Bty. 7 May 1916 8-inch howitzers	4 Cdn. Siege Bty. 29 Jan. 1917
	165 (Cdn.) Siege Bty. 16 June 1916; formed in UK 9.2-inch howitzers	5 Cdn. Siege Bty. 29 Jan. 1917
5 Overseas Bty. Siege Arty. 12 Apr. 1916; Prince Edward Island	272 (Cdn.) Siege Bty. 15 Oct. 1916 8-inch howitzers	8 Cdn. Siege Bty. 29 Jan. 1917
6 Overseas Bty. Siege Arty. 13 Apr. 1916; McGill University	271 (Cdn.) Siege Bty. 6 Oct. 1916 8-inch howitzers	7 Cdn. Siege Bty. 29 Jan. 1917 6-inch howitzers (in 1918)
7 Overseas Bty. Siege Arty. 14 Apr. 1916; Saint John	167 (Cdn.) Siege Bty. 10 June 1916 8-inch howitzers	6 Cdn. Siege Bty. 29 Jan. 1917 6-inch howitzers (in 1918)
8 Overseas Bty. Siege Arty. 20 Apr. 1916; Halifax (RCGA)	273 (Cdn.) Siege Bty. 15 Oct. 1916 6-inch howitzers	9 Cdn. Siege Bty. 29 Jan. 1917
		10 Cdn. Siege Bty. 10 Jan. 1918; formed in UK 6-inch howitzers
		11 Cdn. Siege Bty. 7 Nov. 1917; formed in UK 6-inch howitzers
		12 Cdn. Siege Bty. 1 Jan. 1918; formed in UK 6-inch howitzers

lery groups supporting the Canadian Corps on the Somme on 30 September and 3 October 1916.[38]

The British Expeditionary Force's (BEF's) assignment of heavy and siege artillery to the corps general officers commanding Royal Artillery (GOCRAs) for effective coordination of fire had placed too heavy a burden on a single commander. The solution was to appoint corps heavy artillery commanders who controlled the heavy and siege guns under the direction of the corps

GOCRAs. The Canadian Corps Heavy Artillery headquarters, under a British officer, Brigadier-General A. C. Currie, RGA, stood up in April 1916, with British heavy artillery groups under his command. When, in December 1916, the Canadian Corps took up position in the vicinity of Vimy Ridge, the corps' heavy artillery was reinforced by additional heavy artillery groups, scattered among which were the two Canadian heavy batteries and all of the siege batteries. Meanwhile the headquarters 1st Canadian Heavy Artillery Group, a total of about thirty personnel, had been forming in England, under Minden Cole, who regained his substantive rank of lieutenant-colonel. Major W. G. Beeman, a graduate of Royal Military College and a career officer in the permanent force artillery, succeeded Minden Cole in command of the 97th (Canadian) Siege Battery.[39] Early in January 1917, the new headquarters joined the Canadian Corps near Vimy Ridge and took control of four of the Canadian siege batteries.

At that time, the siege batteries were re-designated with distinctive Canadian numbers "at the urgent request of Canadian authorities." (See table 4.2.) The final three batteries raised in Canada, by McGill University, the PEI Heavy Brigade, and the RCGA at Halifax now became the 7th, 8th, and 9th Canadian Siege Batteries.[40] They arrived in France in late March and early April 1917, and immediately moved to Vimy Ridge.

On 1 April the 2nd Canadian Heavy Artillery Group joined the operations in the Vimy sector under Lieutenant-Colonel F. C. Magee of the 3rd (New Brunswick) Regiment, who had led the 1st Canadian Heavy Battery since 1914. He was succeeded by his second in command, Major C. F. Inches, another 3rd Regiment officer who had volunteered in 1914.[41] Although the two Canadian Heavy Artillery Group headquarters functioned as integral parts of the Canadian Corps, Canadian batteries frequently moved to British groups, including those supporting other corps, and British batteries frequently joined the Canadian groups.

The 9th Battery, raised by the RCGA at Halifax, was the last formed garrison artillery unit to come from Canada, but some thirty reinforcement drafts, varying in size from fifty to more than 200 soldiers, followed in 1917–1918. Of these, seventeen drafts came from Nos. 9 and 10 Depot Batteries, Siege Artillery, which had been organized at Saint John and Halifax in the summer and fall of 1916. Both depots ran through the complete syllabi of siege artillery training that had been developed and supervised by instructors from the Royal School of Artillery at Halifax. The RCGA also dispatched three drafts, as did, periodically, the PEI and Montreal Heavy Brigades and the Cobourg Battery, although the militia units did not have facilities to conduct the same level of training that took place at Saint John and Halifax. The depots at Halifax and Saint John pleaded to be sent overseas as complete batteries, as they had done earlier in the war, but Canadian military authorities overseas now insisted on employing officers and senior noncommissioned officers who had proven themselves at the front.[42]

The success of the militia garrison artillery in sustaining the flow of reinforcements overseas—a total of perhaps 3,000 personnel—was all the more notable because of increased pressure on the coastal artillery at home during the last two years of the war. A fresh and devastating U-boat campaign forced the Royal Navy to begin convoying Atlantic shipping in the spring and summer of 1917, with Halifax and Sydney, Nova Scotia, becoming two of the major assembly ports. Yet neither the Royal Navy nor the newly belligerent United States could spare anti-submarine warships for Canadian waters. More than ever, the security of war shipping in the approaches to the major Canadian ports depended on the coastal artillery, including new defenses established by the Halifax garrison at Sydney. Pressure to keep fully efficient crews available around the clock increased during the last months of the war, when three U-boats operated off Nova Scotia and southern Newfoundland in August–September 1918.

Overseas, the drafts from militia units enabled the Canadian siege artillery to double its gun strength. In the latter part of 1917, the War Office expanded each siege artillery battery from four to six guns, as had earlier been done with the field and heavy artillery. In October–November 1917, sections of sixty to seventy soldiers joined each of the nine Canadian siege batteries to crew the additional guns. These personnel came from three new batteries—the 10th, 11th, and 12th—which had organized in England from reinforcement drafts and which were now broken up to augment the existing units.[43]

Another new battery, initially designated the 13th, was already mobilizing from a new draft of 202 officers and men from McGill University. It arrived in England during September 1917. In response to a personal plea from the Duke of Connaught, the former governor-general of Canada, that the draft should maintain its link to McGill, the Headquarters Overseas Military Forces of Canada (HQ OMFC) in England went to extraordinary lengths to replace the officers and senior noncommissioned officers with experienced people from Montreal. Thus the officer assigned to command was Major L. C. Ord, who had come overseas from the Montreal Heavy Brigade with the 1st Siege Battery and subsequently served as the second in command of the 5th Canadian Siege Battery. The new McGill unit landed in France on 14–15 March 1918 under the designation of the 10th Canadian Siege Battery.[44] It was shortly followed on 3 April by a new 11th Canadian Siege Battery, under the command of Captain J. P. Hooper, from the PEI Heavy Brigade and one of the original officers with the 2nd Canadian Siege Battery.[45] Finally, on 2 June 1918 a new 12th Canadian Siege Battery arrived under the command of Major F. A. Robertson, who before the war had served in the 5th Regiment under Arthur Currie, commander of the Canadian Corps as of June 1917. Robertson had first gone overseas with the 47th Infantry Battalion, lost an eye in the assault on Regina Trench during the Somme campaign, and transferred to the artillery, commanding a British siege battery before taking over the new Canadian unit. Seriously wounded again in the Amiens offensive in August 1918, he lost a leg and was succeeded in command of the battery by Major Colin MacKay of the 3rd (New Brunswick) Regiment, who, after a tour with the Canadian unit at St. Lucia, had reached England and been posted to the Royal Garrison Artillery.[46]

In late 1917 and early 1918, the loosely organized heavy artillery groups of the BEF became large brigades with as many as six batteries permanently assigned. The objective was to combine in each brigade a cohesive mix of the diverse gun and howitzer types that would enable them to carry out different missions without shifting batteries among groups.[47] In January 1918, the two existing Canadian Heavy Artillery Groups became the 1st and 2nd Brigades, Canadian Garrison Artillery. In May, the 3rd Brigade, CGA came into action, under the command of Lieutenant-Colonel W. G. Beeman, promoted from command of the 1st Canadian Siege Battery, where he was succeeded by Major W. H. Dobbie of the 3rd Regiment, second in command since the organization of the 1st Battery in 1915.[48] The three brigades, with all fourteen Canadian heavy and siege artillery units under command, operated a total of eighty-four guns and howitzers. The new garrison artillery brigades of the BEF were still employed fluidly, attached to different armies and corps as needed. One or two of the Canadian brigades were often under the Canadian Corps, and all three came together for a notable role in two of the corps' great successes in the final push to victory, the offensive at Canal du Nord and Bourlon Wood in late September 1918 and the assault on Valenciennes in early November 1918, shortly before the Armistice.

This formidable artillery striking force, not contemplated before the war, was the creation of the militia garrison artillery in eastern Canada and British Columbia, whose determined efforts and the strong support of their communities produced the twelve siege batteries, a considerably larger number than envisioned by the general staff in Ottawa. The officers, experienced prewar members of the militia and permanent force, filled most of the battery and brigade commands—successfully—from the first deployments through to the Armistice.

It is difficult to discover precisely how many men the garrison artillery sent overseas, but between 7,000 and 8,000 would be a reasonable estimate. Sailing lists for the formed units that went overseas from 1914 to 1916 show some 1,000 personnel with previous service in the militia and permanent force units. The militia and permanent force units at home, moreover, recruited all of the personnel who went overseas and provided a full syllabus of training for most of them. Thus, the expertise and experience of the prewar garrison gunners was an indispensable nucleus that generated fourteen heavy and siege units for service overseas. That scarce talent had to be managed carefully. Garrison gunners also had to worry about defending the Canadian coastline and ports. Those roles became paramount because of the German naval threat. Canada had to take measures to defend vital ports that were so crucial to transatlantic shipping. Not every garrison gunner who wanted to go overseas could go overseas—not all at once, anyway. But they managed. In fact, the apparently divergent pressures of the garrison artillery's two-front war ultimately sustained one another as headquarters in Ottawa accepted the pleas of the coastal artillery units and allowed them regularly to dispatch trained, experienced people overseas and replace them with new recruits.

CHAPTER 5

"Returning Home to Fight"

Bristolians in the Dominion Armies, 1914–1918

KENT FEDOROWICH AND CHARLES BOOTH

On 31 October 1914, a picture of Canadian soldiers marching through Shirehampton Park, near Bristol, appeared in the newly-launched fortnightly *Bristol and the War* (see Figure 5.1). In a column four abreast, men of the 11th Battalion, Canadian Expeditionary Force (CEF) smile and wave to the camera. Wearing their distinctive roughrider hats, this "fine body" of men from the Canadian prairies had arrived in Avonmouth on the 11,000-ton Royal Line passenger liner-cum-troopship RMS *Royal Edward*, which had quietly slipped into its home port on Sunday, 18 October. Owing to the *Royal Edward*'s early morning arrival, residents had been taken unawares; but as *Bristol and the War* enthusiastically reported, those who did witness the event gave their colonial cousins a warm and hearty welcome. As "the great liner swept majestically into the entrance harbour," the journal recorded, "there came from her decks and port holes cheer after cheer. Clad in Khaki, these bronze-featured soldiers from the Dominion shouted enthusiastically their greetings to Britain's shores."[1] As debarkation proceeded, "bugles and drum and fife bands announced to the people of Avonmouth the fact of their arrival. The inhabitants speedily turned out of their houses and gave the Canadians a rousing reception," until these men departed in special trains to Salisbury Plain, where they joined the rest of the 31,000-strong 1st Canadian Contingent, most of which had arrived in Plymouth four days previously.[2]

The *Bristol Times and Mirror* commented on "the warmth of the reception accorded to those who represent England's strength from across the sea."[3] The 18 October arrival, in fact, marked the beginning of a long wartime association between Bristol and soldiers from the colonies of white settlement, especially Canada. In fact, the *Bristol Times and Mirror* quickly identified seven "Old Bristolians," several with impressive sporting credentials in boxing, cycling, association football, and rugby, who had emigrated to Canada prior to the war and were now returning "home" to help defend "King, Country and Empire." "In a word," boasted the newspaper, "Bristol has a grand showing of her sons, who have left their land of adoption to give their best for the Mother Country."[4]

Sir Charles Lucas, in his five-volume history *The British Empire at War*, observed that one of the hallmarks of the dominions' participation was that, by the end of the conflict, they were no longer considered imperial "accessories"; rather, like their British cousins, they had willingly taken up the "gauntlet and made and shouldered the war."[5] In this partnership, the mobilization of dominion manpower, an aggregate of 1.3 million men and women, had been a critical factor in the empire's victory. Of this total, 978,000 saw service overseas.[6] Manpower was also sourced through British reservists and dominion personnel joining British Army units in the opening stages of the war. For instance, there were 6,500 South Africans either of British birth or British extraction who returned home to enlist in imperial units over the course of the war.[7] In Canada, there were 3,294 British reservists residing in the dominion, of whom 2,779 returned home, while some 150 joined the CEF. Moreover, an estimated 50,000 Canadians served with British forces, either enlisting directly into British units or, once overseas, transferring out of the CEF to join the British Army, the Royal Flying Corps, the Royal Naval Air Service, and, after 1 April 1918, the Royal Air Force.[8] But there was another huge pool of dominion manpower that has yet to receive the scrutiny of military or migration historians: returning migrants.

Until recently, migration historians have not considered soldiers a worthy subject or a fruitful field of investigation. There are a few exceptions, but even these isolated works have focused on government sponsored ex-service migration schemes, largely ignoring the importance of soldiers as agents of the greater migratory and diasporic processes themselves.[9] Military and social historians have made important observations in their studies of troops garrisoned in particular towns, cities, regions, and overseas territories, especially concerning soldier interactions with local populations and military contributions to the local economies. Much less is known, though, about the role of

soldiers in the processes of cultural transference between the imperial metropole and the colonial periphery, or, in the case of the United Kingdom, how
these soldiers helped construct a wider British identity and culture overseas
that in turn fed a broader Britishness, some of which was exported back
"home."[10] Using the analogy of the soldier as "tourist," several antipodean
scholars have explored the apparent contradictions in identity formation that
emerged between dominion forces and their British hosts.[11]

But what of soldiers as "migrants?" Ulbe Bosma has convincingly argued
that 6 million European soldiers serving in colonies primed the pump for
nineteenth-century colonization and made significant contributions to the
growth of settler societies in areas as diverse as Algeria, Australia, Cuba, the
Dutch East Indies, and South Africa. His clarion call is for the "writing of
these colonial soldiers back into migration history," even when, for the purposes of this chapter, we are talking about return migration.[12] The unprecedented number of dominion and colonial soldiers who found themselves in
Europe, Africa, and the Near East between 1914 and 1919 is an excellent example of both mass migration and global Britishness at work. The war did
not undermine the imperial connection. Quite the contrary, it raised the consciousness of many of these men about their role and place in the empire.[13]
This new interpretation challenges a longstanding tenet that the Great War
broke or at least severely undermined imperial ties and therefore helped shape
new national identities. Recent scholarship has challenged these assumptions,
suggesting more nuanced interpretations.[14]

This chapter makes a similar plea for the examination of those tens of
thousands of British-born migrants who returned home to fight in the dominion contingents during World War One. Using Bristol as a case study, it
explores several interlocking questions concerning migration, identity, and
war. At its core is what is meant by Britishness, the contours of which are still
being mapped by British World scholarship. The digitization of passenger
lists, school magazines, honor rolls, newspapers, dominion attestation papers,
personnel records, nominal rolls, and repatriation files allows us not only to
trace more confidently, and with greater accuracy, the outward migration of
these men, but also to chronicle a unique phase of return migration to the
United Kingdom. This complements the revolutionary way online records
have been used in local studies of military service in the United Kingdom,
what Richard S. Grayson has labeled a "military history from the street approach."[15] In addition, these digital resources help locate and chart strands of
the English diaspora, something that has been a challenging and, until now,
understudied chapter of the British migratory process.[16] Crucially, the exist-

ing scholarship needs to break away from the confines of a "nationalist" agenda. In the early 2010s, Jonathan Vance made the observation that only "recently have [Canadian] historians turned back to Britishness, seeing it as something more than a sign of youthful immaturity."[17] Vance argues that, in the Canadian context, Britishness must be seen as a Canadian hybrid because it allows one to gauge and comprehend one of the great mass migrations of the twentieth century—the return of close to 1 million Canadians to the United Kingdom during the two world wars.[18] It was an entirely natural response for people who saw themselves as belonging to a "Greater Britain," which included the home islands and the "white dominions."[19]

They were products of a "British World" that grew out of mass migration from the British Isles.[20] Its core were the "neo-Britains," where migrants found they could transfer into societies with familiar cultural values. The United States remained the main beneficiary of British settlers from all parts of the United Kingdom throughout the nineteenth century—an estimated 62 percent. By the turn of the twentieth century, however, that had changed. Between 1901 and 1910, nearly half of the 1,670,198 souls who left Britain chose imperial destinations—primarily the dominions of Canada, Australia, New Zealand, and South Africa. This rose to 68 percent in 1910–1911 and to 78 percent in 1913, and it showed no signs of abating by the time war broke out in 1914.[21] Even more illustrative, Canada, the "senior" dominion, experienced six of its ten largest annual immigration levels ever recorded—over 200,000 each year between 1903 and 1913. Many came from the "mother country," with well over 1 million British immigrants settling in Canada between 1900 and 1914, the largest immigration flow of any ethnic group in those years.[22]

The immigration experience of the Pacific dominions was similar. A net influx of almost 121,000 arrived in New Zealand between 1900 and 1914, two-thirds from the British Isles and one-third from Australia. Attracted by a reenergized economy and new employment opportunities, this wave of immigrants was also encouraged by the reintroduction of government assisted passage schemes in 1904 and 1906. Farmers constituted one-third of the assisted passages.[23] A similar pattern was echoed in Australia between 1910 and 1914. The Western Australian government's "Land for Opportunities" campaign, coordinated in London, helped. In 1911, a peak of 9,562 government-aided British immigrants chose a new life in the state.[24] As elsewhere in the settler dominions, these new arrivals would be the first to rally to the colors in August 1914.

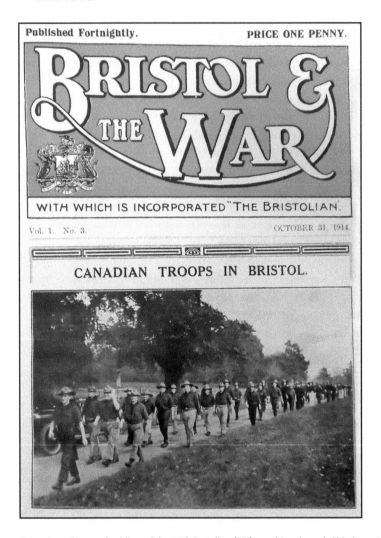

Published Fortnightly.   PRICE ONE PENNY.

BRISTOL & THE WAR

WITH WHICH IS INCORPORATED "THE BRISTOLIAN".

Vol. 1. No. 3.   OCTOBER 31, 1914.

CANADIAN TROOPS IN BRISTOL.

FIGURE 5.1. A contingent of soldiers of the 11th Battalion (CEF) marching through Shirehampton Park, near Bristol, October 1914. Photograph courtesy of Bristol Central Library, England.

Bristol and the British World: Return Migration and Remembrance

In October 1914, Private Thomas G. Spoors, was one of the 1,197 CEF volunteers on board the *Royal Edward* and on their way to Bristol, where his family lived in the arboreal Bristol suburb of Bishopston.[25] Spoors, who was born in 1891, was among the tens of thousands of British migrants who had been attracted to prewar Canada by the promise of free land, higher wages, and a better life, and had emigrated there in 1912. His destination was Winnipeg, the provincial capital of Manitoba—gateway to the Canadian prairies and the "last, best West."[26] Formerly an office clerk, he had decided to become a farmer, and, as such, was eagerly sought after by local emigration and steamship agents, who secured Canadian government bonuses for desirable settlers such as agriculturalists and female domestics.[27] Whatever had enticed this young bachelor to the western plains, Spoors was one of the many British-born migrants who immediately answered the call to the colors when war broke out. In September 1914, he enlisted in the 11th Battalion CEF at Valcartier, Quebec, where he found that close to 80 percent of his unit was British-born. After a brief period of training, he journeyed across the Atlantic in a thirty-two ship convoy, escorted by units of the Royal Navy. He would no doubt have been heartened by the warm reception at Bristol, and it is probably safe to assume that he had some contact with his family while in Bristol or while on leave from training at Salisbury Plain.[28] What we do know for certain is that he survived the war, returned to Bristol when he demobilized, got married in March 1919, and lived out his remaining days in Westbury-on-Trym.[29]

Spoors was one of thousands British-born migrants who returned home to fight with the CEF. This pattern was repeated throughout the war by thousands of others who had emigrated to Australia, New Zealand, and South Africa; they either volunteered in their adopted dominion forces, as in the case of some 1,100 Bristolians, or they returned to enlist in British regiments.[30] Little is known of this returning group of migrants, however. Military historians from the former dominions have long acknowledged the ethnic composition of their respective national armies during the Great War. Nearly 70 percent of the 1st Canadian Contingent was British-born, for example. And when Canada's second contingent was raised in November 1914, more than 60 percent of its 22,000 men were British-born and bred. In fact, by the end of 1915, when the dominion had recruited 213,000 men, 70 percent of CEF soldiers were British-born.[31] Although the proportion of British-born naturally declined as the war continued, even by the end of the conflict nearly half were still of British birth.[32]

Smaller, but similar, patterns of ethnicity were replicated in the antipodes. In New Zealand, according to Paul Baker, British-born recruits made up one-quarter of the strength of New Zealand Expeditionary Force (NZEF) Main Body and the early rounds of reinforcements that fought at Gallipoli.[33] Native New Zealanders may have outnumbered their British brethren, but, for the prodigy of British migrants, the bond of "kith and kin" was a powerful glue that bound the two communities to each other. "Far from regarding the empire as a constraint upon their freedom," notes Ian McGibbon, "most New Zealanders saw it as a positive benefit and were proud to be part of it."[34] Their loyalty was absolute and for most they were British to the core. The Australian case was similar. New research suggests that one in five soldiers of the Australian Imperial Force (AIF) were British-born.[35] Nonetheless, as Charles Bean, Australia's official historian and a keen promoter of the Anzac legend noted, the men who streamed to the state enlistment centers—whether Australian or British-born— did so because "the British connection had always been sacred."[36] "Loyalty to Britain," as Joan Beaumont has recently observed, "was much more than strategic pragmatism"; it was a "core value" of Australian Federation.[37] Undoubtedly, the exploits of Australian troops at Gallipoli and Flanders helped forge a new Australian national spirit. However, according to Graham McInnes, the British-born author who spent his formative years in Melbourne before embarking upon a career in the Canadian diplomatic service, it was to England that these young Australians gazed as they enlisted. "England was still Home," he wrote in his autobiography, and in England's hour of need "the call to the heart and the mind of the unseen yet well-loved Homeland" was uncontrollable. McInnes also made another shrewd observation about the recently arrived British newcomers who had flocked to the recruitment centers: the "emigrant vessel was coming home."[38]

At the battalion level, Australian units had an equal, if not higher, proportion of British-born migrants, which, in turn, reflected settlement patterns in the various regions of the Commonwealth. In the early stages of recruitment, despite attempts by the Australian command to kindle a sense of regional identity, old country and imperial identities flourished. The 2nd Battalion AIF, for example, possessed a genuine "imperial" flavor with men from New Zealand, Great Britain, Canada, and South Africa who had settled in Sydney and northward along the coast to Queensland.[39] The 3rd Battalion AIF, which initially drew its recruits from Sydney, proudly claimed how valuable was the contribution that British ex-regulars had made in the early days of mobilization. Many of the original noncommissioned officers (NCOs) were "seasoned campaigners" who had seen active service in India and Africa: "Quite naturally their influence played no small part in the making of the battalion."[40] The 11th Battalion AIF also boasted that Western Australia attracted the "best of the manhood from the British Isles"; many of its men had previous war service in India, Africa, and China, and they were deliberately selected as NCOs to "stiffen" the raw recruits.[41] The Australian governor-general, Sir Ronald Munro-Ferguson, made an interesting observation when he reviewed the last batch of 5,000 troops embarking for Europe in December 1914: "They looked more like veterans, being older men, than new levies. There are a great number of Scotch NCOs in several of the Battalions."[42] In fact, there was a "good seasoning of veterans" throughout the first Australian contingent with "nearly two-thirds having had some military training before enlistment."[43]

The waves of British migrants who flooded the recruitment stands in Canada testified to the determination of newcomers to preserve that all-important imperial connection. Harold Baldwin, a British-born migrant from Burton-on-Trent who enlisted in Saskatoon, Saskatchewan, summed it up nicely: "The majority of us were Britishers who had left the Old Country to try our luck in the new land; but many were veterans of other wars who wanted to get in to the game again."[44] Prince Arthur, the Duke of Connaught and Canada's governor general (1911–1916), confirmed the same sentiment when he inspected the first contingent at Valcartier in October 1914.[45] And no one could doubt the depth and passion that many Anglo-Celtic Canadians felt towards the mother country.[46]

Canadian units had stronger and more identifiable British elements in their expeditionary forces, at least in the earlier stages of the conflict. For example, it was estimated that three-quarters of the 10th Battalion, whose recruits were drawn largely from Winnipeg and Calgary, were British-born, including a colorful smattering of ex-regulars who had recently arrived from Australia, Egypt, India, Malta, and South Africa.[47] According to one veteran, Sergeant Christopher Scriven, "H" company (120 men) was composed entirely of "seasoned Imperial troops," with many others scattered throughout the remaining seven. A similar pattern was reflected in the recruits from the 13th Battalion (Royal Highlanders of Canada), where between 65 and 75 percent were from the "Old Country."[48] The regiment was also kilted, so Scottish-born migrants were eager to join.[49] Other Canadian Highland battalions within the 1st Canadian Division mirrored the overwhelming "Scottishness" of the 13th Battalion. These units included the 15th Battalion (48th Highlanders) from Toronto and the 16th Battalion (Canadian Scottish), in which half the officers and 80 percent of the other ranks were from the British Isles.[50] By the end of the war, half of the 268 officers who had served in the 16th Canadian Scottish were British-born, as were 3,300 out of the 5,223 soldiers of other ranks.[51] Among them was twenty-nine-year-old Private Frederick G. Flook of St. George in Bristol. He was wounded on 20 May 1915, while fighting with his battalion during the battle of Festubert, at La Bassée in France.[52]

The politics of Scottish identity and its invented traditions was not confined to Canada alone.[53] In Australia, the 5th Battalion, affectionately known as the Victorian Scottish regiment, clung to longstanding Scottish connections in that state centered on Melbourne. In South Africa, Scots rallied to enlist in the Cape Town Highlanders, the 1st and 2nd Transvaal Scottish, and the Cape-based Duke of Edinburgh's Rifles. The 4th South African Infantry (also known as the South African Scottish) formed part of the South African Brigade, which served as part of the 9th (Scottish) Division in France and which also reflected an interesting demographic between South African and British-born recruits. The brainchild of mining magnate William Dalrymple, the 4th Regiment was formed by recruiting through various Caledonian societies, which eventually raised 1,282 troops of all ranks. According to John Buchan, the official historian of the South African forces in Europe, 337 of the unit were Scottish-born, 258 were English, 30 were Irish and 13 were Welsh. There were also 595 South African-born in the regiment, but a large proportion of them were first-generation South Africans of Scottish descent.[54] Ethnically driven appeals for volunteers were not limited to communities of Scottish heritage, as Richard S. Grayson argues in chapter 2 of this volume on Irish identities in the British Army.

"Imperial seasoning" was crucial in providing the backbone of these dominion contingents during early war days, as they transformed from an enthusiastic civilian rabble into disciplined military forces. Some 18,959 members of the CEF were ex-British regulars, who, as Canadian historian Desmond Morton has observed, were "barely 3.1 per cent of the total but conspicuous in almost every unit history and memoir."[55] A large but unspecified number of these soldier migrants had joined the Permanent Force, Canadian militia, and other auxiliary units after migrating to Canada prior to the war. Of fundamental importance were those ex-imperials from the noncommissioned ranks, especially those who had served in South Africa or India. Often placed in pivotal positions such as regimental sergeant-major (RSM) or company sergeant-major (CSM), these men provided a steadying hand during the initial stages of basic training.

For instance, there were two sergeants from Bristol who enlisted in "B" company, 15th Battalion CEF, recruited out of Toronto: Frederick J. Harcombe and Henry W. Hooper. Both Harcombe and Hooper had served in the 6th Battalion, Gloucestershire regiment, before emigrating to Canada in April and May 1912, respectively. There is no indication how long Harcombe served with the Bristol-based Territorial Force battalion, but Hooper had served six and a half years. Soon after their arrival in Toronto, these friends both joined the 48th Highlanders of Canada, which later formed the core of the 15th Battalion. Badly gassed at the battle of Second Ypres in April 1915, Hooper was invalided back to the United Kingdom to convalesce. Continuing to suffer from the effects of poison gas, he was made an assistant training instructor and served out his military career as an acting CSM at a host of Canadian training facilities in southern England until his demobilization in

1919.[56] Harcombe was taken prisoner during the fighting at St. Julien and sat out the rest of the war in Germany. This "seasoning" also occurred among the South African Scottish. According to John Buchan, sixty-four men had served in the regular army, and many of the 760 who had been in the territorials, the volunteers, the yeomanry, or the militia had seen active service during the South African War.[57] In both cases these men brought with them their military skills, their operational experience, and, perhaps most important for this inquiry, their Britishness.

A Few Bristolians at War

To help illustrate the interconnection between British World identities, transnationalism, and return migration, let us examine five examples of Bristolians who fought with dominion forces, starting with Cecil Garnet Stiff. Born in Bristol, he worked as a trainee blacksmith at the colliery in Frampton Cotterell, a small Gloucestershire village northeast of the city. In May 1908, this single young man emigrated to Canada from Liverpool on the Dominion Line passenger ship SS *Kensington*. Upon landing, he traveled by rail to Winnipeg, Manitoba, where he intended to start a new life. While there, he joined the local militia, the 106th Regiment, Winnipeg Light Infantry. Formed in 1912, this unit eventually supplied wartime reinforcements for a number of Canadian units overseas. Stiff joined the CEF in early June 1915 and was drafted into the 61st (Winnipeg) Battalion.[58] Shortly after arrival in England, the 61st was absorbed into the 11th Reserve Battalion based at Shorncliffe in Kent, where the Canadians had established their training facilities. When sent to France as reinforcement, Private Stiff was attached to the 44th (Manitoba) Battalion, with which he eventually fought at Vimy Ridge (9–12 April 1917). Stiff was seriously wounded in the back and abdomen at Vimy, one of more than 7,000 wounded in a battle that remains a focal point of Canada's coming-of-age story. Despite being evacuated from the battlefield and repatriated to a hospital in Cardiff, Stiff eventually succumbed to his wounds. His body was returned to Frampton Cotterell, where it now lies in the tranquil grounds of the parish church. Stiff had come full circle. The poignancy of his story is neatly captured in the inscription on his Commonwealth War Graves Commission head stone, itself emblazoned with the Canadian maple leaf: "He Loved Canada / His Adopted Home / And Died For His Native Country."

An equally rich story, which displays the British World and its multifaceted networks, concerns two brothers: Harold and Lancelot Bacchus, "prominent farmers" from Manakau (near Auckland),[59] who enlisted together with the

New Zealand Rifle Brigade in February 1916. Harold was born (1875) in Sarawak, where his father, Captain George Henry Bacchus, late of the 7th Dragoon Guards (The Princess Royal's), was serving as the commandant of the local defense forces. For whatever reasons—the debilitating climate or professional advancement—shortly after Harold's birth, the Bacchus family left Borneo for Australia, where Captain Bacchus took a commission in the New South Wales artillery. In the meantime, his wife, Constance, who was a daughter of the first principal of the University of Sydney (John Woolley), gave birth to Lance (1877). Captain Bacchus died seven months after Lance's birth, leaving his widow with three young boys to raise on her own.[60] She returned to England, where she chose Bristol as their new place of residence. Between 1887 and 1889, Harold and Lance attended nearby Clifton College and played for the Clifton Rugby Club.[61] The Bacchuses did not stay put for long. In 1899, the family returned to Sydney, where Lance married and began raising a family of his own. A few years later, the family moved again, this time to New Zealand, allegedly because the boys' mother thought Australia too hot a climate for raising Lance's newborn son. Whatever the reason, the entire family moved across the Tasman Sea and settled in New Zealand in 1902.

When war broke out twelve years later, the two brothers resisted the temptation to enlist, at least initially. Instead, they worked their farms and provided food for the war effort. However, they eventually volunteered in early 1916 and were attached to a reinforcement draft for the 1st Battalion, 3rd New Zealand Rifle Brigade. They went straight to France and pretty much straight into the Somme campaign with the New Zealand Division in September 1916. Harold and Lance, who were both lance corporals by this time, were detailed as stretcher bearers. Although the New Zealanders achieved their preliminary objectives, the toll of life was the worst the division had experienced to that time—7,000 casualties, including more than 1,500 killed in just three weeks of fighting.[62] Both men were killed by a German shell while they were carrying a wounded comrade back to an aid station. Lance, who was described by the *Wanganui Chronicle* as a "quiet, unassuming young man," had been an "enthusiastic and first-class [field] hockey player and a lay reader in the Anglican Church." He was thirty-eight when he died. He and Harry, who was forty-one, have no known grave and are commemorated on the Caterpillar Valley Memorial.[63]

When the Anzacs hit the beaches at Gallipoli on 25 April 1915, several Bristolians were among the earliest casualties. Twenty-four-year-old Private Harold James Pring, who was serving under the pseudonym William Clarke, was one of them. Pring lived in his native city and worked as a blacksmith's striker until January 1908, when he enlisted in the Royal Navy. His naval career was far from stellar, however. Five entries in his service record indicate that he served between three and ten days in the brig. He was twice charged with absence from duty and refusing to work, convictions for which he was sentenced to forty-two days hard labor. Finally, after almost four years of questionable service, he jumped ship in Colombo, from where he eventually made his way to Western Australia, where he hewed railway sleepers until enlisting in the AIF in September 1914. He did so under the name William Clarke, no doubt to avoid censure by the Royal Navy.[64] At any rate, after two months of preliminary training near Perth, he set sail from Fremantle on HMAT *Ascanious*. Originally drafted into "D" company, 11th Battalion AIF, Pring, who had attested to having seven years' experience in the Royal Navy, underwent further training and acclimatization in Egypt as well as the Greek island of Lemnos, from which the Gallipoli campaign was launched. When 20,000 Anzacs assaulted Gallipoli on the disastrous morning of 25 April 1915, Pring, now attached to "H" company, went missing. A court of enquiry held in Flêtre, France, almost a year later pronounced that he had been killed in action. His remains were eventually discovered by an exhumation team in early August 1921 near Mortar Ridge opposite Quinn's Post. His leather identity disc permitted the team to verify the dead soldier, who was then interred at Quinn's Post war cemetery, near Anzac Cove.[65]

The travels of another immigrant to Australia, Royal H. S. Bailey, also make for interesting reading. When war was declared, this head teacher from a rural school in Myrrhee, Victoria, was rejected for AIF service on medical grounds. Undaunted, he took passage to England to enlist, but when his ship docked at Durban, he seized an opportunity to join the Umvoti Mounted Rifles, an Active Citizen Force unit that saw action in German South West Africa. When hostilities there ceased in July 1915, Bailey once again sought passage to England. In August 1915, he enlisted with another mounted unit, the North Somerset Yeomanry, which deployed to France, where Bailey served throughout 1916. He must have impressed his superiors, because in January 1917 he returned to England for officer training and commissioning. In August 1917, after four months at Fleet, he was gazetted to the Royal Marine Light Infantry (RMLI). He crossed to France in December and joined the 1st Battalion RMLI, which was part of the 63rd (Royal Naval) Division. Just over a fortnight later, on 5 January 1918, while the rest of the battalion was supplying work parties for their sector of the line, he led a patrol to assess German intentions in Villers Plouich. Meeting heavy machine gun and rifle fire, he ordered his men to return to their trenches, then proceeded to probe the enemy position himself. His body was recovered three days later. His wife later wrote to the Victoria Department of Education: "He always cherished very happy memories of the kindness he had met with in your country [Australia], and had hoped to return there."[66]

Conclusion

The use of soldiers as a lens through which historians can view the migratory process is long overdue. As demonstrated above, this approach offers some fascinating avenues for future research at many levels—local, regional, national, and transnational. For military historians who are preoccupied with the grand strategies of national forces, the deployment of armies during war, and battle, the soldiers themselves are too often "lost," nameless cogs in a vast military machine. Individuals matter. And we now have the ability to look at where they came from and what they did. The revolution provided by the World Wide Web and the subsequent digitization of personnel records, regional newspapers, and passenger lists has provided a plethora of material through which to examine individual soldiers. The surfeit of military records allows one to chart their return "home," plot their careers on the battlefront, and chronicle how they were commemorated by friends, family, and community. Migration historians, in particular, have benefited from the digital revolution that has provided them easier and greater access to material that allows them to pursue a more in-depth interrogation of not just the British migratory process, but also the stories and journeys of return migrants.

What preliminary conclusions can we draw from this study of those Bristolians who emigrated to the far reaches of the empire and returned home to fight between 1914 and 1919? Geographical proximity and Bristol's long-standing commercial links with Canada meant that the largest share of Bristolians who returned to England during the First World War did so with the CEF. Not surprisingly, distance and expense (even with sporadic government sponsorship after 1902) meant fewer men travelled to the Pacific dominions where they might have enlisted with the AIF or the NZEF. South Africa was different. British migrants hoping to start new lives there required capital and/or particular skills, imperatives that narrowed the categories and restricted the flow of potential migrants to this region. Nevertheless, it is certain that Bristol's connection to a wider British World had become well established prior to 1914 and that Bristolians used the migration channels available to them to start new lives and exploit opportunities overseas. Critically, when the "mother country" was threatened, British-born migrants were almost always first to answer the call to arms, most often as soldiers, not officers. Although many had not acquired the social capital in their respective dominions to enlist as officers, early trends indicate that many of the returning Bristolians did have previous military experience that proved invaluable, particularly in providing NCOs, the men who proved so foundationally important during the formative stages in the construction of the dominion armies. Of course, these men also became the first casualties during the early campaigns at Ypres and Gallipoli in April 1915. Most of the men whom we have tracked emigrated to one dominion and then returned home in their adopted country's expeditionary force once war was declared. The circumstances of some, such as Garnett Stiff from Frampton Cotterell, also demonstrate that others traveled full circle—migrating overseas, returning with a dominion contingent, dying of wounds received in battle, and being buried in the yard of the parish church where they had worshipped as boys. Equally intriguing are those examples of men who emigrated to one particular colony or dominion and then used the first destination as a stepping stone to pursue employment in another. The Bacchus brothers are cases in point in which multiple empire destinations, including a sojourn back to Bristol, were experienced before the family finally settled in one of the dominions. As such, it is not a simple matter of traveling from the metropole to the periphery, but of traveling from one part of the British World to another before returning "home" to fight. More mapping needs to be completed before a fuller understanding of the life histories and networks of these returning soldier-migrants can be reached. By piecing together individual soldier stories and incorporating them into the broader migratory developments at work, we can better chart those patterns. If migration is at the heart of the British World, it is also fundamental to understanding both the local and transnational forces at work regarding war, identity, and memory.

CHAPTER 6

Martial Race Theory and Recruitment in the Indian Army during Two World Wars

Kaushik Roy

Armed forces constituted the ultimate line of defense against both the internal and external threats of the British government in India (GOI). The most important component of the GOI's armed forces was the Indian Army, the rank and file of which were Indians, the commissioned officers of which were British. The army numbered anywhere from 150,000 to a quarter-million men in peacetime, and it consumed the bulk of the government's revenue. During the two World Wars, it expanded dramatically—by a factor of five during the First World War and a factor of nine during the Second—and functioned as a sort of imperial reserve. Indian troops fought in places such as northern France and Belgium, Gallipoli, East Africa, Mesopotamia, North Africa, Italy, and Burma. This chapter examines manpower mobilization for the Indian Army and deals with four issues: which communities were recruited, the reasons for recruiting only certain communities, the actual mechanism of recruitment, and measures undertaken by the imperialists to keep the colonial soldiers loyal. Further, this chapter shows the shifts in the theory and practice of recruitment that enabled the colonial Indian Army to wage "Total War" instead of merely "small wars." During the two world wars, as we will see, the Raj not only updated the martial race theory but also replaced the regimental recruitment system with territorial/area recruitment.

Recruitment in the Indian Army before the First World War

The GOI had long used Indian troops to supplement the garrisons of British soldiers stationed on the subcontinent. Ad hoc employment of Indian troops by the British started in 1683, when the Bombay presidency raised 200 Rajput soldiers, but the credit for raising the first Indian regiment goes to Robert Clive, the victor of the battle of Plassey in 1757. He organized the Lal Paltan battalion, which comprised 700 sepoys officered by the British regulars. That was a start. By the first half of the nineteenth century, Indian soldiers were organized in four separate armies: the Bengal Army (the largest), the Bombay Army, the Madras Army, and the Punjab Frontier Force. The arrangements worked well enough for internal security and for extra-Indian wars in places such as Burma, Afghanistan, and China, until 1856, but it was also a somewhat tenuous business. In 1857, for example, some 120,000 troops of the Bengal Army rebelled, and it took two years to crush the mutiny with the aid of British troops and the Punjab Frontier Force, which was comprised of Sikhs and Pathans who had been recruited from central Punjab and the North-West Frontier Province.[1] Even after the 1857 Uprising, the GOI maintained Indian soldiers in Indian regiments because they were four times cheaper than British soldiers and better acclimatized to the South Asian environment. Indian soldiers fell ill far less frequently than their British counterparts, and there was also the benefit that they did not come with the costs associated with expensive deployments to and from Britain.[2] There was also the cold calculation that Britain simply did not have enough troops to garrison India. Eventually, in 1895, the four regional armies were amalgamated in the Indian Army, as part of the centralizing policy of the Raj.

The Indian Army never lacked for men to fill its ranks. A dearth of comparable economic opportunity elsewhere was one motivating factor for potential enlistees. Soldiering was a lucrative occupation for a young man from the arid and infertile Salt Range of west Punjab, for example. A permanent job, with regular pay, a gratuity, and a pension in cash, constituted an attractive offer. Military service was also considered in Indian society to be honorable and respectable. Most Indians joined as sepoys (infantry, who during the Second World War were known as *jawans*), and a lesser number as *sowars* (cavalry). Very few were allowed to join as *golundazs* (gunners). After the 1857 Uprising, the British were loathe to let the Indians operate artillery. In fact, until the Second World War, Indians could serve as gunners only in the mountain artillery. They were, however, permitted to serve as noncommissioned officers

(NCOs) and viceroy's commissioned officers (VCOs) in the infantry or the cavalry. VCOs were lower in rank than British subalterns (but superior to British warrant officers) and were a go-between for British commanders and the Indian soldiery in matters of discipline. The Indian Army troops were long-service soldiers. Generally, sepoys served for about twenty-five years before being eligible for a pension. Long-service engagements contributed to long-term stability in the army, and discipline was generally good. Large-scale mutiny like that which occurred in 1857 was an anomaly in the Raj's military history. During 1870–1875, for instance, desertions affected less than 0.5 percent of the strength of the force.[3] Surprisingly, though, there was no centralized recruiting system. Instead, all regiments sent out recruiting parties to scoop up recruits and bring them to the regimental training depots. This system, known as the regimental recruiting system, was adequate for meeting the relatively small number of recruits required in peacetime. Before the First World War, the annual intake of recruits was about 15,500 men.[4] This small manpower was adequate as the Indian Army was engaged in conducting small wars ("butcher and bolt" expeditions along the North-West Frontier, occasional forays into Afghanistan) and internal policing of the subcontinent.

The Indian princes, who ruled roughly one-third of India, also maintained their own armies and provided contingents of Imperial Service Troops (IST), who were trained and officered by the British and equipped with weapons provided by the GOI. In 1913, the strength of the IST was 22,479 men, and twenty-nine states maintained IST units.[5] Together, the Indian Army, British units stationed in India, and the IST constituted what became known as the Army in India.

British attitudes toward caste and race affected the Raj's perceptions of Indian soldiers. Before 1857, the GOI recruited mostly high-caste sepoys (Brahmins and Rajputs from Awadh and Bihar), who were known as Purbiyas. The thinking was that higher caste allies of the Raj would be more reliable. The 1857 Uprising forced a rethinking of that rationale.[6] After 1857, race replaced caste as an organizing feature of the Indian Army. British discourse on race was influenced by both religion and Victorian "science." Before 1850, races represented communities of different geographical locales and their differing positions on the ladder of progress. In the last decade of the nineteenth century, race came to be understood in more fixed terms, as an immutable biological set of observable characteristics. This was the pseudo-science that connected supposed race markers such as skin color, head size, and nose shape to what were believed to be inborn/genetic characteristics such as courage, honesty, servility, deceitfulness, or even martial prowess. Heather Streets writes that the assumption that some communities were biologically and culturally predisposed toward warfare operated both in the core and in the periphery of the British Empire. Representations of savage masculinity, which was at the heart of martial race ideology, was the by-product of the imperial response to the 1857 Uprising, as well as a number of other crises, including Russian expansion in Asia, recruiting problems of the British Army, and emerging Indian and Irish nationalism.[7] The construction of martial races was a sort of "Orientalist" discourse, initiated in the military dispatches, memorandums, and regimental handbooks authored by British officers of the Indian Army from the late nineteenth century onward.[8]

The British officers who introduced the martial race theory in the 1880s argued that in India some races were martial and others effeminate. And, they believed, for reasons of combat effectiveness, only the martial races ought to be recruited in the Indian Army. They assumed that martiality was an inherited trait, and, since blood was the medium responsible for transmission of hereditary features, a strange biological determinism, supported by anthropological ideas, sat at the bedrock of scientific racism. The other strand of martial race theory was a climatic-environmental element. Hilly regions with cold climates, proponents of the martial race theory believed, produced people with martial characteristics, while hot and humid climates produced effeminate people. The cool and bracing climate of the Nepalese Himalayas, for example, produced Gurkhas who were more physically robust and mentally superior to the degenerate plainsmen of swampy and humid Bengal. The Raj actually manufactured a Gurkha identity from the Magars, Gurungs, Limbus, Rais, Sunwars, and Tamangs of Nepal. The *kukri* (curved knife), Nepali cap, and so on were crucial ingredients of this constructed identity.[9]

Martial race thinking affected army policy, particularly when it came to recruitment. In 1882, Field-Marshal Frederick Roberts (commander-in-chief of India from 1885 to 1893) asserted that the races of Bombay and Madras provinces were martially inferior to the hardier races of the north. So, the Madrassis (Tamils and Telegus) and the Marathas of the army should gradually be replaced with Sikhs, Pathans, and Gurkhas. Roberts believed that nearly 100 years of peace had quenched whatever little martial spirit was there among the people of Madras and Bombay presidencies. And the Purbiyas were considered disloyal as a result of their rebellion in 1857. Not so the peoples of northern India, where cold weather had kept them virile and continuous warfare on the North-West Frontier had proved them loyal and combat effective.[10] As a result of that thinking, the recruiting focus shifted from southern and northern India to north-west India, and it more or less remained that way until 1945. British Indian Army authorities also considered rural people to be superior to the urban proletariat and landless laborers. Rural people were hearty and well fed, while urbanites were weak and malnourished. The supporters of the martial race theory therefore spoke against the recruitment of men from urban centers. Generally, younger sons of the small peasant communities were recruited. The big peasant communities were not interested in joining the army as they earned more from their farms. Meanwhile, even the low castes were regarded as nonmartial communities. The British feared that the induction of low castes in the army would reduce the prestige of soldiering among the Indian masses. And then higher and middling castes would shun army service. Thus, the martial race theory had both an ideological and instrumental component. Just before the First World War, the Indian Army had 150,000 personnel, most of whom were from the "martial races," including the Gurkhas from central Nepal, Sikhs, Dogras, and Jats from south-east Punjab, Punjabi Muslims from west Punjab, and Pathans from the North-West Frontier.[11]

The examples of Punjab and Nepal illustrate how martial race theory and the recruitment policies informed by it shaped the Indian Army. Punjab, despite a relatively small population of 24 million in 1913, was the most intensely recruited region of India. On the eve of the First World War, some 100,000 men of the Indian Army were from Punjab. And between 1914 and 1918, roughly 360,000 men of the Indian Army (almost half the total number of combatants raised in India during the war) came from Punjab. Of these, more than half were Punjabi Muslims (from tribes such as the Ghakkars, Awans, Janjhuas, and Tiwanas).[12] The Sikhs comprised only 12 percent of Punjab's population and only 2.5 percent of India's population.[13] However, a large proportion of the Sikh community served in the Indian Army during the two world wars. Just before the Great War, there were 33,000 Sikhs in the army. During the war, another 88,925 Sikhs joined the Indian Army, and 6,369 joined the IST.[14] In Nepal, the male population during the war was 907,000.[15] Between 1914 and 1918, an astonishing 200,000 Gurkhas served in the Indian Army.[16] Recruitment from Nepal peaked in 1916, while overall recruitment peaked in 1918.

Manpower Mobilization during the First World War

When the First World War started, a wave of enthusiasm spread among educated Indians. Indian elites believed that if India aided Britain during the latter's time of need, they would be politically rewarded for it.[17] The same elites also assumed that brown soldiers fighting alongside white troops would raise the status of the colonized. And the Indian princes supported the Raj in order to strengthen their position with the British authority, vis-à-vis the rising nationalist movement in their own kingdoms. Indian newspapers also supported recruitment, albeit with some qualifications. For instance, the newspaper *Panjabee*, published from Lahore, noted on 6 August 1914 that Indian loyalty was passive, not active, because no Indians had yet been allowed to occupy top slots in the Raj's administration.[18] The *Panjabee* was fairly typical in supporting the agenda of moderate Indian politicians who argued that, if a full-on Indian war effort was reciprocated with promises of reform and Indianization in both the civil and military spheres, support for Britain would intensify. That seemed to be the direction that things were heading politically, and recruiting did not seem to be a problem.

Even so, the Raj's managers were troubled by certain changes in Indian society, most notably the emergence of an extremist group of Western-educated Hindus. They drew their strength from the Hindu religious revival, which had developed from the late 1880s, partly in reaction to the spread of Western material culture. Increased competition among Western-educated Indians for jobs also played an important role in generating anti-imperialist sentiment amongst high-caste Hindu youths of Bengal and the puritan Hindu militant community of Arya Samaj in Punjab.[19] The failed Ghadar conspiracy (February 1915), fueled by Sikh émigrés who wanted to overthrow British rule, made the authorities apprehensive about conditions in Punjab and the North-West Frontier.[20] They also worried about a pan-Islamic movement. In 1914, there were 57 million Muslims in India, many of whom had pan-Islamic sympathies, and the Raj feared that their identification with Ottoman Turkey could present a threat.[21] British officials worried that the Muslim soldiery recruited by the Raj, if deployed against the Ottoman Empire, would experience a clash of loyalties that might precipitate a jihad against the British Empire.[22]

This was not so far-fetched a notion. In November 1914, when the Ottoman Empire entered the war on the side of the Central Powers, the *amir* of Afghanistan, Habibullah, informed the governor-general of India, Lord Hardinge, that he would remain neutral. But Habibullah was under pressure from the *mullahs* and *sirdars*, who were led by his brother, Nasrulla. They argued that Afghanistan should take advantage of Britain's difficulties and end British control over Afghanistan's foreign policy. Nasrulla's party believed that Britain's overseas commitments provided an opportunity for Afghanistan to regain its lost possessions. Arnold Roos-Keppel, the chief commissioner of the North-West Frontier Province, noted that if the Afridis rebelled, other Pathan tribes could also turn against the Raj.[23] Accordingly, the Raj took several measures to check desertions among the Pathans. They were recruited only when recommended by political officers (who were mostly British military officers seconded to the political/foreign department), and the recruits had to pay for their arms, equipment, and ammunition. Further, they had to get their villages and tribes verified by the political officers.[24] And to keep the North-West Frontier quiet, the army in India had to launch punitive raids. All these developments had an adverse effect on the Indian Army. In 1914, there were about 5,000 Pathans in the Indian Army, and half were Afridis. By June 1915, over 600 Afridis had deserted. Moreover, there were many more dismissals and discharges for misconduct. In November 1915, all recruitment of the Pathans stopped. By the end of 1918, there were fewer than 1,800 Pathans in the Indian Army. Still, for the war's duration, internal security remained an important issue for the GOI. Thus, it kept 50,000 British and 180,000 sepoys in India.[25] There was less concern about the dependability of Indian soldiers serving abroad. Among the sepoys deployed overseas, only one mutiny occurred. It involved the 5th Light Infantry at Singapore in February 1915. Inefficient leadership by British officers had riled the sepoys, and their anger spilled over when rumors spread that they were to be deployed against the Ottoman Turks.[26]

How soldiers in the field thought about their own military service and how their family members and relatives thought about conditions on the home front also concerned the Raj's officials. In general, soldiers and their relatives displayed loyalty toward the Raj, but there were some voices of dissent. On 26 January 1916, one Maratha soldier, writing from Lady Hardinge Hospital Brockenhurst, told Narain Nawle in Deccan that his son Gunda Singh should not be allowed to enlist in the army because conditions in France were terrible.[27] Authorities grew concerned that if any bad news in soldiers' letters reached the domestic audience, recruitment could suffer. The Military Censor Department analyzed letters written by relatives and friends in India to the soldiers deployed in France, Egypt, and Mesopotamia. By the beginning of February 1916, authorities were alarmed that large number of letters from home to soldiers at the front mentioned drought and high prices of grain in rural India.[28]

In addition, imperial visual propaganda (especially photographs, pictures, and the like) played an important role in sustaining morale of the Indian soldiers and the home front. The British successfully waged the battle for propaganda. Sepoys who were grievously wounded in France during 1914–1915 wrote discouraging letters to the higher authorities and to their relatives back home. In response, the Raj not only censored these letters but also went on a propaganda spree. Photos and sketches of valiant Gurkhas and Sikhs standing heroically with their arms in the different battlefields (Flanders, Gallipoli) and of smiling wounded soldiers who were taken care of in the clean and beautiful hospitals were circulated widely not merely among the soldiers but also back in India.[29]

One way the Raj's strategic managers tried to dissipate dissent was through the granting of land. Land grants were a big reason why Indians joined the army because land ownership gave one social status and economic security. At the start of the war, the Punjab government put at the disposal of the commander-in-chief of India 180,000 acres of irrigated land for allotment to those VCOs and men who served with distinction in the field. He also set aside 15,000 acres for reward grants to those who provided aid in raising recruits.[30] The scheme proved relatively successful, although not through any sense of altruism or heartfelt loyalty to the Raj. Punjabi landlords and chieftains collaborated with the Raj for their own interests. They provided recruits in the hope of gaining *jagirs* (land grants) and titles, which would bolster their wealth and their position in the local community. To encourage recruitment, they in turn provided land tax remission to tenants whose male family members joined the army.[31] Factional rivalry among the landlords and chieftains also resulted in competition to provide larger numbers of recruits.

Indian soldiers were not entirely cynical, however. They may not have cared about great power rivalries, but they trusted their officers, and they had affection for the king-emperor, to whom they generally felt bound. Since they had eaten the *namak* (salt, actually meaning they had accepted wages) of the Raj, they were *naukars* (servants or employees). Hence, it was their *dharma* (religious duty) to display soldierly valor and undergo sacrifice for their employers (the British) without caring much for who the enemies were.[32] Sometimes it was a sense of personal honor. Historian DeWitt C. Ellinwood, after analyzing the war diary of Amar Singh, a Rajput commissioned officer of a princely state, came to the conclusion that Singh, like many others, went to war to fulfill his duty as a member of the warrior class. Military service allowed him to express his sense of honor.[33]

As demand for manpower rose during the war, the GOI had to adjust its recruiting practices. Decentralized regimental recruiting was not working. In October 1916, the adjutant-general took control of recruiting for all branches of the army. The recruiting section of the adjutant-general's branch was expanded into a directorate with three sections: combatant and military departments, laborers and followers, and technical classes (artisans).[34] Gone were separate recruiting officers for the Sikhs, Punjabi Muslims, and so on. This localized system had made the tapping of new regions difficult. Moreover, several communities were often found in the same area, which resulted in overlapping jurisdictions for recruiting officers. Class-based recruiting went away, and territorial recruitment became the order of the day. Under the new system, a recruiting officer drew from all the communities in his area of responsibility. Area recruiting also made for effective cooperation with the civilian agencies. In addition, the Raj utilized the services of village administrators to bring in recruits. It helped that most village officials were retired soldiers and VCOs who had been nominated to their offices by the British administrators. In Punjab and North-West Frontier Province, all the recruiting divisions were under the authority of army officers who worked in close cooperation with the provincial recruiting boards. In the other provinces, the recruiting machinery was partly civilianized, however. In Bombay, Central Province, Bihar, and Orissa the divisional recruiting officers were Indian Civil Service personnel.[35]

Monetary incentives were another effective recruiting stimulant. In August 1916, the GOI offered a war bonus to recruiters. Due to competition between combatant and noncombatant branches of the army for recruits, the pay of both was raised in August 1918. The pay of a sepoy, for example, rose from rupees (Rs) 11 to Rs 20 per month, and gratuity and bonuses were introduced. A newly trained soldier proceeding overseas received a gratuity of Rs 65. And after completing six months service, NCOs, sepoys, and sowars each received a war bonus of Rs 24.[36] For reference, a healthy male consumed about 30 seer of wheat or rice, 3 seer of pulse, 7 seer of sugar, and 14 chattak of tobacco per month. I maund was equal to 40 seer and 1 seer was 2 pounds or 16 chattaks. During wartime, the prices of essential goods skyrocketed. The price of 1 maund of salt rose from Rs 1 to Rs 2 and wheat rose from 13 seer for Rs 1 to to Rs 2.5. In addition, the cost of rice went up from 10 seer at Rs 1 to Rs 3. The average soldier had to take care of his wife, two children, his parents, and one sister until she married. Most of the women at the time were homemakers.

Monetary incentives were also raised for the noncombatant recruits but at a somewhat lesser scale. Monetary incentives, combined with more efficient recruiting practices, land grants, and measures to quell dissent, helped keep a vastly expanded Indian Army up to strength throughout the First World War.

From a population of about 300 million, India mobilized 877,008 combatants organized in twenty-four divisions and 563,369 noncombatants.[37] When the war came to an end, there were 943,344 Indian Army soldiers serving in four active theaters of war, the largest contingent being in Mesopotamia.[38] They had their share of sacrifice. In total, 121,598 Indians became casualties, 53,486 of them fatal.[39]

FIGURE 6.1. India enlisted 2.5 million men for the Second World War, including many from the so-called martial races, such as Gurkhas, Dogras and Jats, Punjabi Muslims, and Pathans. In this photo of the Battle of Imphal-Kohima, soldiers of the 10th Gurkha Rifles and British troops of the West Yorkshire Regiment advance along the Imphal-Kohima road. Image source: © Imperial War Museum, IND3469.

Manpower Mobilization during the Second World War

During the First World War, the British strategic managers promised power and privileges to the Indians. However, just after it ended, Britain faced a financial crunch and also suffered from a sense of powerlessness due to the presence of so many Indians with military experience. Therefore, Britain attempted to go back on its promises. And this had devastating consequences for the Raj. The Indians were already angry due to soaring inflation, influenza epidemic, and British foot-dragging over granting *swaraj* (self-rule). The Rowlatt Act (February 1919), which allowed trying of Indian politicians and several communities arbitrarily, was the straw that broke the camel's back. Indian anger culminated in the Jallianwala Bagh Massacre on 13 April 1919. The event occurred when an Indian military detachment comprised mainly of Gurkhas under Brigadier-General 'Rex' Dyer, a highly decorated soldier fired on unarmed civilians (including women and children) in a walled garden (known as Jallianwala Bagh) at Amritsar in Punjab. The Indians protested against this massacre and the "black act." The spontaneous uprising was channeled by hitherto loyal M. K. Gandhi and the Non-Cooperation Movement (1920–1922). A disillusioned Gandhi at this stage realized that not sweet words but only acts (mass movement) would force concessions from the Raj. He had no faith that display of loyalty would enable the Indians to get concessions from the grateful British. Britain now appeared as "perfidious Albion" in the eyes of the moderate Indians. However, the point to be noted is that the Indian Army remained loyal both during the Jallianwala Bagh Massacre and the Non-Cooperation Movement. About 1,500 Sikhs (the lowest estimate was 400 died) died at Jallianwala Bagh in Amritsar city of Punjab. And Punjab was the principal recruiting ground of the Indian Army. In the end, regimental spirit and the special collaborative relationship between the Raj and its "faithful" Punjabi soldiers held the army's loyalty mechanism intact. The British, however, understood the gravity of the situation and both London and the GOI decided to fast track Edwin Montagu's declaration. As early as August 1917, Montagu, who was secretary of state for India, had declared in the House of Commons that the ultimate objective of Britain was to grant India self-rule. The Government of India Acts of 1919 and 1921 finally put India on the road to self-government. And this had indirect effect on the Indianization of the Indian Army's officer corps.[40]

At close to 2 million men under arms, the Indian Army of the Second World War was even bigger than the Indian Army of the First World War, and slightly more Indian. Due to "nationalist" pressure, after the First World War, the GOI had initiated a slow process of Indianization of the Indian Army's officer corps. Indianization was a series of measures designed to increase the proportion of Indian officers and, by corollary, decrease the proportion of British officers. In 1923, the Army Department implemented the Eight Unit Scheme, whereby eight regiments would integrate newly trained (and king's-commissioned) Indian officers into their establishments. Where would these new officers come from? Indians had been attending Sandhurst since 1917, but the output was low. So, in October 1932, the Raj established the Indian Military Academy, which was modeled on Sandhurst and had a Sandhurst Wing for infantry and cavalry cadets and a Woolwich Wing for engineer and artillery cadets.[41] Progress was slow, though. In October 1933, the total establishment of commissioned officers in the Indian Army was 2,972 and included 112 Indians.[42] Six years later, there were only 577 Indian officers (none above the rank of lieutenant-colonel) in an officer corps that numbered some 3,200.[43]

Finding sufficient numbers of recruits was not a big problem. Just as during the opening stages of the Great War, so at the beginning of the Second World War, a wave of enthusiastic loyalty spread throughout India. On 29 September 1939, a British official in Jhelum wrote to Governor-General Lord

Linlithgow: "Recruits are panting to come forward in large numbers; and martial classes. . . . Surely the Indian Government will take advantage of the present enthusiasm."[44] They fought for more than the tangible incentives of monetary packages and land grants. Mercenary motives could not totally explain the group solidarity that held units together. This had a lot to do with the fact that *jawans*, NCOs, and VCOs remained with the same units for their entire careers. Recruitment based on ethnicity, region, and class was intended to strengthen group solidarity within regiments, battalions, and companies, and it did. When a recruit expressed a desire to go to a particular unit due to family connections, he got his way. There are many examples of families with successive generations of men in particular units.[45]

As was the case during the First World War, Sikhs, Punjabi Muslims, and Nepalese were heavily recruited for the Indian Army. Most of them were farmers, who either owned land themselves or were tenants. In Punjab, the Unionist government declared full support for the British war effort. By the beginning of 1941, Punjab had contributed 48 percent and Nepal contributed 11 percent of all recruits for the army.[46] During the war, almost a quarter million Nepalese served in fifty-five Gurkha battalions. Severe land shortages, high rates on agricultural tenancies, extravagant rates of interest, and rigorous forced labor exactions in Nepal encouraged the Nepalis (Gurkhas) to join the Indian Army. The Magars, Gurungs, Limbus, and the Rais among the Gurkhas joined, because they were not allowed to rise above the post of captain in the Nepalese Army. And the Limbus were in high debt to the high-caste Hindus of Nepal.[47]

The martial race mentality never really went away either. In July 1943, Lieutenant-General George Noble Molesworth (secretary of the Military Department, India Office) quoted Roberts when he noted that the virile races were the Sikhs, Punjabi Muslims, Rajputs, Dogras, Pathans, and Jats. He continued: "The population of Bengal, Bihar, Orissa, parts of the United Provinces and Central Provinces, Madras and Bombay began to come into the suffocating penumbra of Victorian and Edwardian peace and . . . lose all interest in war themselves."[48] Between 1939 and 1945, Punjab provided over 700,000 recruits and the North-West Frontier Province another 100,000.[49] The recruiting regime reflected an enduring faith in the martial race theory as well as a concomitant emphasis on Punjab and Nepal. India was divided into distinct areas, each under a recruiting officer (RO).[50] Under each RO was an Assistant Recruiting Officer and paid recruiters (generally ex-soldiers). These paid recruiters earned Rs 2 for each recruit in 1942. Some recruits were also brought in by VCOs and civilians. Training battalions and units sent their forecast of requirements to the ROs. Recruiting staff collected recruits in each area in batches and sent them to the training centers. In provinces such as Uttar Pradesh and Punjab, where recruiting was very intense, there were several recruiting areas. In places such as East India, which were seen to be deficient in martial peoples, there were fewer ROs and recruiting districts. One RO in Calcutta, for example, was responsible for the three large provinces of Orissa, Bengal, and Assam.

Dealing with dissent, especially in the Army, was also a concern for British authorities in India. There was real reason for unease. Some 15,000 Indian soldiers of the 50,000 or so who surrendered to the Japanese at Singapore in February 1942 joined the Japanese-sponsored Indian National Army (Azad Hind Fauj) under the leadership of Captain Mohan Singh. And another 4,500 Indian POWs, who had been captured by the Axis forces in North Africa during 1942, joined the German-sponsored Indian Legion under Subhas Chandra Bose.[51] These two Axis-sponsored armies constituted the greatest threat to the loyalty of Indian soldiers serving with the Raj. The concern was that they would attract defectors or even encourage similar rebel enterprises, so the GOI took action to prevent any such eventualities. To start, in early 1942, the government announced a welfare scheme for soldiers and their families. And, from January 1943 onward, the *jawans* were trained and educated for jobs in the civilian sector for the postwar scenario. Since most of them came from rural areas, education corps staff prepared them for work in the agrarian sector. Training centers were set up and pamphlets issued for training demobilized soldiers and their families in animal husbandry and a host of other agricultural enterprises.[52] The government also tried to put soldiers' minds at ease about what was happening at home. When *jawans* in Burma became anxious about the effect of food shortages on their families in India, the GOI responded by providing rations (wheat, sugar, and kerosene) to the soldiers' families.[53]

These measures, combined with other incentives and long and deep attachments to regiments, had a positive effect. In mid-1942, when the Indian nationalists under the banner of Indian National Congress launched the Quit India movement in Bihar and Bengal, the GOI used fifty-seven battalions (most of them Indian) to crush the uprising.[54] There were no further mass desertions or mutinies.

For continued loyalty of the Indian Army much credit is due to Field Marshal Claude Auchinleck, who was appointed Commander-in-Chief India for a second time in June 1943. He successfully fought against the ridiculous notion of Winston Churchill that the Indian Army was a Trojan Horse and needed to be demobilized. He also challenged Churchill's assumption that only the Muslims could be trusted. Thanks to "Auk's" efforts, the Indian Army continued to expand and enlisted Hindu groups such as the Marathas and Madrassis in large numbers. The Marathas were given martial status, and the Madrassis were included in the technical branches. Further, Auchinleck did away with all discriminations that Indian commissioned officers faced vis-à-vis British officers in the spheres of pay and promotion. This made possible the creation of a robust well-disciplined army, which liberated Burma from the Japanese in 1944–1945 (see Figure 6.1).[55]

Conclusion

Including noncombatants (who came from the so-called non-martial races), the Indian Army during the Great War and the Second World War enlisted 1.2 million and 2.5 million men from a population base of 300 million and 390 million, respectively. British Indian authorities managed to raise these armies without having to resort to conscription. The vast population base of India helped. So too did targeted recruiting of groups believed to be the most martial (or at least loyal) and incentives to keep soldiers in long-service commitments. The Raj attempted to broaden the base for its recruitment policy by diluting the martial race theory as well as the practice of recruitment. During both the world wars, Jats from United Provinces and the Marathas from Maharashtra were enlisted in the combatant branches, and they were given the status of martial races. And the Madrassis of Madras presidency, especially during the Second World War, were enlisted heavily in the noncombatant technical branches. So, in principle, the martial race theory seemed to be elastic enough to accommodate the increasing demands of manpower during the era of Total War. One could pose a counterfactual question— namely, what would have happened if the First World War continued even in 1919? In such a scenario, the British would have done exactly what they did in 1942. Instead of depending mainly on Punjab, they would have brought the hitherto nonmartial groups of United Provinces and Maharashtra under the recruiting net. During Second World War, this policy was so successful that there was a surge in the pool of available recruits. And after 1943, the Indian Army did not require to expand any further. So, we can say safely that the martial race theory was quite successful in allowing the Indian Army to tide over the two World Wars.

In addition to theoretical flexibility, innovative changes in the mechanism of manpower procurement (the shift from regimental to area recruitment and the introduction of ROs) also helped. Moreover, in caring for the soldiers and their families during both world wars, the colonial state functioned somewhat like a welfare state especially for those who collaborated.

It is striking that after 1947 the Pakistan and Indian armies continued to rely on the so-called martial races. The Pathans and Punjabi Muslims from the Potowar region of Salt Range were the favored martial races of the Pakistan Army. And the Indian Army has continued to rely heavily on the Gurkhas, Dogras, Sikhs, and Jats. Further, military identities, like those of the Sikhs, Gurkhas, and Pathans, constructed by the colonial state, continue to operate in post-1947 South Asia.

CHAPTER 7

Manpower, Training, and the Battlefield Leadership of British Army Officers in the Era of the Two World Wars

GARY SHEFFIELD

> England is the most class-ridden country under the sun. It is a land of snobbery and privilege. . . . Still, it is a family. It has its private language and its common memories, and at the approach of an enemy it closes its ranks.
>
> George Orwell, "The Lion and the Unicorn" (1941)

To understand the British army officer corps in the two world wars, it is essential to locate it in the context of the hierarchical, class-based society in which it was rooted. Orwell's famous dictum captures one of the central facets of British society in the first half of the twentieth century. [1] It was class-based, but it possessed some unity. Without denying the tensions that undoubtedly existed, we can say that members of different social classes were not necessarily antagonistic. Indeed, in some spheres, including the army, different classes could come together in a relatively harmonious and productive fashion. Social class was not identical with economic status, although there was a close relationship between the two. An individual's class was defined by, among other things, education, accent, dress, manners, behavior, and lifestyle. Classes were porous: it was perfectly possible for children to rise to higher social classes than their parents if they were sent to the "right" schools. A key concept was respectability. This was a division within the working classes, for example, between those with a steady job and others. [2]

British social classes were conventionally divided into three: "working," "middle," and "upper." All three were characterized by nuances of status, as captured in a letter written from a passenger ship by an army officer in 1926:

"The passengers are somewhat amusing at times. There are several of the right kind and a lot on the borderland, and one or two very queer! There are only two more people in the Army, excluding an R[egimental].S[ergeant].M[ajor]. Both subalterns."[3] Class was all pervasive. Jimmy Perry, born in 1923, claimed that one of the first words he learned was "common," as in "Don't shout in public . . . that's what common children do." During the Second World War, Perry was asked by an officer why he spoke like a public (that is socially exclusive and fee-paying) school boy. His reply, that he had attended such a school, was met with a baffled "But you're only a sergeant! . . . Why aren't you an officer?"[4]

Until 1945, and arguably later, there was a widespread belief that skill in military leadership could be equated an individual's position in society. This was a modern version of the ancient belief that "war is the occupation of the nobility and gentry."[5] By the early twentieth century, in practice this meant that most regular army officers had a private income and had been educated at a public school, although these did vary in their prestige. Because only a small proportion of the population attended public schools (defined broadly)—in England, around 300,000 per year in the 1930s—this drastically limited the number of potential candidates for commissions. In 1914, only some 2 percent of British regular army officers had formerly been "rankers" (other ranks, or ORs), and some of those may have been "gentlemen rankers," impecunious men of some social standing who enlisted as privates, many in the hope of gaining a commission.[6] Some auxiliary (that is, Territorial) officers were, however, from a somewhat lower social bracket than most of their regular counterparts. This is not to say that the social profile of the officer corps remained static. Indeed, sending a son to a public school, the Royal Military College, Sandhurst, and then into a smart regiment was a recognized path to social respectability. The abolition of purchase in 1870 and its replacement with a competitive examination made a difference to the composition of the officer corps, as did declining revenues from many landed estates. Upper-middle-class boys increasingly followed their fathers into the army. There was also a pecking order among regiments, and aristocrats were increasingly concentrated in a few socially elite ones such as the Household Cavalry and the Grenadier Guards.[7]

As war with Germany became increasingly likely, the prospect grew of the army undergoing a major expansion. However, little was done to prepare to officer a greatly expanded army. The class-based nature of the army militated against obvious solutions: to commission talented and experienced ORs on a large scale and make it easier for poorer men to join the army as officers. A 1907 report recognized that, on mobilization, the expeditionary force would be short of 4,419 regular and 3,901 auxiliary officers. Although the authors of the report knew that some officers in other armies came from the ranks, this option was dismissed because Britain did not have conscription. The implicit assumption was that, while conscripts were drawn from all parts of society, in Britain only the poor volunteered for noncommissioned service. The existing social basis of the officer corps was to be preserved: the 1907 report led to the formation of the Officers Training Corps (OTC), based at universities and elite schools. Thus, although the officer shortage was acknowledged, a major source of potential officers was ignored.[8]

There were some dissenters. In 1910, General Sir Ian Hamilton, the adjutant-general, feared for the reliability of the supply of officers from the customary "limited class" and suggested that junior noncommissioned officers (NCOs) could be commissioned in wartime.[9] One small step in that direction came with the 1909–1910 decision of the Army Council to commission some carefully selected NCOs on mobilization. In 1914, plans had advanced to commission up to fifty NCOs when war began. But even this modest step was controversial. Field-Marshal Sir John French was wary of large-scale commissioning from the ranks because he feared this would change the "exceptionally happy" existing relationship between officers and ORs.[10] His view reflected the (not entirely unfounded) belief that working-class soldiers wanted to be officered by their social superiors.

The problem was partly cultural, as officers had both to fit in to the society of the mess and to live the opulent life of an officer. It was also financial because living that lifestyle practically demanded a private income. A very few, very dedicated individuals, famously William Robertson, were poor men commissioned from the ranks, who, through living abstemiously, managed to live off their pay. There was no systematic attempt to address this problem. Indeed, even after the salutary experience of the First World War, when the mass commissioning of officers from nontraditional backgrounds was a success, the failure in the 1920s and 1930s to undertake fundamental reform led to a renewed officer recruiting crisis during the Second World War.

In August 1914, Lord Kitchener, the newly appointed secretary of state for war, made the decision to raise a mass volunteer army.[11] The 733,514 regulars and various types of reservists were supplemented by the 2.5 million men who enlisted between August 1914 and December 1915, and large numbers of new units were formed. As Kitchener recognized, the demand for trained officers greatly exceeded the supply, so he resorted to various expedients. Retired officers, unkindly nicknamed "dugouts," rejoined the colors. The Sandhurst and Woolwich courses were shortened, fees were suspended, and immediate commissions given to OTC certificate holders. Officers of the Indian Army on leave in Britain were diverted to newly raised units. This was a misuse of resources, as the Indian Army was to make a significant contribution to the imperial war effort, and British officers with the requisite linguistic skills were a prized asset. Another example of the inefficient use of manpower was the raising of units such as the University and Public Schools Brigade of the Royal Fusiliers from men with elite educations. The ranks of middle-class Territorial "class corps," such as the London Scottish, also contained many potential officers. Some civic-raised "Pals" battalions also contained many men who, by education and social status, were deemed suitable officer material. While many of the ORs in these categories were eventually commissioned, others died on the battlefield as other ranks.

After the fighting started, the army responded pragmatically to heavy casualties among officers by instituting mass commissioning from the ranks. In late September 1914, 105 warrant officers and NCOs became officers. The financial problem was partly overcome by a larger grant for uniforms and equipment, and, of course, messing expenses were much lower on active service than in a peacetime garrison. Giving other ranks commissions had already begun in some units at home. In November some Territorial class corps soldiers received battlefield commissions into regular units. Moreover, regular officers were posted to regiments other than their own, as the need arose. This led to a significant weakening of the bonds of the regiment. From February 1916, the creation of officer cadet battalions (OCBs) rationalized the officer training system. Often based at ancient universities, they sought to give men a veneer of social respectability by teaching them "gentlemanly" manners as well as providing military training. A major difference between OCBs and prewar Sandhurst and Woolwich was that officer cadets at the former were taught leadership, which involved the transmission of gentlemanly "country house" values of paternalism. Before the war, "gentlemen cadets" needed no such social training. The pragmatic opening of the officer corps to talented but impecunious lower-class soldiers, who had demonstrated battlefield leadership, provided the vast citizen army, which engaged in heavy attritional fighting, with sufficient officers to lead it. Eventually, most officer candidates (with a few exceptions) had to first serve in the ranks. These commissions were temporary, although it was possible, if not easy, to convert these into regular commissions. In 1918 some 40 percent of officers were of working or lower-middle class origin. Such drastic changes in the officer corps did not occur without some opposition, although it was largely limited to snobbish comments about temporary officers being "temporary gentlemen."

Providing senior regimental leaders for the expanded army presented particular challenges. Many serving and retired regular officers were promoted to battalion and company command (or equivalent). In 1914, Territorial units were commanded by a mixture of Territorial Force (TF) and regular officers. But suspicion of the competence of Territorial officers was fairly widespread, based on the not unreasonable belief that amateur soldiers could not be as well trained or experienced as regulars. At Gallipoli a TF brigade was commanded, very unusually, by a Territorial, Noel Lee. This was a rare accolade even for "an exceptionally good and capable officer" such as Lee. Nonetheless, Lieutenant-General Hunter-Weston, commander of VIII Corps, ordered a regular officer, William Marshall, to shadow Lee in the trenches of Cape Helles, in effect to show the Territorial how to command his brigade. This embarrassed both men, not least as it rapidly became clear to Marshall that Lee was a highly competent brigadier.[12]

As the war went on, a rough meritocracy emerged, and military authorities became more pragmatic by appointing sizable numbers of nonregulars to command units at the major and lieutenant-colonel levels. On the battlefield, officers were able to demonstrate their competence as a platoon and company commander, or in temporary command of a battalion (or their equivalents) and thus "catch the selector's eye." The huge size of the army and the heavy turnover of officers meant there were always plenty of opportunities for the advancement of competent leaders. The line between regular and nonregular officers at the regimental level never disappeared, but it was blurred to a substantial degree.[13]

After 1918 the officer corps mostly reverted to the prewar status quo: no officers rose from the ranks between 1919 and 1922. There was, however, a modest alteration in the social profile of officers.[14] Although the 1923 Haldane Committee stated that officers should no longer be drawn from "any one class of the community," and its proposals aimed at "democratising" the process of officer recruitment, with more candidates being sought from grammar and even secondary schools, little was done in practical terms to address the financial hurdles preventing lower-class men becoming officers.[15] As before 1914, life in the officers' mess was expensive.[16] Moreover, there was still no career path for warrant officers to become officers. Even if it had been financially viable, why should a sergeant major, a respected figure, exchange his position for that of a lowly subaltern? However, in the 1930s, there were renewed fears for the supply of officers from traditional, and limited, sources. Among other factors, the backlash against the losses of the Great War and the emergence of the disillusioned/futility narrative, which produced a short-lived period when pacifism was intellectually fashionable, made military service unfashionable with the public school classes.[17]

This was the context in which the War Office looked to broaden the social base of the officer corps. The Willingdon Report of December 1937 envisaged that a proportion of officers should be commissioned from the ranks and that the wider "the net is cast, the greater the chance of securing men of ability to officer the Army." Grammar schools, selective and fee-paying but not as expensive or exclusive as public schools, were seen as potential sources of officers, as they had been during the Great War.[18] However, Willingdon was overtaken by the introduction of conscription in 1939. In any case, the report's recommendation did not find favor with some of the Army Council. In a very revealing comment, General Sir Walter Kirke argued against "drastic measures to attract a new class of officer, whose entry in any considerable numbers would probably have the effect of curtailing the existing supply from the *superior classes*." [emphasis added]. This view is reminiscent of a 1923 comment on a proposal for using the ranks of the Territorial Army (TA, as the TF had been renamed) as a source of officers in a future war: the door might be "inconveniently wide."[19] By 1939, thirty places at Sandhurst and six at Woolwich were reserved for regular NCOs of twenty-three years or younger, under special financial arrangements. However "a fair proportion" of ranker officers were "of the class most suitable for officers," but had opted for this path to commissioning because their parents could not afford to send them to Sandhurst or Woolwich.[20]

Thus, on the eve of war, "the exclusivity of the [regular] officer corps remained intact," overwhelmingly dominated as it was by the products of public schools.[21] The steps taken by the War Office to obtain officers for the expanded army in 1939 were in theory a more efficient and egalitarian use of manpower than in 1914. Some immediate commissions were granted to suitably qualified men (for instance, those with OTC certificates), but once immediate needs were satisfied, all bar a limited numbers of specialists, officer candidates had to first serve in the ranks. On the surface this represented an approach that was in line with Willingdon's recommendations. But old patterns soon reasserted themselves. In the early part of the war, candidates for commissions were largely ex-public schoolboys and regular NCOs. The picture was not so very different from 1914–1915.[22]

The same Territorial-regular tension regarding command appointments that had marked the mobilization of 1914–1918 resurfaced during the Second World War. In March 1940 the Army Council decided to remove some prewar TA commanders and replace them with regulars. This process had already begun. Lieutenant-Colonel Donald Dean, a Great War Victoria Cross winner, was removed from command of 4th Buffs in October 1939, when his divisional commander told him that he did not "want to have any Territorial

C[ommanding] O[fficer]s" because they could not "possibly be as efficient as a regular officer of similar length of service."[23] Dean was the victim of a major weakness in the army of 1939–1940—namely, the lack of standardized training. Much depended on the views of individual commanding officers, and, lacking the extensive prewar training of the regulars, TA units were particularly vulnerable to poor quality leadership.[24] So the clear-out of Territorial commanding officers (COs) was understandable, if somewhat harsh on individuals such as Dean. It might also have been a misuse of talented commanders. Thus, during both world wars, the regular army provided commanders for a number of Territorial units and formations, sometimes displacing existing Territorial COs, and imposed a "glass ceiling" that made it extremely difficult for non-regular officers to achieve promotion above lieutenant-colonel. It must be questioned whether this was an appropriate use of available manpower.

By 1941, there was considerable concern at the numbers and quality of potential officers. The army faced competition from the Royal Air Force (RAF). Much the same sort of men who became infantry subalterns in the First World War became aircrew in the Second.[25] The RAF was a glamorous and technologically based service, with a reputation for being less stuffy and less concerned with bullshit than the army. The army's struggle to adjust to the demands of a mass citizen force in a people's war was epitomized by David Low's reactionary newspaper cartoon figure "Colonel Blimp"—fat, pompous, slow-witted, and tradition-bound—who seemed to have taken multiple corporeal forms.[26] But the officer responsible for sorting out officer recruitment was anything but Blimpish. The adjutant-general, Sir Ronald Adam, was liberal-minded and willing to make radical changes. He faced multiple challenges to attract the best sort of officer candidate and in sufficient numbers. Not the least of these challenges were financial barriers and disincentives. Adam's reforms in 1941–1942 ameliorated this problem to a degree, for instance by speeding up promotion and placing limits on daily messing charges.[27]

However, there were still problems in getting enough high-quality candidates. Some COs were unwilling to put able rankers forward for commissions because they wanted to keep their best men. Even if potential officers cleared this hurdle, they then had to pass an interview board. These tended to be biased against candidates from nontraditional backgrounds, or, more subtly, in favor of ex-grammar school boys—a social step down from the public school boy, but regarded as the next best thing. By spring 1941, some three-quarters of newly commissioned officers did not have a public school background, but this figure concealed continued class bias in officer selection. Around a quarter of the men selected for an Officer Cadet Training Unit (OCTU) failed to complete their training, which led to shortages of officers; and the quality of some OCTU products left something to be desired. The 1942 introduction of personnel selection officers (talent spotters) and War Office Selection Boards (WOSBs), which included psychiatrists and psychologists, was a breakthrough. The failure rate at WOSBs was high—140,000 men appeared before them, but only 60,000 were "recommended for officer training." Even so, the supply of candidates rose by 65 percent by mid-1942. In 1943–1945, the rate of failure at OCTUs was down to 8 percent. Although imperfect, the system introduced by Adam in 1942 did result in a distinct improvement in the quality of officers being commissioned, and, generally, the system was seen as fairer (see Figure 7.1).[28]

Nonetheless, the system struggled to keep up with the demand for officers, especially for the infantry. As on the Western Front twenty-five years earlier, high-intensity attritional fighting, such as in Italy and Normandy, took a heavy toll on infantry officers. By 1944, the logistics and support "tail" rivaled the "teeth" portion of the army in terms of size.[29] This led to vacancies in posts that were far from sinecures, but that allowed officers to avoid the highly dangerous job of infantry platoon commander. One soldier turned down commanding a platoon in favor of being commissioned as a lieutenant quartermaster; this would build on the administrative skills he had acquired in the army, the implication being that it would help him in his postwar career. Left unspoken was the fact that this post also minimized his risk of being killed or wounded.[30] The shortage of infantry officers was ameliorated to some extent by the CANLOAN scheme, by which volunteer Canadian officers were seconded to British units. These officers proved highly successful, which says something for the compatibility of different armies of the imperial family.[31]

In both world wars, the regimental officer's role was in part managerial, to train his men and to look after their welfare, thus enhancing their morale and combat motivation. Paradoxically, the other part involved putting men into danger by sending them, or physically leading them, into battle. Building trust between the leader and the men was a critical part of both roles. This could place great demands on officers. A newly commissioned subaltern wrote of the strain of constantly "setting an example to the men," being well aware that his charges "are always watching."[32] During the First World War, trust was aided by the essentially deferential nature of Edwardian society, rising working-class industrial militancy notwithstanding. The concept of officership was based on country house values: inter-rank relations were underpinned by the deference of rankers in return for paternalistic, even self-sacrificial, leadership on the part of the officers. In theory (and to some extent in practice), although different classes remained in separate spheres, there was a good deal of mutual respect and a limited amount of intimacy was even pos-

FIGURE 7.1. Associating social class with leadership ability affected British officer production in both world wars. However, in both conflicts, the army eventually devised sound, meritocratic officer production systems. This photo shows a group of prospective officers undergoing assessment at a War Office selection board OCTU in October 1943. Image source: © Imperial War Museum, H33543.

sible.[33] In May 1915, for example, Second-Lieutenant R. F. E. Laidlaw, an upper-middle-class Scot, was posted to 1st Royal Munster Fusiliers at Gallipoli. He remembered that his platoon "treated me in a fatherly way which could not give rise to any ill feeling, or any indiscipline and I soon felt an affection for them which it was difficult to disguise. Later, in the trenches I often heard them around the traverse discussing 'th' orficer bhoy,' often in jokes to which I had given rise, but with almost the same affection that I had conceived for them." Officer-man relations in an Irish regular battalion early in the war may be something of an extreme example, but let it stand for many others.[34]

Officer training in the Great War taught paternal values to men who lacked a public school background. Paternalistic leadership led to generally excellent officer-man relationships, which in turn were critical in maintaining morale during the grueling attritional struggles. Conversely, poor morale was often linked to poor leadership. Moreover, if good leadership was not forthcoming from officers, other ranks were perfectly capable of making their views known and of taking action in their own, rather than the army's, interests. The situation in the Second World War army was similar, but not identical. The things common to both were that soldiers tended to judge their officers by a simple set of criteria. Were they paternal and "fair"? Were they courageous? Were they competent? To some extent, although less so in 1939–1945 than in 1914–1918, if an officer scored highly in the first two categories, he could get away with a less-than-stellar performance, especially if he was inexperienced. Needless to say, reckless officers, the ones likely to get men killed, were unpopular in either war.

Harmonious paternal/deferential relationships were not always the norm in units of the large British Army stationed in the United Kingdom in 1940–1944. The basic problem was that this semi-peacetime existence was not conducive to forging closer, more informal "active service" relations between officers and other ranks, all of whom lacked combat experience. Moreover, under wartime conditions, the regimental system, the bedrock of the interwar army's social structure, came under severe strain, and the army struggled to ensure that adequate numbers of paternal officers were available. These problems were exacerbated by the sheer boredom experienced by many soldiers. Indeed, some astute officers recognized the problem of keeping up morale in an army that was becoming stale and over-trained.[35]

The problem ran deeper than that, however. Societal changes had produced a citizen conscript army that was less deferential, more cynical, and more questioning of authority. As Jonathan Fennell argues in his chapter in this volume, the question of consent was at the heart of manpower and morale problems in the British army of 1939–1945. The Great War itself had contributed to these changes by, to some extent at least, discrediting the ruling or "officer" class. For much of the 1930s, films, fiction, and journalism had often portrayed the First World War as "futile." The failure of the army in campaigns such as France 1940 and Singapore 1942, as well as defeats in the Desert in 1941–1942 further undermined confidence in the upper echelons of the army. Many soldiers were less inclined to respect officers simply because they wore pips on their shoulders, and the rank and file grew more resentful of officers' privileges and the way that they were treated by the army. As a general rule of thumb, the higher a soldier's social class, the greater the resentment tended to be; older men and trade unionists also tended to be more critical. Fighting for a cause was not enough to unite the ranks. Many soldiers had little idea why Britain was at war.[36] Officer-man relations need to be placed in the context of the swing to the left that resulted in the victory of the Labour Party in the 1945 general election.

Such soldiery needed careful man-management, but the army was falling down badly in this area. In a circular letter of March 1943, Adam tackled this problem head on. Failures in "man-management" led to poor officer-man relations in some units: while outwardly discipline might appear to be sound, "it rests upon an insecure foundation in the absence of mutual confidence." Adam stated that "sound discipline and morale are the natural outcome of mutual confidence between all ranks. Discipline of other ranks, therefore, depends directly upon a high standard of 'man-management' among regimental officers." In a circular of June 1943, Adam was even blunter: "Although there has been a definite improvement in the general standard of man-management and the standard is high in field force units; it is still bad in some units and below standard in far too many. Responsibility is, of course, that of the regimental officer and particularly the junior officer."[37] That Adam felt the need to make these statements about something that had been a central tenet of the officer's credo in 1914–1918 illustrates the extent to which things had changed since the Great War.

Officers of conservative views placed the blame for poor man-management on officers from nontraditional, that is non–public school, backgrounds, who simply lacked (as one particularly reactionary CO of an OCTU, Lieutenant-Colonel R. C. Bingham notoriously—and publicly—put it) the "attitude of mind" of looking after '"their people"'—noblesse oblige, in other words. In this view, man-management could not be taught, but with ex–public school boys "this was instinctive and part of the philosophy of life."[38] This conveniently overlooked the great success of First World War OCBs in taking men from humble backgrounds and training them to become effective and paternalistic leaders. Further, this view begs the question of whether the type of man being commissioned in the Second World War was very different from his Great War counterpart. The answer was no. However, many "ranker-officers" spent more time in training in the United Kingdom than did their First World War counterparts and therefore lacked combat experience (many had none at all at the point they became officers). That may have been a barrier to developing their officership. Or, perhaps officer training in the Second World War was simply not as effective in teaching this aspect of leadership to men. This seems highly likely, although further research in this area is needed. Some radical critics agreed with Bingham's views on nontraditional officers. Alan Wood, an Australian-born ranker in the Royal Artillery (RA), thought that "instead of supplementing the Old Etonian officer with the qualities he lacks, they merely duplicate his deficiencies . . . They have no snob appeal . . . [and] no particular knack of handling men."[39] A thoughtful senior officer argued that while the "pre-war regular officer . . . was . . . apt to treat his men as chattels . . . at least he recognized that his first duty was to see that they were fed and housed and administered well and justly." So, for an officer, a public school background was "not essential, but it is definitely helpful."[40]

Over time, matters did improve, especially as the reforms in officer selection and training brought in by Adam began to take effect.[41] In 1942, for instance, John Gorman attended a Royal Armoured Corps OCTU at Sandhurst, where he was taught "leadership, and the motivation of one's men, and the code of behaviour expected of a British Officer." An article on one particular OCTU listed the subjects studied, concluding with "most important of all, something of leadership and man management . . . and then some!"[42] However, as Adam clearly recognized, some officers resented being instructed on man-management. Historian Jeremy Crang's judgment is damning: "a number of commanding officers seemed unable to gasp the importance of . . . [man-management] in a citizen army." Some "were simply not interested in their men" and too often, junior officers took their cue from this attitude.[43]

In sum, the pragmatic approach to officer selection and training, which had served the army so well in 1914–1918, was neglected during the early years of the Second World War. Some ground was clawed back, but significant problems remained at the end of the war. All this amounted to a profound change in the ethos of the officer corps since the First World War, all the more astonishing because many of the unit commanders had seen service in the earlier conflict. The quality of individual COs had a bearing here, as did the effectiveness of the prewar army in preparing officers to handle men. Adam admitted that "we had not considered the problem of morale and selection in a conscript army sufficiently before the war."[44] This lesson from 1914–1918, it seems, had been forgotten. When added to the class prejudice displayed by some officers, all this suggests that the radical critics of the army's "Blimpocracy" had a point.

Officer-man relations on active service were generally more harmonious, especially in teeth-arm units. As in the First World War, other ranks and officers shared the dangers and, up to a point, the hardship of campaigning, although the privileges and comforts enjoyed by the commissioned ranks could be considerable. On campaign, officers had much greater opportunities than they did at home to demonstrate leadership that made a difference to, and was appreciated by, the men, who might also recognize the additional pressures of responsibility borne by officers. Under such circumstances, the gulf between the ranks could narrow to some extent, and soldiers might regard, however grudgingly, officers' privileges as having been earned. In September 1942, a private wrote home from the Middle East: "The officers and men get on together better out here. Very little saluting etc. and all that[,] apart from in a new mob just out from Blighty, and then it soon wears off. Our old O.C . . . used to chat with the lads at night and come round joining in the brew [tea-making] schools. Imagine that in Blighty."[45] In 1944 in Normandy, an OR commented of his new battalion, 6th Green Howards, "Our officers and NCOs are . . . O.K. and muck in with the lads. Everyone is in the best of spirits and confident of victory."[46] Nine months later, a private of 2nd Seaforth Highlanders wrote home from Germany that "the Army looks after us here, plenty of comforts and fags [cigarettes] and the officers are kinder to us than they were in England." At about the same time, a platoon commander of 1st Black Watch indicated why inter-rank relations in infantry battalions could be particularly close: "I . . . have formed a very strong bond of friendship with my men. This [is] partly due to the fact that as an infantry man I am closer to my boys than any other officer in the other branches of the Army. We often share a trench and even perhaps the same knife and fork or last mug of tea, *all tending to make us a team instead of individuals*."[47] [Emphasis added.]

Territorial units tended to have looser discipline and somewhat more relaxed inter-rank relations, which made for distinctive esprit de corps and officer-man relations, although these often eroded as the original TA officers were replaced, especially by regulars. Bill Cheall, a prewar Territorial soldier of 6th Green Howards, could be cynical about the army, but he took a sympathetic and even admiring view of his officers. He praised Major Leslie Petch as "a good, kindly man . . . a gentleman farmer in civilian life . . . he never forgot that the lads were human beings as well as soldiers." Cheall's officers were effective leaders in battle; he gave them much credit for holding the battalion together during the retreat to Dunkirk.[48]

That is not to say that officer-man relations on active service were always good, but where there were problems, individual officers tended to be at fault. There was outrage in the 2nd Royal Gloucestershire Hussars, veterans of desert fighting, when a new CO arrived from England and attempted to impose a "surfeit of 'spit and polish'" (this was a TA yeomanry regiment, so unused to the "regular" approach to discipline). Officers were very angry, but the response of ORs was telling: "Many fellows have written home to their M.Ps. and others to the Higher Command out here."[49] This characteristic response of disgruntled Second World War rankers was much less common during the Great War.

Very large numbers of soldiers remained in the United Kingdom, or in base areas such as India and Egypt, doing jobs that were basically civilian, such as repairing and servicing equipment or working in offices as clerks. Such men were denied the opportunity to experience the increased inter-rank comradeship that helped to compensate for their loss of personal freedom. They required a particular sort of handling, which was not always forthcoming. A senior officer commented in 1942 that "technical units . . . the Ordnance and Signals, for example—are defective in management." Things gradually improved. In August 1942, the censorship report for the Middle East frankly noted that at long last positive comments on officers from training and base units exceeded unfavorable ones. This was notable, not because it reflected the general upturn in morale that occurred after the arrival in Egypt of the new command team of General Sir Harold Alexander and Lieutenant-General Sir Bernard Montgomery, but because of the volume of "adverse criticism" that had preceded it and had more in common with inter-rank relations in the United Kingdom than those in combat units in the Middle East.[50]

It is interesting to compare Laidlaw's reception at his unit on Gallipoli with the experience of Lieutenant R. Lyle, when he arrived direct from a UK-based OCTU to a tank regiment in Italy in November 1944. Lyle was described in the diary of one of the ORs, Trooper Jack Merewood, as "'a real 'twerp.' He was a 'rookie' and after the Troop Leaders we'd had, this one had no idea how to handle men—especially some of whom had been abroad and roughed it for years." There are several points of interest here. The emphasis on man-management skills at OCTU does not seem to have prepared Lyle for command of a veteran tank troop. This problem was exacerbated by the fact that an officer who was part of a tank crew was inevitably thrust into a greater degree of intimacy with his charges than, say, an infantry platoon commander. Moreover, the lack of automatic deference given to Lyle, simply because he was an officer, is striking. But this was the beginning, not the end, of this relationship. Merewood's comments, based on his diary entry of 6 January 1945, are revealing: "We were gradually training our Mr. Lyle and introducing him to our way of life. He began to realize that the only way to live in harmony was to be, to a certain extent, 'one of the boys.' We didn't take advantage of him, after all he was an officer and had a lot of responsibility as our Troop Leader; but it was impossible for him to try to live the life here he'd been taught in an officers' training school." The leadership techniques that Lyle had been taught at an OCTU collided with the reality of life on campaign, and within two months of arriving in theater he had had to adjust his leadership style accordingly. But ORs recognized the importance of boundaries. Even in the cramped confines of a tank, to some extent, officers and ORs existed in separate spheres.[51]

There are, of course, examples of novice officers who immediately demonstrated good leadership on operations.[52] Some regular officers displayed leadership that would not have been out of place on the Somme twenty-five years earlier. Private Patrick Devlin of 1st Royal Ulster Rifles gave a glowing account of Major F. R. A. Hynds. About forty years old, Hynds was "to lads like me, 20 years old, . . . like a father," even though Hynds was a Baptist and Devlin a Roman Catholic from the Irish Free State. Conversely, Devlin was sharply critical of another officer who was killed on patrol in June 1944: "although he was a brave man he obviously died that night because he blundered."[53] The basics of battlefield leadership and the paternal/deferential dialectic did not differ fundamentally from the Second to the First World War.

The question of the effectiveness of regimental officers' leadership in battle needs to be located in the wider context of the combat performance of the British Army. Older works tend to stress its weaknesses and ineffectiveness.[54] Modern historians stress that in both wars the army underwent a learning process and over time became highly effective.[55] In 1918 and in 1945, fighting as part of a coalition, the army won major victories, and recent scholarship suggests that regimental officers played a key role. Mark Connelly, for instance, has convincingly refuted the overly negative views of the official historian on the leadership shown by junior officers in 1918, while Peter Hodgkinson paints a generally positive picture of battalion commanders in that year. David French stresses that the reforms of 1942 had, by 1944, produced highly effective regimental leadership, and Daniel Marston argues for the importance of British and Indian regimental officers in the victorious campaigns in Burma.[56] Thus, conflation of social class with leadership ability distorted the production of officers in both wars, but, after false starts, effective recruiting and training systems were established. Ironically, the more rational Second World War approach was less effective in reality than the flawed but pragmatic methods for recruiting and commissioning officers in the 1916–1918 period. During the Great War, a Military Medal and a proven combat record did a great deal to overcome the handicap of an officer lacking the right social and educational background. For all that, regimental-level leadership was of crucial importance in the British Army's path to victory in both world wars. As a report stated in 1944, regimental officers were "match winners" who could "come from any social class, providing they possess the right qualities, and are fully trained."[57]

CHAPTER 8

Legitimacy, Consent, and the Mobilization of the British and Commonwealth Armies during the Second World War

JONATHAN FENNELL

> If it is a case of the whole nation fighting and suffering together, that ought to suit us, because we are the most united of all the nations, because we entered the war upon the national will and with our eyes open, and because we have been nurtured in freedom and individual responsibility. . . . Our people are united and resolved, as they have never been before. Death and ruin have become small things compared with the shame of defeat or failure in duty.
>
> Winston Churchill, "The Few" speech,
> 20 August 1940

Churchill's speech still resonates today. As Britain faced the prospect of invasion, the prime minister and those around him remained confident that citizens would do their duty and sacrifice everything for the state. The strategic calculus driving the army's deployment later in the war, in the Middle East, Europe, and the Far East, was hardly different. "The Empire would rely enormously on the 'poor bloody infantry', the ordinary citizen soldier, and his willingness, when called upon, to mobilize, fight, and if necessary die for the cause."[1]

Such calculus was not without logic. The countries that provided the core contingents of the British and Commonwealth Armies in the Second World War contained a combined population of no fewer than 470 million.[2] The great armies of the Soviet Union and Germany were built from populations far less numerous. Nevertheless, the question of mobilization has become one of the key debates of the war. "In the end," as one prominent historian has put it, "manpower became the chief limiting factor on Britain's war effort."[3]

The manpower problems that were to become so prevalent from 1942 onward were not, however, overwhelmingly an issue of demographics. They were, to a significant degree, a question of consent. As John Horne has argued in relation to the First World War, the conflict "cast doubt" on the supposed moral unity of the polity "by resuscitating sectional divisions." Such tensions "strained the legitimacy of the state and nation and intensified the pressure on governments and military commands" to arbitrate between different perceptions of what was right or wrong, fair or unfair, in the context of "total war."[4] Only by succeeding in this endeavor, could states properly mobilize and remobilize for war.

In many ways, this chapter argues, Britain and the Commonwealth faced significant manpower mobilization challenges—namely, to convince their complex mix of citizens (with all their varied loyalties and attachments) that the war was necessary (for them) and that it was being fought in a fair and procedurally just manner. In spite of the many millions that served willingly and the proud story and traditions that they represent, the empire struggled at times to mobilize its people for war. This would have profound implications for the performance of the British and Commonwealth Armies on the battlefield.

Mobilization

We have, perhaps, become too accustomed to the narrative of the Second World War being a "good" war, a "People's War," and we have lost sight of the powerful and destructive forces let loose by global conflict. For Britain, the commencement of the war was characterized as much by disunity as unity. It was only with Churchill's rise to power in May 1940 and the formation of a coalition government including the Labour Party that a significant degree of political accord was achieved. In India, the start of international hostilities ignited a full-blown political crisis. The Indian National Congress (INC) asserted that support for the war would be forthcoming only if London renounced imperialism and promised independence. When Lord Linlithgow, the viceroy, offered little more than a review of the 1935 constitution, the Congress ministries resigned en masse.[5]

The question of unity was as profound in the dominions. In numerous ways, Canada entered the war a "divided country." Many French Canadians had little time for what they perceived as "Britain's war." Total war, it was feared, would wreck national unity. In this context, W. L. Mackenzie King, the Canadian prime minister, decided against forming a government of national unity; a policy of "limited liability" would characterize Canada's early war effort. Similar perspectives were just as prevalent in the Antipodes. In New Zealand and Australia, efforts to form governments of national unity faltered repeatedly, to the extent that in October 1942 Peter Fraser, the New Zealand prime minister, admitted in Parliament that "the basis of unity in the country" had "been destroyed—irretrievably destroyed." In South Africa, the slide to war dismantled the short-lived stability created by the interwar Fusion government. Antiwar feelings among a proportion of Afrikaners came close to driving the union in the direction of neutrality; in some parts of the country, such sentiments catalyzed support for the Germans and for a Nazi victory.[6]

The struggle for unity, so visible among political elites, was echoed in many ways in the attitudes of citizens to mobilization for the war effort. Conscription was introduced in the United Kingdom, except Northern Ireland, from the beginning of hostilities, a policy replicated by New Zealand not long after. It was concluded in both cases that voluntary enlistments alone would not supply the necessary numbers for the services, an assessment that proved "well founded." In the United Kingdom, an effort to avoid military service was made by at least 10 percent of those called up. "With special deferment schemes for those in the higher echelons of society, the fighting fell predominantly to those in the lower-middle and working classes" (see table 8.1).[7] In New Zealand, where exemptions due to public interest (e.g. essential industries) were granted on an individual basis, appeals were lodged by or on behalf of 47 percent of conscripts, about 39 percent of these on the grounds of hardship or conscience.[8] The 2nd New Zealand Expeditionary Force (2NZEF) had a disproportionately small percentage (14.8 percent) of the professional classes as compared to the population at large (25.1 percent). Skilled workers were also underrepresented (23.7 percent, as opposed to 28.2 percent). Unskilled workers, by comparison, were represented to a disproportionately high extent (25.5 percent in the 2NZEF as compared to 12.1 percent in the general population) (see table 8.2).[9]

In Canada and Australia, a "hybrid solution" to the trials of mobilization developed, "not least due to ethnic tensions and widespread opposition to conscription."[10] Both dominions introduced compulsory service, but only in a limited manner. Conscripts were restricted, at least hypothetically, to home service; only volunteers could be sent overseas. In Canada, this policy led to noticeably unrepresentative armed forces. French Canadians made up only 12 percent of the Canadian Army Overseas; this was in a country where 30 percent of the population was French speaking.[11] In Canada, much as in New Zealand, it was the semi-skilled and unskilled classes who were particularly represented in the army (see table 8.3). In Australia, a widespread reluc-

Table 8.1   Social class breakdown of 2.5 million other ranks in the British Army, 1944

CLASS	GENERAL POPULATION		ARMY
	1931 CENSUS*	1951 CENSUS*	1944*
I Professional	2%	3%	1%
II Intermediate	13%	15%	4%
III Skilled	49%	53%	68%
IV Partly Skilled	18%	16%	11%
V Unskilled	18%	13%	15%

Source: Jonathan Fennell, *Fighting the People's War: The British and Commonwealth Armies and the Second World War* (Cambridge: Cambridge University Press, 2019), 84.

*Male only.

Table 8.2   The 2NZEF by social class

CLASS	1966 CENSUS	ARMY
I Higher Professional	6%	5%
II Lower Professional	19%	10%
III Clerical & Highly Skilled	13%	13%
IV Skilled	28%	24%
V Semiskilled	21%	23%
VI Unskilled	12%	26%

Source: Fennell, *Fighting the People's War*, 83.

tance to "commit to the war" led to a situation in which only 38 percent of the army was made up of "direct volunteers." By the end of August 1941, 188,587 had enlisted voluntarily from a population of 7 million (only about 2.7 percent). In comparison, during the first two years of the First World War, 307,966 out of a population of 5 million volunteered (about 6.2 percent).[12]

In the extremely charged political surroundings of the subcontinent and South Africa, conscription was simply "out of the question." It would be necessary to expand the Indian and Union Armies by volunteerism alone. At first glance, the Raj was highly successful in this regard. The Indian Army, which eventually reached a size of 2.25 million, became one of the largest volunteer armies in history, a considerable achievement. However, it was recruited from a populace of nearly 400 million and thus "represented only a small proportion of potential Indian manpower, roughly three per cent of the entire adult male population."[13] Mobilization in South Africa was similarly undermined by sociopolitical dynamics, to the degree that there was even danger of a civil war. "Black" and "coloured" and Afrikaner South Africans "proved far less likely to serve than their British South African compatriots."[14]

Table 8.3   The Canadian Army by social class

| | 1951 CENSUS | | | |
CLASS	ENGLISH*	FRENCH**	TOTAL	ARMY
I Higher Professionals	1%	1%	1%	1%
II White Collar	12%	10%	11%	10%
III White Collar + Higher Blue Collar	8%	4%	6%	7%
IV Higher Blue Collar + Lower White Collar	9%	5%	7%	4%
V Skilled Trades	36%	31%	34%	39%
VI Semiskilled	17%	25%	20%	20%
VII Unskilled	17%	25%	21%	20%

Source: Fennell, *Fighting the People's War*, 85.

* English-speaking
** French-speaking

Sixty-six percent of the Union Defence Force (UDF) was English-speaking as compared to 34 percent Afrikaans speaking, in a population where 59 percent of white men spoke Afrikaans and 41 percent spoke English. Only 11 percent of recruits came from classes I (higher professionals) and II (white collar) compared to 18 percent among the white population more generally. This discrepancy was particularly prevalent among English speakers; only 14 percent came from classes I and II compared with 26 percent in wider society. Skilled workers, many of whom were extremely poor, made up the majority of the UDF (see table 8.4).[15]

Thus, throughout the Commonwealth, "levels of enthusiasm for war reflected levels of public morale, the socio-political context, and perceptions of state legitimacy." In numerous ways, "the act of enlisting, or of being conscripted, reflected 'a dialogue' between the soldier and the state 'about citizenship' and about rights more generally." Conscription and enlistment "added layers of duty and obligation to the social contract. They were very much 'political' moments." Mobilization, it is apparent then, was not exclusively a question of numbers, but also a matter of "negotiation and consent."[16] Manpower policy, and the degree to which the individual states could compel citizens to serve, played out in the demographic makeup of the British and Commonwealth Armies. In Britain, where special deferment schemes were in place for those in the higher echelons of society and where many partly skilled and unskilled workers were drafted into the wartime economy, the fighting was left to those in the lower-middle and upper-working classes. In countries where mobilization was reliant to a greater degree on volunteerism,

Table 8.4   The Union Defence Force by social class

CLASS	1946 CENSUS			ARMY		
	ENGLISH	AFRIKAANS	TOTAL	ENGLISH	AFRIKAANS	TOTAL
I Professional	8%	1%	4%	4%	1%	3%
II Intermediate	18%	10%	14%	10%	4%	8%
III Skilled	67%	68%	67%	74%	76%	75%
IV Party Skilled	5%	14%	10%	9%	11%	10%
V Unskilled	2%	7%	5%	3%	8%	5%

Source: Fennell, *Fighting the People's War*, 85.

a larger, if still disproportionately low, fraction of the army was made up of professional and intermediate classes. It was those most connected to Britain and least able to avoid conscription (by deferment or due to their economic position) who joined up.[17]

The British Army and the Beveridge Report

In this context, the state's treatment of soldiers, their families, and their communities mattered. The issues of social justice and fairness resonated for soldiers throughout the war years and had considerable impact on mobilization as well as combat performance. For the British Army, this dynamic played out most powerfully in the reaction of the soldier to the agenda for social change encapsulated in Sir William Beveridge's report on "Social Insurance and Allied Services." The Beveridge Report, as it became widely known, appeared in December 1942. It presented a vision of "cradle-to-grave" social security, assuring all citizens of a basic minimum standard of living. It included proposals for a commitment to full employment, a state system of medical care, and a regime of family allowances.[18] Beveridge's aim was "not merely to abolish physical want, but to give a new sense of purpose to democracy, to promote national solidarity and to define the goals of the war."[19] It captured the public imagination, and "it soon achieved the status of a kind of social 'Magna Carta'."[20]

Government foot-dragging on the plan desperately disappointed the troops. The 1943 censorship summaries from First Army in Tunisia noted that "the Beveridge Report meets with general approval."[21] Over the next number of months, the censors commented on growing interest in the report and other matters relating to politics, along with concerns about postwar conditions and troops' families in the United Kingdom. A soldier in the 10th Battalion

Rifle Brigade wrote that "whenever there is any news about the Report there is always a number round the news sheet."[22] A soldier in a Light Anti-Aircraft Regiment commented:

> Chaps are still arguing about the Beveridge Report. . . . It seems to me a good step in the right direction and it is a pity that the Govt. can't be big minded enough to do something about it now. . . . Churchill . . . is I think an admirable man for the present task, but for the future he is too bellicose and too steeped in Toryism. He must not handle the peace. . . . What sort of Govt. is this when the elected person to bear a responsibility avoids his duty. . . . This much is certain, that the fellows in the Army are more than ever left-wing in their politics.[23]

In the absence of trust in the political sponsorship of the Beveridge Report, morale and motivation suffered, exacerbating existing manpower problems.[24] Britain had, by 1942, substantially mobilized its population for service, either in the armed forces or in the wartime economy. Consequently, the manpower resources of one sector could only be expanded at the expense of another.[25] Casualties in 1943 complicated this calculus. The fighting in Tunisia cost the British and Commonwealth Armies dearly; the First Army suffered 25,742 casualties among its imperial troops, while the Eighth Army suffered an additional 12,618.[26] Sicily cost the British Army a further 9,617 casualties.[27] The fighting in 1944 was no less attritional: British and Commonwealth forces in South-East Asia lost around 40,000 casualties between January and June;[28] by the end of August, the British Army in Normandy had suffered an additional 63,865 casualties,[29] while British infantry divisions in Italy had suffered on average 10,750 casualties each between September 1943 and November 1944.[30] Replacements "broadly kept up with" battle injuries during this casualty-intensive phase of the war, but they did not compensate for other forms of "wastage." In Italy, for example, illness rather than injury was responsible for more than three-quarters of hospital admissions in 1944. During a period when medical professionals were "conquering" epidemic diseases such as dysentery, malaria, and jaundice (infectious hepatitis), it was the increase in sick admissions connected with different factors, such as morale, "that caused the most serious concern."[31] Indeed, medical professionals and commanders were confident that sickness, battle exhaustion, desertion/Absence Without Leave (AWOL) and Self-Inflicted Wounds (SIWs) "reflected the state of the men's morale as much as any other factor." "The medical state" of the army, according to Bernard Montgomery, the commander of 21st Army Group in North-West Europe, was not "dependent on the doctors alone." In June 1944, Major D. J. Watterson, the psychiatrist attached to British Second Army in Normandy, concluded that the figure for exhaustion cases in a unit was an excellent "index to that unit's quality of men and of its wellbeing and morale." In fact, he said, "it is as good a guide to the unit's state of mental health as is the temperature chart in a case of fever."[32]

The official historian of the British Army Medical Services in North-West Europe, F. A. E. Crew, noted similarly that there was a close association between military crimes, such as desertion, AWOL, and SIW, and battle exhaustion. In fact, he maintained that these issues could reasonably be understood as two sides of the same coin. "Whereas some men went sick and were evacuated, others suffering from much the same condition ran away, were charged and awarded penal servitude. The psychological escape of the former and the physical escape of the latter were expressions of the same mechanism."[33] Other reports produced around this time lend support to this contention. A study on "'Soldiers under Sentence' for Such Offences as Desertion, Cowardice, Mutiny etc., Whose Cases Have Been Reviewed in British Second Army," compiled in June 1945, found that the "great majority" of prisoners were found to be "good personality types, only too anxious to be given the opportunity to redeem their characters." According to the report, their crimes were "in a large majority of cases not premeditated, but occurred on the 'spur of the moment' when under great stress." The report determined that "the percentage of 'real bad eggs' has been small" and that "the outstanding impression gained" was "the great similarity there exists between many of the cases reviewed and those that are referred through medical channels for psychiatric opinion." The only conclusion to be deduced from the study was "that the majority of deserters" were not "true cowards" and that issues relating to morale, just as with cases of battle exhaustion, were the key drivers in the behavior of soldiers.[34]

Of course, morale was not solely determined by socioeconomic policy and postwar prospects during this period; it was influenced by a complex range of multidimensional factors that go beyond the Beveridge Report.[35] But it must be recognized that even in the last months of the war, morale reports pointed to a clear deficit in meaning when it came to the men's emotional armor. The report for British soldiers in South-East Asia, covering the period of Fourteenth Army's great "Capital" offensive in 1945, noted:

Of any widespread appreciation of a higher purpose in the war there is at present little sign, and there would appear to be an urgent need for the Government at home, by word and deed, to present the troops with a cause worth fighting for. . . . Lack of faith in the Government and in politicians generally continues to be the prevalent mood among the troops.[36]

The British Army suffered over 95,000 admissions for sickness during the North-West Europe campaign. Of these losses, 13,255 were due to battle exhaustion. The figure for sick admissions in the Eighth Army (all nationalities) in Sicily and Italy was extremely high at 250,284, with the British battle exhaustion figure not far off that experienced in North-West Europe. Additionally, between July 1944 and April 1945 there were 5,737 courts martial convictions for desertion and AWOL in the 21st Army Group in North-West Europe. Courts martial for desertion among British troops in Italy between October 1943 and June 1945 came to 5,694. The total number of cases of AWOL and desertion by British troops reported to General Headquarters 2nd Echelon for the Central Mediterranean Forces July 1943 to June 1945 (which included Sicily, Italy, North Africa, and Greece) came to a remarkable 12,929. One historian has gone so far as to argue that the desertion rate in the Eighth Army in the winter of 1944 "was the worst of any Allied army in the whole war." In fact, so great were concerns about desertion and AWOL that the question of reinstating the death penalty for desertion and cowardice came to the fore in 1944, in Italy.[37]

By October 1944, venereal disease (VD) had become so prevalent in the 21st Army Group that it too began to act as a drain on manpower. By the end of the campaign, the British had suffered 4,390 losses to VD. It was an even greater problem in Italy; between 17 October 1943 and 31 March 1945, the Eighth Army was temporarily deprived of the service of 15,140 men due to VD. The results of all these deficiencies (casualties, sickness, battle exhaustion, desertion/AWOL, SIW, and VD) were severe. In North-West Europe, Montgomery was forced to disband the 59th Staffordshire Division in August 1944 and the 50th Northumberland Division, which had landed on Gold Beach on D-Day, in November/December. In Italy, at the end of September 1944, General Sir Harold Alexander, commander of the Allied armies in Italy, ordered that the 1st Armoured Division and two brigades be disbanded and every British infantry battalion be cut from four to three rifle companies (a 25 percent decrease).[38] By the summer of 1944, British infantry battalions in the Fourteenth Army were, as in Europe, short of men, some 3,500 in June, rising to 10,000 by October. Most battalions were now operating 18 percent under establishment.[39] The two British divisions in theater, the 2nd and the 36th Divisions, had become "wasting assets." By May 1945, British personnel made up only 13 percent of the Fourteenth Army.[40]

High casualties were undoubtedly a fundamental cause of this manpower crisis, but issues relating to morale and the soldiers' relationship with the state also played a part. Mobilization, and remobilization during the later years of the war, was left in no small measure to the soldiers themselves. They came to realize, through army education, that they could, in the perceived absence of a government-sponsored vision for a postwar world, take control and advance their own idea for social change (the concepts encapsulated in the Beveridge Report). In time, through use of the franchise, the men would get the chance to ensure the future of the country coincided with their desires; they would vote overwhelmingly for Labour, the party most associated with the Beveridge Report. The "road to 1945" passed through the battlefields of Africa, Asia, and Europe.[41]

The New Zealand Army and the Furlough Mutiny

In New Zealand, the soldiers' frustration with the manner in which the war was managed led not only to manpower problems but also to outright mutiny, as Ian McGibbon explains in chapter 13 of this volume. By 1943, the British and Commonwealth forces fighting in the Mediterranean were, according to one report, "tired, not only in body, but in spirit also." Censorship reports on the mail of soldiers identified that many believed that their long period in action "morally entitle[d] them" to leave.[42] In light of the prevailing mood, the New Zealand Government decided to give 6,000 men in the 2NZEF furlough, or leave, back home (see Figure 8.1). This equated to about 20 percent of 2NZEF's men in theater and a third of the 2nd New Zealand Division. Those 6,000 men lucky enough to return home were appalled by what they found. The government had promised, in the interest of sharing the wartime burden, to "conscript wealth" as well as men. However, in reality, the war only exacerbated inequalities between tiers of New Zealand society. By 1943, there were 35,000 Grade "A" men, meaning those fit enough to go overseas, still holding jobs in "essential industry" in the dominion. Dismayed by this apparent injustice, the furlough men insisted that these "essential industry" workers replace troops who had already done their duty in the Middle East.[43] The government refused to bend, which incensed the furlough men and led to a revolt that would result in only 13 percent of the men returning to the Middle East.[44] The "Furlough Mutiny" would eventually develop into "the most severe outbreak of indiscipline in any British and Commonwealth force in both world wars."[45] The most serious example of group disobedience in the First World War, the Étaples mutiny, had developed due to the treatment of veteran soldiers in a training camp. The Furlough Mutiny, by contrast, was driven by criticisms of the government's management of the war effort.[46]

FIGURE 8.1. A soldier on furlough, Wellington, New Zealand. Soldiers who came home on furlough grew furious over the large numbers of fit men kept out of the army and in essential jobs. Many of these troops, feeling let down by the government, refused to return to the Middle East. Image source: 1/4-002053-F, Alexander Turnbull Library, Wellington, New Zealand.

It can be equated, perhaps provocatively, with the French mutinies of 1917, a succession of incidents that embodied "the most significant internal challenge to the prosecution of World War I in any of the victorious powers."[47]

News of the mutiny, needless to say, had a profound effect on those not fortunate enough to have been sent home. Back in the Mediterranean, by the onset of the second battle of Cassino (in February 1944), censors remarked that there had been a "decided drop in morale, and letters are distinctly gloomy." The existing conditions had "made the men 'furlough conscious,'" with 10 percent of writers commenting on the mishandling of the scheme back home and the thousands of "essentials" who could be sent to take their place at the front. Seven days later, an "alleged announcement" that further

furlough schemes were no longer being considered for overseas personnel received considerable comment "[against] the Gov't," and the assertion that
people in New Zealand didn't "know that there is a war on" became widespread. In the lead-up to the third battle of Cassino, censors again identified "a
slight drop [in morale] over the whole of the Div," and by the start of the battle,
on 15 March, they gauged morale as being only "fairly good." Without question, the furlough scheme and the news of the escalating mutiny back home in
New Zealand were having a "psychological effect" on those remaining at the
front.[48] The departure of the furlough men from the Middle East left many remaining soldiers wondering why they should not go home, too.[49] The censors
confirmed that "the question of home leave" continued to "exercise the minds"
and that many were "becoming restless at delay in continuing the scheme."[50]
There was a real fear that the mutiny could weaken "authority and control and
risk spreading disobedience."[51] News of the mutiny created "discontent and
bitterness" and left many questioning the "sincerity of the [New Zealand] Government." Some started to believe that the furlough scheme had been only a
"vote catcher" (with respect to the 1943 New Zealand general election).[52] Other
censor reports commented that the thought of 35,000 "essential services" men
living safe and lucrative lives at home became "rather a blister" for the men in
Italy, as it had been for the furlough men in New Zealand.[53]

The mutiny moreover deprived 2NZEF of a great number of its veteran
troops, just as it was about to tackle one of its most challenging operations
of the war. In September 1943, W. G. Stevens, officer in charge of administration in 2NZEF, had informed Wellington that "there was a maximum" total
of men that could be lost to the division due to furlough "beyond which it
would NOT repeat NOT be safe to go." He insisted that at a minimum 3,500
"old hands" be returned to the Middle East (about 60 percent of the furlough
draft) and that the total draft returning should amount to at least 5,000.[54] In
the end, only 13 percent of the first draft returned, with only 3,400 (mostly
new recruits) embarking from New Zealand in mid-January 1944, a figure
well below the 5,000 that had been envisaged.[55] The New Zealand Division,
therefore, had a shortage of reinforcements for the coming campaign season
and would have a "very high" proportion of new personnel.[56]

As a consequence, veterans in Italy felt decidedly let down, and reinforcements, pushed prematurely into battle due to manpower shortages stemming from the mutiny, suffered from feelings of inferiority due to a lack of
proper battle preparation. Morale and combat effectiveness suffered accordingly.[57] A quantitative assessment of morale in the 2NZEF for this period reinforces the argument that problems developed during this critical phase of
the campaign in Italy. The sickness rate, "a good barometer" of morale, rose

in the lead up to the third battle of Cassino.[58] Between departing for Italy and the onset of the New Zealand Division's involvement at Cassino in March 1944, the sickness rate for other ranks rose by 96 percent and that for officers by a remarkable 162 percent.[59] The battle exhaustion rate was also noteworthy. Whereas only 9 percent of casualties were attributed to battle exhaustion and neurosis during the heavy fighting in December 1943 (around Orsogna), they made up 34 percent of casualties in February and 36 percent in March 1944. The desertion rate had also increased dramatically, although it compared favorably with some of the British formations in Italy. In the second half of 1942 in North Africa, desertions in the New Zealand forces had averaged about three per month. In Tunisia they averaged about one per month. In Italy, the average rose to eight per month.[60]

Lieutenant-General Sir Bernard Freyberg, commander of 2NZEF, accepted that by 1944 the division was a "tired force as compared with previous years" and could not "easily absorb indifferent personnel."[61] In June, a few months after the third battle of Cassino, he wrote to the New Zealand prime minister that "after careful consideration," he saw "strong reasons why 2NZEF should be withdrawn to New Zealand." While he was certain that the division "could carry on and add fresh honours to its record," there were "various factors affecting the efficiency of the Force," which had to be taken into consideration, and "signs" were "not lacking" that many of the old hands required "a prolonged rest."[62] As mostly volunteers for a war effort on which the fate of the Western world rested, the men felt distinctly badly treated, and, in particular, they believed that they had been let down by their countrymen on the home front. In this context, and given that it was highly unlikely that the 2NZEF would be sent home, Freyberg came to a difficult conclusion: discipline and coercion would have to be as important to motivation as the more traditional and positive influences on morale. As he put it:

> We have got to a stage which was reached in the last war where by encouragement and discipline people have got to be made to fight . . . we have to fight now with some second-class material. The Germans are doing it and we have to harden our hearts and make as many fight as possible.[63]

The Union Defence Force and the "Blue Oath"

The story that materializes from the South African experience of the war aligns to a significant extent with that of the furlough mutineers. As early as the mid-point of 1941, the UDF was seriously short of fighting men. In the aftermath of the fall of Tobruk in June 1942 and the loss of 10,722 South Africans as prisoners of war, a second mobilization was initiated to try and make good the manpower deficit. These efforts, which became known as the "Avenge Tobruk" campaign, centered more on urban areas than those previously undertaken and, as a consequence, attracted a higher percentage of intakes from social classes I and II (13 and 18 percent for 1942 and 1943 as compared to 11 and 8 percent for 1940 and 1941; see table 8.4). Recruitment rose 46 percent as a consequence of these campaigns. However, by the end of the year it had fallen again, to well below its original alarming level. It appeared that many soldiers were warning friends and relatives "against joining up" because they themselves were "dissatisfied with service conditions."[64]

With the return of the 1st South African Division to the union in early 1943 (after the victory at El Alamein), attention turned to yet another (third) round of mobilization. To replace the 1st South African Division in the field, General Jan Smuts, the South African Prime Minister, set out to raise troops for two armored divisions (ideally constituted under a South African Corps). To recruit these men, and ensure that they could accompany the Allied armies in the Mediterranean theater (at that time, South Africans were expected to serve only on the continent of Africa), Smuts announced, on 11 December 1942, that he would ask Parliament to sanction a new oath for general service anywhere in the world. Parliament passed the motion to allow persons who signed the new General Service Oath, also known as the "Blue Oath," to fight outside of Africa. As long as 60 percent of serving soldiers also took the oath, South Africa would be able to play a full part in the closing stages of the war in North Africa and in the campaigns beyond.

Overall, though, the response was decidedly lukewarm, despite an initial surge in recruiting during the first quarter of 1943 (a 30 percent increase in white and 42 percent increase in black enlistment). Thereafter, recruitment dropped considerably and did not pick up again during the remainder of the war. A staggering 77 percent of soldiers already in service declined to take the new oath that would extend their service outside of Africa. The 23 percent who did sign up were mostly English-speakers (76 percent). Only 17 percent of Afrikaners, as compared with 26 percent of English-speakers, opted to take the new oath. Smuts, who had intended to send two armored divisions to Italy, would have to settle for one.[65]

A central issue appeared to be the need for "fairness." The perception was that some families made all the sacrifices, while others benefited from the booming war economy. This "unfairness" factor, combined with the overwhelming desire to be reunited with family, played with the motivations of soldiers. A South African Military Censorship Special Report on "Reactions to [the] New Oath" tried to engage with the question of "why the men were not coming forward in a better spirit." The veteran 3rd Armoured Car Company of the 1st South African Division was most negative about the oath, 75 percent being against it. Much like the New Zealand furlough mutineers, they felt unfairly treated. They had, in their view, already done their bit. Interestingly, the report showed that of three infantry battalions assessed the higher the percentage of Afrikaans speakers in the unit, the less likely the unit was to support the oath. Indeed, according to the censors more broadly, the men were "reluctant" to leave their families again "for any considerable length of time"; the "call from their homes seemed to be stronger than comradeship" and "loyalty" to their country.[66]

As the conflict continued, the risk grew that soldiers and their families would disengage from the war effort. Censors remarked that "surprisingly few" soldiers seemed to have "patriotic motives for their decision" to take the new oath. A survey on morale, compiled in September 1943, noted a "disturbing increase of despondency in the UDF." It was clear that "war-weariness" was now prevalent among South African troops and that "the issues of the war had been lost sight of." These sentiments were captured in the men's letters: "I honestly feel that I do not care who wins this war as long as it ends soon"; "the papers write how we are itching to go into action. I laugh, the fellow who wrote that does not know how our hearts ache to return to our loved ones"; "I feel no obligation to this country or any country any more. I had my ideals when the war started but they no longer exist." The censors concluded that a "very large number of writers" could find "no justification for their sacrifice."[67]

As Ian van der Waag demonstrates in his chapter later in this volume, it is clear that the South African state failed to rise to the challenge of mobilization for the second half of the war. Far fewer men joined up in the later years of the conflict than had done so during the great crises of 1940 to 1942. These dynamics caused great bitterness in those families who had loved ones in the services,[68] and the dramatic drop in recruitment after 1942 meant that many units struggled to keep up to strength.[69] As a result, South Africa had to reconsider its whole contribution to the Allied armies in the second half of the conflict.

The Canadian Army and the "Zombie Mutiny"

Problems with manpower were also acute for the Canadian Army in the concluding years of the war, as Daniel Byers examines in detail in chapter 11.

Much like the British Army in North-West Europe and Italy, by August 1944, the Canadians were running out of men to fill their infantry battalions. The Canadians lost just under 18,500 killed, wounded, or captured in Normandy between 6 June and 23 August.[70] They lost 6,500 casualties in the battles of the Scheldt Estuary (October–November 1944) and another 4,500 in the battles of the Gothic Line in Italy (August–September 1944).[71] These battle losses were exacerbated by issues relating to morale. During the whole of the North-West Europe campaign, the Canadian Army suffered the loss of 44,000 men due to sickness, of whom 4,991 were the result of battle exhaustion and no fewer than 7,000 from VD. During the Italian campaign, the Canadians suffered at least another 5,000 battle exhaustion cases and many more sick. Only about one-third of such men ever returned to full duties in the field.[72] The number of men lost to desertion and AWOL was also high, about 2,400 cases in the Mediterranean theater alone.[73] In these circumstances, it became necessary to tap into the reserve of trained Canadian conscripts—who were, at this time, not expected to fight overseas.[74] At first, the government tried persuasion, but these efforts met with little success. Only 694 men of 60,000 home-based conscripts volunteered for overseas service during the first three weeks of a new recruitment campaign.[75] Reluctantly and at the urging of his generals, Mackenzie King, the Canadian prime minister who had promised to avoid conscription for overseas service, decided that 16,000 home-service conscripts would have to be directed to go overseas: 16,000 conscripts (or "Zombies" as they were for unknown reasons called) would be sent to North-West Europe.[76]

The decision had profound consequences that resonated, in many ways, with those of the New Zealand Furlough Mutiny and the story of the "Blue Oath" in South Africa. Most of the trained Canadian conscripts were stationed in British Columbia. When news of the government's adjustment of policy reached them by radio, several disturbances ensued, the most serious of which took place at the base in Terrace. There, a sit-down strike by two companies of the Fusiliers du St. Laurent ignited further demonstrations involving the majority of the recruits in camp; for days, conscripts refused to obey orders from their officers. Some of the protestors looted storerooms and grabbed ammunition and weapons, including Sten and Bren machine guns. On 25 November, a big group of disgruntled conscripts marched through the camp at Terrace carrying banners with slogans such as "Down with Conscription" and "Zombies Strike Back." The commander in the Pacific region, Major-General Pearkes, informed Ottawa that the situation had escalated into a "mutiny." It was without doubt the most egregious breakdown of discipline in any Canadian force during the war. Another large demonstration took place two days later, when about 1,600 men paraded through the town, some carrying loaded weapons and exhibiting threatening behavior toward officers. Additional small disturbances took place in Vernon, Nanaimo, Prince George, Courtenay, Chilliwack, and Port Alberni.[77]

By December, discipline had been reestablished, "mostly through a process of negotiation," and by January 1945 all the available trained conscripts in Pacific Command had left for the journey to North-West Europe. Many of the mutineers, however, did not intend to cross the Atlantic. Like those of the Furlough Mutineers, the actions of the "Zombie Rioters" were animated by "a broader frustration and dissatisfaction with the overall management of the war effort." They were either politically opposed to any form of conscription for service outside of Canada or willing to serve overseas only if there was a more general conscription of wealth and industry as well as manpower. The issue of political legitimacy was fundamental to the remobilization process.[78] One local newspaper commented:

> Among the English-speaking draftees one can hear many remarks smacking of class warfare, ideological struggle and party politics. "We can win this war right here at home," meaning the war for "economic democracy," and similar phrases were common enough during the riots staged by the Zombies.[79]

It was "small wonder" then that "many" of the mutineers "took their embarkation leave as the occasion to desert."[80] Some 7,800 of the 16,000 men (48.8 percent) ordered overseas went absent as their units moved from British Columbia to Halifax. Many simply overstayed their embarkation leave, but, by the end of March, 4,082 men still remained unaccounted for. In the end, the army managed to get 12,908 conscripts overseas and into the reinforcement system, although only 2,463 "Zombies" actually made it to frontline units before the conclusion of hostilities.[81]

Conclusion

This chapter has argued that "deeply political questions of will and consensus lay at the heart of the mobilization process."[82] As John Horne has argued in relation to the First World War, but with considerable relevance to the situation that unfolded during the Second, "the terms and language of national mobilization and 'self-mobilization'" were "a vital dimension of 'total war' without which neither the combatants' tenacity nor the duration of the conflict is readily explicable." The "radical heart" of the war lay in the encounter between the state and those tasked with manning the front line. This interaction, or negotiation, "tested the legitimacy" of states and the "sense of national community to the limit." The way ordinary soldiers rationalized their experience on the front line, "and either rebelled or kept fighting, had a good deal to do with the varying capacity of different powers to keep mobilizing their soldiers' will to continue."[83] Recognizing that this interaction did not always deliver the results anticipated should not diminish the dedication and sacrifices of those many thousands who did serve with unswerving commitment. It should, however, remind states that it matters enormously, as Oliver Cromwell put it, that men should know what they fight for and love what they know.[84]

CHAPTER 9

"Enemy Aliens" and the Formation of Australia's 8th Employment Company

PAUL R. BARTROP

In the late summer of 1940, a ship filled with "enemy alien" internees arrived on the shores of Australia. Less than two years later, most of them would be enlisted as soldiers in an Australian Army labor corps and working as noncombatants to do their part in the war against the Axis powers. Most of them were from Germany or Austria, and most of them were Jewish. Their story is one of the most remarkable episodes in the immigration history of twentieth-century Australia, and it is also an intriguing story of manpower management in a country that was manpower poor.

Not since the middle of the nineteenth century had Australia received the unwanted of Britain, transported across the world for the purpose of incarceration. In 1940, however, a single instance revived this practice at the height of Britain's fight for survival against Nazi Germany. That summer, Britain was fighting for its life.[1] The so-called Phoney War had ended on 10 May with the German invasion of the Low Countries and France, and Britain stood alone awaiting a German invasion. Its resources were stretched beyond capacity, and new security considerations began to confront British decision makers, not least of them the home secretary, Sir John Anderson, who declared that the British government would draw a clear distinction between enemy aliens and refugees from Germany and Austria. Accordingly, alien tribunals were set up classifying those bearing German nationality into three categories:

A. persons to be immediately interned as not being absolutely reliable;
B. persons left at liberty, but subject to certain of the restrictions applicable to enemy aliens under the Aliens Order of 1920; and
C. persons who should be free from all restrictions under the Aliens Order, except those applying to friendly aliens.

Both the B and C categories were classified as refugees from Nazi oppression and generally considered sympathetically by the British people. In fact, these made up the great majority of aliens from enemy countries in 1940—about 6,800 were deemed category B, while some 65,000 were classified as category C.[2] Aliens tribunals found only 568 to be category A aliens and interned. With the invasion of the Low Countries and France, however, panic swept through Britain, and all enemy aliens, whether refugees or not, came to be seen as potential fifth columnists, spies ready to spring into action once the Germans invaded the home islands. On 12 May, Anderson issued an order under which all German and Austrian males, aged sixteen to sixty and living in the coastal regions of England and Scotland, would be interned (excluding invalids or those who were infirm). All other male aliens in the same age group, regardless of their nationality, were subjected to restrictions, such as having to report daily to the nearest police station; not using any motor vehicle (other than public transport) or bicycle; and having movement and activity restricted by nighttime curfews.[3] A second order at the end of May authorized the immediate internment of all category B persons, male or female. Finally, at the end of June 1940, an order was issued for the general internment of all adult males of enemy nationality. The great majority were category C, including many who were engaged in work of national importance as scientists and educators or studying at various schools, colleges, and universities.

Accompanying the panic measures to intern all enemy aliens were calls for their deportation from Britain. On 3 June, Prime Minister Winston Churchill suggested the deportation of 20,000 internees, and on 7 June the dominions secretary asked the high commissioners for Canada and Australia if they could take some of the internees off Britain's hands. Both dominions agreed, and ships bearing nearly 9,000 internees began leaving Britain before the end of June.[4] One of the transports, the *Arandora Star*, carrying 1,213 internees, never reached its destination. It was torpedoed by a U-boat a few hours out of Liverpool, with considerable loss of life. Some 444 survivors were plucked from the water by British and Canadian warships and later reembarked on board another ship, the Hired Military Transport *Dunera*, which left Liverpool for Melbourne and Sydney on 10 July. Altogether the *Dunera* carried 2,732 internees of all ages. Most were German and Austrian Jews. Mixed in with them were also 251 German prisoners of war, several dozen Nazi sympathizers, and 200 Italians.[5] It was intended that the *Dunera* would be the first of several transports to Australia, but, in the end, it was the only ship to bring internees to the Commonwealth.

The long sea voyage saw an appalling journey during which instances were recorded of the most gross injustices and mistreatment perpetrated by the guard detachment charged with security on board. The guard included companies in the British Pioneer Corps and members of the Royal Norfolks, Suffolks, and the Queen's Own Regiment. During the voyage the internees were subjected to a variety of beatings, looting, robbery, torture, and intimidation by some of the guards, who, having fought in France and survived the beaches of Dunkirk, were determined to mete out the harshest of punishments to the "Nazis" in their care. *Dunera* reached Australia on 26 August, stopping first at Fremantle.[6] Subsequent stops offloaded internees at Melbourne and Sydney. Those who disembarked at Melbourne went on to camps at Tatura in northern Victoria, while the remainder, who left *Dunera* at Sydney, went by train to Hay, some 725 kilometers due west. At Hay, internees were divided into two groups: Camp 7, which consisted mainly of Jews; and Camp 8, which was made up of political internees and Catholic Germans. The internees then quickly began to settle into an existence intended to enable them, efficiently and, so far as possible, comfortably, to survive the experience of captivity and perhaps even gain something positive from it.

Established Australian policy regarding Jewish refugees complicated matters somewhat. Before September 1939, policy was based on a 1933 determination that "no undue influx" of Jews should be permitted.[7] If Australia accepted vast numbers Jewish refugees fleeing Nazi Germany, some felt that the country's racial homogeneity—97 percent British according to racial purists—would be diluted. Worse, in some quarters, was the fear that Australia would fall under Jewish "domination" and that consequently the Australian standard of living would drop.[8] On the other hand, if the Australian government deliberately excluded refugees, the Commonwealth would surely miss the opportunity of acquiring some useful skills and capital brought to the country by potentially "good" Jews who did not fit the stereotype.[9] Australia would then also miss the chance of adding to the country's white population at a time of considerable apprehensions about under-population and fears concerning Japanese expansionism. After weighing the pros and cons, the Commonwealth government took a compromise position. *Some* Jewish refugees would be accepted. In this way, Australia would not be seen as renouncing its humanitarian obligations, and the nation's racial composition would remain essentially intact. Unquestionably, the government adopted racial criteria when determining its policy, which resulted in a rejection rate of 90 percent for all eligible applications. In August 1938, the assistant minister for the interior, Victor Thompson, stated coldly that it was "necessary to defer or reject many applications *which would have been considered satisfactory* if the necessity had not arisen to limit the number of approvals. . . . Under present conditions [the increase in Jewish refugees from Germany] . . . only about one in ten applications can be approved."[10] And it got worse. At the outbreak of war in September 1939, the Commonwealth government announced that all applications for landing permits by "enemy aliens"—including Jews residing in Germany or German-controlled territory—would henceforth be refused.[11] Australia would not take Jews if they originated from within Nazi Europe.

Given these policies and attitudes, there was little reason to suspect that the Australians should have welcomed the arrival of over 2,000 Jews from Britain in September 1940—and every reason for the government to want them to leave once their internment was over. Yet for the internees, a constant theme running through their entire experience, before they left Britain and after they arrived in Australia, was their desire to be released so that they could contribute to the war effort against the common enemy. And as will be shown, after the entry of Japan into the war, when Australia itself was threatened, the Australian government did provide the internees with the opportunity of demonstrating their loyalty by joining the Army in a noncombatant labor role. Almost all who had not yet returned to Britain took advantage of the offer.

As *Dunera* arrived in Australia, questions were being asked in the British House of Commons about the arbitrary nature of the arrests that had transformed the refugees into internees in the first place. The upshot of these questions was a set of exemptions from internment, which affected most of those who had been sent to Australia on the *Dunera*.[12] The change of heart facilitated the release of thousands who had been interned in Britain and threw open the status of those who had been sent overseas. In light of the new exemptions, in November 1940, the British government requested that Australia consider the release of eligible internees for transmigration to the United States, Palestine, and other countries.[13] To help facilitate this, the Home Office sent to Australia a liaison officer, Major Julian Layton, who acted as a go-between for the British government, the internees, and the Australian authorities.[14]

Layton went quickly to his work. On 10 April 1941, he made his first visit to the internees at Hay. While some anxious internees thought it a "great day" that would lead to their release, Layton himself cautioned that there was much to be done before they could leave the camp.[15] Australian authorities did not want internees released into the territory of the Commonwealth, so plans had to be put in place to send them somewhere else. In the meantime, Layton did manage to improve conditions for the internees by relocating them in May 1941 from the forbidding climate of Hay to the altogether better climate of Tatura—a move that was both needed and appreciated by the internees. Once at Tatura, they joined another consignment of nearly 300 Jewish internees who had been sent to Australia from Singapore in late September 1940.[16] Layton also managed to repatriate several hundred internees to Britain, where they joined the Pioneer Corps, a condition of their transfer to the United Kingdom.

As for those who remained in Australia, authorities deliberated throughout 1941 on the possibility of limited releases for highly skilled internees who could be of use to the war effort. Security would remain paramount—concerns persisted that the internees might actually pose a risk—but, in November 1941, the Department of the Army made a formal proposal to the War Cabinet that highly skilled internees, such as toolmakers and machine-manufacturing experts, be released to work on projects of national importance. Cabinet approved the proposal on 20 November, and, accordingly, a few of the most highly skilled internees were released into the Australian work force.[17]

The situation for the remainder of the *Dunera* internees changed dramatically with Japan's entry into the war in December 1941. More than 100,000 Australian men were called up for full-time service; many of those who had previously been in reserved occupations were now conscripted, and a labor crisis began to emerge. There were also shortages of agricultural labor. The Commonwealth now needed more than just the highly skilled internees. It now needed every all able-bodied man—and internee—for the defense of the country. As a result of the sudden manpower crunch, the minister for the Army, Frank Forde, quickly arranged for the establishment of a labor corps, organized along the lines of the British Pioneer Corps and comprising unskilled internees. In some respects, it was a *fait accompli* because it was so much easier than shipping internees back to Britain. As Layton later recalled, the Japanese entry to the war made it now "very difficult to get shipping back to the United Kingdom," and it "was almost impossible to get accommodation" on whatever ships were available in any case.[18] By mid-December rumors of a soon-to-be-formed labor corps began circulating among the internees.[19] They liked the idea, which sounded to them like a way out of the camp and an opportunity to contribute to the war effort.

The labor shortage occasioned by the war did not give the authorities many alternatives when it came to releasing the internees—and not just for the Australian Army's labor corps. In the fruit-growing areas surrounding

Tatura, the usual itinerant labor required for the harvest could not be found, so some internees were permitted to take up the work of harvesting fruit in the Goulburn Valley region, not far from Tatura. The fruit growers of the region eagerly accepted the help, and the internees eagerly gave it. As one released internee wrote to his "mates" still in the camp: "As you all know we left you by car to reach a race course . . . where we camped in the "Grand Stand" where we met those who had left us before. There was an atmosphere absolutely different from your camp; everybody was gay, smiling, in the best of spirits, we jumped to the parades and roll calls willingly. . . . There was no barbed wire, no guards, officers and soldiers, nothing but friendliness and we felt like being their guests. . . . To cut a long story short: we were happy."[20] There were no uniforms at this time, and those on fruit-picking duty had to buy their own food and cook their own meals. They did, however, have free accommodation and were paid at award (or minimum) wages. Restrictions were few: "Only the boss has to inform the police by phone once a week that 'the gang is all here.' We work 9 hours a day on 5 days and 3 hours on Saturday. Then we are free on the week-end, free to move wherever we want, to Melbourne etc. No restrictions whatsoever besides changing the domicile."[21] Internees were aware that the fruit-picking experiment could serve as "a stepping stone to lead us back in our own occupation if vital for the war work." Indeed, the minister told the internees that "he has another job for us in mind."[22]

Fruit-picking did in fact serve as a precedent for a more general enlistment into the already-advertised (although not-yet-activated) labor corps. This had been long been a subject of speculation, and now the changed conditions brought about by the Japanese threat made a revision of internee status more necessary than ever. After all, those working at fruit-picking had to be guarded by troops who could be put to better use elsewhere. The logic of manpower management dictated that, for every internee who swore an oath to the king and put on a uniform, a native Australian soldier could be released for combat.

And so the labor corps was formed. In total, thirty-nine employment companies, comprising about 15,000 men, were formed over the course of the war, eleven of them made up of so-called aliens.[23] They performed essential labor tasks in support of the home-front war effort as well as the fighting forces. These unarmed companies deployed to places such as Tocumwal and Albury on the New South Wales/Victorian border. There they worked on the trains, loading and unloading military supplies, foodstuffs, and armaments. Across the country, the employment companies were also directed to factories to assist with the packing and transport of goods. Others worked on wharves, repaired roads, and drove trucks loaded with military equipment. There was to be no prospect of transfer to combat duty. In the words of one internee, labor corps troops would serve as "coolies."[24] Even so, internees still rationalized that this would remain operative only "until the necessity becomes probable," and hopes remained high that their war service would involve more than simply loading and unloading boxes.[25]

The labor corps comprising the *Dunera* and *Queen Mary* internees formed on 7 April 1942 as the 8th Employment Company under the command of Captain Edward R. Broughton, a career officer who had seen service in three armies dating from the time of the Boer War.[26] The war diary for April 1942 describes initial war establishment strength of four officers and 453 other ranks.[27] The first internees to volunteer for labor corps service were actually set to work fruit-picking, probably much to their annoyance, but only these initial volunteers were required to do so—between January and April 1942—while the unit was being formed. Subsequent intakes went straight into the army. The option to join remained open throughout the war, with the last internee enlisting in September 1944. Their status as "enemy aliens" still remained unchanged until February 1944, when the government granted them "refugee alien" status.[28]

The 8th Employment Company was a most unusual organization. Comprised exclusively of Jewish men with no prior experience of Australia or of military conventions or discipline, its soldiers-by-default soon found army life to be very different than it was in the internment camps, and they often found themselves in unaccustomed roles. This highly intelligent and motivated group of what would today be termed "achievers" often found the demands of the military bewildering and illogical, and they gave back as good as they got. Captain Broughton was reputed to have said on one occasion that after service in three armies across a forty-year career, the 8th Employment Company was the only unit he had ever encountered in which, when he gave an order, the reply inevitably came back, "Why?"[29] Such good-hearted tongue-in-cheek chutzpah notwithstanding, when it came to military matters the men were well-disciplined. They respected Broughton and their other officers, and they made a useful contribution to the war effort.

That said, the work in which the men were engaged was "hard, backbreaking, [and] monotonous." It involved "loading and unloading on the dock, at depots and dumps."[30] Those on such duties were often unaccustomed to such work, being "professional men with fine brains and specialized training." They were, however, "bent on helping to win this war," given that "fascism to them had a real meaning." Thus, "they . . . learned to use their muscles,"[31] working at duties that were far from inspiring. The tasks on

FIGURE 9.1. Members of the 28th Australian Employment Company perform manual labor, Alice Springs, Australia, December 1942. This was one of thirty-nine such companies raised to perform labor on the home front. Eleven labor companies were made up of so-called aliens. For example, the 8th Employment Company comprised exclusively non-Australian Jewish men who had been arrested in Britain as enemy aliens and transported to Australia as prisoners. Image source: Australian War Memorial, 028348.

which they were engaged were mundane, as a lyric to one of their company songs captures so well: "Our only chance to travel / Is fetching sand and gravel."[32] And as in any military organization, it took little time for the men of this unusual company to learn how to gripe, as one of them said later, "like real soldiers": longing for leave, complaining about an unending diet of bully beef, and awaiting mail from families, who, unknown to them, had all too often already been consumed by the Holocaust (see Figure 9.1).

While the 8th Employment Company was a mobile unit traveling to wherever there was a need for muscle power, its bases—first in the Melbourne suburb of Caulfield, and then at Camp Pell in Carlton, close to the inner city central core—provided opportunities for entertainment and personal growth that did not exist in the internment camps. One former internee described this aspect of his new life in khaki in the following manner:

> I wrote you in my last letter that I have been to the concert by the Melbourne Symphony Orchestra. I do not want to miss a single concert if I can help it. You know yourself how few concerts are taking place in Melbourne. On Sunday afternoon I went to the concert by the

Melbourne Conservatorium Orchestra under the conductor Craw-ford. . . . Every evening from 5 o'clock onwards we have open camp. That means we can do what we like. I am going to the city almost every night. Unfortunately Melbourne cannot offer very much entertain-ment except dancing, pictures and cabarets. . . . I do not miss any amusement or show which is worthwhile seeing. I have supper in town almost every evening and have a bath almost every other evening, as there are no hot showers in camp, which is very primitive. . . . In the evenings I usually come home not before 12 o'clock. Therefore I only get 5 hours of sleep.[33]

For this ex-internee—one of many—"military life is no pleasure, but I can think of worse conditions." Indeed, his greatest fear was that he would be moved to the countryside: "I only pray that we will stay in Melbourne because it will not be half as good in the country. All the other aliens' compa-nies are stationed in the country by now, I hope we shall not suffer the same fate."[34] The location of Camp Pell was also convenient in that it was close to the nearby University of Melbourne, where some studied to matriculate and others read for degrees. Of course, this could be done only while the men were off-duty, but now that they were in the army, their prospects for an edu-cation were enhanced through the Army Education Unit. By the end of the war, at least fifty ex-*Dunera* men had obtained degrees, and twelve were actu-ally on the faculty at Melbourne.[35]

When on leave, 8th Employment Company men found ways to enter mainstream Australian society—going to dances, meeting women, attending movies, and building relationships. For the most part, they were able to miti-gate the worst effects of their internment experience in such a way as to en-hance their life options. Most of those who had been on the *Dunera* were released by the end of 1942, and by November 1945 some 785 former *Dunera* men were still in Australia, their war service having forced the Common-wealth government to rethink the permanency of the migration and let them stay. Of those left in Australia, 417 were in civilian employment and 368 were still in the army.[36] The remainder returned to the United Kingdom or trans-migrated elsewhere.

The 8th Employment Company was exceptional in many respects. A unit of the Australian Army comprised of non-Australians, it was exclusively Jew-ish and created in circumstances that were also remarkable. Its men were ar-rested as enemy aliens in Britain, transported halfway around the world as prisoners, released gradually from internment to make up labor shortages in the Australian economy, enlisted as soldiers in the Australian Army labor corps to release others for combat service, and, at the end of their wartime service, allowed to remain as permanent residents, even at a time when Jewish immigration had essentially been closed down.

Looked at in this sense, the 8th Employment Company was indeed an oddity, but one that, fortunately, was comprised of men who were to play an important role in the development of postwar Australia—in the arts, in education, in science, and in the law (among other endeavors).[37] As an army observer noted in April 1943, "To these men their Australian uniform is a symbol of tolerance, decency. Australia and Australians have revived their flagging faith in mankind. We can be proud of that."[38] Or, in the words of an ex-*Dunera* internee who chose to return to Britain in October 1941, and therefore missed out on the opportunity of enlisting in the 8th Employment Company, "By and large we all done well and are proud of our heritage" as *Dunera* alumni.[39]

The Australian authorities concurred, expressing an attitude that the ex-internees, now army veterans, should be offered the opportunity to remain. In March 1944, the War Cabinet approved a proposal that those internees still under internment (of whom there were very few) could be released later.[40] By this stage, most of those under discussion were in the army, still considered to be interned but "on parole." In fact, it was not until after the war had ended that serious consideration was given to allowing former *Dunera* internees the opportunity to stay in Australia, regardless of whether they had served in the army or not. This was never a sure thing. At one point, in November 1945, Frank Forde, still in his capacity as minister for the army, proposed that the ex-internees should all be repatriated back to Britain now that the war with Japan was over.[41] The minister for labour and national service, E. J. Holloway, spoke for many when he objected strongly to Forde's proposal: "Where any of these people, who have worked loyally and well since being released in Australia, desire to do so, they should be permitted to become permanent residents and citizens of Australia."[42] More ministers were with Holloway than with Forde, with the result that those *Dunera* men who sought to remain and who had served the country during the war were accepted in line with Holloway's preferences and in due course became Australian citizens.

CHAPTER 10

The Body and Becoming a Soldier
in Britain during the Second World War

EMMA NEWLANDS

In February 1942, twenty-year-old Alan Bad-
man was recruited into the ranks of the Royal Engineers. Having passed a
medical examination, Alan completed three months of training at Chatham
Barracks in Kent. Sixty years later, in an interview for the Imperial War Museum, he reflected on his early experiences of military life:

> [Barracks] were like a prison regime really. Fighting to get up in the
> morning to see if you could get to the toilet. You had no excuses. You
> had to bark to orders. There was no you can't do this or you can't do
> that, blame anybody else. If you can't get it, you fight somebody else
> for it. . . . In the end you start to enjoy it. You start to get a bit of pride
> cos they'd say you were a shower of shit. All day long, you've done this
> wrong and you've done that wrong. Then they say "oh look." It's like
> you can be indoctrinated to the stage where you were rebelling against
> it one minute then taking pride in it the next.[1]

Alan was one of over 3.5 million men who joined the British Army between
1939 and 1945.[2] The majority of these men were conscripts, enlisted under
the government's National Service Acts, which imposed liability for military
service on all males aged eighteen to forty-one (and later fifty-one).[3] Historians have examined the ways that the military authorities adapted doctrine
and organization to meet the needs of this new civilian intake, including

changes in selection, leadership, and education.[4] However, the experiences of the recruits themselves remain relatively unexplored.[5]

This chapter complements the others in this volume by looking closely at an underappreciated but essential aspect of raising manpower for a mass army: the processes used to transform raw civilians into disciplined, fit, battle-ready soldiers. It examines the transition from civilian to soldier during basic army training in the Second World War by focusing on the recruit's body. Various theorists have drawn attention to the formal organizational control of soldiers' bodies within military institutions, as well as to connections between the male military body and hegemonic masculinity.[6] Yet, this work has rarely been grounded in the physical development of service personnel.[7] Scholarly studies of the Second World War have examined the contribution of military medicine to manpower efficiency in overseas theaters, as well as the treatment and rehabilitation of wounded and disabled servicemen in hospitals back in Britain.[8] We know much less, however, about the ways that men were physically prepared for war.

This chapter explores the methods used by army training officers and instructors to mold, treat, and transform the civilian bodies that they were presented with. It examines the qualities considered ideal, the skills taught, and the strategies used to inculcate military values, including close regulation of diet, dress, sexual activity, and exercise. To do so, this chapter draws on the instructional material produced for army training staff between 1939 and 1945. The first codified set of guidelines was published in 1908 as the *Manual of Physical Training*, largely in response to concerns about the poor physical condition of recruits during the South African War. According to James Campbell, by the First World War, military physical training had reached a "point of professional maturity," with exercises and sports fully ingrained in army doctrine in order to prepare soldiers' bodies for the demands of modern conflict.[9] There were several revisions to physical training regulations before and during the Second World War, which, I argue, reflected military requirements and wider ideas about health.

This chapter is also rooted directly in the experiences of army recruits— men like Alan Badman, whose story reveals a great deal about what it was like to become a British soldier during the Second World War. He explains that he had to get up at a certain time, go to the toilet at a certain time, and obey orders all day long. Alan was no longer able to employ or to rest his body as he saw fit. Indeed, he compares this regime to a prison sentence. Yet Alan ultimately recounts his transformation as a success, stating that, in the end, he took pride in being able to keep up with the army's demands. This raises questions about the extent to which Alan was able to exercise agency or had internalized military control. To explore these issues, this chapter utilizes a range of personal narratives, including diaries, memoirs, responses from *Mass Observation* (a British program that used volunteers to record their everyday life experiences), and a selection of oral history testimonies from the Imperial War Museum sound archive.[10] All of the accounts included come from men recruited into the rank and file of the army. Like the majority of servicemen in this period, all were aged between eighteen and thirty at the time of enlistment.[11] All went on to serve in combat operations overseas. While these sources are subject to all of the caveats that surround the use of personal testimonies, they are nonetheless highly revealing.[12] They provide glimpses into the daily experience of routines and treatments as told by men at the receiving end of army discipline.[13] They also reveal the extent to which recruits complied with the demands of their instructors, their reasons for engaging in behaviors deemed to be unhealthy or unsafe, and the meanings they attributed to their own bodies. Analyzing the feelings, expectations, and motivations of recruits in this way opens up a number of themes, including control, agency and resistance, gender and class identities, and emotional responses to military service.

"Then You're under Control": Settling In

For the majority of army recruits during the Second World War, training lasted for about four months. At the start of the war, men were enlisted directly into regiments and received basic training in depots. However, officers soon discovered that recruits were being allocated to roles that did not best suit their abilities. So, in July 1942, the army introduced the General Service Scheme. From then on, recruits spent their first six weeks in primary training centers, where they underwent basic infantry training, as well as aptitude and intelligence tests. They were then posted to corps training centers to receive instruction specific to their arm of the service. This ranged from sixteen weeks for infantrymen to thirty-two weeks for signalers.[14] Whatever his eventual destination, every new recruit began basic training by undergoing the same rituals and practices, all of which were designed to strip away his civilian identity and submit him to the authority of his officers and instructors. Upon arrival at the camps, men were given an army number, a uniform, and a regulation haircut and assigned a space to sleep. Albert Hunter volunteered for the Rifles just before the outbreak of war in 1939. Describing his initiation at Winchester Barracks, he stated, "They take all your clothes off you. They give you a bunch of canvas clothes called fatigues, and issue you with a knife, fork, spoon, razor, comb and lava brush in a holdall, a bed in a barracks, and then you're under control"[15] (see Figure 10.1).

The issue of military clothing, in particular, elicited a range of emotional responses. An anonymous *Mass Observation* respondent wrote in his diary on his second day at Queen's Barracks in Perth in 1942, "We were dressed in our denims (work suit) and I for one felt even more depressed. We sent all our clothes home and now the complete break from civilian life was accentuated."[16] Miner's son, James Wyndham, on the other hand, was enthusiastic about his uniform because it meant that he was better clothed than he had been before. James, from Abergavenny, had struggled to find work since leaving school at sixteen. He described training at Bedford Barracks as "heaven" because "I had two pairs of navy boots, two pairs of underwear, which I'd never had before. I had an overcoat, the first overcoat in my life, and woolen vests."[17] For others, the uniform had more symbolic value. In November 1940, recruit Henry Novy recorded in his diary at a Leeds depot that "the pride taken in the uniform is that of being part of a well-organized and efficient machine."[18] At a time when inclusion in the armed forces signified increased masculine status, new soldiers also enjoyed looking different to their civilian counterparts.[19] Peter Holyhead was called-up for military service in 1943. As one of thirteen siblings, including eight brothers, he welcomed the extra attention from his father, who "when I went home in uniform, tended to make more of a fuss of me than he did the other boys."[20] Twenty-year-old Leslie Gray trained with the Gloucestershire Regiment in 1940. He also recalled that his father, a First World War veteran, "never took any notice of me because the Victorian parents didn't and me being the last, he didn't take any notice whatsoever, not when I was a child. But when I went in the army he wanted to show me off, cos he was an old soldier. He'd take me down the pub in full uniform, because you couldn't be in civilian clothes in those days."[21]

From day one, recruits were expected to be neat and tidy in their appearance and to maintain good personal hygiene. In September 1940, an army training memorandum emphasized the importance of good grooming habits to the acquisition of a soldierly mindset by stating: "A dirty soldier is invariably a bad soldier, slovenly in action and in thought; whereas the alert, clean man reflects his characteristics in his turn out."[22] Army regulations included shaving daily, a practice with which many young recruits had little experience. Sixteen-year-old John Dray lied about his age to enlist in 1944. On his first day at Britannia Barracks in Norwich, the sergeant-major asked, "Shave boy?" When John replied "No sir, I don't shave." The sergeant-major said "You do now, boy."[23] William Dilworth was eighteen when he was called up and sent for basic training with the Rifle Brigade at York in 1942. When asked by his sergeant-major how often he shaved, William replied that he had never shaved before because he had no facial hair. This was his first lesson in army discipline:

> He called one of the corporals and he said, "Take this man to the ablutions and see that he shaves immediately." So the corporal marched me off across the square to the toilets and he said, "Well, shave," and I said, "I've never shaved." So he says, "Get your razor out," so I got the razor, which the army gave me and opened it up and I said, "Well, I haven't got a razor blade," so he says, "Put it all back together again and go through the motions, soap your face and then make out you're shaving." So, without a razor blade in I went through the motions of shaving and everything, washed my face and was marched back to the parade ground, marched up to the sergeant-major and the sergeant-major looked at my face and said, "That's bloody better, man. Now in future you'll shave every morning."[24]

Early on, the army also sought to establish control over the body's inner functioning. Instructors had received some basic knowledge of anatomy since before the First World War. Increasingly, they were expected to apply this knowledge to training regimens as the century progressed.[25] The 1941 manual *Physical and Recreational Training* recommended "the systematic development and strengthening of the whole body," based on "physiological principles." These included "good nutrition" and "careful regulation of smoking and drinking."[26] By 1944, a replacement publication, *Basic Battle and Physical Training*, dedicated an entire chapter to "Body Mechanics and Applied Physiology." Comparing the human body to a combustion engine, it stated that "the petrol must be ample, and a free air entry assured, together with accurate timing of ignition and efficient clearing of the exhaust."[27] Thus, the recruit was fed, rested, and cleansed of his bodily waste products.

Against a backdrop of wider advances in physiology and growing professional interest in nutrition, feeding the soldier became something of a science during the Second World War.[28] At the start of hostilities, the army established twenty-four cookery schools where civilian experts in dietetics trained army cooks in both nutrition and variety.[29] As a result, recruits in training received four meals per day, made up of meat, fish, vegetables, pulses, and cereals. These included "body-building proteins, energy-producing carbohydrates and fats, and protective vitamins and salts." Rest, defined as "all degrees of absence from work, from sleep in the lying position to relaxation in the upright" was considered equally important to allow the body time to absorb food and encourage the removal of products "for disposal and excretion through lung, bladder and skin." Official advice stipulated that men secure eight hours sleep per night along with sufficient rest periods throughout the day. Specifically, each meal was to be followed by half an hour of relaxation time to "help the digestive processes get underway."[30]

Soldiers' responses to the army diet appear to have been framed largely by social class. While men tended to describe the same sorts of meals being served, differences in satisfaction depended on what they had been used to before joining the service. Miner's son James Wyndham recalled that there was "good grub. I'd never really had seconds. We had liver and bacon and gravy for the first meal."[31] Nineteen-year-old David Evans was also from a Welsh mining family. Enlisted into the infantry in 1940, he later recalled in his memoir that "I hadn't been accustomed to anything better and was, at least, being well-fed, with solid and regular meals, for the first time in my life."[32] Robert Ellison had been raised in difficult circumstances by a single mother after his father's death in a colliery in the North East of England. Robert described the food at a primary training center in Cheshire as "pretty good. . . . You ate things there you'd never eaten before. Like I remember the first time in my life that we had peas that had not been taken out of the pod. . . . I thought my goodness pea pods for your lunch [laughs]."[33]

There was, however, a general feeling among recruits from all backgrounds that the army diet was sufficient, especially in light of wider food shortages. Twenty-one-year-old former grammar-school boy Walter Chalmers volunteered with the 1st Battalion, Liverpool Scottish, and recalled that "the food was very much better than one would be getting in civilian life at that time."[34] Roy Bolton, another grammar-school graduate and former county council clerk from London, trained at Richmond Barracks in York in 1943. Although he "took to the food as best I could" and "didn't always like it," Roy was still surprised by the complaints that came from the men in his barracks. He stated that "it was as though they'd been brought up to dine at the Ritz or somewhere. . . . I used to wonder what on earth they were accustomed to at home."[35] Even men who had been used to eating more noticed the benefits of developing new habits. John Gray explained that "I found at first that I used to be hungry after meals but there was no more so you couldn't have it." With time, however, John felt that he "certainly became much fitter. Even I realised that. So although the food didn't appear to be as much, it did me a damned sight better."[36] John Dray likewise recalled that at Britannia Barracks the food "did take a bit of getting used to" because "the quantity wasn't terribly great but the army convinced us boys that if we overfed that we'd be fat and hungry and no good. To keep us hungry is the way to build life. In the diet we had, we used to have lectures on this by the MO [medical officer], that the dieticians had worked out all the vitamins and so forth we needed to grow to be big strong men so we accepted it."[37] It appears, then, that over time recruits came to trust in the expertise of army staff, and they accepted changes to their diets, particularly when they experienced positive physical effects.

"He Wouldn't Be Scruffy for Long": Monitoring and Surveillance

Having set out what was expected of recruits regarding their appearance, personal hygiene, diet, and digestion, the authorities used a range of methods to monitor men's adherence to standards. Kit inspections and parades were a routine feature of life in barracks, designed to ensure that men prepared their uniforms in strict accordance with army regulations. James Wyndham described how he put soap in his trousers and slept on them the night before, because "when I got up they were as if I'd ironed them." He also recalled that any recruit who was "slovenly" and "unclean" was taken by the lance corporals to the ablutions and "scrubbed viciously with a scrubbing brush." The effect was that "he wouldn't be scruffy for long."[38]

From the outset of training, men were also subject to regular physical examinations so that medical staff could identify and fix any problems. On his first day at Retford Barracks, William Dilworth had "a thorough examination, your ears and every other part of your body." This included a dental examination during which he had a tooth "drilled and filled."[39] Particularly prominent in soldiers' accounts are the army's "short arm" inspections that were used to detect venereal disease. These most intimate of assessments were often performed en masse, with medical officers paying little attention to matters of confidentiality. James Wyndham remembered "a big house where the doctor was. You were assembled there to drop your trousers and have a medical FFI [free from infection]."[40] Recalling one particularly embarrassing experience with a female medic at an infantry camp on Salisbury Plain in 1939, Bert Scrivens described what happened to one unfortunate man in his unit:

> It was quite funny because the RSM [regimental sergeant-major] was standing there and he said, "Right it's a lady doctor, behave yourselves. Any man who doesn't goes out of here at the double." One bloke, well her method of doing the inspection, she had a long something like a pencil and lifted the penis up and put it down again. One bloke got

aroused and the Sergeant-Major said, "That man, out," and as soon as he got outside the marquee he got a bucket of cold water over him, clothed and all."[41]

Medical examination was therefore something of a spectacle in which men were expected to submit to the demands of the medical inspector. Those who did not obey, even unwillingly, were publicly shamed, as a deterrent and a warning to other men.

Recruits also experienced considerable restraints on their personal movements, especially during the early stages of training. Men were usually confined to barracks for the first six weeks to let discipline take hold. Roy Bolton recalled that "very early it was made clear to us at the barracks that there was no way we'd be allowed to go out and show ourselves in public until we knew how to behave as proper soldiers."[42] Leslie Gray likewise recalled, "We didn't get out until about eight weeks. You had to be a fairly trained person before they'd let you through the gates. I think they thought you'd not come back again."[43] Within barracks, surveillance was enhanced through a timetable, which scheduled every moment of the soldier's day. Even the most natural bodily functions were regulated by time. James Wyndham recalled one incident at Bedford Barracks in January 1940:

> You had to be regular in your motions as well. You had to be up with the lark, get your breakfast, come back you've got to have done your crap and you've got to be ready. If you were caught short in the middle of the morning, I've known chaps to say to Corporal Sears, "Corporal, I've got to go to the loo." "You bloody well won't." Then suddenly [makes noise of someone defecating]. He's got the shits and you've got him doubled-up around the barrack square. Oh I've seen that, terrible. You know, the man couldn't help it because he probably had one or two pints the night before or ate something that didn't agree with him. But I've seen Corporal Sears ruthless. He wouldn't let the man fall-out, even when he had diarrhea.[44]

Confining men to barracks also allowed army superiors to monitor sexual behavior—important for controlling venereal disease. The frustrations that men felt are clear in their testimonies. Sherwood Foresters recruit Neville Wildgust recalled that "for the first sixteen weeks we were hard and fast locked in and there was no sex life at all."[45] A *Mass Observation* respondent named Leonard England noted in his 1941 diary that the men in his unit had to find "sexual release" by describing "moments of passion" and reading love

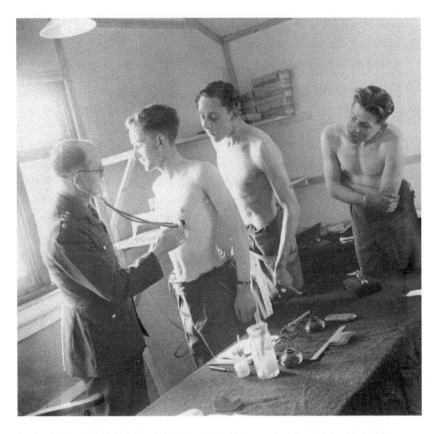

FIGURE 10.1.   During the Second World War, the British army transformed about 3.5 million civilians into hardened, battle-ready soldiers. These recruits, undergoing a medical officer's examination at an infantry training center in April 1942, are just beginning the arduous transformation process. Image source: © Imperial War Museum, H18457.

letters to each other.[46] Such accounts can be read as displays of masculinity, based on virility and heterosexuality, leading men to engage in competition with each other. Indeed, some recruits believed that bromide had been added to their tea to, as one man claimed, "keep your sexual fantasies down."[47] This was a widespread myth within the armed forces that reinforced traditional notions of masculinity, based on the assumption that only chemicals could cause a reduced sex drive.[48] The reality was that men's libidos were probably affected by the change of lifestyle.

While it is unlikely that the army chemically tempered men's impulses, welfare officers did try to encourage abstinence by providing healthy recreations like libraries, games rooms, and supervised all-ranks dances. William Dilworth remembered that at Retford Barracks:

we would have a dance I think it was every Saturday night in the barracks and women who wanted to come to the barracks, there'd be
army lorries sent into the town and all those that wanted to come, they
just piled in and when the lorry was full they would bring them to the
camp, you know. But then the dance would finish at ten o'clock and all
the women had to get back on the lorries and [be] taken back to town
and they were all checked and everything to make sure nobody was
staying behind."[49]

Such wholesome recreations were not, however, enough to deter amorous
recruits, such as men stationed close to Auxiliary Territorial Service (ATS)
camps. A *Mass Observation* respondent named Morris, who was based at an
infantry depot in Essex in 1942, reported that "the men keep their urges fas-
tened on such females as may be in range," especially "the girls in the can-
teen."[50] In June 1941, Leonard England likewise proclaimed that "the ATS are
far more in demand as girlfriends."[51]

Within barracks, soldiers also had sex with each other. Despite being a
crime in both civil and military law, homosexuality, as personal accounts reveal, was openly practiced in some units.[52] At Blanford Camp, Private R. H.
Lloyd Jones observed two recruits whose "behaviour all day was perfectly
proper. It was therefore a little surprising sometimes, when awakening in the
morning to see the two of them sharing the same bed."[53] Morris described in
detail the evening activities at his barracks in Essex:

It is a quite well-recognised fact that such activities do occur, and that
those who participate will freely admit to them. This may be due to the
fact that recruits include all types, not omitting those already well
versed in these arts . . . and the outside opportunities for the "working
off" of sex. . . . There are a certain number who are definitely treated
as females by the others. They are referred to by feminine pronouns
and use feminine first names (Sheila, Nora, Elsie). Some of these men
go so far as to "make up" in the evening with eyebrow pencil, rouge
and lipstick, and a certain neighbouring public house is supposed to be
the favourite haunt in fixing any rendezvous. . . . These men-women
often refer avidly to their officer gentlemen friends and a certain few
N.C.O.s are popularly supposed to utilise their services.[54]

Morris therefore acknowledged the influence of the enclosed all-male environment, which could force men to rethink their sexual orientations. However,
at a time when thousands of homosexual men were recruited into the armed
forces, Morris recognized that recruits could have been acting on preexisting

sexual preferences.[55] What is also interesting is that Morris describes these encounters as moments of collusion between the recruits and their superiors. His account suggests that away from the formal training environment, where monitoring and surveillance became more relaxed, officers and men found safe spaces in which to pursue their own agendas.

"Bigger and Better": Physical Transformation

Training was a two-pronged process. While exerting control over recruits' bodies, army instructors also sought to transform them: to equip them with the capabilities and skills needed for effective soldiering. This began with physical training (PT), a daily forty-five minute session in the gymnasium or outside. Part of army training since the mid-nineteenth century, PT was designed to create a base level of fitness by instilling five main physical attributes.[56] These were mobility; strength; endurance; agility, dexterity and speed; and carriage. Men took part in exercises including running, marching, skipping rope, heaving, climbing, vaulting, and games.[57] All activities were given "reality of purpose" by being associated with command objectives. For example, in preparation for long periods on the move, recruits were taught about energy efficiency by learning to relax all muscles not required for walking, running, crawling, climbing, lifting and pulling.[58] In addition to improving fitness, PT was valued for building character and morale.[59] *Physical and Recreational Training* claimed that PT "gives a man confidence in himself, his performance and his powers of endurance."[60] This sentiment was echoed three years later in *Basic and Battle Physical Training*, which advised that PT "is not merely a means of developing the physique, but it also helps to train and influence the mind. . . . Achievement will promote complete self-confidence and lead the solider, through the conviction of his own fighting efficiency and that of his comrades, to an indomitable will to victory. . . . It will create the fighting spirit."[61] By linking physical fitness with moral attributes, army training doctrine in this period reflected traditional notions of military masculinity based on the warrior ideal.[62]

Having mastered basic PT, recruits progressed to battle training, which applied these fundamental physical skills to military activities, including route marches, running, assault courses, climbing and scaling, lifting and carrying, swimming, landing by parachute, close combat, and weapons handling. Often known as "field craft," battle training had become central to military training during the First World War.[63] Exercises were, as far as possible, carried out under realistic war conditions to develop the tactical thinking required for combat. An Army Training Memorandum from September 1940 explained: "In war, amid the general noise and confusion of battle, nerves will be strained, time will be pressing, the situation may be vague, orders may arrive late, and messages may be ambiguous. Officers and men must be trained to expect such conditions and their imaginations must be roused. Deliberate disregard of warlike conditions in training must not be allowed."[64] To develop "night-mindedness," recruits participated in night exercises and patrols lasting up to a week.[65] By day, they learned to move and conceal their bodies in different environments and landscapes. Robert Ellison remembered "galloping about fields and woods" and "creeping about the grass. . . . We were given an objective to get to without being seen."[66] Roy Bolton similarly recalled learning "how to move, advancing, covering people, who were going in front of you and then moving to catch up with them, throwing yourself down when commanded."[67] Assault courses taught recruits how to surmount obstacles such as walls, trenches, parapets, and ramps that were likely to be encountered in the field. John Dray remembered, "We used to swing across a ditch full of barbed wire and all sorts of horrible junk, on a rope and if you let go they just told you that you were an idiot when you fell among the barbed wire and had to get yourself out."[68] As a result of repeated practice, however, men would learn to read obstacles ahead of time and maintain momentum. Robert Ellison recalled that "when we did it [an assault course] the first time they said that was it, yes, but it had to be done twice as quick as that and by the end of the week we were doing it very, very quickly." At the same time, instructors who were "screaming mad" encouraged the men to be aggressive.[69]

For even more realistic training, recruits could be sent to "battle drill" schools where they took part in field exercises in all weathers and conditions. Established in mid-1941 in response to military defeats overseas that were linked to poor morale, battle drill courses aimed to bolster men's resilience by exposing them to the sights and sounds of war. This meant that troops experienced live firing and, in some instances, were taken to abattoirs to witness the sight of blood.[70] Vic Emery, who attended a four-week course at a battle drill school at Featherstone Park in Northumberland during February 1942, recalled that "we were out all day crawling about, being fired on," while the regimental sergeant major shouted, "When you see Germans there's no good calling for your mother."[71] Kenneth Johnstone trained at the battle drill school at Barnard Castle in Durham in 1942 and described a "great urge to really induce a great deal of toughness. We were carrying buckets of pigs' blood and throwing them over figures of Germans and instructors were shouting 'Can you kill a German?' in your ear."[72] Training staff clearly sought to effect both physical and psychological changes through bodily channels.

Again, there was a definite feeling among recruits that PT and battle training did inspire confidence, as men experienced higher states of physical fitness than they had attained before enlistment. An anonymous *Mass Observation*
respondent recorded in his diary in August 1940 that "I used to pride myself
on my fitness before I entered army life but this daily physical training has
developed my stamina tremendously."[73] Bert Blackhall, an apprentice me-
chanic from the East End of London who had left school at fourteen, explained
that "I was a street corner boy and this was something new to me, physical
jerks, something to tune me up, and I felt tuned-up. I felt good."[74] County council clerk Roy Bolton, who weighed nine stone at his army medical examination
and described himself as "all skinny" at enlistment, also remembered "heavy
physical exercise all the time. Not just PT but you marched everywhere at the
double. . . . Practically everything we did seemed to be of a physical nature, to
which I just wasn't accustomed to." As a result, Roy "just got bigger and better,
which," as he remembered, "did me a lot of good."[75] These accounts suggest
that men of all backgrounds experienced positive changes to their bodies as a
result of entry into the army, and they felt the effort was worth it for looking
and feeling better.

Conversely, some recruits were simply not robust enough to keep up with
the army's demands. PT sergeant Ian Sinclair explained that "it was very hard
and made some of them wish they'd never been born. To have to go on a
three-hour route march killed them. They were falling out by the wayside."[76]
Robert Ellison recalled that "some couldn't do it. Absolutely fatigued, you
know. . . . There was no way they could get them fit. . . . I don't know exactly
what happened to them."[77] One option was for officers to refer men for medical regrading. An investigation by the Directorate of Medical Research at the
end of 1942 revealed that as many as fifty men in every 1,000 were being
medically downgraded at primary training centers. This was due to both the
physical strain of training as well as differences in judgment between the
civilian medical boards that had initially examined men for service and army
medical officers. Those who were downgraded were either medically discharged or assigned to noncombatant units, such as the Pioneers or Service
Corps.[78]

Alternatively, recruits who were considered physically underdeveloped
could be sent to an army Physical Development Center (PDC). Initially established in response to manpower shortages during the interwar years and revived in 1941, PDCs focused on building up men's bodies with diet and
exercise.[79] Nineteen-year-old Ernest Harvey was called up in May 1942. He
described himself as "somewhat underdeveloped" as a result of suffering
from rheumatic fever as a child. After six weeks of basic training at a Durham

depot, Ernest was sent to No. 70 PDC in Skegness. For two months he did "nothing else but PT unarmed combat and route marches" to "build muscle power."[80] Anthony Bashford was transferred from a training battalion at Bovington to No. 30 PDC at Kingston-upon-Thames because, as he explained, "the army decided that I was underweight for my height." Anthony spent six weeks "marching in battle order around Richmond Park, running along the tow path, a lot of gymnastics and a lot of track running." Although he felt "slightly miffed" at being identified as underdeveloped, he believed that the course did him a lot of good because "it gave me a physical stamina that I might never have developed for myself."[81] Both Ernest and Anthony were posted back to their original regiments, where they completed their training. Certainly, the results obtained at PDCs were encouraging, with over 80 percent of men in early cohorts achieving higher physical standards.[82]

Not all recruits were equally motivated, however, and some purposely tried to avoid physical training activities. In a diary entry for January 1941, Leonard England described "a very strong resentment to P.T., which is held out in the open at 8.30 in vest and shorts. Over 50% I should say attribute their coughs and colds and ailments to it and all sorts of excuses are used to get out of it."[83] These men literally used their bodies to resist by malingering. Another strategy was to cheat. Sixteen-year-old Percy Bowpitt had lied about his age to enlist in May 1942. He was assigned to the Queen's Own Royal West Kent Regiment in Maidstone, where training soon came as a shock, particularly the weekly cross country run: "Our route took us out of town, through farms and fields and back through the town. This had the advantage that when the edge of town was reached it was possible to hop on a bus. . . . Provided the bus stopped some way from the barracks all was well but often the conductor would deliberately pass the stop we needed and then stop nearer to the barrack where would be standing Regimental Police waiting to catch anyone too slow off the mark."[84] Even eager volunteers, therefore, tried to undermine the army's intentions. Yet as Percy's account tells us, their efforts met with mixed success.

"A Proper Soldier Now": Unit Cohesion

While conditioning individual bodies to withstand the rigors of war, PT and battle training also enhanced the unit cohesion required for success in battle.[85] During PT lessons and field exercises, for example, men were split into groups in order to inculcate "team spirit."[86] Competitive games and sports also promoted "esprit de corps," "comradeship," and "an unselfish attitude for the good of the side."[87] Rooted in the nineteenth-century public school tradition and incorporated into army training during the First World War, regimental sports included boxing, swimming, football, hockey, and rugby.[88] Collective physical training, such as marching, likewise induced a sense of solidarity as men experienced a feeling of shared hardship. Even reluctant recruit Henry Novy admitted feeling pride when recounting a route march:

> This marching was queer—at the beginning I felt for the first time, almost in spite of myself, that pride in numbers, marching numbers, squad after squad in step. I saw it in many men's eyes, looking proudly to the passers-by. They were happy to be carrying full kit and marching, squad after squad, over 400 men. When we had our kits on, two of my mates remarked: "Here we go boys, real soldiers now." The little coalminer said: "You feel a proper soldier now, don't you?" When we came in, tired, all tried to say they loved it and felt no effects. A lad with bad feet dropped out. His mate remarked: "I'd rather be dead than drop out of a route march, I would honest." To my shame I must say I felt the same, a pride of being a soldier, well disciplined, in step, doing hard work.[89]

It was, therefore, when he fell in line with the other men that Henry suddenly experienced the feeling of becoming a soldier. He also describes the march as a rite of passage, with the ability to endure central to acquiring a soldierly identity. Ultimately, Henry seems to have felt helpless to stop the changes that were happening, as he was immersed into the collective body of men.

This was also the chief function of drill, a highly regimented exercise in which men performed exact movements and gestures to an external rhythm imposed by the commands of the drill sergeant. The result was that recruits came "physically to act and perceive themselves on parade as one man."[90] As such, drill produced the uniform response to orders needed to achieve battlefield objectives. According to *Basic and Battle Physical Training*, the synchronized repetition of movements was designed to "free the conscious brain to concentrate on summing up the actions and intentions of the enemy."[91] Recruits themselves depict this sensation in their accounts of drill, although in a more sardonic way.

John Gray claimed that "the idea was to teach you that you would do as you were told and you would do it at once. . . . You stopped thinking and you just did as you were told. If they said "stand on your head" you stood on your head. If they said "try flying" you would try flying."[92] Ron Gray, who completed basic training at Bulford Barracks in Wiltshire in 1941, remembered, "You stamp up and down and you march and you halt and you march and you halt and you march, as though it's designed really to crush your brain power [laughs], to turn you into an automaton."[93] Using similar language, James Wyndham described "weeks and weeks of this sodded square-bashing until eventually you were automatons. You were doing it in your sleep. Suddenly you had a soldierly bearing and suddenly you had a measuredly step and you were a good marcher. Without knowing you were doing it."[94] These testimonies convey a sense of disembodiment, as the men developed instinctive and immediate obedience.

Drill also exposed bodily limitations, as men struggled to perform the complex sequences of movements required. Kenneth New trained with the Hampshire Regiment in Colchester. He recalled that "drill was very awkward. For some unknown reason I didn't know right from left."[95] Roy Bolton also remembered: "I didn't take to it at all well because in those days anyway I was somewhat clumsy I think, in a sort of bodily way. I found the marching and even keeping step, not too difficult keeping step, but not entirely easy, and then the sudden changes in direction, the right turns, the left turns, the about turns, these I did find tricky. Occasionally I distinguished myself by marching off in the wrong direction."[96] Again, this story can be read as one of failure on the part of Roy's body, which was literally out of step with his fellow recruits. He blamed his noncompliance on his clumsy body. It seems that although he wished to comply with the army's orders, his physiological make-up prevented him from doing so. On the other hand, the fact that Roy recounts this as failure also suggests the success of military discipline because he had internalized control.

Raising soldiers for war between 1939 and 1945 was, therefore, not simply a question of "man-management."[97] The process was undoubtedly physical. Troops in training were told what to wear, when to wash, what to eat, how to exercise, and how to move their bodies as one. Basic training in the army was indeed a context of extreme militarization and control. Soldiers' accounts tell us, however, that the body was consistently at the forefront of the experience of barrack life for recruits themselves. The body was a source of enjoyment, pain, embarrassment, and constraint. It was a marker of class and masculine identity and it was a site of negotiation and resistance between the soldier and the state.

CHAPTER 11

Canada and the Mobilization of Manpower during the Second World War

DANIEL BYERS

Over the past forty years, Canadian historians have become increasingly critical of their country's efforts to raise armed forces between 1939 and 1945. Those views have been shaped particularly by the memory of political and social differences between English- and French-speaking Canadians over whether the federal government should compel men to serve outside their country in times of war. In 1917–1918, imposing conscription led to a divisive wartime election and major cleavages between the two linguistic groups for years afterward. As a result, Prime Minister William Lyon Mackenzie King, who led the country for much of the interwar period and throughout the Second World War, was determined not to repeat the same apparent mistake as 1914–1918 of creating large armed forces based on little more than the enthusiasm of early-war voluntarism, only to find that that alone could not maintain those forces as the war wore on.[1] Yet after 1939 not only the Canadian Army but also the Royal Canadian Navy (RCN) and Royal Canadian Air Force (RCAF) ultimately expanded to sizes larger than the country has ever known. At their peak, in late 1943 and early 1944, they totaled roughly 775,000 men and women, or approximately *ninety* times their combined full-time strength at the start of September 1939. In total, almost 1.1 million people served in uniform at some point during the war. Upward of 3 million more worked in war industry or agricultural production, all out of a total national population of approximately 11.5 million.[2] While such numbers may not have matched the scale of mobilization of the war's largest combatant nations, it was a significant undertaking, and among the reasons why Canada came to play a role out of all proportion to its tiny share of the global population both during and after the conflict.

This led to problems maintaining war establishments however. As early as the 1950s, one of the country's senior wartime officers, E. L. M. Burns, pointed out that a higher proportion of the Canadian Army's personnel had been assigned to administrative and other tasks than was the case with the armies of other countries, thus implying a certain level of inefficiency.[3] Prime Minister King's biographer, R. M. Dawson, was more critical a few years later in arguing that what evolved into another divisive political crisis over sending conscripts overseas in 1944 to rival that of 1917 was caused by the army expanding too quickly and with too little oversight.[4] In the first detailed study to tackle manpower policies of all types during the war, J. L. Granatstein and J. M. Hitsman suggested that, when the most important decisions about army expansion were being made during the first half of the war, the army's leaders ought to have known that the large forces they asked for could not be maintained over the long term by voluntarism alone.[5] More recently, in a book whose title *Canada's Greatest Wartime Muddle* makes clear its underlying theme, Michael Stevenson concludes that the civilian bureaucracy that mobilized men and women for the armed forces and other tasks "did not constitute the comprehensive, forward-thinking blueprint for managing Canada's manpower resources ... that the situation *should have* warranted."[6] Richard Walker has gone even further, stating that the country's top generals openly misled and even coerced civilian leaders into accepting too large an army, for their own personal and professional reasons, regardless of the political or other consequences.[7]

Yet such pessimistic views of how Canada mobilized its human resources during the Second World War bear more than a little of the mark of hindsight. In particular, we tend not to consider three major military events—Germany's defeat of Western Europe in the spring of 1940, the German invasion of the Soviet Union in the summer of 1941, and Japan's entry into the war that December—as the strategic crises they were for the people who lived through them. Canadian views have also been shaped since the 1970s by reliance on the personal diaries of Mackenzie King, an incredibly rich resource that provides insights into almost every aspect of national decision-making related to Canada's war effort, but also one that describes these events almost entirely from King's point of view.[8] Instituting conscription had led to open rioting in the largely French-Canadian province of Quebec in 1917, a more violent confrontation in Quebec City on Easter weekend 1918, and even the first stirrings of separatism as a political movement. A majority of French Canadians remained opposed to it in 1939–1945, and had heavily voted for King's Liberal Party for most of the period since 1919, as opposed to the Conservatives who had led the charge for conscription during the First World War, partly for that reason. Thus, he was justifiably preoccupied with avoiding any return of conscription for overseas service. Yet that was not necessarily the concern of every Canadian at the time, and we have perhaps focused a little too much on King as the primary guide to Canada's war effort. Moreover, we seem to assume that there is some perfect way to create the kind of huge bureaucratic organizations necessary for mobilizing societies on so grand a scale, when our experiences with such bodies in the modern day might suggest that such undertakings can sometimes be difficult. Thus, we should not be surprised that mobilizing the country's human and other resources meant having to negotiate among many competing personalities and constituencies, all of which came to exercise their own influence over decision-making (and despite what King himself may have wished, and tried to prevent). Wartime mobilization was in fact a considerable success, and one that allowed Canada to make contributions to the conflict well above what might have been expected based upon its status in the world in 1939.

As Canadians went to war that September, few of them had any concept of the degree to which their society would eventually be mobilized. Initially, Canada's guiding principle was "limited liability," a policy shaped primarily by domestic influences, but that also reflected Britain's prewar policy of the same name. In both countries, key political leaders hoped they would not have to devote massive ground forces to combat, preferring instead to make their largest commitments at sea and in the air, where casualties were expected to be much lower. The land forces Canada initially promised (one infantry division) were intended to underline its determination to help resist the aggressions of Adolf Hitler, alongside the much larger armies of France and other Western European nations. Canada would also concentrate on producing industrial goods, food, and other raw materials needed by its allies. To King, these limited commitments would help avoid the need for conscription to maintain a large army.[9]

Influenced by this policy, as well as by the relatively limited way the conflict progressed following the defeat of Poland, Canada's early mobilization was very measured. Even before it had officially declared war on 10 September, the federal cabinet agreed to permit the army to raise two divisions through voluntary enlistment, one to serve overseas and the second to act as a reserve. Recruiting went well, and by the end of the month almost 60,000 men were in uniform, or well over ten times the prewar permanent force strength of about 4,300.[10] The RCN, meanwhile, concentrated on taking up, fitting out, and

Figure 11.1.   (From left) Defense minister J. L. Ralston and C. D. Howe at the unveiling of Canada's 500,000th military vehicle produced during the war, 19 June 1943. Despite competing demands for the nation's manpower, the Canadian government managed to sustain its ambitiously large armed forces while operating an industrial and agricultural production program that generated significant quantities of materiel and food for the Allies. Image source: Library and Archives Canada/James Layton Ralston fonds/e011201532.

manning a number of suitable government- and civilian-owned ships to back the seven destroyers and four modern minesweepers that made up its existing naval forces. It also organized the first convoys for the thousands of merchant ships it would escort across the Atlantic Ocean and elsewhere for the rest of the war. Over the winter of 1939–1940, it ordered some ninety new minesweepers and Flower-class corvettes for construction in Canadian shipyards. Calling out reservists and adding new volunteers close to tripled the RCN's strength to 5,500 by the spring of 1940, from a peacetime figure of fewer than 2,000.[11] Canadians also drove hard bargains with the British to supply wheat, bacon, and other agricultural goods over the winter of 1939–1940. Aside from small orders to supply Canada's own military forces, industrial production did not significantly expand, mostly because the largest potential purchaser, the government of Neville Chamberlain in Britain, was also attempting to limit spending during the war's early months.[12]

Furthermore, King was happy to receive a September 1939 request from the British government to expand a much more modest prewar plan to train a small number of British pilots and aircrew. Known in Canada as the British Commonwealth Air Training Plan (BCATP) and in other parts of the Commonwealth as the Empire Air Training Scheme, the new agreement would take advantage of the country's large, open skies and safe distance from the battlefields in Europe to train thousands of airmen from Britain and the other dominions. It also fit nicely with King's desire to limit Canada's liability and avoid the sort of large-scale casualties that had led to conscription during the First World War: air forces were expected to suffer fewer casualties than land forces, and in any event a good bulk of the RCAF's manpower would be occupied running the program rather than serving overseas. By the end of March 1940, the RCAF had expanded from 2,000 to over 10,000 full-time personnel, and was expecting to grow more than twenty-fold to 45,000 by the time the BCATP was fully in operation. As part of the negotiations, King demanded that the British government publicly acknowledge it as Canada's major contribution to the war. He also suggested in his private diary that, had he received Britain's request to create the program a little sooner, he might have resisted more strongly his government's commitment to send the 1st Canadian Infantry Division overseas that fall—although it is likely that in that case public pressure from Canadians to make a prominent land contribution to the war, combined with the country's collective memory of the accomplishments of the Canadian Corps in 1914–1918, would have overridden his own wishes.[13]

Things changed with the collapse of Allied forces in Western Europe during April–June 1940. Within a few weeks, Denmark, Norway, the Netherlands, Luxembourg, Belgium, and France all fell, and Italy joined the war on the Axis side. Suddenly, the largest forces with which the Allies had planned to face the Germans were gone, and, until the Soviet Union and United States entered the war in 1941, the British Empire was left to carry on almost entirely on its own. It now had to rely on Canada, the other dominions, and India to make up a much larger part of future Allied forces. Canada responded accordingly. The 2nd Canadian Division proceeded overseas, and cabinet authorized the mobilization of the 3rd and 4th Canadian Divisions. Canadian units relieved British garrisons in what was then the separate colony of Newfoundland, as well as the West Indies, and Iceland.[14] The RCAF sent its only fully equipped fighter squadron overseas in time to participate in the later stages of the Battle of Britain, and it sped up organizing the BCATP. By November, the RCAF had more than doubled the plan's original projected output of trainees for 1941, and in real numbers it reached double that again before the end of the year and it doubled again in 1942. By 1943, the RCAF had tripled the planned strength of its own personnel, as well, in order to meet its commitments to the BCATP and other operations.[15]

While the RCAF was expanding, the RCN rushed the bulk of its available destroyers from Canada's east coast to the British Isles, starting in the summer of 1940. Losing most of Western Europe to Germany meant that U-boats would be able to extend their operations across the Atlantic, so contracts for further corvettes and minesweepers were authorized, along with smaller patrol vessels, and the RCN began to pursue ambitious plans to build the first of several Tribal-class destroyers in Canada. It also took responsibility for manning six (and later a seventh) out of fifty First World War–era destroyers the United Kingdom acquired that September in the famous "destroyers-for-bases" deal between Prime Minister Winston Churchill and US president Franklin D. Roosevelt. By January 1941, the RCN's strength had tripled since the previous spring to roughly 15,000. By the following January it had doubled again, and by 1943 it was above 50,000 and still expanding, eventually reaching 90,000 and comprising hundreds of smaller ships, destroyers, two cruisers, and two escort carriers.[16]

Canadian industry had to step up as well, and it did. In April 1940, Canada's American-born federal cabinet minister, C. D. Howe, assumed responsibility for a new Department of Munitions and Supply, with a mandate to significantly increase industrial production. Over the next few years, Canadian industry expanded so that by the end of the war it had manufactured 5 percent of all small arms and infantry weapons used by the Western Allies and almost 8 percent by dollar value of all of the Commonwealth's munitions. This put it far behind the United States and United Kingdom as a Western industrial power, but well ahead of any of its next closest contenders.[17] The output included finished ships, aircraft, artillery, radios, radar sets, tanks, and other military vehicles (the latter, numbering 850,000, amounted to one-fifth of all such Canadian, American, and British vehicles put together); semi-finished products such as aluminum (one-third of all Allied production), steel, plywood, and lumber; and raw materials such as coal, oil, and various metals. Farmers did their part by supplying Britain with 89 percent of its wartime pork imports, along with large quantities of poultry, wheat, and other agricultural goods.[18] Between 1939 and 1945, Canada devoted approximately $20 billion in goods and services to the war effort, the largest proportion between 1940 and 1943. Half came in the form of direct wartime manufacturing. This compared with a figure of just $5.6 billion for the country's total national gross domestic product in 1939.[19]

Mobilization of Canada's industrial manpower and armed forces was managed under the National Resources Mobilization Act (NRMA), which the prime minister drafted and steered through Parliament in June 1940. Based largely on Canada's preexisting War Measures Act (WMA), as well as the Emergency Powers (Defence) Act, which had recently been passed in the United Kingdom, the NRMA was intended to acknowledge the gravity of the current situation by highlighting the wide array of powers it already had under the WMA to mobilize the population for all-out war. But its key focus quickly became conscription, albeit with such service limited to "Canada and the territorial waters thereof."[20] In this way, King hoped to balance public calls for a greater war effort with his own worries about the dangers of introducing compulsion for overseas service. The early conscripts received thirty days of training, in camps initially separate from those preparing volunteers for overseas service. In the winter of 1940–1941, however, based on recommendations from the army's chief of the general staff (CGS), Major-General H. D. G. Crerar, the government merged the two programs, requiring conscripts to complete the same four months of training as volunteers and to serve for the duration of the war. This, he hoped, would release volunteer men from home defense units and allow them to proceed overseas. His proposal was well calculated, since it meant that the army would have all the soldiers it needed, at least for the immediate future, while allowing his political superiors to avoid having to extend conscription any further. In the end, almost 160,000 Canadians were enrolled into the army as conscripts between 1940 and 1945.[21]

Historians have repeatedly questioned the behavior and motivations of the Canadian generals who called for this expansion, Crerar in particular. A veteran of various command and staff positions in the Canadian artillery during the First World War, he had been groomed for even higher posts throughout the interwar years, before proceeding overseas to organize the army's wartime headquarters in London in 1939–1940. He was personally ambitious, but also professionally devoted to improving the army's postwar status by making it as large as possible, in order to win a strong wartime reputation and resist postwar retrenchment.[22] Thus, when large numbers of men called up under the NRMA began to volunteer willingly for service outside the country (partly thanks to the various positive sides to their being in uniform that they came to experience, such as the sense of personal and group pride Emma Newlands describes among British conscripts in chapter 10), he hit upon the idea of mixing NRMA men with direct-intake volunteers so as to encourage further conversions and thus expand his overseas forces even further. And he could do it without having to worry about provoking political opposition. The scheme paid off. Almost 60,000 (or 10 percent) of the army's total overseas volunteers came from NRMA enrollees during the war, and conscripts who chose not to "go active" still freed another 60,000 volunteers from home defense duties. An additional 5,000 transferred to the RCAF, and another 750 to the RCN. An estimated one-third of all men who volunteered for the overseas army but who were never officially recorded as conscripts also did so after receiving their initial call-up notices under the NRMA.[23]

Historians have tended to focus on the political motivations and concerns behind Crerar's actions, but the general really did consider the demands of the war itself. After the fall of France, British planners suddenly found themselves having to find men to rebuild their own country's army. Following Germany's invasion of the Soviet Union in June 1941, the situation appeared even more desperate, as the latter's defenses seemed to crumble. To confront a German force of an estimated 191 divisions in June 1940 and 250 divisions a year later, they hoped to raise a total of fifty-three divisions, plus another twenty-one independent brigades. The British were looking for as much assistance as they could get from the Commonwealth to reach that total.[24] As the senior officer in Canada, whose government and a large majority of its population were supposedly devoted to aiding the British as much as possible, it was Crerar's duty to help meet this need, and he did emphasize these factors in presenting his growth plans to his political superiors. By January 1941, he had convinced them to send 3rd Canadian Infantry Division and what became 5th Canadian Armoured Division overseas before the end of that year, and, in November, he submitted proposals to convert 4th Canadian Infantry Division into an armored division and send it as well. Canada was also expected to maintain sizeable formations in North America—another legacy of the crisis of 1940, during which President Roosevelt and Prime Minister King had created the Permanent Joint Board on Defense (PJBD) to coordinate continental security. Canada's ground contribution under the PJBD was two divisions.[25] On top of that, after the summer of 1940 Canada also took over responsibility for the defense of Newfoundland.[26] The result was that the total size of Canada's wartime army came to seven divisions. This was not exactly what the prime minister wanted, but in the crisis atmosphere of 1940–1941, and with the NRMA seemingly providing enough backing to support such ambitious plans, he was willing to let Crerar and the general staff proceed.[27]

The final stage in the growth of Canada's wartime military commitments came after Japan's entry into the war in December 1941. Two Canadian battalions participated in the ill-fated defense of Hong Kong in December 1941. In response to public panic on the west coast, the RCAF and the army mobilized several home defense squadrons, anti-aircraft artillery regiments, and the better part of an eighth army division. It is worth emphasizing that the military's leaders were not the ones calling for this expansion. It was King who attempted to take advantage of the panic, as he began to worry that he was permitting his cabinet to authorize too large a force for Europe, and thus increase the potential of having to send conscripts overseas. In the words of journalist Grant Dexter, King "egged Brucie [Hutchison, another Ottawa journalist] and me on to keep banging away at the generals"—King's aim being to build up forces in Canada such that the generals would be forced to scale back their plans for a big army in Europe.[28] But King did not always control everything, and, to his dismay, the cabinet agreed to expand the army both at home and overseas, and it even began debating extending conscription for overseas service. Ever conscious of the political ramifications of any such action, King decided to seek a mandate through a national plebiscite that the government be permitted to send NRMA men overseas—should such action become necessary. The April 1942 vote—64 percent in favor overall, but 73 percent opposed in Quebec—revealed a continuing split between English- and French-speaking Canadians over the issue.[29] Yet partly because of King's own actions, the end result was to expand Canada's armed forces to a size beyond which even Japan's entry into the war might not otherwise have been expected to lead.

One last consequence of these developments was that, by the end of 1941, King and his colleagues had begun to worry about the degree to which they would need to introduce civilian as well as military controls over the country's human resources. Here, too, he and his ministers had tried to learn from the First World War, when the federal government had exercised little to no control over wages, working conditions, or inflation. Canada still did not have national collective bargaining or union recognition laws in 1939, but that November cabinet had extended peacetime legislation requiring workers in public utilities and mines to wait through a compulsory cooling-off period and take part in formal conciliation before they could strike to apply to all war-related industries. With inflation now threatening to become problematic as industrial production began to ramp up, they enacted wage and price controls in October 1941. At the end of March 1942 they created a body known as National Selective Service (NSS) to coordinate manpower resources themselves more directly to meet the needs of industry, agriculture, and the armed forces. They also proclaimed a list of nonessential occupations, in which no physically fit man between seventeen and forty-five could be employed. In May and September, two national registrations were held (in addition to one in August 1940, which had laid the foundation for calling out conscripts under the NRMA) to identify all unemployed males and then women between the ages of twenty and twenty-four. These sorts of measures were not that well received by workers, since most of the government's actions were aimed primarily to prevent strikes and other disruptions to war production and clearly favored employers. During the war, union membership more than doubled from 359,000 to 832,000, support rose for Canada's socialist political party, the Co-operative Commonwealth Federation, and strike activity over wages, union recognition, and government controls rose to one of the highest levels in Canadian history, peaking with a loss of 1 million man-days of work in 1943. Prodded by these developments, in February 1944 cabinet enacted Order-in-Council P.C. 1003, which enshrined unions and collective bargaining and laid the foundations for Canada's system of industrial relations as it still exists today.[30]

The mobilization of Canada's human resources also affected Canadian women dramatically. By October 1943, the number in paid employment rose to a peak of 1,075,000, a two-thirds increase from the 1939 figure of 638,000. Another 750,000 were estimated to be contributing to operating family farms. Eventually, childless married women, and later even those with children, were encouraged to work. Women already possessed the right to serve in uniform as nursing sisters, but in mid-1941 they gained the opportunity to join a new Canadian Women's Auxiliary Air Force (later the RCAF Women's Division) and Canadian Women's Army Corps (CWAC), and a year later the Women's Royal Canadian Naval Service, all to help free more male servicemen to proceed overseas. Over the course of the war, 21,624 women served in the CWAC, 17,018 in the RCAF, 6,781 in the RCN, and at least 4,518 in the various medical services.[31]

After 1942, Canada's major priority was simply to maintain the commitments it had made. Decision-makers came into conflict over competing needs as pools of available manpower drained more quickly than anticipated. It did not help that, before 1941, no one was quite sure what manpower resources were actually available. Canada's most recent decennial census had taken place almost ten years earlier, and at nearly the lowest point of the Great Depression when industrial activity was much reduced.[32] This was not a solid statistical foundation on which to build mobilization plans. In fact, the army's early projections were based simply on extrapolations from Canada's First World War effort, the principal assumption being that the country could raise at least the same size army twenty years later, even after taking into account the increased manpower demands for the other armed services and industry, because a 30 percent increase in the population ought to allow it.[33] After

August 1940, cabinet members gained slightly better information, thanks to data collected through the national registration for the NRMA. Yet a June 1941 report based on that data, and prepared by the Economics and Statistics Branch of the Department of Munitions and Supply rather than the army, still concluded that "it appears clearly that the man-power of Canada is adequate to meet both the anticipated demands of the armed services and those of war and essential civilian industries."[34] Only as cabinet began to debate the final steps in the expansion of the three armed services a few months later did they decide to create a Labour Supply Investigation Committee (LSIC) to review the figures more thoroughly. That committee soon warned of a number of projected manpower shortages. Granatstein and Hitsman argue that these warnings ought to have led cabinet to limit its further liabilities.[35] But we need to remember that the war was going badly for the Allies at this time, and it looked like it could continue to go poorly. Canadian cabinet ministers felt they had little choice but to proceed with their extensive mobilization plans and then somehow find the necessary resources afterward.

There also remains the question of whether the various military and civilian organizations involved in applying these measures actually utilized existing manpower as efficiently as possible. By mid-1943, for example, the BCATP was producing more men than any of the Commonwealth air forces expected to need for the rest of the war, and the RCAF soon began to scale it back. Even then, thousands of men remained engaged in aircrew training a year later, when they could have been used much more effectively as infantry reinforcements for the army. As Allan English has argued in his study of RCAF manpower policies during the war, in 1941 and 1942, as the BCATP was being spooled up, it was difficult to predict exactly how many aircrew would be needed for the various air forces of the Commonwealth. The program could not reasonably be scaled back until authorities were near-certain of future requirements, because it would be very difficult to ramp up again if circumstances demanded it.[36]

The army faced similar challenges in the later years of the war, having had to create a very large training system to facilitate its own expansion. Furthermore, the minister of national defense, J. L. Ralston, had grown frustrated that his senior officers could not produce detailed statements of their manpower needs in 1941–1942, even as they were moving forward with plans for a five-division field force. Ralston fired B. W. Browne, who as the adjutant-general was responsible for managing the army's human resources, and brought in H. F. G. Letson, who did put in place a more rigorous system for tracking them.[37] What is more, the civilian NSS machinery that had been created to mobilize manpower for industry and agriculture also experienced difficulties managing a mobilization effort that had grown so much, and so quickly.[38]

Lastly, it should be noted that it was more difficult to avoid disputes and personality clashes between cabinet ministers at the highest political levels than historians sometimes seem to assume. Ralston, in particular, was criticized both at the time and afterward for conveying the army's demands too strongly at the cabinet table and for privileging its needs over those of civilian industries and agriculture.[39] Yet it was his duty as minister to do that. And, if his colleagues disagreed, then ultimately it was their duty to decide collectively whether other priorities were more vital. Instead, from Ralston's point of view, it seemed that C. D. Howe as minister of munitions and supply succeeded more often than not in advocating his own department's requirements over those of the army. As early as 1940, Ralston had to agree to requests from his colleagues to provide indefinite agricultural leave to any soldier whose family was engaged in farming. By mid-1942, men could be released for up to six months to work in essential industries or seasonal occupations, even though their unavailability to the army for prolonged periods frustrated its planning. In 1943, Howe advocated similar exemptions for the logging, coal, and mining industries, in which working conditions were tough and pay was low, and men had to be fit and healthy—the same type of potential recruit the army was competing to attract. Yet as the adjutant-general's branch noted when reviewing some of these requests, Howe could produce no actual statistics to support his claims, acting instead on anecdotal information and criticisms from individual employers.[40] At Howe's behest, the army did return some 1,900 UK-based men of the Canadian Forestry Corps that December to make them available to civilian lumber companies in Canada. Only about one-third of that number actually transferred, however. Many of the identified men were merely filling administrative posts and had no experience in forestry. Others stayed in the army because they preferred its rates of pay and other benefits.[41]

Debates over how the NSS was finding men to put in uniform resulted in increasingly acrimonious exchanges between Ralston and the ministers responsible for administering that body: J. T. Thorson, and later L. R. LaFleche, as ministers of national war services for most of 1942, and then Humphrey Mitchell as labor minister for the rest of the war. For the army's reinforcement system to work efficiently, every training center had to function near maximum capacity so that staffs were not sitting idle. But the problem was that the army had to take such recruits as NSS assigned them. And, as more and more potential conscripts were called out, many were not available because they had already joined the armed services, were working in vital civilian occupations, were below the necessary medical or other standards, or simply refused to answer their summons. Cabinet increased the ages of single men liable for training and widened the eligible classes to include married men, but that was only marginally helpful. From late 1943 to early 1944, NSS had to call up 185,000 men just to find 34,000 recruits for the training centers.[42] Even at that, C. D. Howe still felt impinged upon. As he wrote Ralston and Thorson: "My Department is at its wits' end to decide on steps to protect essential war production in the face of the call to service of men extending upward to age 40."[43] A few months later, he noted that several primary industries faced major cuts in production if the army continued to receive preference for men.[44]

In a perfect world it might have been possible to manage Canada's manpower such that there were enough men for the army, the other armed services, agriculture, and industry. But, in the imperfect world of 1944, Canada seemed to be reaching the limits of its ability to manage an all-out war effort—at least without imposing more rigorous mobilization measures that the public might not be willing to support (or "consent" to, as Jonathan Fennell explains in chapter 8).[45] As it was, by the autumn of 1944, Canada was making major contributions to the Battle of the Atlantic, the bombing campaign in Europe, other wide-ranging naval and air operations, and the ground war in both Italy and North-West Europe. Its industrial production was greater and more sophisticated than it had ever been. This was when the conscription issue resurfaced with a vengeance. After several weeks of acrimonious debate, and the loss of two ministers (Ralston, who supported sending NRMA men overseas to provide necessary infantry, and C. G. Power, the minister responsible for the RCAF but also a Quebec member of Parliament who opposed it for political reasons), King agreed to send 16,000 conscripts to Europe, enough to meet the immediate demand. As winter approached and operations in North-West Europe and Italy slowed down, Canadian troops gained a reprieve that allowed the reinforcement system to catch up. And the war in Europe ended in May 1945, before any new difficulties arose. Yet King managed to retain the support of a majority of French Canadians, who understood that he had done everything he could to avoid conscription while the Conservative opposition did everything it could to move the measure forward.

In the end, then, King and his colleagues were able to fight the war on a scale no Canadian had imagined before 1939, while at the same time avoiding the worst of the linguistic and cultural cleavages of the First World War. This accomplishment was not the result of King's political genius alone. Nor did Canada just "muddle through," as historians who get lost in the many political and bureaucratic debates that occurred in Canada throughout the conflict tend to argue. Instead, when we attempt to put events into perspective, what should be more remarkable is how effectively the country *was* in fact mobilized, despite the many complications involved.

CHAPTER 12

South African Manpower and the Second World War

Ian van der Waag

Jan Smuts, deputy prime minister of the Union of South Africa, spent part of July 1939 on holiday in Central Africa, from which he returned keen and refreshed. That was a good thing because he faced huge political struggles soon after his return and, as it turned out, for the rest of the Second World War. To start, the United Party government, in which he had been partnered with Prime Minister J. B. M. Hertzog since 1934, broke up in September 1939 over the issue of Union neutrality in the war.[1] The split occurred on largely language lines, with Afrikaners supporting Hertzog's position of neutrality, and the English-speaking minority and some Afrikaners supporting Smuts, who wanted to join with Britain and take up the Union's "rightful place of another segment in the bastion that the free world was hurriedly throwing up to meet the gravest challenge to human liberty that modern man had ever faced."[2] Smuts won that first battle. The day after Hertzog lost a 4 September parliamentary vote on neutrality, he became prime minister when the governor general asked him to form a new government. He was firmly in charge as both prime minister and minister of defense from 5 September, but mobilizing the country for war would not be easy, mostly because of the language and ethnic cleavages within the Union's 9.5 million people. In addition to the opposition of the Hertzogites could be added the nationalist Afrikaners of Dr. D. F. Malan's Purified National Party. There was also some opposition to the war from the disenfranchised black

South Africans. Smuts had to steer through very troubled waters in order to stitch together a reasonable contribution to the British Commonwealth war effort.

That was no easy task. Having suffered years of peacetime neglect, the Union Defence Force (UDF) was small, ill-prepared, and in a dismal state. In September 1939, the UDF comprised 5,384 officers and other ranks in the permanent force, 14,408 in the Active Citizen Forces (ACF), and 122,000 rifle association men, of whom only 18,000 were trained to any reasonable extent.[3] There were also shortages of equipment, ammunition, and good leadership. Smuts wrote to a friend at the end of that November: "Most of my time has been taken up with the recasting of the defence department and the recruiting and training of our new defence forces."[4] The defense policy of the interwar Union governments had been based on fighting an African opponent to the immediate north or defending against Japanese attack through Lourenco Marques, not combatting the Germans or the Italians. Necessarily, war plans had to change.

The UDF obviously had to be brought onto a war footing, but it soon became clear that prewar estimates of trained and available manpower had been exceedingly optimistic. More men would have to be enlisted and trained, and the Union policy of not allowing "non-European" South Africans to serve in combatant roles complicated matters greatly.[5] According to the 1936 census, the white male population of the Union was just 651,000 (approximately 7.23 percent of the total population), of whom 452,369 (approximately 5.02 percent of the total population) were between the ages of eighteen and forty-four.[6] Mobilization plans for the UDF required something like 140,000 trained men for the Mobile Field Force, but the Defence Act limited the service of the ACF to southern Africa, and any discussion of conscripting men for service beyond the region would have been political suicide.[7] The Smuts government, as a result, decided that any expeditionary forces must come from an army of volunteers (who took an oath to serve anywhere in Africa) and that this volunteer army would be "South African in spirit, outlook, leadership and tactics, and not an integral part of the British Army as in the Great War."[8] Finding volunteers was not easy, however. By 17 August 1940, nearly twelve months after the outbreak of hostilities, the number of all ranks serving was just 92,809.[9]

Predictably, the response to the call to enlist was uneven. Figure 12.1 shows the percentage increase in the strength of the ACF infantry regiments over the last three months of 1939. That September, only four regiments had two battalions. By the end of December, second battalions had been added to four further regiments, while the Transvaal Scottish gained a third battalion,

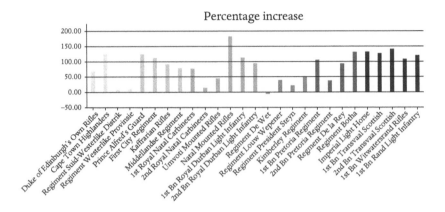

FIGURE 12.1. Percentage increase in strength in ACF Infantry Regiments, 30 September–31 December 1939. Image source: Drawn from various files in the archives of the Adjutant General, Department of Defence Archives, Pretoria.

and two new regiments were created. Most of the growth came in Natal (with a predominantly British white population) and the urban areas of the Transvaal. Some traditional regiments had their local mobilization plans: the Transvaal Horse Artillery was the first ACF regiment to mobilize, while the Prince Alfred's Guard recruited to full war strength of 926 all ranks by 21 October. Despite the patriotism and early enrollment of volunteers, however, there was little hint of actual mobilization. Men eager to join the air force converged on Roberts Heights, but only a few were taken on immediately, and others were registered for later call-up. Some 100,000 volunteered, but, by the end of 1939, only 38,000 had been called up.[10]

Why was that the case? There were several reasons. Some reservists were turned away. Others, unwilling to take part in "the government's war," refused the oath. Some were just too young. The Dukes lost nearly 300 of their strength due to minors who could not produce parental consent and an additional fifty who refused to take the oath. The numbers were higher in other units, in some cases much higher. This came at a time when recruitment was slowing down, and, as noted, 140,000 recruits were needed for the Mobile Field Force (the "teeth" portion of which comprised two infantry divisions) in addition to 4,000 for the Home Defence units, command staffs, and headquarters personnel.[11] These figures showed that the UDF would be unable to provide the necessary personnel from volunteers to complete establishments. In August 1940 there was an immediate shortage of 31,000 men, and, more alarmingly, defense officials predicted that, even with an annual intake of 8,000 youths, estimated wastage rates of 15 percent would mean net losses of about 5,000 per year. The Mobile Field Force, as planned, was not sustainable. It either had to be reduced in strength or supplied with men conscripted for service outside southern Africa.[12] Neither choice was ideal. The chief of the general staff, General Sir Pierre van Ryneveld, refused to consider the first, and Smuts avoided the political minefield of the second.

Smuts made matters worse. In 1940, he offered Whitehall a second South African Division, for service in North Africa—this in addition to the 1st South African Division already deployed in East Africa. And that 1st South African Division was already facing a significant manpower crisis. The divisional commander, Major-General George Brink, calculated that disease and other casualties meant that most of his units were a quarter to a third under strength. His 1st Infantry Brigade Group suffered sickness at a rate of 150 casualties per day, and at the conclusion of the Juba River operations it was 778 short of establishment. The number of men in the fighting units decreased with each passing week. And the trickle of reinforcements from the Union—146 reinforcements arrived on 22 March 1941—never made up the shortfall.[13] How was South Africa to keep two fighting divisions in the field?

As early as September 1940, after the first contingents had left for East Africa, officials began investigating ways of freeing up white labor for the fighting divisions and the other armed services. Authorities appealed to some of the Union's largest employers. South African Railways and Harbours (SAR&H) soon employed women in office and clerical roles, while positions such as porters, laborers, and lorry drivers were filled with black and coloured workers.[14] This allowed more than 15,000 railwaymen to enlist in the armed services.[15] The mines, which employed 44,880 white workers (32,600 of them of military age), were encouraged to do something similar as SAR&H, as was the South African Police (SAP).[16] Twenty-eight engineer companies were formed, and so was a police brigade that saw service in Italy.[17] More would have to be done.

Smuts believed the need for combatant troops could be best met by enlisting black volunteers, who would free up white soldiers for front-line roles.[18] Van Ryneveld opposed the idea and suggested instead a "dilution policy," whereby drivers and other noncombatants were gradually replaced by the Cape Corps (CC) and later by Native Military Corps (NMC) personnel. Soon, however, the demand for drivers, stretcher bearers, cooks, batmen, and laborers outstripped all initial estimates. By the end of 1940, CC reserve motor transport (RMT) companies were barreling across the Kenyan Northern Frontier District, unarmed and, in many cases, unprotected. As a result, an armed white soldier was attached to every vehicle, which made nonsense of the whole policy of "dilution." In January 1941, the ever practical Brink recommended the only sensible course: arming all CC, Indian and Malay Corps

FIGURE 12.2. During the Second World War, South Africa, like other British Commonwealth nations, turned to nontraditional sources of manpower to keep deployed forces up to strength. For instance, by late 1940, Cape Corps Reserve Motor Transport Companies, manned by coloured soldiers, were operating in East Africa. These South African troops are fighting at Anzio, Italy, 13 March 1944. Image source: © Imperial War Museum, NA12862.

(IMC), and NMC drivers and providing each RMT company with an establishment of CC anti-aircraft gunners.[19]

The Smuts government scrounged manpower wherever it could get it. Brink's prodding from Nairobi led to the attestation of women in the armed services. The first contingent of the Women's Auxiliary Army Services, the "Mossies" (Afrikaans: "Sparrows"), arrived in Kenya in September 1940.[20] Further personnel came from north of the Union's borders, from South West Africa and the Rhodesias. Some 1,400 Rhodesians later served with the 6th South African Armoured Division in Italy, where each of the regiments of the 11th Armoured Brigade had its Rhodesia squadron. The 12th Motorized Brigade's First City/Cape Town Highlanders also had a strong contingent of Rhodesians.[21] South Africa was hardly alone in turning to nontraditional sources of workers and recruits. In chapter 9, Paul Bartrop explains how Australians admitted into their army interned Jewish "aliens" from Germany and Austria. And in chapter 13, Ian McGibbon examines how New Zealand mobilized women, aliens, and the Maori community for the national war effort.

Recruiting in the Union remained unsatisfactory, however. At the local district level, recruiting had proved inefficient, even during the uptick that coincided with the European disasters of May–June 1940. And it got worse when local units departed their districts for East and North Africa. To ameliorate the situation, the deputy adjutant-general (DAG), Lieutenant-Colonel G. C. G. Werdmuller, proposed a nationwide publicity program utilizing all media, which would, to some extent, make up for influence lost when regiments left their home bases. The appeals of Defence Liaison Committees to employers and local residents needed some kind of a boost. The press, theaters, radio— all had to be exploited to the maximum. Military bands, recruiting marches, loudspeaker vans, and similar methods also had a role to play. And ongoing consultations had to occur with all of the main recruiting centers to monitor the work of local organizations and tailor recruiting programs to suit local conditions. This aggressive recruitment campaign demanded a substantial monetary investment and political support.[22] Frank Theron, the adjutant-general (AG), endorsed Werdmuller's initiative, but Smuts demurred on the whole publicity package.[23] The dicey political situation was such that he had to avoid antagonizing nationalist sentiment and inflaming the antiwar camp.

Even so, Smuts did pursue a few recruitment initiatives. One, almost counterintuitively, was to link the recruiting campaign to Afrikaner identity. Taking the pattern of the Trek Centenary of 1938, recruiting officers staged similar "roadshows." Two recruiting "commandos"—the "Steel Commando" and later the "Air Commando"—toured the countryside. Military bands, armored vehicles, and a variety of weapon systems drew crowds, while a mobile loudspeaker broadcast Smuts's message that all South Africans had an interest in resisting the enemies of the freedom they so cherished. The recruiting "commandos" had tremendous novelty value, particularly in rural areas that were generally deprived of almost any form of organized outside entertainment. There was political opposition, but for the most part political sentiments took second seat to curiosity and the long-standing interest of these communities in weaponry.[24] Film was also used to reach wider English and Afrikaner audiences. The Bureau of Information (BOI), created in late 1939 to counter subversive propaganda, commissioned African Film Productions (AFP) to produce an English-language documentary called *Fighters of the Veld* (1940), a thirty-minute film dealing with the South African effort during the first year of the war.[25] AFP also produced the Afrikaans-language film entitled *Noordwaarts* (Northward), which chronicled a young Afrikaner soldier and his explanation for why he joined to fight beyond the region of southern Africa. It starred a well-known Afrikaner actress, Lydia Lindeque, and it drew large audiences. Other films followed on this success. AFP, again commissioned by the BOI, produced a series of short films based on footage taken by F. D. Dixon, an AFP cameraman who had enlisted with the bureau, of the South African forces operating in East Africa and later North Africa. Productions included *The Springboks Trek North* and *With General Smuts up North*. These films and those that followed were shown in Twentieth-Century-Fox cinemas, of which there were about fifty in the Union, as well as from cinema vans that toured the whole country.[26] They may have drawn crowds, but the films produced no appreciable increase in the numbers of volunteers, all of which was a reflection of how difficult the recruiting problem was for the Union government.

Some recruitment was more targeted. The recruitment and training of technicians and skilled mechanics received special attention due to the simple fact that the UDF and South African industry needed them. A labor committee set up by the director-general of war supplies in July 1940 regulated the supply of labor, and a controller of industrial manpower (CIM) determined which industries were controlled, regulated the movement of labor, and fixed wages and working hours. Allowances enticed youths to enter apprenticeships, and employers were encouraged to employ young apprentices in the third years of their programs. In the war's early years, fourth- and fifth-year apprentices were released from their indentures and taken on as artisans in war production. Abbreviated basic trade training, offered through the Central Organisation of Technical Training (COTT), was another measure to redress the shortages of technical personnel for both industry and the UDF. Training centers popped up in the major towns and, in July 1940, the COTT had accepted more than 1,400 trainees. This did not entirely solve the technician deficit problem for the UDF, however. Intakes of trainees into the COTT system gradually declined, particularly when trainees were required to take the "Africa" oath (to serve anywhere in Africa) and later the "General Service" oath (to serve anywhere in the world). Even so, by April 1945, the scheme had produced 26,000 technicians, 85 percent of whom went to the technical branches of the military.[27] The trouble was that some of them could not be deployed to North Africa, or later to Italy, because they had not taken oaths to serve outside southern Africa.

The twin disasters of Sidi Rezegh (November 1941), when the 5th South African Brigade suffered a staggering 3,800 casualties from a pre-battle strength of 5,800 men, and Tobruk (June 1942), when the 2nd South African Division surrendered nearly 12,000 prisoners, brought Union manpower problems to a head. The sudden loss of 15,000-plus UDF soldiers killed, wounded, or captured pretty much shattered all existing manpower management models and measures. Maintaining two expeditionary infantry divisions was out of the question. In November 1942, therefore, Union authorities withdrew the 1st South African Division from the desert and returned it to the Union, where some of the men took the new oath and joined the 6th South African Armoured Division. This made sense, at least in terms of manpower. South African infantry divisions had war establishment strengths of 22,490, while an armored division required only 14,195 all ranks. Moreover, casualty rates for armored divisions were much lower than for infantry divisions.[28] This new formation, under the command of Major-General Evered Poole, assembled in Egypt, starting in February 1943, and eventually took part in the Italian campaign, which required the "general service" oath of volunteers to serve outside Africa. But even a reduced expeditionary commitment, based on an armored division, would require reinforcements for casualties and normal wastage. Where would they come from?

The Union government tried desperately to "comb out" potential soldiers from numerous organizations and agencies. A short-lived Civil Service Manpower Board, for example, was created to "comb out" civil servants, but the body had only two desultory meetings due to resistance from the heads of government departments.[29] No one seemed particularly keen on having their people combed out of their offices, factories, or farms and combed into the ranks of the UDF. Complaints regarding the misuse of military manpower came from all quarters. These complaints took several forms. Some were lodged at Defence Liaison Committees, others through liaison with other government departments, and still others were aired in the press. Even when individuals could be combed out and coaxed to volunteer, there were complaints that they were not employed in ways that were commensurate with their levels of skill and knowledge. The misplacement of men with specialist qualifications was a perennial complaint. In some cases, young pilots, tired of waiting for a South African Air Force (SAAF) call-up, actually joined the army.[30] In June 1942, eleven men trained as machine tool operators were found to be painting and doing other "menial work" at Zonderwater. The simple fact of the matter was that the UDF had not been organized to cope with the type and scale of operations it faced from September 1939, and the urgency to recruit and train, without comprehensive occupational planning, had more or less made misplacements inevitable.

Another problem related to the question of "balance" in the forces. There were too many engineers for UDF requirements, while there was a dramatic shortage of gunners and artisans for the armored division then being formed.[31] The accumulation of superfluous officers, a large proportion of whom were old and redundant, exacerbated the imbalance. By late 1942, Smuts and Van Ryneveld were determined to resolve this problem. Age limits were tabled for anyone below the rank of brigadier. This made room for younger and more suitable officers. By August 1944, most superfluous officers had been released to other government departments, although trained suitable officers were not always easy to find.[32] Manpower was undoubtedly poorly managed and resulted in a large force with few teeth.

Many manpower problems persisted because there was no central military control of this resource for all three armed services. The different services and heads of sections jealously guarded their own personnel and resisted attempts by the AG to control the growing number of reserve depots and training centers. The Engineers, "Q" (Quatermaster Services), and Technical Services, for example, each ran their own training centers and, as a result, controlled their own manpower. Smuts had at first refused to deal with the issue, but gradually, he managed to assert tri-service control of manpower under the AG. Not until August 1944 were two tri-service manpower boards established: a Manpower Board to comb out every available man for service in the operational theater and a Conservation of Manpower Board in the Central Mediterranean Theater to examine all establishments and make recommendations on postings, reassignments, and reductions.[33] These were positive developments for the management of manpower, but it had taken a very long time to enact them.[34]

Of the nation's approximately 452,000 white males of military age, 186,000 volunteered for full-time service in the UDF.[35] Alongside them, 25,000 white women and 123,000 coloured, Asian, and black men served on the same basis. Another 63,000 white South African men served in part-time units. Taken together, some 398,000 South Africans served as volunteers in the full-time and part-time units of the UDF. This represented only 4.15 percent of the country's population. There is a growing literature on these volunteers, on who they were and why they volunteered. Early examinations were made by Albert Grundlingh on the Afrikaner volunteers, and by his brother, Louis, on black volunteers.[36] In 2005, Neil Roos published a study on the white volunteers as a group.[37] What is clear is that there are several gradients. Thanks to the clerks in the AG's office, we have reasonably accurate statistics for the enlistment of black South Africans into the NMC. Here there was a definite provincial gradient. Of the 77,000 men who joined the NMC, the overwhelming majority, some 69 percent, came from the Transvaal Province.[38] Here the failure of the mielie crop, together with the droughts of 1941 to 1943, pressed black farmers and farmworkers to join the UDF, and, as a result, the northern districts of the Transvaal became the foremost recruiting grounds for the NMC. Much as was the case for the white poor, the UDF provided a refuge for the rural unemployed and those left destitute by the famine.[39] Roos has suggested that there were two waves of white volunteers. The first wave of white and poor recruits was largely returned to industry deemed essential to the war effort. It was left instead to white men from rural districts—the unemployed of the towns and cities, many of whom may have been Afrikaans-speaking—to fill the army's ranks in the first eighteen-months of recruitment. A second wave followed from the end of 1941, when the intake numbers of poorer whites had started to falter. The changing nature of the UDF's war, which became more technical and necessitated investments in the South African Engineer Corps (SAEC), SAAF, and armor, also demanded recruits who could be trained quickly to work sophisticated equipment. In this wave, the demand for manpower shifted from infantry to more technical trades, including mechanics, electricians, and ship repairmen. Naturally, Roos argues, to find such men, recruiters targeted "the white urban working and middle classes."[40]

But were there in fact two waves of recruitment? Figure 12.3 represents approximately two thirds of wartime attestations and shows no indication of waves. In fact, it shows steady decline. Recruitment, at first, steadily dropped off. The result of the call for the Non-European Army Services (NEAS) for service in Africa is clearly visible. Of the 64,037 men enlisted in 1941, no less than 36,657, or 57.24 percent, were "non-European." This figure fell to 44.98 percent in 1942, to 38.94 in 1943, and, finally, to 6.21 in 1944, when South African attention was focused on the campaign in Italy.

Men, naturally enough, enlisted for a variety of reasons.[41] James Ambrose Brown, writing with considerable hindsight, noted "the ignorance, naïveté and willingness of the young men" who volunteered.[42] First and foremost, patriotism and the idea of "South Africanism," with its apparent inclusivity, were no doubt important, stressing as they did the ties with Britain and the fifty-fifty power-sharing approach to white society.[43] This appealed to English-speakers, while assuaging at least some Afrikaner fears. In many ways, Smuts, a former Boer general, a British lieutenant-general, and leader of the United Party, seemed to personify the unity of the state. A veteran of two previous wars and speaking with the highest authority, Smuts reminded the troops assembled before him at Zonderwater on 14 June 1940: "Whatever you do, whatever situation in which you might find yourselves, always bear in mind that South Africa's honour is at stake."[44] Mike Sadler, then a young student and something of a pacifist, "could not help being affected by the strong

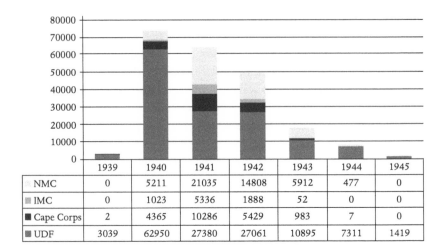

	1939	1940	1941	1942	1943	1944	1945
NMC	0	5211	21035	14808	5912	477	0
IMC	0	1023	5336	1888	52	0	0
Cape Corps	2	4365	10286	5429	983	7	0
UDF	3039	62950	27380	27061	10895	7311	1419

Figure 12.3. Attestations in the Union Defence Force, 1939–1945 (n = 216,869, or 64.87 percent of the population). Image source: Drawn from table 2.2 in Jonathan Fennell, *Fighting the People's War: The British and Commonwealth Armies and the Second World War* (Cambridge, 2019), 73.

emotions of patriotism that were sweeping through the country."[45] And as Major J. F. Reitz, who was a South African military law officer, recounts, far from being a divisive factor, Afrikaans came to play an interesting role during the war, as a kind of cement for all South Africans serving with various formations overseas: "It proved in all cases to be the 'Open Sesame' when fellow South Africans encountered one another," even when they possessed only rudimentary knowledge of the language.[46] Nonetheless, within the Union, as elsewhere, the early patriotism was later supplanted by grim sense of duty and responsibility.

Still, for many, the war also brought the promise of fun and enjoyment, as well as an opportunity to relish comradeship. In groups, men joined the colors, often of local, district-based units and regiments. Later in the war, recruits volunteered to serve in specific units, where they may have had friends or relatives. The authorities recognized the value in this "regimental family" incentive and attempted, where possible, to post volunteers for service with units of their choice.[47] While serving with friends or people from the same region, soldiers might enjoy the strangely wonderful sights of a foreign campaign. This is what Albert Grundlingh referred to as "the touristic potential of the war."[48] Sergeant Schalk Wolhuter, of Die Middellandse Regiment, records how "proud and excited" they were at sailing north from Durban.[49] For Sampie de Wet, a young woman with the South African Women's Auxiliary Services (SAWAS), service in Italy "offered an experience . . . and with it the chance of really doing something to help win the war."[50] Foreign campaigns, of course, held other attractions for healthy young men removed from female company and the restrictions of home surroundings. The opportunity for pleasure-seeking, casual sex, and intemperance was always there, with appetites fueled by the horror of war and contemplations on the possible brevity of life. This was the concern of more than one mother.[51]

There were other satisfactions, such as taking part in something of great meaning. For Major "Chooks" Blamey of the 1st Natal Mounted Rifles, "the call came as a relief for, ever since the declaration of war, we had been living in a constant state of tension wondering when we would be called out. It was difficult to settle down to anything or to make plans for the future."[52] This is finely caught in Smuts's exhortation to the departing men of the 1st Brigade in June 1940: "Go forth as crusaders, as children of the Cross, to fight for freedom itself. You are volunteers of your own choice. . . . You are going forth to meet danger, hardship and sacrifice."[53] And with it came the satisfaction of eventually succeeding in a shared endeavor.

Personal reasons, too many to count, played a part as well. The army offered employment, regular income, housing, and medical services for many impoverished young men. Politics may very well sometimes have taken a second seat to "economic conscription." Gunner Gert de Waal, of the 2nd Field Regiment (Natal Field Artillery, NFA), who had been a troubadour traveling with a circus in the Carolina district of the Eastern Transvaal, responded to the call of the "Steel Commando" in June 1940, just to spite his girlfriend.[54] A study of the letters sent home from the operational theater shows just how common the political divide within families and between spouses appears to have been.[55] For Major Reitz and his wife, the war brought things to a head. His posting to Italy, no doubt, brought relief to both parties.[56] For many, enlistment was an escape from creditors, from poor employment, or from failing relationships. Others simply followed in their fathers' footsteps. Many South African families had a tradition of military service that extended over many generations and many wars. When the Police Brigade formed in 1940, Lennox van Onselen was called in by his station commander, Head Constable F. A. Holton, handed a pen, and told to "sign here." Van Onselen's father had served under Smuts during the Anglo-Boer War and then with Holton in the South African Mounted Riflemen. Service was accepted as a matter of course.[57]

For most volunteers any single motive or combination of motives could have been resonant. This was certainly the case for two young students, David Brokensha and his brother Paul:

[We volunteered] partly from patriotism, partly from what we saw as the adventure and glamour, and partly because neither Paul nor I was content in our respective institutions. Paul was too impatient to be away from the restrictions of school, and I was too immature to be taking advantage of my time at university. Influenced by Guy, who was already a decorated pilot in the Fleet Air Arm, we aimed to join the South African Air Force. Guy was an irresistible model and hero to his impressionable younger brothers.[58]

For black South Africans, eager to win political points and at the same time confront an unjust political system at home, enlistment was a particularly complex issue. "A decision to enlist," Kenneth Grundy has noted, "is always a product of a highly personal perception of one's overall career and social prospects in the context of a particular set of situational determinants. Black recruitment is a two-way process involving the absence of opportunity in civil society and the attraction of the armed forces."[59] Albert Grundlingh concludes that for most black South Africans their primary motive was economic.

The UDF was in a poor state in September 1939. The reorganization could only be done from outside the Defence Department and if backed by unquestionable authority. This rested in one person, Smuts himself. His was the task to marshal South Africa's 9.5 million people and, in preparing for a large war, exhort, enlist, encourage, and husband the men and later the women who entered the UDF between 1939 and 1945. Ideas concerning how, where, and when the UDF would be deployed were hotly contested. As had been the case in 1914, the mobilization was from the start beset by difficulties emanating, in no small part, from the limitations imposed by the Defence Act. In effect, only white males could be used as fighting troops and then only in direct defense of the Union. The pool from which soldiers could be drawn—white male volunteers—was small and inadequate for the task ahead. Defense authorities had to face the fact that many units were under strength and had little prospect of being brought up to strength quickly, and even less prospect of being sufficiently reinforced once committed to battle. And matters reached a near catastrophic stage with the disasters and Sidi Rezegh and Tobruk. Expeditionary forces were reduced to a single armored division and special measures were adopted to enlist women as well as men from the disenfranchised black, coloured, and Asian communities. Yet, despite this, only a small portion of South Africa's 9.5 million people actually *fought* the war or contributed directly to the national war effort.

CHAPTER 13

Manpower Mobilization and Rehabilitation in New Zealand's Second World War

Ian McGibbon

New Zealand's initial role in the war, precipitated by Germany's invasion of Poland on 1 September 1939, was much the same as it had been during the First World War. Prime Minister Michael Savage encapsulated the dominion's approach to the crisis in a broadcast to the nation on 4 September. New Zealand aligned itself with Britain: "Where she goes, we go, where she stands, we stand."[1] Although the dominion's apparent subservience has drawn criticism, this statement was an acknowledgment that New Zealand's fate depended on the outcome of the British Commonwealth's war effort, and in 1939, as in 1914, the center of that war effort would inevitably be where the hub of the Commonwealth, the United Kingdom, was most threatened—in Europe. But the Second World War would not be a rerun of the earlier conflict because this time New Zealand found itself under direct threat. And the dominion faced challenges far surpassing those it had confronted in 1914–1918, not least being greater demands on its manpower. In contending with this crisis, the role of the state would be greatly enhanced. The controlled economy that emerged from the war would have pervasive and enduring consequences.

For those who had lived through the First World War, New Zealand's initial efforts in 1939 had a familiarity about them. Not only would New Zealand contribute to the Allied military effort overseas—an approach that was made possible by the lack of any immediate or direct threat to the dominion's

home islands—but it would also supply Britain with vital food and other resources. This latter effort meshed nicely with New Zealand's economic dependence on the British market and was to New Zealand's advantage, provided
the sea routes between the dominion and Britain could be kept open. The
first priority was to form and dispatch an expeditionary force comparable in
size to the 25,000-strong contingent of the First World War. As in 1914, the
2nd New Zealand Expeditionary Force (2NZEF) initially formed on the basis
of voluntary enlistments. But, also as in the former conflict, conscription had
to be introduced. Not enough men were coming forward to sustain an infantry division overseas, so the dominion government introduced conscription
for overseas service in 1940, and it did so with very little opposition. Labor
leaders who had opposed conscription in the First World War—Peter Fraser,
who succeeded the deceased Savage as prime minister in March 1940, had
been imprisoned for sedition in 1917—were by 1940 more amenable to the
idea than they had been in 1916–1918. They were also more willing to regulate manpower for industry and agriculture, both of which continued to produce apace. It all seemed manageable for a while.

That changed with Japan's entry into the war in December 1941, which
commenced the second phase of New Zealand's war effort. From that time,
the dominion had to contend with the difficulties of maintaining its expeditionary force overseas *and* providing for the defense of the home islands, to say
nothing of sustaining its industrial and agricultural output. Needless to say, all
of this compounded New Zealand's manpower problems and led to an exten-
sion of conscription to civilian labor in a way that had not occurred during the
First World War. New Zealand's need to provide for its own physical security
introduced a new element, involving major strategic and domestic policy decisions. Civilians also found themselves under direction, but resources were still
stretched.

September 1939–December 1941

The divisional-size 2NZEF got off to a promising start. With a population at
1.5 million in 1939, New Zealand had nearly one-third of a million men of
military age (nineteen to forty-five), which should have been enough to keep
a division going.[2] In fact, more than 12,000 men came forward as volunteers
in the first week alone.[3] No problems occurred in filling the ranks of the first
echelon, which departed on 5 January 1940. But difficulties soon emerged in
finding enough volunteers for the second echelon, although a recruiting
surge in December ensured that, by the end of January 1940, some 25,140

New Zealanders had enlisted.[4] Although voluntary enlistment initially sufficed to form 2NZEF, the provision of reinforcements to keep it up to strength was difficult. Part of the problem was that New Zealand now had three armed services that demanded manpower. Men had to be found for the two cruiser–strong New Zealand Division of the Royal Navy and the Royal New Zealand Air Force, as well as 2NZEF.

As in 1914–1918, the removal of so many men from the labor market inevitably had adverse economic consequences, which the dominion government anticipated and acted to counter. Since 1936, a planning body called the Organization for National Security (ONS) had been preparing for possible involvement in a major war effort. A Manpower Committee of the ONS addressed the problem of manpower management. When war began in September 1939, its composition soon expanded, to include representatives of three existing councils—Industry Emergency (including both employer and worker members), Primary Production, and Factory Production.[5] In November 1939, the Manpower Committee gave way to a Manpower Advisory Council (which became the National Service Advisory Council in June 1940). Chaired by Paddy Webb, it planned and directed the "utilization of manpower necessary to maintain services and production and to secure the greatest effort of expansion."[6] This body faded out after being superseded by the War Council in 1940.[7]

The Manpower Committee oversaw the first efforts to coordinate wartime manpower. Not every man who wanted to enlist in the armed services could be allowed to do so, not if the dominion was to maintain a sufficient level of industrial and agricultural output. Even before the war, deliberations of the Manpower Committee produced a "Schedule of Reserved Occupations in the Initial Stages of a War" to guide, or even restrict, recruiting officers.[8] At first, men whose occupation appeared on the list were rejected outright for enlistment into the armed services—600 before November 1939 alone.[9] This seemed a bit draconian and not particularly efficient. A more nuanced approach that treated each case on its own merits had to be adopted. Army area officers, of which there were twelve, advised the names of fit volunteers to local Labour Department placement officials, who after investigation could recommend postponements or grant enlistments.[10] Appeals by men unhappy at being denied enlistment in the army, navy, or air force and complaints by employers anxious not to lose key workers were at first heard on an ad hoc basis. In due course, however, rulings fell to sixteen district advisory manpower committees, which were set up to protect essential industrial activities. These committees, which included employer and worker representatives, began hearing appeals in May 1940.[11] This seemed the best way to ensure that key people were not lost to the military. By this time, the schedule of reserved occupations was replaced by a "Schedule of Important Occupations" to reflect the more flexible approach.[12] These constructive changes notwithstanding, no sense of urgency underlay New Zealand's preparations as the Phoney War—the term coined to denote the period of relative inactivity on the Western Front following the outbreak of war—dragged into 1940.

All this changed when the Germans burst into the Low Countries and France in May. Jolted out of its complacency, the New Zealand government took a series of actions that set the pattern of the country's manpower management for the rest of the war. The state intruded much more dramatically in people's lives. Under the Emergency Regulations Amendment Act of 31 May 1940, the government assumed wide powers to direct all aspects of the economy and populace.[13] Regulations gazetted soon afterward deemed all persons and property to be at the disposal of the dominion government, a situation later described as "constitutional autocracy."[14] As Prime Minister Peter Fraser put it: "Every person in the Dominion, every atom of the country's services, must be subordinated to the requirements of the Dominion and the British Commonwealth."[15] A new agency, the National Service Department under J. S. Hunter, assumed responsibility for all administrative aspects of manpower, both military and civilian.

The new legislation immediately changed the basis for sustaining 2NZEF. Pressure for conscription had been building, not only among officials and senior soldiers grappling with manpower requirements, but also among a public receptive to the idea of equality of sacrifice. The matter posed difficulties, however, for a government that included several men, the prime minister among them, who had been imprisoned for opposing conscription during the 1914–1918 war, but it nonetheless became the law of the land in the summer of 1940. One last-minute surge of men seeking to secure the perceived (to them) higher status of volunteer brought the 2NZEF strength to 63,740.[16] With another 16,000 men volunteering for the air force and 3,000 for the navy, about one in four men of military age were under arms or had offered their services before conscription was introduced.[17] The termination of voluntary enlistment for 2NZEF marked a significant change from practice during the First World War, when voluntary service had continued and conscription was used simply to make up the numbers required.

Conscription for army service began in October 1940, at first for home defense purposes. It was based on a system that prioritized liability for service according to age and family responsibilities. All eligible men aged sixteen to forty-five were deemed to be part of a general reserve, which was subdivided into three categories: the first included all single men aged nineteen to forty-five, the second, married men nineteen to forty-five, and the third, all other residents sixteen and older. The National Service Department determined who was available for conscription, beginning with the first division of single military-age men, all of whom had to register in August 1940. Ballots were done on a district basis for service in the home-defense units of the Territorial Force, and the results of the first two ballots brought in 50,000 men by early November. These ballots, for part-time home service only, would be extended in 1941 to include eighteen-year-olds.

There were exemptions. Apart from "non-citizens," Maori were the main group excluded from the first two divisions of conscriptable men. In September 1939, there were 12,800 Maori aged twenty-one to forty-one, making them 5 percent of the military-age cohort.[18] Some 3,506 Maori volunteered for service with 2NZEF from 1939 to 1945, most going to an all-Maori unit, the 28th Battalion, one of seventeen infantry battalions of the 2nd New Zealand Division.[19]

In due course, the government began conscripting men for 2NZEF. The first 14,000 of them received their call-up notices on 4 December 1940, and a second draft for 19,000 followed on 4 March 1941. These men were all aged twenty-one to forty.[20] Some of them had already been called up for the Territorial Force, which caused confusion. To remedy this problem, ballots for Territorial service were henceforth confined to men ineligible for overseas service (that is to say, younger than twenty and older than forty, later forty-five). During 1941, the remaining men who were single and of military age received draft notices. Nineteen thousand were conscripted for overseas service on 7 May and another 24,000 in August. By December 1941, then, all fit single men had been called up for service either overseas or in the Territorial Force.[21] In early 1942, all conscription, mainly of married men, was for Territorial service. This lasted until June, when a change of policy meant that every man (unless he was Maori) was deemed to be liable for service "wherever he is required, whether in New Zealand or elsewhere."[22]

Not all those who were conscripted wanted to serve in the army, navy, or air force. As in 1916–1918, there were conscientious objectors, men who were determined not to serve for personal, mainly religious, reasons. To rule on their appeals, in 1940 the government established six armed forces appeal boards, and later added three more. The nine appeal boards heard from men who did not want to serve overseas or who identified as conscientious objectors. Separate appeal committees at the district level heard the cases of men who wished to be exempted from service in the Territorial Force. In June 1942,

Figure 13.1.   During the Second World War, the New Zealand government, facing acute manpower shortages for the armed forces and essential industry, strove to make the best use of the nation's human resources. Maori made important contributions to both essential industry and the army. This photo shows reinforcements for the 28th Battalion, an all-Maori unit and one of seventeen infantry battalions of the 2nd New Zealand Division (November 1940). Image source: Australian War Memorial, 004333.

when the distinction between Territorial and 2NZEF ballots was removed, all these boards and committees were amalgamated, leaving an apparatus of twenty-six statutory appeal boards.[23]

With 45 percent of conscripts for overseas service either seeking exemptions or having their enlistment challenged by employers, the appeal boards were busy.[24] By December 1944, they had heard 18,653 cases.[25] The bulk were "on the ground of public interest," although a "fair proportion" had hardship as their basis. The National Service Department actually submitted some of the appeals, intervening in cases where employers or conscripts refrained from appealing. Success rates were high. Nearly four in five appeals resulted in at least a temporary postponement. Industries or occupations for which postponements were most common included farming, coal mining, sawmilling, butter and cheese production, tanneries, engineering, railways, shipping, police, and clergy.[26] By December 1940, more than 15,000 fit men had been granted service exemptions for essential industry.[27] Conscientious objectors were "by far the most difficult section of the population to deal with in the matter of national service."[28] By 28 February 1943, more than 5,800 conscientious objectors had appealed, and 18 percent (about 550) of the 3,000 cases actually heard by the boards were upheld.[29] About 800 refused to accept the rejection of their appeals. They were imprisoned.

Despite these difficulties, reasonable processes and measures were in place to manage New Zealand's limited manpower. By December 1941, 81,000 men were under arms, more than half of them overseas.[30] Because 17 percent of all men in industry had been removed from the economy, the female work force expanded substantially—from 180,000 to 214,000 between 1939 and 1941.[31] That worked well enough for a while.

December 1941–August 1945

In December 1941, Japan's entry to the war transformed New Zealand's situation. Its response to the now global conflict was two-phased. In the first, the crisis period of the first six months of 1942, defense became the prime consideration and demanded drastic action. In the second, the counteroffensive period from August 1942, the emphasis shifted to supporting American efforts to take the fight to the Japanese. In both periods, manpower was an acute problem.

As Japanese forces swept south in late 1941 and early 1942, a "new spirit of driving urgency" infused New Zealand's war effort.[32] With Japanese forces bombing Australia and penetrating into the Solomon Islands, the possibility of direct attack on the home islands seemed very real. The situation demanded "a complete reorientation of the war effort," based on universal service and military preparedness.[33] Men and women of working age found their freedom of action in the work place severely curtailed as the war administration endeavored to stretch the manpower elastic to keep the economy running.

Did home defense requirements now demand the return of New Zealand's best trained force, the 2NZEF? Such considerations gained additional weight when two of the three Australian divisions in the Mediterranean were redeployed to Australia.[34] There were, however, practical difficulties in bringing home the 2NZEF, not least shipping availability, given the priority of moving the Australian divisions. And with Japanese naval forces marauding the Indian Ocean, the safety of such a transfer soon became a concern. Under the circumstances, the dominion government decided that the safer alternative to bringing the 2NZEF home was to have American troops reinforce New Zealand. The first Americans began arriving in mid-June, just after the US Navy defeated the Japanese at Midway.[35]

In early 1942, then, New Zealand adhered to the overall strategy of the Allies to defeat Germany first, and the dominion took what measures it could to keep the 2NZEF fighting in the Mediterranean and to bolster its position in the South Pacific. A force of 3,700 New Zealanders already in Fiji when the Japanese offensive began soon found itself bolstered to 10,000, using men who had originally been earmarked for the 2NZEF in the Mediterranean.[36] At home, the Territorial Force and the National Military Reserve (created in May 1939, and including ex-Territorials and NZEF soldiers up to the age of fifty-five)[37] mobilized to provide three weak infantry divisions. On 20 January 1942, 27,000 men were called up for full-time Territorial service, which built the force up "to a level which was far beyond anything previously contemplated."[38] All married men up to age forty-five with children were balloted.[39] This meant that by the end of 1942, all single and married men aged eighteen to forty-five—283,000 in all—had been called up.[40] One-third of New Zealand's work force was in uniform by September 1942, up from 10 percent at the end of 1940.[41] Such was the gravity of the situation.

The crisis forced New Zealand to grapple with the problem of enhancing home defense while sustaining its economic contribution to the war effort. The country had to be put in a position to defend itself against a scale of attack far greater than previously envisaged. In addition to filling the ranks of the Territorial Force cadre units for full-time service, this entailed carrying out the construction of defense works at likely invasion sites, which was also manpower intensive. Much needed to be done to bolster fixed defenses. This included installing pillboxes at likely invasion beaches, creating gun positions, and building air raid shelters. Diverting men for this urgent construction effort put additional pressure on an already strained labor force. For the time being, reinforcement of the 2NZEF became impossible, and only a few air and naval personnel were seconded to the Royal Navy and Royal Air Force.

Drastic measures were also needed to meet the shortfall in workers available for the economy. There were several ways to find labor for essential industries. First, employers in key industries continued to have the ability to claw back conscripted workers using the appeals system, which remained in place. Many appeals against conscripted Territorial service had already been judged by appeal boards in 1940–1941 and usually dismissed because Territorial service was then limited and could be accommodated with work requirements. But when Territorial service became full time during the invasion scare of 1942, industry faced grave problems. Employers accordingly relodged some 7,000 appeals, about half of which succeeded.[42] As the year proceeded and the age of those called up for military service increased, more and more essential workers were caught in the dragnet. In the final ballots, appeals of men in their forties rose to more than 70 percent.[43] Those whose appeals were upheld had the essentiality of their work assessed.[44] And the government at last began to use powers it had taken in May 1940 to control the labor market through what was popularly known as "manpowering." Even before Japan's onslaught, National Service officials had been increasingly convinced that only direction of labor could alleviate the shortages developing in key industries. What in 1941 had seemed desirable now became imperative.

On 10 January 1942, the government urgently amended the National Service regulations to provide specific powers, as opposed to the general powers it already had. Now legally empowered to declare an industry essential, the government began doing so immediately, and to significant effect. Workers of an essential industry could no longer leave to accept higher paying positions in nonessential industries. Appeals against military service for workers in an essential industry were now almost invariably successful. And there was also a "steady stream of directions" into essential industries of those engaged in "less-important occupations" or not employed at all. By March 1943 nearly 31,000 directions had been made, though 3,000 were later withdrawn. The result was that, by March 1944, roughly 40 percent of the work force (about 255,000 people) was employed in essential industries.[45]

Another source of manpower, both military and civilian, was groups not so far subjected to state direction, starting with women, who provided by far the largest pool of potential labor. In the armed forces, they filled noncombatant roles to free up fit men for the fighting units. This process had begun in late 1941 with the establishment of women's elements of all three services, and a thousand were in uniform by December.[46] Initially channeled into office and clerical jobs, they were then directed into a broader range of occupations. Some found themselves driving, manning motor launches, or operating searchlights in port defense artillery units. New Zealand women made an even greater contribution in the civilian sphere. The "manpowering" of females "was to secure an adequate labor supply for priority undertakings and to prevent people already employed in essential industry from taking other work."[47] From January 1942, all twenty- and twenty-one-year-old civilian women had to register for essential work. Registration was later extended to all women up to the age of thirty in 1943 and forty in 1944, the exemption being for women with children under the age of fifteen. In all, 147,000 women registered before March 1944. More than 6,000 were directed to essential industries before March 1943, and at least 37,000 complied with orders to change jobs before the end of the war. Thousands more were held in jobs that were declared essential.[48] By the end of 1943, the female work force had increased to 228,000, not including 8,000 serving in the armed forces.[49]

Yet another source of manpower was New Zealand's 40,000 Maori, who may not have been liable for military service, but who could be conscripted for labor. The direction of many Maori into essential industries in cities set in motion a trend toward urbanization that continued after the war. Hitherto, except in certain areas, Maori and Pakeha (European-origin New Zealanders), had tended to live in parallel societies. The new development had immense long-term positive significance for Maori-Pakeha relations. The exploits of 28th Maori Battalion in the 2NZEF were equally significant in changing attitudes.

If the industrial conscription of Maori and women helped New Zealand to surmount its manpower problems during the crisis period, the second phase of its war against Japan would bring little relief to those juggling New Zealand's resources to meet commitments. Even when home defense anxieties eased in the second half of 1942, manpower demands remained high. Complicating the government's myriad problems was its determination that New Zealand, for political reasons, should play an active part in the Solomons campaign that began with the US invasion of Guadalcanal in August 1942. The idea of recalling the 2nd New Zealand Division for these purposes came up, but, in the end, the government opted to leave the 2NZEF in place until at least the end of the North African campaign.[50] Instead, the 3rd New Zealand Division, formed from units then stationed in Fiji, was deployed to New Caledonia in November 1942. This two-brigade, 14,000-strong division would ultimately go forward to the Solomon Islands and take part in several minor offensive actions in 1943.[51] Alongside this army effort, the air force steadily increased its strength in the theater, reaching 7,000 in 1945.

This commitment ensured that labor problems became acute in early 1943. The Department of National Service noted: "[New Zealand] was facing simultaneous urgent demands for man-power from every branch of the armed forces and from all the major producing and processing industries. An all-round man-power shortage, far transcending anything which could have been foreseen a year earlier, was in immediate prospect, and strong and clear-cut action, affecting both industrial and man-power control simultaneously, was seen to be vitally necessary."[52] An increasingly obvious measure to address the shortage of workers was to reduce the number of men serving full time in the home defenses, especially as the danger of invasion had diminished following the American victory at Midway and the arrival of American troops in New Zealand. In March 1943, the government decided "to entirely remodel the whole of our home defense policy."[53] This was when the demobilization of the Territorial Force began. It started with a reduction of 25,000 men, and it accelerated from there. Indeed, so many Territorials were demobilized that "the home forces, as a military organization, practically disappeared."[54] Unfortunately, much of the manpower savings were eaten up by the 2NZEF. The press of overseas commitments meant that fewer than 10,000 of 36,000 formerly full-time Territorials were actually available for industry by the summer of 1943.[55]

Maintaining an active division in the Mediterranean posed problems for both the government and the men involved. They came to a head in the incident surrounding the furlough of long-service men at the end of the North African campaign in May 1943. It was then that the War Cabinet agreed not only that the 2nd Division should remain in the Mediterranean and fight in Italy, but also that a furlough scheme should be instituted for men who had served the longest with the division. As a first step 6,000 men of the three initial echelons of the 2NZEF were to be brought home on a three-month furlough. As Jonathan Fennell discusses in chapter 8, the scheme did not work well. When the first 4,000 furlough men arrived home in July 1943, they were incensed by the situation they found, especially the number of fit men held back in essential industries.[56] These troops fumed that no man should be forced to go overseas twice before all had gone once. By the time the furlough men were set to return to the Mediterranean in early 1944, only 1,600 of the 6,000 were still available. Many had obtained medical discharges. Others had readily found employment. Nearly a thousand of them refused to embark, although roughly one-quarter were eventually persuaded to do so. The rest, 547, were court-martialed and convicted for desertion (a verdict that was later quashed). Similar problems were experienced with the second, 1,900-strong contingent of furlough men, who arrived in February 1944, with 111 refusing to re-embark when it was time to return.[57] The government stopped the furlough scheme in September 1944 and instead instituted a replacement scheme for men with three years' service. That was not a "cheap" manpower option. It required more than 9,000 men to just to keep the 2nd Division up to strength, and this requirement was met from men of the returned 3rd New Zealand Division and its supporting troops.[58] The disbandment of this division had become inevitable following the withdrawal of 9,000 men, half its strength, from the Solomons for essential industry between April and August 1944.

Repatriation

By 1945, New Zealand had reverted to its early war position of sustaining one division overseas and a very small home-defense establishment to meet a now nonexistent home invasion threat. The 2NZEF was supposed to take part in the invasion of Japan, but the sudden end of the war in August 1945 overtook these plans. Instead, a brigade-sized force joined the British Commonwealth Occupation Force in Japan. By this time, however, Wellington's focus had shifted to the problem of repatriating and reincorporating the remaining men and women of the 2NZEF into society.

New Zealand's repatriation and rehabilitation policy in 1945 built on lessons that had been learned in the decade that followed the First World War. Back then, for the men coming back from overseas, "employment was of the utmost concern and seen as the key to successful repatriation."[59] The whole process was flawed, however, and the onset of economic depression only compounded the problems. Men installed on unproductive land struggled to survive financially, and many of them were forced to walk off. In the early 1940s, there was a pervasive view among the public that the country had failed its veterans of the previous war. Reflecting this opinion, the government determined to do better this time. As early as 1940, Prime Minister Michael Savage, was adamant that the men who returned would not face "an unseemly struggle for the right to live."[60] This was a difficult problem that all countries of the Commonwealth faced after the end of the war, as Meghan Fitzpatrick examines in chapter 14. A key aspect of rehabilitation then was to ensure no repetition of the post-1918 speculative investment boom and the ensuing depression. Stabilizing land prices was key to preventing speculation. To this end, legislation decreed that the price of land should remain at the September 1942 levels. Wartime restrictions, such as price-fixing, would be maintained to ensure the successful rehabilitation of New Zealand's warriors, another publicly acceptable cause.

The framework of New Zealand's rehabilitation scheme was set up in 1941–1943. Legislation passed in October 1941 provided for the establishment of an advisory National Rehabilitation Council. Oversight of rehabilitation was in the hands of a Rehabilitation Board, established in February 1942 under the minister in charge of rehabilitation, decorated returned serviceman C. F. (Jerry) Skinner. At first, the board used various departments as its agent, but from November 1943 it was supported by a new Rehabilitation Department, which took over the National Service Department's soldier rehabilitation functions. The new department had the "immediate and basic responsibility . . . to give all ex-servicemen and ex-servicewomen the opportunity of returning to civil life on terms at least as favorable as those which would probably have applied . . . if they had not been required to serve in the Armed Forces."[61] Accordingly, the department developed a comprehensive scheme for reintegrating returning men and women, and officers went overseas to educate the troops about what they could expect in terms rehabilitation assistance. The Rehabilitation Department also established a country-wide apparatus. Local rehabilitation committees (of which there were 110 by March 1944) provided the first port of call for returned service members seeking assistance. These bodies had the main responsibility in determining "the extent of assistance of all kinds merited by ex-servicemen applicants." But the Rehabilitation Board had the final say on whether assistance was provided.[62] Much cooperation and coordination was required with other departments and agencies to make it all work. War pensions, for example, remained the responsibility of the Department of Social Security, and the National Service Department (from 1 April 1946 the National Employment Service) continued to be responsible for placing men and women in work once the Rehabilitation Department had retrained them.[63] And a steady stream of returning sick and disabled soldiers, 22,000-plus by March 1944, received help from the Disabled Servicemen's League, an organization that had been operating since the First World War.[64]

Throughout this period, the Rehabilitation Board had two main areas of action: preparing former soldiers to take their place in the economy or encouraging them to establish their own businesses. The thousand returned servicewomen were not overlooked, even if, as with their more numerous home service counterparts, marriage was considered their main form of rehabilitation. [65] Vocational training, focused on trade and occupational training, took place in rehabilitation training centers. For small business creation, rehab loans were available, and more than 11,000 obtained them in the decade after 1945. But given that New Zealand's economy was still overwhelmingly rural-based, land settlement remained "the traditional response to the problem of rehabilitating soldiers."[66] It was inevitably difficult because land had to be found for these purposes. With limited undeveloped land available, most rehab farms had to be carved out of existing farms. In all, 1.4 million acres were acquired by 1954. Most of the land was purchased by the state, but 0.3 million acres (21 percent) was appropriated.[67] Both in sales and seizure, the problem of valuation was contentious due to price fixing at 1942 values. The issues were addressed by land sale committees, and there was a land court judge to resolve outstanding disputes.[68]

The principle applied was that returned men would be established only on farms that were productive and only when the soldiers had the necessary farming skills and knowledge. There was a system in place to ensure these conditions. Local farm subcommittees, set up to cooperate with local rehabilitation committees, made sure that men with farming expertise oversaw the first step in the process for new soldier-farmers. These committees considered applications and recommended training, depending on previous experience. An aspiring soldier-farmer approached his district rehabilitation officer as a first step; the latter would refer his application to the farming subcommittee and thence to the local rehabilitation committee. If deemed suitable, he might be approved for immediate establishment on a farm or for training, if that was necessary. The final step was installation on a farm. The program proved popular. In March 1944, only 264 returned soldiers were on rehab farms.[69] Ultimately, though, some 13,000 men settled on farms, 90 percent of them before 1955. As historian Jane Thomson noted, "It was a programme built upon faith in the duty and the ability of the state to regulate economic activity for social ends."[70]

Establishing men and women in jobs or businesses, including farms, was only part of the Rehabilitation Board's responsibility. The aim was also to restore veterans to society. Properly accommodating the returning soldiers was another key element in this process. Overall, 64,000 housing loans were made to ex-servicemen. Fifty percent of the state's vacant housing stock was reserved for returned men, and more than 18,000 preferential state house allocations were made under the rehabilitation scheme.[71] But the government's efforts were hindered by a severe housing shortage. The freeze on house prices proved counterproductive. Under-the-table payments and other schemes proliferated as sellers sought to get around the restrictions. Rising building costs also undercut the value of loans available to returned soldiers.

New Zealand mobilized its manpower for war and then restored its demobilized soldiers to the economy in a much more efficient way than it had during and after the First World War. It met the challenges of deploying expeditionary forces to the Mediterranean and the Pacific, providing for adequate home defense, and returning both physically able and disabled soldiers to civilian life by using an unprecedented level of state intervention—whether it was conscription to grow the armed services, price controls to control inflation when resettling returning soldiers, or creating government bureaucracies to administer veterans and resettlement schemes. There were some inevitable problems. Controls on the economy put a brake on economic development. And widespread dissatisfaction, especially in relation to land price-fixing, contributed to the defeat of the Labour government in the general election of 1949. The new National government loosened some economic control measures, but retained others, ensuring that the wartime experience of government intervention had a lasting legacy.

Chapter 14

Caring for British Commonwealth Soldiers in the Aftermath of the Second World War

Meghan Fitzpatrick

> In every capital of the Allied World Civil Servants plucked neatly-ribboned files from pigeon holes. These were the blue-prints from which the shape of the brave post-war world would be fashioned. It was only a matter of some necessary details . . . before these plans could be implemented. And the very first set of blueprints concerned the soldiers themselves. Nations were grateful: they wished to reward their soldiers and speed their return to civilian life. This set of plans bore the file title, "Rehabilitation."
>
> Colin McDougall, *Execution*

Over 6 million people from the United Kingdom, Canada, Australia, and New Zealand served in the armed services during the Second World War (1939–1945). To this day, it remains the largest ever mobilization of British Commonwealth manpower. Many of these men and women returned home bearing the physical and psychological scars of war. This chapter addresses how Britain and the dominions tackled the needs of veterans in the decade that followed the Second World War. It explores how they grappled with the challenge of demobilization on a vast scale, and it reviews how the legacy of the First World War shaped the rehabilitation process that began in 1945. The chapter also examines the thorny business of awarding pensions, measuring disability, and quantifying human suffering. It assesses what these countries provided veterans in terms of compensation, benefits, and medical care, and it looks at how millions of veterans gained unprecedented access to economic and educational opportunities. It also considers how the same systems failed some of the most traumatized.

Demobilization

Plans for demobilization started pretty much as the Second World War began. Officials in Britain, Canada, Australia, and New Zealand recognized the scale of the challenge they faced, and, as early as December 1939, they struck cabinet committees and formed advisory groups to study the problem.[1] In most countries, planners eventually formulated points systems whereby they would release the majority of soldiers, sailors, and aviators in staggered groups, based on age, rank, and period of service. Officials initially planned to discharge 10 percent of individuals early because of their value to postwar reconstruction and economic development, mostly those in industrial occupations such as mining and skilled trades such as building.[2] Across the Commonwealth, officials designed demobilization to be as honest and even-handed as possible. As Rex Pope points out, "The virtues of this arrangement were its obvious justice (long service promised early release) and its simplicity. It was easily understood and not readily open to manipulation."[3]

Early demobilization planning owed much to the dismal legacy of the First World War. Financial and industrial need had played a far greater role in shaping the system and determining groups assigned priority for early release in 1918. As a result, the first soldiers out of uniform were also those with the skills best suited to "adapt industry to peacetime purposes."[4] But this often meant demobilizing men who had spent less time in uniform. A system so heavily based on economic considerations was also open to manipulation and failed to take the psychology of the average soldier into mind.[5] Transportation delays for dominion soldiers slowed the process even further, and the 1918 influenza pandemic intensified the misery of troops waiting to return home, with disaffected servicemen eventually turning to violence.[6] In early 1919, New Zealand troops at Sling Camp in Wiltshire rioted, and Canadian servicemen rampaged in Wales.[7] And, over the ensuing months, Australian soldiers were involved in more than twenty major riots.[8]

Demobilization was no less complicated in 1945; officials just handled it more efficiently. From 1945 to 1946 alone, officials discharged over 100,000 New Zealanders, 500,000 Australians, 700,000 Canadians, and 5 million Britons from military service.[9] Not that the demobilizations were problem-free; shipping delays again meant that many service personnel had to spend yet another Christmas in uniform, and again there were a number of predictable altercations. Four thousand New Zealanders marched in protest of transport delays from Indonesia in December 1945, and less than a month later, disgruntled members of the Royal Air Force's Transport Command walked out of work at bases in the Middle East, India, and Ceylon.[10] Incidents like this proved isolated, however, because demobilization was still proceeding in accordance with points systems that were well articulated and understood. In contrast to the demobilization of the First World War, politicians and policymakers went to great pains to ensure the release system properly acknowledged the sacrifices of ordinary men and women. In doing so, they secured widespread public support and paved the way for rehabilitation to begin.

Pensions and Rehabilitation

Authorities across the Commonwealth also thought about how to reintegrate and compensate returning veterans. Once again, the experience of the First World War informed their efforts. In 1918, soldiers in Britain, Canada, Australia, and New Zealand had come home with high hopes for the future, including promises of generous pensions and full employment. British Prime Minister David Lloyd George best encapsulated those hopes in a November 1918 speech at Wolverhampton. Describing his government's plans, Lloyd George explained to the assembled crowd: "What is our task? To make Britain a fit country for heroes to live in. . . . I cannot think of what these men have gone through. I have been there at the door of the furnace and witnessed it, but that is not being in it, and I saw them march into the furnace. There are millions of men who will come back. Let us make this a land fit for such men to live in. There is no time to lose. . . . Don't let us waste this victory merely in ringing joybells."[11] But promises of a land "fit for heroes" proved illusory in Britain and the dominions.[12] The United Kingdom, Canada, Australia, and New Zealand all struggled under the weight of high inflation, industrial strife, and rampant unemployment in the immediate aftermath of the First World War. Legislation provided compensation for the sick and injured, but nations struggled to pay generous pensions.[13] In *War Come Home: Disabled Veterans in Britain and Germany*, Deborah Cohen argues that "successive British governments [during the interwar years] . . . limited the state's liability for the disabled, as for the unemployed. Fearful of committing . . . to open-ended expenditure, civil servants . . . aimed to delegate tasks they could to the voluntary effort."[14] Poorly designed education and vocational training schemes also did little to prepare ex-service members for the harsh realities of the postwar labor market. For instance, as Ian McGibbon discusses in chapter 13, New Zealand's Repatriation Department placed returning soldiers in jobs and issued study grants, but it prematurely ended its work in 1922, before many had even secured permanent employment.[15] Veterans from all over the Commonwealth came back to social and economic instability—and governments poorly prepared to receive them. As Nancy Taylor asserts, they quickly became "the flotsam and jetsam of the First World War, old soldiers for whom nothing had gone right, who through lost opportunities, lack of capital, wrong decisions, bad advice or sheer bad luck, let alone physical damage, drinking or fecklessness . . . lived precariously in good times and worse in bad."[16]

Fearing another lost generation, Britain and the dominions began to plan for the reintegration of Second World War veterans almost as early and diligently as they did for demobilization. From the beginning, the goal of both the pension system and rehabilitation programing was to return ex-service members to work. All four countries called for veterans to take their place in the civilian labor market.[17] The Canadian pamphlet *Back to Civil Life*, which was issued to all of the dominion's servicemen and women in 1945, explained that "the object of Canada's plan for rehabilitation of her Armed Forces is that every man or woman discharged . . . shall be in a position to earn a living."[18] In Canberra's *Return to Civil Life*, the authors similarly argued that "national considerations . . . demand your rapid return to civil life so that you can assist in the great tasks which face Australia." It also promised that "every assistance . . . will be provided to enable you to assume your rightful place in the community again."[19] Policymakers did not want to encourage dependence on the state; nor did they intend pensions, allowances, and benefits to be "handouts." Instead, they saw payments as compensation for lives interrupted and rehabilitation as a path to self-sufficiency and independence.[20]

To facilitate this process, all four nations passed extensive legislation that included basic financial gratuities calculated on the basis of rank, length of service, and time spent overseas.[21] Granted to all returning veterans, these reestablishment payments provided ex-servicemen and women with some temporary financial independence and purchasing power.[22] This money could help finance anything from the purchase of a home to the cost of household items such as furniture.[23] Rehabilitation legislation also supplied veterans with low-interest loans to support new business ventures. These loans were not lavish, but they did help to supplement the recipient's existing financial resources.[24] The New Zealand government, for example, issued loans up to £500 at less than 4 percent interest for the first two years—and with a flexible repayment plan.[25] In all four countries, the state also offered specialized employment services or counseling to assist veterans seeking work. Moreover, government hiring practices gave veterans preference for appointments in the civil service.[26] Programs like this ensured that the majority of returning veterans quickly secured employment in national economies that needed their labor. For example, over 650,000 Canadian veterans entered the job market in

1946. Nearly 85 percent of those who used government counseling services secured a job within only two months of discharge.[27]

Similar to business loans, land-settlement schemes proved particularly popular in Canada, Australia, and New Zealand, where government programs offered financial assistance and preferential terms to those willing to settle down to the business of farming.[28] Canada's Veterans Land Act of 1942 "provided $4,800 financed at 3.5 per cent interest to acquire a full sized farm or a half-acre hobby operation."[29] But officials were exceedingly careful in how they screened applicants and distributed land. Here again, they took account of the post–First World War experience, during which so many land settlement programs had failed miserably. Nearly a third of all Australian veterans deserted their properties in the post-1918 period, as did many in Canada and New Zealand.[30] The problem was combination of bad land and lack of agricultural know-how on the part of the veterans. But regulations imposed in 1945 made sure that failure rates were not nearly so high. In New Zealand, for example, veterans interested in farming had to apply to local rehabilitation authorities, which assigned regional farming subcommittees to assess the applicant's skill level and make a determination whether or not additional training would be required before land could be allotted and funds dispensed.[31] Land-settlement schemes in New Zealand and the other dominions proved more successful in the post-1945 period than they did in the post-1918 period. Within a decade, the New Zealand government had settled nearly 12,236 veterans on state-held acres. Australia's War Service Land Settlement Scheme similarly provided comprehensive training and farms to 12,000 returned soldiers.[32]

Rehabilitation legislation provided veterans with equally transformative opportunities for education and training. Ex-servicemen in the United Kingdom were entitled to six months of free vocational training through the Ministry of Labour and National Service.[33] Meanwhile, Canadians could spend as many months in training as they had spent in the military, and they could also apply for university scholarships and living allowances.[34] Australia and New Zealand proved to have the most generous policies.[35] Under the Commonwealth Rehabilitation Scheme, Australian ex-service members could receive "university education, or technical and apprenticeship training, with the aid of generous scholarships, sustenance, and training allowances," for up to two years.[36] New Zealanders could spend up to three years on education, with grants for textbooks and full-time bursaries part of the package.[37] While Taylor observes that "rehabilitation sought to put the serviceman where he would have been without the war," it did more than that.[38] It gave veterans financial security and social mobility. Commenting on Australia's reconstruction, historians Graeme Powell and Stuart Macintyre rightly point out that "many from lower income families acquired university degrees and diplomas and joined professions that would have been beyond their reach in pre-war times."[39]

In all its rehabilitation programming, Britain proved less generous than Canada, Australia, and New Zealand. Veterans from the dominions returned to buoyant economies, but the same could not be said of their British counterparts. Six-plus years of total war had taken a toll on the British economy, which lay in tatters in 1945. The government, which had amassed huge foreign debts to finance the military effort, faced the painful process of repaying its creditors.[40] Throughout the late 1940s, the country faced continued economic instability and a housing crisis.[41] The British state simply could not afford to finance veterans' programs as generously as did Canada, Australia, and New Zealand. It relied more heavily on the private sector and charity, as a result.[42] The government expected veterans and civilians alike to "muck in and help rebuild a country physically shattered by war and struggling to survive."[43] British authorities shared the same goal of returning ex-servicemen and women to full employment; they just could not do it in exactly the same way as did governments in the dominions.[44]

But not all veterans could take full advantage of reintegration programs or return to the workforce so easily, especially those whose lives had been blighted by disability and disease. Pensions were the primary way of acknowledging sacrifice and compensating injury. Britain, Canada, Australia, and New Zealand all granted two types of pensions: service and disability. They issued the first type to veterans who had deployed overseas in an active theater, and officials calculated compensation based on age, rank, length of service, and other factors such as marital status and responsibility for dependents.[45] They awarded disability pensions to men and women whose impairment had resulted "from injury or disease or aggravation thereof incurred during military service."[46] In a 1950s study of the Canadian pension system, the word "disability" was broadly defined as "the loss or the lessening of the power to will or do any normal physical or mental act."[47] Remuneration for disability depended on the severity of the handicap, which could range anywhere from 5 to 100 percent.[48] Made on a weekly or monthly basis, disability pension payments were adjusted to align with cost of living.[49] Severely disabled veterans or those assessed as 100 percent impaired could access additional grants for unemployment, marriage, and child support. They could also apply for home nursing care.[50] And the law entitled former prisoners of war to similar compensation measures.[51]

To administer the new compensation programs, legislators in Britain, Canada, Australia, and New Zealand assembled vast new departments of civil servants.[52] The process of applying for a disability pension began by filing a claim, which triggered a review of service medical files by a panel of assembled physicians. Once complete, the applicant's petition went to a war pensions committee for adjudication. These varied in size and composition from country to country, but typically they consisted of three or four appointees, who were usually veterans themselves and prominent members of the community.[53] In New Zealand, regulations dictated that a member of the medical profession also be included.[54] The assembled committee assessed if a claim warranted financial remuneration and decided the appropriate level of compensation. War pensions committees were legally obliged to give all appellants the benefit of the doubt; the "onus of proof" that a disability did not relate to service rested with the government. Applicants also received free legal advice and an advocate paid for by the state.[55] If a war pensions committee rejected an application, the veteran could appeal the decision indefinitely, provided he or she presented new evidence. The United Kingdom was the only exception. There, applicants could not launch new appeals beyond seven years from date of discharge.[56]

Veterans were also entitled to free medical care upon their return home. In Britain and the dominions, veterans undergoing medical care could receive pay and allowances commensurate with their rank for up to one year, if they began treatment within thirty days of discharge. A disability pensioner could even receive lifetime access to free medical treatment for service-related conditions.[57] Classified as priority patients, handicapped veterans could also access a number of vocational and industrial rehabilitation programs designed to help them reenter the workforce. For example, the British Ministry of Pensions and National Insurance funded any local authority or voluntary organization willing to provide work for disabled ex-service members.[58] One such company, Remploy Limited, employed over 6,000 disabled veterans and civilians in its factories. The British ministry also opened eight homecraft centers for the severely injured, which taught the skills of woodwork, leather work, and light metal work.[59] Similarly, Canada's Department of Veterans Affairs agreed to underwrite a portion of a disabled veteran's salary, until he or she could perform at the same speed as his or her able-bodied counterparts and agreed to cover extra premiums charged to the employer by provincial workman's compensation boards.[60]

Pensions and ready access to health care benefited thousands of ex-service personnel returning home. Medical advancements such as artificial limbs and hearing aids allowed these men and women to take up the threads of lives left behind.[61] In Britain, doctors at Stoke Mandeville hospital in Aylesbury used physiotherapy and exercise to reduce the long-term impact of paralysis and sparked the beginnings of an international sporting movement for the disabled.[62] The Canadian government financed four specialized spinal cord rehabilitation centers in Montreal, Toronto, Winnipeg, and Vancouver. These centers returned more than 70 percent of patients to life in the wider community, pioneering the idea that the disabled could eventually return to productive and rewarding work.[63] Australia opened modern occupational therapy centers in repatriation hospitals across the country and provided veterans with the opportunity to access extensive outpatient services, something that the Commonwealth had not done before.[64] Military doctors returning to New Zealand ran a number of plastic surgery units that made groundbreaking contributions in the field of reconstructive surgery.[65] There can be little question that numerous medical innovations paved the way for the successful reintegration of disabled veterans.

But for all the good they wrought, the pension and rehabilitation systems were not without their flaws. The British Commonwealth nations, like most countries around the world, still struggled over the course of the twentieth century to care for veterans bearing the psychological scars of war. Following the First World War, the sheer number of veterans who claimed pensions for psychological or neurological reasons overwhelmed Britain and the dominions alike. A decade after the war had ended, close to 9,000 Canadians continued to claim compensation for psychological conditions, and two decades after the armistice of 1918, roughly 120,000 former British servicemen and women were "still in receipt of pensions or had received final awards for primary psychiatric disability."[66] And mental health problems accounted for well over half of all disability pensions issued to Australian veterans who served from 1914 to 1918.[67] In light of the cost to the public purse, government officials were eager to avoid a repetition of these chronic problems and costs. Meeting in 1939, British policymakers went so far as to rule out the possibility of pensions for the psychologically traumatized altogether. But as the war progressed, public opinion and pressure from the medical community forced the government to reverse its position and concede eligibility.[68] Nevertheless, securing a pension for psychological injury remained a daunting prospect.

Pensions and rehabilitation programs facilitated the recovery of many physically disabled veterans, but the same cannot be said for the psychologically disabled. Planners did not design rehabilitation systems with these men and women foremost in mind. Indeed, they calculated pension rates based primarily on how the loss of key physical abilities such as strength and mobility affected earning capacity. But they failed to quantify the impact of depression, anxiety, and other psychological symptoms.[69] In addition, the wording of pension legislation was imprecise and wholly inadequate to address the

FIGURE 14.1. During and after the Second World War, Britain and the dominions implemented veterans pension and rehabilitation programs that, while far from perfect, proved much better than those for First World War veterans. The Canadian soldiers in this photo await interviews with rehabilitation counsellors, Toronto, 1944. Image source: Library and Archives Canada/National Film Board of Canada fonds/c049434.

complexities of mental trauma. By law, veterans were entitled to receive a disability pension for an "incapacity arising out of or aggravated by 'active service,' in war."[70] But as Australian author Stephen Garton has argued, "the terms *arising* and *aggravated* are vague," and while "it seems clear that legislators intended that pensions should be for those conditions that were a 'direct' consequence of service . . . the ambiguity in the terms . . . points to the difficulty in any such determination."[71] Military authorities and medical personnel also embraced a model of mental health that stressed the importance of predisposition to psychological breakdown. Consequently, it became almost impossible for veterans who had either a personal or a family history of psychological illness to link their current condition to war service.[72] Officials in some countries, such as Canada, also claimed that compensation hurt rather than helped its recipients. They contended that regular pension payments encouraged psychologically traumatized veterans to prolong their symptoms rather than seek treatment.[73] Therefore, policy stipulated that the government should deny compensation to anyone who did not provide "positive proof" that his or her condition resulted from service.[74] What is more, they would award funds only in the event that treatment at a recognized institution had already failed.[75]

The composition of war pensions committees presented an additional obstacle. Medical panels assessed all applications, but the final decision on compensation rested with war pension committees. Drawn from a variety of educational and professional backgrounds, committee members did not receive any specialized training for their role. Nonetheless, states asked them to adjudicate a vast range of complex and co-morbid conditions.[76] Despite the best intentions, archival evidence suggests that the ill-preparedness of the committees adversely affected the results of pension proceedings, especially in cases of psychological injury. One British official at the Ministry of Pensions and National Insurance got to the heart of the issue when he wrote to a colleague in December 1957: "It is exceedingly doubtful whether the War Pensions Committees as they are constituted are really competent to judge the medical issues in the cases which now come before them."[77]

Like their physically disabled comrades, psychologically traumatized veterans were entitled to free medical treatment for pensionable conditions and could receive care at a variety of institutions, including general hospitals, private care homes, and asylums. By the mid-twentieth century, outpatient facilities may have been on the rise, but inpatient treatment remained the norm for the treatment of chronic mental health problems.[78] Military hospitals that specialized in the care of psychological trauma were rare, which meant that ex-service personnel often had to travel far from family and friends to get help.[79] What is more, government officials frequently underestimated the demand for treatment. For instance, Australia's Repatriation Commission projected in 1941 that "[0].5 per thousand or less" of veterans would seek treatment for mental health reasons, and, based on that wildly imprecise projection, it concluded that "it should be practicable to allot . . . one ward in each large hospital for this purpose," or 160 beds in total.[80] By 1946, they estimated that they needed nearly seven times the number of beds.[81] Repatriation hospitals simply could not cope with the demand, which forced public healthcare systems to take on an increasing share of the burden. Underfunded and chronically overcrowded, state-run mental institutions had little room to accommodate additional patients.

Service patient programs, originally developed after the First World War, were designed to ensure that psychologically disabled veterans received an adequate standard of care, if not a higher quality of treatment than that which was generally available in state-run mental hospitals. After the Second World War, officials continued to use these schemes to improve the lives of ex-service personnel who found themselves in the civilian healthcare system. Upon admission to hospital or asylum, veterans received treatment on separate wards and wore distinctive clothing that distinguished them from their fellow patients.[82] But this did not fully protect service patients from discrimination at the hands of doctors or the state itself. For example, British officials revoked psychiatric pensions for the duration of hospital treatment. Issuing a replacement allowance, they made deductions from this payment if the veteran remained in hospital for more than five years. These deductions were more "severe than those made for any other type of patient in receipt of a treatment allowance."[83] Throughout the United Kingdom, the quality of treatment also varied depending on rank. Former officers could expect to receive care in private homes, and they could access their own financial resources, with the permission of an attending physician. In contrast, the other ranks generally received treatment at public institutions. Moreover, attending physicians could deny these patients access to their own finances indefinitely.[84] The British government failed to address these practices until the early 1970s, when the Ministry of Pensions and National Insurance reviewed its policies, only to discover that they did not meet modern standards.[85] As one civil servant bemoaned, "There [is] little internal consistency and some of our practices in terms of contemporary standards [are] not merely indefensible but positively offensive."[86]

Once released from hospital, psychologically disabled veterans encountered yet more obstacles in accessing vocational and industrial rehabilitation. Few government programs adequately addressed the challenges that mentally ill pensioners faced in returning to the civilian workforce. This meant that veterans often had to turn to private charities. These included groups such as the British Ex-Services Mental Welfare Society, which ran a residential scheme in Surrey, where patients could undergo occupational therapy and get other forms of counseling. In addition, they offered a small sheltered employment scheme, where they hired patients to "[assemble] cardboard boxes for blankets made by [company] Thermega Limited."[87] But specialized charities like this one remained rare. The group's small size meant that they could offer treatment and hope of recovery to only a limited number of individuals.[88]

It is hard to know just how many Commonwealth veterans secured a disability pension for psychological reasons following the Second World War.

Historians estimate that mental trauma accounted for approximately 10 percent of all disability claims lodged. It is even more difficult to establish the number of servicemen and women who did not come forward at all.[89] For many, the stigma associated with mental illness outweighed the benefits of seeking treatment, and, while some recovered and thrived, others struggled to leave the battlefields behind them. A former member of the Seaforth Highlanders of Canada, Charles Miller, suffered from nightmares of his experiences at the Battle of Ortona for years afterward. The memories were no less poignant and intrusive when he was an elderly man. Speaking to the *Memory Project* in 2010, he explained, "It's a horrible feeling and it'll always be there, I know it will. It's like a tattoo, it's on your brain and it'll never leave you."[90] One Australian veteran interviewed by historians in 2007 remembered not being able to settle down for years after the war, moving to more than thirty-five different towns.[91] Another recalled the continued struggle to communicate with his family: "I've got a chest full of medals and I don't think my family even know what they're for."[92] A veteran of Canada's Le Régiment de la Chaudière, Conrad Landry described his own struggle with postwar reintegration: "They marched us out to tell us that the Armistice had been signed. I didn't feel good. You can never be happy after something like that. I went to the Iles-de-la-Madeleine after the war. Nobody knew anything about that [the experience of war]. There was no doctor for that. They knew we had fought in the war. They knew that we had both our arms and legs. We were supposed to be fine. I have been depressed ever since then. I have never been able to be happy since those days, but I'm still alive."[93] The weight of stigma and social convention forced many veterans like Landry to deal with symptoms like depression and anxiety in a private way. Some took refuge at the bottom of a bottle and in other forms of destructive substance abuse.[94] The invisible scars of war irreversibly transformed countless lives and the generations to come. As Kristy Muir has argued in the *Australian Journal of Human Rights*, "the . . . implications of poor mental health transcend the individual, and affect families, communities and the nation."[95]

Britain, Canada, Australia, and New Zealand faced an unprecedented challenge in 1945: the demobilization and reintegration of millions of men and women in uniform. By all accounts, they succeeded in doing just that. Peter Neary has gone so far as to describe Canada's Veterans Charter as an "investment of unmatched success."[96] Across the Commonwealth, the "precise mechanisms differed [but] each government tended to craft a similar blend of financial reward, transitional funds, training/education provisions, employment support/advantages, access to loans for land or business development, disability pensions and other miscellaneous measures."[97] This facilitated access to property, education, and social mobility. Pensions and revolutionary medical care also allowed thousands of severely disabled veterans to rejoin the civilian workforce in spite of their injuries. Innovative social programs helped lay the foundations of the modern welfare state and build public expectations of the state's obligations to its citizens in peace and at war.

But the demobilization legacy of the Second World War is more complicated than it first appears. The pension system was more generous than ever before, but it remained difficult to access for the psychologically traumatized. Policymakers did not design compensation law or medical rehabilitation programs to respond to their needs. Most importantly, the pernicious idea that compensation only harmed veterans combined with the social stigma surrounding mental illness ensured that these men and women did not share in the benefits their fellow veterans so rightly enjoyed. Advancements in medicine and the liberalization of social attitudes have helped to change this for a younger generation. Increased investment in mental health programming over the past decade has also significantly improved the lives of psychologically scarred service personnel around the world. Nonetheless, the legacy of the Second World War continues to shape pensions and rehabilitation systems to this day. Faced with a new generation of veterans from Iraq and Afghanistan, policymakers will undoubtedly encounter the same challenges as their predecessors in creating better and more responsive systems to help veterans return home one step at a time.

Conclusion
The Many Dimensions of Mobilizing Military Manpower

Douglas E. Delaney and Andrew L. Brown

Defeating twentieth-century challengers to the British Empire and Commonwealth demanded careful management of military manpower. This was the problem that most vexed military planners from Whitehall to Wellington. Building big armies to meet big enemies was an exceptionally complex business because in August 1914 and again in September 1939 none of the empire's national armies had sufficient forces-in-being, even in aggregate, to fight the Germans or their allies. Britain, India, and the dominions all had to assemble, train, and maintain field formations without impairing their ability to arm, equip, and feed them, to say nothing of impinging on their capacity to put forces in the air and on the sea. The preceding chapters have examined a wide range of army manpower issues: putting enough citizens into uniform and training them; balancing army requirements against those of the other services, industry, and agriculture; sustaining public support for recruiting and conscription programs; demobilizing soldiers; and caring for veterans. During and immediately after the First World War, it all occurred on a scale that no one in 1914 saw coming, so manpower planning occurred in a reactive and fitful way. Even in 1939, very few anticipated the scale of the war to come, despite best attempts to limit liabilities; but at least the soldiers and statesmen of 1939 had the experience of 1914–1918 to inform manpower management when national commitments ballooned well beyond any limits authorities sought to impose. This time, governments knew that manpower allocation demanded interdepartmental planning and coordination with other British Commonwealth constituencies. This time, they understood that their nations could yield only so many men for the army without jeopardizing other national efforts or, in the case of Canada and South Africa, national unity. This time, they accepted in advance that going to war meant assuming liability for veterans' care that would last decades. And yet, it was still difficult to do, and there were still problems—so vast and complex was the management of national manpower in time of total war.

What observations can be made based on this collection of essays that has probed the three themes of recruitment and conscription, training and the soldier's experience, and demobilization and postwar care? One is that identities mattered, especially when it came to recruitment and voluntary enlistment. Jean Bou's chapter explains how imperial sentiment and a persistent sense of Britishness drew tens of thousands of volunteers to the Australian Imperial Force (AIF) in 1914–1915 and led the Commonwealth government to make commitments that were hard to maintain. Prime Minister William Morris "Billy" Hughes beat the drum in his country for a total war effort and even berated British officials for their supposed lack of backbone. Australia's First World War effort was impressive, even though Hughes twice failed to impose conscription by national plebiscite. Outsized ambitions did not prevent a country of fewer than 5 million citizens from putting five infantry and two mounted divisions in the field. It helped that a good proportion of the population of Australia comprised British immigrants or the descendants of recent immigrants from England, Scotland, Ireland, or Wales. Kent Fedorowich and Charles Booth explore that identity theme in their examination of British emigrants from the city of Bristol, who returned to fight for the empire as soldiers in the dominion armies. The proportion of British-born migrants in dominion armies was significant. One-half to two-thirds of the Canadian Expeditionary Force (CEF), for example, was British-born.

Appealing to distinct *communities* was part and parcel of the expansion of armies in war. Richard S. Grayson explains how the British Army tapped Irish pride, mobilizing "Irish" regiments and offering a chance to serve alongside kinsmen. This was essentially the only way to mobilize Irish manpower because the Military Service Act of 1916 exempted Irishmen from conscription for overseas service. The army even assembled divisions that made overt appeals to sectarian sentiments, drawing both unionists and nationalists to their ranks. To preserve the identity of Irish regiments, the army invoked policies to keep them filled with Irish soldiers—similar to practices for Scottish and Welsh units. Sometimes, communities were a class, as Gary Sheffield explains in his essay on the British Army's tendency to draw almost exclusively on the public-schooled upper class for officers—except when army expansion during the two World Wars forced authorities to look more to the middle class and, to a lesser extent, the working class for officers. The Indian Army, as Kaushik Roy explains, had long drawn recruits from the communities of supposedly "martial races"—Sikhs, Pathans, Gurkhas, and others. This policy, which endured until 1945, was based on the most dubious British reasoning that certain ethnic groups from the subcontinent's cooler and hillier regions possessed inherent military talent. British Indian authorities, as a result, had little room in the army for people from regions such as Bengal or Madras, where heat supposedly drained men of their martial spirit. Also unwelcome were the less-hearty urban dwellers and low-caste Indians who could tarnish the prestige of soldiering. Such narrow and blatantly racist policies might seem counterintuitive to raising large armies, but India's massive population allowed it to work. The martial communities were so populous and so impoverished that the Indian Army never wanted for enough recruits, and authorities, therefore, never had to reach deeper into the nation's "nonmartial" regions.

National affiliations and regional identities mattered in the dominions as well. Australia, Canada, New Zealand, and South Africa all raised "Irish" and "Scottish" regiments. Sometimes authorities appealed to a more local sense of identity. As Roger Sarty explains in his chapter, the Canadian Garrison Artillery raised forces for the CEF by appealing to the communities in which garrison artillery units had been stationed, places such as Halifax and Esquimalt. In raising batteries that represented cities and towns, the Canadian Garrison Artillery harnessed local pride, and that helped the dominion generate much larger artillery forces than the general staff had ever contemplated. None of this was new practice. City regiments had long been a tradition in Britain and in Canada, but extending the practice to specialist corps such as the artillery and engineers was a bit of a novelty. Ian van der Waag tells us how South African military authorities also recognized the attraction of district-based regiments that drew men in groups at a time during the Second World War. Appreciating that "regimental families" attracted recruits who wanted to serve with family and friends, the Union Defence Force (UDF) allowed South African men to serve in whatever units they wanted, wherever and whenever possible.

When the war effort demanded it, governments looked beyond traditional sources of manpower and took unorthodox measures. Paul Bartrop explains how the Australian Army trained "enemy alien" detainees to serve in eleven of thirty-nine labor companies, a measure designed to free up able-bodied Australians for the combat arms. This was a direct response to the threat of Japanese invasion in 1942. One company, the 8th Employment Company, comprised mostly Jewish Austrians and Germans, whom British authorities had rounded up in the United Kingdom and transported to Australia for internment. Anti-Jewish sentiment may have run high in Australia, but the Commonwealth profited from the hard work of these men, who were only too happy to assist in the defeat of Nazi Germany. Many even settled in Australia after the war. New Zealand also raised manpower from nontraditional sources. As Ian McGibbon explains, to free fit men for combat units, the New Zealand government, like all British Commonwealth governments, enacted measures to bring women into factories and create noncombatant women's auxiliary services for the armed forces. New Zealand authorities also conscripted Maori men to work in essential industries. While the country exempted Maori from conscription for military service, the army eagerly welcomed volunteers for an all-Maori unit, the 28th (Maori) Battalion. In the Union of South Africa, when there were insufficient white male volunteers for the fighting units and formations of the UDF, authorities tried to squeeze more of them out of noncombatant roles by enlisting women in auxiliary services and by placing black, coloured, and Asian volunteers in noncombatant jobs.

It is difficult to ignore what these manpower-scrounging measures implied about societal pecking orders. Decision-makers would not have dipped into these pools had the manpower demands of war not forced them to do so. They were expedient measures only, and they certainly did not reflect equality of status. Women in various auxiliary corps were paid far less than their male counterparts (60–80 percent), and nearly all of the women's services were disbanded within eighteen months of August 1945. This was commensurate with what happened on home fronts across the British Commonwealth, when women had to leave their factory jobs to make room for returning servicemen. In South Africa, black, coloured, and Asian men who had volunteered for noncombatant roles were not only demobilized in 1945, but also soon found themselves living under an apartheid regime erected by the National Party government of Daniel F. Malan (1948–1954). The mobilization of 2.5 million Indians for the war effort did not fundamentally change the composition of the Indian Army, which was still dominated by British officers who led soldiers recruited from the so-called martial races, while Hindus remained under-represented as a percentage of the army. Understanding how governments handled these matters yields important context for understanding postwar women's movements, the rise of the African National Congress (ANC), and the Indian independence movement.

It may not always have been fair, but governments at least had to appear even-handed in their handling of manpower mobilization during the Second

World War. As Jonathan Fennell argues, Britain and the dominions had to demonstrate to their populations that everyone had some stake in the war and that there would be fair treatment and compensation at the end of it—mostly because people were less deferential in 1939 than they had been in 1914. Governments had to convince potential and serving soldiers that the state would treat them fairly. When people were unconvinced of even-handedness in the war effort, fewer men came forward to fight, morale dropped among forces in the field, and national mobilization programs suffered. Thousands of furloughed New Zealand soldiers mutinied in 1943 when they returned home to find so many able-bodied countrymen safe in essential-industry jobs, enjoying the good life and high rates of pay. Many of the furloughed men sought medical exemptions to avoid returning to the Mediterranean. Some simply refused to go back. Many were court-martialed. In South Africa, when the government introduced a new oath that would allow for deployment outside of Africa, serving South African soldiers reacted with anger. They felt that they had already done their fair share, while others were still at home and profiting from a booming economy—much the same grievance as their New Zealand counterparts. The new oath was a bust in the end, and South Africa proved unable to mobilize enough soldiers to meet the government's military aims after 1942. The Union went from having two infantry divisions in the Mediterranean in 1942 to having one (much smaller) armored division in Italy by 1944. And in Canada, some of the 16,000 home defense conscripts designated to reinforce flagging infantry battalions in Europe staged sit-down strikes and protest parades in late 1944 because they objected to what they saw as the uneven conscription of the dominion's resources. Several thousand of these soldiers also absented themselves without leave and disappeared before the army could ship them overseas. Incidents like these made clear to governments across the British Commonwealth that they could not reach their mobilization goals without the consent of the mobilized. Fairness and recognition of service were important. This is why all governments announced plans for pensions, veterans' care, and benefits long before the Second World War was over.

They did a better job of that than they had done during the First World War. As Jessica Meyer explains in her chapter on British manpower conservation during and after the First World War, government authorities in the United Kingdom thought more in terms of returning wounded and disabled veterans to a state of self-reliance, so that they would be available for employment in industry and agriculture. Part of that was tied to the disincentive of difficult-to-get and low-paying disability pensions. It was not exactly fair recompense for sacrifice. By the time of the Second World War, though, countries across the British Commonwealth designed demobilization plans that were fairer than those offered the previous war's veterans. As Meghan Fitzpatrick explains, almost from the outset, governments planned demobilization schemes with "fairness" uppermost in mind. This time, soldiers came home to decent financial gratuities based on rank, time in service, and time overseas. Disability pensions were generous, far more so and easier to get than those offered their fathers, and they also came with ongoing health care benefits. Veterans also received low-interest loans for start-up businesses and farms, employment placement services, preferential hiring for government jobs, vocational training, and education programs. Benefits and terms of benefits varied a bit from country to county, but Britain and the dominions all offered a similar blend of packages.

These benefits and programs, designed to meet the expectations of a less-reverential soldiery, resulted from more careful manpower planning all around. In Britain, a subcommittee of the Committee of Imperial Defence began looking at manpower management, national service in particular, as early as 1920. The dominions took a little longer to take the matter seriously. New Zealand started planning to manage wartime manpower in 1936. When war broke out in 1939, as Ian McGibbon explains, structures and processes were in place for managing the dominion's total manpower requirements. Conscription legislation ensured enough men for the 2nd New Zealand Expeditionary Force (2NZEF) and the home defense army. A National Service Department managed manpower for both civilian and military purposes. In fact, even when the threat of Japanese invasion seemed highest, the dominion government prevented men and women from leaving employment in essential industries (presumably for the army) and redirected tens of thousands more into those critical industrial enterprises. The Canadian state also intervened dramatically to field larger armed forces than the dominion had ever known, as Daniel Byers tells us. Most of it stemmed from the National Resources Mobilization Act of June 1940, which gave the government full authority to "do and authorize such acts and things requiring persons to place themselves, their services and their property at the disposal of His Majesty in right of Canada."[1] The government soon announced national registration, conscription for home defense, and restrictions on military-age men working in industries deemed nonessential for the war effort. It also established women's divisions for each of the armed services and encouraged women to enter the civilian workforce, especially in essential industries. Canada's manpower management programs were not perfect, by any means—the dominion did wind up having to conscript men for overseas service in November 1944, despite earlier promises not to do so—but, as Byers reminds us, the soldiers and statesmen who managed the dominion's manpower faced exceptionally difficult problems for which there were no easy solutions. The dramatic expansion of the Canadian armed services after the catastrophic defeat of France in June 1940 and the unexpectedly high casualties in the summer and autumn of 1944 could not be resolved without cascading effects that touched all aspects of the national war effort. Even so, Canadians still managed to put 1 million of their 10 million citizens into uniform, all while producing war materiel and foodstuffs on an unprecedented scale.

The magnitude of national mobilizations makes it easy to forget that the great armies of the British Empire and Commonwealth comprised millions of individual servicemen and servicewomen. Their personal experiences and perspectives matter when nations mobilize mass armies because the people who are enticed, pressured, or compelled to serve undergo profound physical and psychological changes in the course of their transformation from civilian to fighting soldier, changes that are deliberate and have to be planned. Emma Newlands's essay on how the British army transformed raw civilians into soldiers during the Second World War helps us understand mobilization at the individual level. Basic training affected men physically and psychologically. The new recruit or conscript, always incapable of doing anything right for his instructors, felt the army strip away his civilian constitution and mindset and replace them with those of a soldier. He bulked up with good diet and hard physical training. Foot drill instilled unquestioning obedience. And battle training built up resilience to the traumatic sights and sounds of combat. Collectively, these measures instilled confidence and churned out soldiers who valued esprit de corps and operated as members of teams. Not everyone made it through, however. For some, the training was just too demanding. Many, as one soldier put it, "wish they'd never been born." Some of them, about 5 percent, were redirected to noncombatant roles, or even back to civilian life, where they probably did better working in industry or agriculture.

Maintaining large armies also necessitated careful consideration of how nations allocated and employed their available manpower. Jessica Meyer shows us why with her chapter on the conservation of British manpower in the First World War. As the war dragged on and as the British Expeditionary Force (BEF) grew well beyond its initial six divisions, the army strove to assign incoming soldiers to the arms or services for which they were best suited. The strong and the fit went to fighting units. The diminutive, the unfit, and the overaged—those unlikely to make good combat soldiers—went to noncombatant forces, such as the Royal Army Medical Corps (RAMC). So did others whose medical conditions precluded duty at the front, including men recovering from wounds or illness. These deliberate measures freed combat arms-fit RAMC men, whom the army "combed out" and sent to combatant units. Meanwhile, the RAMC geared its medical operations toward manpower conservation, which meant not only getting the sick and the wounded back to duty as quickly and efficiently as possible, but also practicing "preventative medicine"—enforcing good personal hygiene to prevent unnecessary wastage from conditions such as scabies and trench foot, for example.

While we hope that this volume takes a good step toward understanding how the British Empire and Commonwealth responded to the military manpower challenges of the two world wars, we also understand that it is in no way the final word on the matter. Much more needs to be done, and can be done, so we offer a few suggestions of still-dark areas where scholars might shed some light. Gary Sheffield's important essay on class in the British officer corps prompts questions about class in the other armies of the empire. Troops from the dominions often prided themselves for not having the overt class distinctions of the British Army, but class distinctions still existed, and we require a better appreciation for how things like education, wealth, and religion affected how nations used manpower to build up their armies. Kaushik Roy, Paul Bartrop, and Ian van der Waag demonstrate that authorities struggling to raise enough manpower called to the colors underprivileged segments of society and ethnic groups that they might not otherwise have called. Surely there is much more we can learn about how governments beckoned their indigenous and other minority communities, and how—or if—their responses altered the places of those groups in society. We know, for example, that the pre-1914 defense acts of South Africa and Australia specifically banned indigenous peoples from combat roles, and we fortunately have two important comparative studies on indigenous soldiers in the dominion armies by Timothy Winegard and by R. Scott Sheffield and Noah Riesman.[2] But we still do not know much about the indigenous subjects in the colonial empire. While there were some 2,580,000 British Empire fighting troops deployed around the globe in October 1918, there were also 560,000 native labor troops filling noncombat roles, a large portion them coming from the colonial empire in Africa, Asia, and the Caribbean.[3] Their stories need telling and could bear examination through the lens of race, the recent work of John C. Mitcham and Jesse Tumblin providing examples of how that might be done.[4] A comparative study of women's auxiliary services in the Second World War begs to be written. Finally, Meghan Fitzpatrick's chapter on veterans' care synthesizes how Britain, Canada, Australia, and New Zealand learned from the First World War and implemented much better rehabilitation and reintegration programs after 1945, but, as she also emphasizes, psychological disorders have received too little academic scrutiny. Surely, there remains room to study how various countries addressed, or did not address, the long-term challenges of mental trauma.

The subject of manpower offers numerous lines of inquiry, all of them worthy of scholarly attention. Raising manpower for the world wars was as much about calling for individual sacrifices as it was about war planning, and the full breadth and depth of the sacrifices made across the British Empire and Commonwealth are as fitting a subject for historical investigation as any other.

Notes

Introduction. Britain and the Military Manpower Problems of the Empire, 1900–1945

1. Memorandum on the Military Policy to be adopted in a War with Germany, 10 February 1903, War Office (WO) 106/46, The National Archives, Kew (TNA).

2. Military Needs of the Empire in a War with France and Russia, 10 August 1901, 48–49, Cabinet (CAB) 3/1, TNA.

3. See, for example, Douglas E. Delaney, *The Imperial Army Project: Britain and the Land Forces of the Dominions and India 1902–1945* (Oxford: Oxford University Press, 2017).

4. See, for example, David French, *The British Way in Warfare, 1688–2000* (London: Unwin Hyman, 1990).

5. H. M. D. Parker, *Manpower* (London: HMSO, 1957). The Interdepartmental Committee on National Service in a Future War became the Sub-Committee on Man-Power in 1924. On interwar efforts to maintain military compatibility, see Delaney, *Imperial Army Project*, 165–229.

6. War Office, *Statistics of the Military Effort of the British Empire during the Great War, 1914–1920* (London: HMSO, 1922), 62–63.

7. Douglas E. Delaney and Nikolas Gardner, eds., *Turning Point 1917: The British Empire at War* (Vancouver: University of British Columbia Press, 2017).

8. Tim Stapleton, "The Africanization of British Imperial Forces in the East African Campaign," in *Turning Point 1917: The British Empire at War*, ed. Douglas E. Delaney and Nikolas Gardner (Vancouver: University of British Columbia Press, 2017), 139–59.

9. John Crawford, "'The Willing Horse Is Being Worked to Death': New Zealand's Manpower Problems and Policies in 1917," in *Turning Point 1917: The British Empire at War*, ed. Douglas E. Delaney and Nikolas Gardner (Vancouver: University of British Columbia Press, 2017), 114–38.

10. The best source remains WO, *Statistics of the Military Effort of the British Empire*.

11. Keith Grieves, *The Politics of Manpower, 1914–1918* (Manchester: Manchester University Press, 1988); Peter Simkins, *Kitchener's Army: The Raising of the New Armies, 1914–1916* (Barnsley, South Yorkshire: Pen & Sword, 2007). See also Ian F. W. Beckett and Keith Simpson, eds., *A Nation in Arms: The British Army and the First World War* (Barnsley South Yorkshire: Pen & Sword, 2014).

12. A. J. K. Piggott, *Manpower Problems* (London: HMSO, 1949).

13. Parker, *Manpower*.

14. Jeremy A. Crang, *The British Army and the People's War, 1939–1945* (Manchester: Manchester University Press, 2000). See also Alan Allport, *Browned Off and Bloody-Minded: The British Soldier Goes to War, 1939–1945* (New Haven, CT: Yale University Press, 2015).

15. J. L. Granatstein and J. M. Hitsman, *Broken Promises: A History of Conscription in Canada* (Toronto: Oxford University Press, 1977); Richard Holt, *Filling the Ranks: Manpower in the Canadian Expeditionary Force, 1914–1918* (Montreal: McGill-Queen's University Press, 2017); and Daniel Byers, *Zombie Army: The Canadian Army and Conscription in the Second World War* (Toronto: University of British Columbia Press, 2016). See also Stephen Harris, *Canadian Brass: The Making of a Professional Army, 1860–1939* (Toronto: University of Toronto Press, 1988); James Woods, *Militia Myths: Ideas of the Canadian Citizen Soldier, 1896–1921* (Vancouver: University of British Columbia Press, 2010); Steve Marti and William John Pratt, eds., *Fighting with the Empire: Canada, Britain, and Global Conflict, 1867–1947* (Vancouver: University of British Columbia Press, 2019).

16. Ernest Scott, *The Official History of Australia in the War of 1914–1918*, vol. 11, *Australia during the War* (Sydney: Angus and Robertson, 1941); Gavin Long, David Dexter, Barton Maughan, Dudley Mccarthy, and Lionel Wigmore, *Australia in the War of 1939–1945: Series One—Army, Volumes I–VII* (Canberra: Australian War Memorial, 1952–1966).

17. Jeffrey Grey, *The Australian Army* (Melbourne: Oxford University Press, 2001); Albert Palazzo, *The Australian Army: A History of Its Organization, 1901–2001* (Melbourne: Oxford University Press, 2001); Joan Beaumont, ed., *Australia's War, 1914–1918* (Sydney: Allen & Unwin, 1995); Joan Beaumont, *Broken Nation: Australians in the Great War* (Sydney: Allen & Unwin, 2014).

18. Paul Baker, *King and Country Call: New Zealanders, Conscription, and the Great War* (Auckland: Auckland University Press, 1988); Crawford, "'The Willing Horse Is Being Worked to Death'"; and Major-General W. G. Stevens, *Official History of New Zealand in the Second World War, 1939–1945: Problems of 2 NZEF* (Wellington: War History Branch, 1958).

19. Ian van der Waag, *A Military History of Modern South Africa* (Johannesburg: Jonathan Ball, 2015); H. J. Martin and N. D. Orpen, *South Africa at War* (Cape Town: Purnell, 1979).

20. Kaushik Roy, ed., *The Indian Army in the Two World Wars* (Leiden: Brill, 2012); D. P. Marston, *Phoenix from the Ashes: The Indian Army in the Burma Campaign* (Westport, CT: Praeger Publishers, 2003); David Omissi, *The Sepoy and the Raj: The Indian Army, 1860–1940* (London: MacMillan, 1994); S. N. Prasad, *Expansion of the Armed Forces and Defence Organization, 1939–45* (Calcutta: Combined Inter-Services Historical Section, 1956); George Morton-Jack, *The Indian Empire at War: From Jihad to Victory, the Untold Story of the Indian Army in the First World War* (London: Little, Brown, 2018).

21. Julie Anderson, *War, Disability and Rehabilitation in Britain: "Soul of a Nation"* (Manchester: Manchester University Press, 2011); Deborah Cohen, *The War Come Home: Disabled Veterans in Great Britain and Germany, 1914–1939* (Berkeley: University

of California Press, 2001); Jeffrey S. Reznick, *Healing the Nation: Soldiers and the Culture of Caregiving in Britain during the Great War*, Cultural History of War Series (Manchester: Manchester University Press, 2011); Marina Larsson, *Shattered Anzacs: Living with the Scars of War* (Sydney: University of New South Wales Press, 2009); Alison Parr, *Silent Casualties: New Zealand's Unspoken Legacy of the Second World War* (Auckland, New Zealand: Tandem Press, 1995).

22. Jessica Meyer, *Men of War: Masculinity and the First World War in Britain* (London: Palgrave Macmillan, 2009); Edgar Jones and Simon Wessely, *Shell Shock to PTSD: Military Psychiatry from 1900 to the Gulf War* (New York: Psychology Press, 2005).

23. Serge Marc Durflinger, *Veterans with a Vision: Canada's War Blinded in Peace and War* (Vancouver: University of British Columbia Press, 2010).

24. Terry Copp and Mark Osborne Humphries, eds., *Combat Stress in the 20th Century: The Commonwealth Perspective* (Kingston, ON: Canadian Defence Academy Press, 2010). See also Mark Osborne Humphries, *A Weary Road: Shell Shock in the Canadian Expeditionary Force, 1914–1918* (Toronto: University of Toronto Press, 2018).

25. F. W. Perry, *The Commonwealth Armies: Manpower and Organisation in Two World Wars* (Manchester: Manchester University Press, 1988); Roger Broad, *Volunteers and Pressed Men: How Britain and Its Empire Raised Its Forces in Two World Wars* (Croydon, UK: Fonthill, 2016); Steve Marti, *For Home and Empire: Voluntary Mobilization in Australia, Canada, and New Zealand during the First World War* (Vancouver: University of British Columbia Press, 2019).

26. Narrative covering aspects of work as adjutant-general, WWII, chap. 1, Manpower, ts [Typescript] 1960, Papers of General Sir Ronald Forbes Adam, ADAM 3 / 13, Liddell Hart Centre for Military Archives (LHCMA) King's College London.

1. The Government That Could Not Say No and Australia's Military Effort, 1914–1918

1. For more on the militias systems before the war, see Craig Wilcox, *Hearths and Homes: Citizen Soldiering in Australia, 1854–1945* (St. Leonards, NSW: Allen & Unwin, 1998).

2. The most recent examination of the AN&MEF is found in Robert Stevenson, *The War with Germany* (South Melbourne: Oxford University Press, 2015).

3. For more detail on the AIF's expansion, see Jean Bou and Peter Dennis, *The Centenary History of Australia and the Great War*, vol. 5, *The Australian Imperial Force* (South Melbourne: Oxford University Press, 2016) 13–17, 27–31. There were several divisional reorganizations for the mounted troops in Egypt / Palestine but space precludes more detail here.

4. Bou and Dennis, *The Australian Imperial Force*, 17.

5. Robert Stevenson, *To Win the Battle: The 1st Australian Division in the Great War, 1914–1918* (Port Melbourne: Cambridge University Press, 2013), 92–93.

6. Charles Bean, *Official History of Australia in the War of 1914–1918*, vol. 3, *The Australian Imperial Force in France, 1916* (Sydney: Angus and Robertson, 1941), 49–52. Hereafter the volumes of the Australian Official History will be referred to by the abbreviation *AOH*.

7. Stevenson, *To Win the Battle*, 92–93.

8. Resulting in 5,500 casualties, the battle of Fromelles remains the bloodiest single day in Australian military history; Stevenson, *To Win the Battle*, 92–93. See also Roger Lee, *The Battle of Fromelles, 1916* (Canberra: Australian Army History Unit, 2010).

9. For a recent examination of the Australian experience of military adaptation, see Jean Bou, ed., *The AIF in Battle, How the Australian Imperial Force Fought, 1914–1918* (Melbourne: Melbourne University Press, 2016).

10. Birdwood had taken temporarily taken over command of the AIF upon Bridges's death in 1915 and then held it on and off through 1915–1916; Bou and Dennis, *The Australian Imperial Force*, 47–49.

11. Geoffrey Serle, "McCay, Sir James Whiteside (1864–1930)," *Australian Dictionary of Biography* (National Centre of Biography, Australian National University, 1986), accessed 8 April 2019, http://adb.anu.edu.au/biography/mccay-sir-james-whiteside-7312/text12683.

12. Chris Clark, "Legge, James Gordon (1863–1947)," *Australian Dictionary of Biography*, accessed 8 April 2019, http://adb.anu.edu.au/biography/legge-james-gordon-7160/text12367.

13. Clark, "Legge, James Gordon."

14. Bou and Dennis, *The Australian Imperial Force*, 48, 56.

15. Ernest Scott, *The Official History of Australian in the war 1914–1918*, volume 11, *Australian During the War*, (Sydney: Angus & Roberston, 1941), 871–72. (hereafter *AOH*, 11).

16. Scott, *AOH*, 11:871–72. Joan Beaumont, *Australian Defence: Sources and Statistics* (South Melbourne: Oxford University Press, 2001), 111.

17. Scott, *AOH*, 11:871–72.

18. Scott, *AOH*, 11:871–72.

19. All recruiting figures are taken from Scott, *AOH*, 11:871–72.

20. The division was eventually required to give up men. Joan Beaumont, *Broken Nation* (Crows Nest, NSW: Allen and Unwin, 2013), 147, 221; Bean, *AOH*, 3:867–68.

21. Beaumont, *Broken Nation*, 374–75.

22. Beaumont, *Broken Nation*, 416; Scott, *AOH*, 11:872. These two citations aside, a similar outline of the manpower situation, drawing on some of the same sources as this study, can be found in F. W. Perry, *The Commonwealth Armies: Manpower and Organisation in Two World Wars* (Manchester: Manchester University Press, 1988), 151–59.

23. Perry, *The Commonwealth Armies*, p. 155.

24. This section on recruiting is based on various reports and correspondence contained in the Australian War Memorial, Australian War Memorial (AWM) series 27, 533/28 and (AWM) series 38, 3DRL, 6673/169 pt. 1.

25. This section is based on a consideration of the ideas put forward in John Donovan, "The Over-Expansion of the AIF in 1916—Effects and Possible Alternatives Then, Implications Now," *Sabretache* 55, no. 3 (2014): 4–19. See also Perry, *The Commonwealth Armies*, 158–59, where he too outlines some of the problems associated with manpower and speculates about the inevitability of reductions in the AIF's divisions if the war had gone into 1919. These two sources and this author's consideration of the matter in Bou and Dennis, *The Australian Imperial Force*, largely constitute the attention given to the topic of the AIF's size, which deserves more thought.

26. Conscription in Australia has an extensive historiography. For two recent treatments of the issue and the associated politics see Beaumont, *Broken Nation*, and John Connor, Peter Stanley, and Peter Yule, *The Centenary History of Australia and the Great War*, vol. 4, *The War at Home* (South Melbourne: Oxford University Press, 2015).

27. This fifth mounted brigade was not a complete one and there were only enough Australians available to form two of the required three regiments. The machine gun squadron was established by disbanding New Zealand's two camel companies, and the brigade's third regiment was made up by using a French colonial cavalry regiment. Jean Bou, *Light Horse: A History of Australia's Mounted Arm* (Port Melbourne: Cambridge University Press 2010), 188–90.

28. Charles Bean, *Official History of Australia in the War 1914–1918*, volume 6, *The AIF in France, May 1918–The Armistice* (Sydney: Angus & Roberston, 1942,1098 (hereafter *AOH*, 6). Total male population is an imperfect measure compared to "eligible males" of the right age, but this was the official history's unit of measure and the figure most readily available. The 1915 War Census identified 600,000 "fit" men between the ages of eighteen and forty-four; Beaumont, *Broken Nation*, 148.

29. Bean, *AOH*, 6:1098. Bean offers a figure of 458,218 Canadians sent overseas or in training as of 1 November 1918.

30. Shane B. Schreiber, *Shock Army of the British Empire: The Canadians in the Last 100 Days of the Great War* (Westport, CT: Praeger, 1997), 21.

31. These figures are from Bean, *AOH*, 6:1098. The New Zealand government's historical website gives a figure of 98,950 men who served overseas. The New Zealand Expeditionary Force's (NZEF's) total enlistments are more obscure due to the character of its call up system. See Ministry for Culture and Heritage, "First World War by the Numbers," accessed 5 May 2019, https://nzhistory.govt.nz/war/first-world-war-by -numbers#q1. The postwar official New Zealand outline of the nation's contribution to the war gives a figure of 124,211men "mobilized," with 110,368 embarked for overseas. See Chief of the General Staff, Headquarters, New Zealand Military Forces, *New Zealand Expeditionary Force, Its Provision and Maintenance*, 1919, 45, accessed 5 May 2019, https:// nzhistory.govt.nz/files/documents/ww1-stats/provision-and-maintenance.pdf.

32. Chief of the General Staff, *New Zealand Expeditionary Force*, 3–6.

33. "New Zealand Expeditionary Force," in *The Oxford Companion to New Zealand Military History*, ed. Ian McGibbon (Auckland: Oxford University Press, 2000), 366.

34. Bean, *AOH*, 3: 32.

35. Beaumont, *Broken Nation*, 146–47.

36. Bean, *AOH*, 3: 862–64.

37. The official history alludes to a connection between Birdwood's ambition for an Australasian army and safeguarding the 3rd Division from disbandment in 1916. Bean, *AOH*, 3: 864.

38. Beaumont, *Broken Nation*, 146–48.

39. Connor, Stanley, and Yule, *The Centenary History of Australia and the Great War*, 4:106–9.

40. One might speculate, however, that they missed a moment to introduce conscription in late 1915 or early 1916, before the costly battle of the Somme, which almost certainly helped the "no" vote.

2. Irish Identities in the British Army during the First World War

1. Thomas Bartlett and Keith Jeffery, "An Irish Military Tradition?," in *A Military History of Ireland*, ed. Thomas Bartlett and Keith Jeffery (Cambridge: Cambridge University Press, 1996), 2 1–25.

2. Terence Denman, "The Catholic Irish Soldier in the First World War: The 'Racial Environment,'" *Irish Historical Studies* 27, no. 108 (1991): 353.

3. Bartlett and Jeffery, "Irish Military Tradition," 1–2.

4. Cited in Keith Jeffery, "The Irish Military Tradition and the British Empire," in *An Irish Empire? Aspects of Ireland and the British Empire*, ed. Keith Jeffery (Manchester: Manchester University Press, 1996), 103.

5. Bartlett and Jeffery, "Irish Military Tradition," 8–12, 18–20.

6. Dan Harvey, *The Irish at Waterloo* (Cork: H Books, 2015), xi. See also Terence Denman, "'Hibernia Officina Militum': Irish Recruitment to the British Regular Army, 1660–1815," *Irish Sword* 20 (1996): 148–66.

7. E. M. Spiers, "Army Organization and Society in the Nineteenth Century," in *A Military History of Ireland*, ed. Thomas Bartlett and Keith Jeffery (Cambridge: Cambridge University Press, 1996), 335–37.

8. David Fitzpatrick, "Militarism in Ireland, 1900–1922," in *A Military History of Ireland*, ed. Thomas Bartlett and Keith Jeffery (Cambridge: Cambridge University Press, 1996), 380–401.

9. Fitzpatrick, "Militarism," 381; *Census of Ireland, 1911. General Report, Cd. 6663* (London: HMSO, 1913), xviii; Richard S. Grayson, *Dublin's Great Wars: The First World War, the Easter Rising and the Irish Revolution* (Cambridge: Cambridge University Press, 2018), 13.

10. David French, *Military Identities: The Regimental System, the British Army, & the British People c. 1870–2000* (Oxford: Oxford University Press, 2005), 10–30; Tom Johnstone, *Orange, Green & Khaki: The Story of the Irish Regiments in the Great War, 1914–18* (Dublin: Gill & Macmillan, 1992), 4.

11. "The Inniskilling Dragoons, a Brief History," The Inniskillings Museum, accessed 6 June 2018, http://www.inniskillingsmuseum.com/the-inniskilling-dragoons-a-brief-history/; J. A. d'Avigdor-Goldsmid, *Short History of the 4th Royal Irish Dragoon Guards 1685–1922, 7th (Princess Royal's) Dragoon Guards 1688–1922, 4th/7th Royal Dragoon Guards 1922–1939* (Aldershot: Gale & Polden, 1949), 1; J. R. Harvey, *The History of The 5th (Royal Irish) Regiment of Dragoons from 1689–1799, Afterwards the 5th Royal Irish Lancers from 1858 to 1921* (Aldershot: Gale & Polden, 1923), 146; "Unit History: King's Royal Irish Hussars," Forces War Records, accessed 6 June 2018, https://www.forces-war-records.co.uk/units/1712/kings-royal-irish-hussars/; William Butler, *The Irish Amateur Military Tradition in the British Army, 1854–1992* (Manchester: Manchester University Press, 2016), 28.

12. Jeffery, "The Irish Military Tradition and the British Empire," 105–14.

13. John Morrissey, "A Lost Heritage: The Connaught Rangers and Multivocal Irishness," in *Ireland's Heritage: Critical perspectives on Memory and Identity*, ed. Mark McCarthy. (Aldershot: Ashgate, 2005), 72.

14. Fitzpatrick, "Militarism," 386, 388.

15. The 1st Dublins, 1st Inniskillings, and 1st Munsters deployed to Gallipoli in April 1915.

16. Grayson, *Dublin's Great Wars*, 34.

17. Stephen Sandford, *Neither Unionist nor Nationalist: The 10th (Irish) Division in the Great War* (Dublin: Irish Academic Press, 2015), 35–36, 40; David Fitzpatrick, "The Logic of Collective Sacrifice: Ireland and the British Army, 1914–1918," *Historical Journal* 38, no. 4 (1995): 1017–1030.

18. "10th (Irish) Division," The Long, Long Trail, accessed 4 June 2018, http://www.longlongtrail.co.uk/army/order-of-battle-of-divisions/10th-irish-division/.

19. *Dublin Evening Mail*, 11 September 1914, 2.

20. Sandford, *Neither Unionist nor Nationalist*, 13–14.

21. Sandford, *Neither Unionist nor Nationalist*, 16–20.

22. Timothy Bowman, "Officering Kitchener's Armies: A Case Study of the 36th (Ulster) Division," *War in History* 16, no. 2 (2009): 189–212; Geoffrey Lewis, *Carson: The Man Who Divided Ireland* (London: Continuum, 2005), 168–69; Timothy Bowman, *Carson's Army: The Ulster Volunteer Force, 1910–22* (Manchester: Manchester University Press, 2007), 174–75.

23. Bowman, *Carson's Army*, 179.

24. Richard S. Grayson, *Belfast Boys: How Unionists and Nationalists Fought and Died Together in the First World War* (London: Continuum, 2009), 35–36.

25. Richard S. Grayson, "Beyond the Ulster Division: West Belfast Members of the Ulster Volunteer Force and Service in the First World War," in *Remembering 1916: The Easter Rising, the Somme and the Politics of Memory in Ireland*, ed. Richard S. Grayson and Fearghal McGarry (Cambridge: Cambridge University Press, 2016), 112–37; Bowman, *Carson's Army*, 173.

26. Keith Jeffery, *Ireland and the Great War* (Cambridge: Cambridge University Press, 2000), 39, 56.

27. *Irish News*, 21 September 1914, 5; Charles Hannon, "The Irish Volunteers and the Concepts of Military Service and Defence, 1913–24" (unpublished PhD dissertation, University College Dublin, 1989), 82–101.

28. Hannon, "Irish Volunteers," 105; National Library of Ireland (NLI), Redmond MS 15, 258: Irish National Volunteers' Strength on 31 October 1914; Terence Denman, *Ireland's Unknown Soldiers* (Dublin: Irish Academic Press, 1992), 38.

29. Terence Denman, "'The Red Livery of Shame': The Campaign against Army Recruitment in Ireland, 1899–1914," *Irish Historical Studies* 29, no. 114 (1994): 208–33.

30. Denman, *Ireland's Unknown Soldiers*, 50–51.

31. John Strachan and Claire Nally, *Advertising, Literature and Print Culture in Ireland, 1891–1922* (Basingstoke: Palgrave, 2012), 206–209 and 212–215.

32. Mark Tierney, Paul Bowen and David Fitzpatrick, "Recruiting Posters," in *Ireland and the First World War*, ed. David Fitzpatrick (Dublin: Trinity College History Workshop, 1988), 47, 50.

33. Tierney, Bowen, Fitzpatrick, "Recruiting Posters," 53, 55.

34. Nuala Johnson, *Ireland, the Great War and the Geography of Remembrance* (Cambridge: Cambridge University Press, 2003), 28–34, 38–53. On nationalists in posters see National Library of Ireland Catalogue, accessed 4 June 2018, http://catalogue.nli.ie/Record/vtls000019673; South Dublin County Libraries, accessed 3 September 2020, http://catalogue.nli.ie/Record/vtls000019673.

35. National Library of Ireland Catalogue, accessed 4 June 2018, http://catalogue.nli.ie/Record/vtls000023826.

36. South Dublin County Libraries, accessed 4 June 2018, http://source.south dublinlibraries.ie/handle/10599/8954.

37. *London Gazette*, 16 February 1915, 1700.

38. Cited in Denman, "The Catholic Irish Soldier," 355.

39. Ibid.

40. Denman, "The Catholic Irish Soldier," 363–64; Jeffery, "The Irish Military Tradition and the British Empire," 104–5.

41. Jeffery, *Ireland and the Great War*, 6–8, 18; Fitzpatrick, "Logic of Collective Sacrifice," 1020; Patrick Callan, "Recruiting for the British Army in Ireland during the First World War," *Irish Sword* 17 (1987): 42–56.

42. Fitzpatrick, "Logic of Collective Sacrifice," 1017.

43. Fitzpatrick, "Logic of Collective Sacrifice," 1023–24.

44. Fitzpatrick, "Logic of Collective Sacrifice," 1025–29.

45. Butler, *Irish Amateur Military Tradition*, 84–87.

46. Grayson, *Belfast Boys*, 10.

47. Sandford, *Neither Unionist nor Nationalist*, 37.

48. Bowman, *Carson's Army*, 173, 177.

49. Timothy Bowman, William Butler, and Michael Wheatley, *The Disparity of Sacrifice: Irish Recruitment to the British Armed Forces, 1914–1918* (Liverpool: Liverpool University Press, 2020), 219–225.

50. "History—1859 to Present," London Irish Rifles Association, accessed 7 June 2018, https://www.londonirishrifles.com/index.php/regimental-history/history-1859-to -present/.

51. "Frank Edwards," Playing the Game, last modified 17 June 2014, https://www .ww1playingthegame.org.uk/content/soldiers/frank-edwards.

52. "King's (Liverpool Regiment)," The Long, Long Trail, accessed 7 June 2018, http://www.longlongtrail.co.uk/army/regiments-and-corps/the-british-infantry -regiments-of-1914-1918/kings-liverpool-regiment/.

53. "Northumberland Fusiliers," The Long, Long Trail, accessed 7 June 2018, http://www.longlongtrail.co.uk/army/regiments-and-corps/the-british-infantry -regiments-of-1914-1918/northumberland-fusiliers/.

54. Cited in John Sheen, *Tyneside Irish: 24th, 25th, 26th & 27th (Service) Battalions of the Northumberland Fusiliers. A History of the Tyneside Irish Brigade Raised in the North East in World War One* (Barnsley: Pen & Sword, 1998), 17.

55. Cited in Sheen, *Tyneside Irish*, 21.

56. Cited in Sheen, *Tyneside Irish*, p. 23.

57. Sheen, *Tyneside Irish*, 33.

58. "Lives of the First World War," Imperial War Museum, accessed 1 June 2018, https://www.iwm.org.uk/lives-of-the-first-world-war.

59. Grayson, "Beyond the Ulster Division," 112–19; Somme Association, accessed 8 June 2018, http://www.irishsoldier.org/.

60. *Irish Independent*, 22 May 1915, 3; *Evening Herald*, 25 May 1915, 2.

61. Cited in Henry Hanna, *The Pals at Suvla Bay: Being the Record of "D" Company of the 7th Royal Dublin Fusiliers* (Dublin: Ponsonby, 1917), 76.

62. *Freeman's Journal*, 21 August 21, 1916, 7.

63. *Freeman's Journal*, 9 March 1917, 6.

64. *The Foggy Dew*, BBC, accessed 20 June 2016, http://www.bbc.co.uk/history /british/easterrising/songs/rs_song06.shtml; David Cooper, *The Musical Traditions of Northern Ireland and Its Diaspora: Community and Conflict* (Farnham: Ashgate, 2009), 129.

65. *Freeman's Journal*, 9 September 1916, 5; 11 September 1916, 5; 12 September 1916, 5; 13 September 1916, 5; 14 September 1915, 5.

66. Denman, "The Catholic Irish Soldier," 355–56.

67. Richard S. Grayson, ed., *At War with the 16th Irish Division, 1914–1918: The Staniforth Letters* (Barnsley: Pen & Sword, 2012), 127. See also Denman, "The Catholic Irish Soldier," 356.

68. 36th Division General Staff Diary, War Office (WO) 95/2491, The National Archives (Kew) (TNA).

69. 9th Royal Inniskilling Fusiliers War Diary, WO 95/2510, TNA.

70. *Belfast Telegraph*, 30 June 1966, 11.

71. Bartlett and Jeffery, "Irish Military Tradition," 18.

72. 9th Royal Inniskilling Fusiliers War Diary.

73. Cited in Philip Orr, *The Road to the Somme: Men of the Ulster Division Tell Their Story* (Belfast: Blackstaff Press, 1987), 166.

74. *Belfast Evening Telegraph*, 30 June 1917, 5; *Belfast News Letter*, 2 July 1917, 8; 1 July 1918, 3; 2 July 1918, 2.

75. Gillian McIntosh, *The Force of Culture: Unionist Identities in Twentieth-Century Ireland* (Cork: Cork University Press, 1999), 15–16. See also Kris Brown, "'Our Father Organization': The Cult of the Somme and the Unionist 'Golden Age' in Modern Ulster Loyalist Commemoration," *Round Table* 96, no. 393 (2007): 707–23; Brian Graham and Peter Shirlow, "The Battle of the Somme in Ulster Memory and Identity," *Political Geography* 21, no. 7 (2002): 881–904.

76. Richard S. Grayson, "Ireland's New Memory of the First World War: Forgotten Aspects of the Battle of Messines, June 1917," *British Journal for Military History* 1, no. 1 (2014): 49–52.

77. "Remarks by President Mary McAleese at Reception on Occasion of the Inauguration," President of Ireland, 11 November 1998, https://www.president.ie/en /media-library/speeches/remarks-by-president-mary-mcaleese-at-reception-on -occasion-of-the-inaugura.

78. *Irish Times*, 12 June 1917, 5.

79. *Dublin Evening Mail*, 9 June 1917, 3.

80. Grayson, "Ireland's New Memory of the First World War," 64–65; Grayson, *Belfast Boys*, 103.

81. Terence Denman, *A Lonely Grave: The Life and Death of William Redmond* (Blackrock: Irish Academic Press, 1995).

82. *Saturday Herald*, 9 June 1917, 1; *Evening Telegraph*, 11 June 1917, 3; *Freeman's Journal*, 11 June 1917, 4, 5; *Evening Telegraph*, 13 June 1917, 1; 22 June 1917, 3.

83. *Freeman's Journal*, 9 June 1917, 5.

84. Joseph Finnan, "'Let Irishmen Come Together in the Trenches': John Redmond and Irish Party Policy in the Great War, 1914–1918," *Irish Sword* 22, no. 87 (2000–2001): 174–92.

85. Nicholas Perry, "Nationality in the Irish Infantry Regiments in the First World War," *War and Society* 12, no. 1 (1994): 65–95.

86. Grayson, "Ireland's New Memory of the First World War," 53–64.

87. Rowland Feilding, *War Letters to a Wife: France and Flanders, 1915–1919* (Staplehurst: Spellmount, 2001 [1929]), 107; Timothy Bowman, *Irish Regiments in the Great War: Discipline and Morale* (Manchester: Manchester University Press, 2003), 154–55; Denman, *Ireland's Unknown Soldiers*, 150.

88. Grayson, *Belfast Boys*, 103.

89. Terence Denman, "The 16th (Irish) Division on 21st March 1918: Fight or Flight?," *Irish Sword* 17 (1990): 273–87.

90. Gary Sheffield and John Bourne, eds., *Douglas Haig: War Diaries and Letters, 1914–1918* (London: Weidenfeld & Nicolson, 2005), 390.

91. Denman, "The Catholic Irish Soldier," 357–361; Bowman, *Irish Regiments in the Great War*, 202.

92. Denman, "The 16th (Irish) Division on 21st March 1918," 287. See also Lynn Speer Lemisko, "Morale in the 16th (Irish) Division, 1916–1918," *Irish Sword* 20 (1997): 217–233; Denman, *Ireland's Unknown Soldiers*, 168–69; Keith Jeffery, *Field Marshal Sir Henry Wilson: A Political Soldier* (Oxford: Oxford University Press, 2006), 222–223; and Johnstone, *Orange, Green & Khaki*, 390.

93. Perry, "Nationality in the Irish Infantry Regiments," 65–95; Nicholas Perry, "Maintaining Regimental Identity in the Great War: The Case of the Irish Infantry Regiments," *Stand To!* 52 (1998): 5–11.

94. Grayson, *Dublin's Great Wars*, 340–41, 344–45.

3. Conserving British Manpower during and after the First World War

1. War Office, *Royal Army Medical Corps Training Manual* (London: HMSO, 1911), 1.

2. J. M. Winter, *The Great War and the British People* (Basingstoke: Macmillan, 1985), 49.

3. Winter, *The Great War and the British People*, 49–50.

4. Winter, *The Great War and the British People*, 50.

5. Winter, *The Great War and the British People*, 59.

6. Peter Simkins, *Kitchener's Army: The Raising of the New Armies, 1914–16* (Manchester: Manchester University Press, 1988), 178–80.

7. Jessica Meyer, *Men of War: Masculinity and the First World War in Britain* (Basingstoke: Palgrave Macmillan, 2009), 101.

8. Winter, *The Great War and the British People*, 53.

9. Adrian Gregory, *The Last Great War: British Society and the First World War* (Cambridge: Cambridge University Press, 2008), 101–8; James McDermott, *British Military Service Tribunals, 1916–1918: 'A Very Much Abused Body of Men'* (Manchester: Manchester University Press, 2011), 15.

10. Winter, *The Great War and the British People*, 154.

11. Winter, *The Great War and the British People*, 155.

12. Ian Whitehead, *Doctors in the Great War* (Barnsley: Pen & Sword, 2013[1999]), 252–53.

13. For a full discussion of these relationships, see Jessica Meyer, *An Equal Burden: The Men of the Royal Army Medical Corps in the First World War* (Oxford: Oxford University Press, 2019), chap. 1.

14. John S. G. Blair, *In Arduis Fidelis: Centenary History of the Royal Army Medical Corps* (Edinburgh: Scottish Academic Press, 1998), 78.

15. After the introduction of conscription in 1916, those appealing conscription on grounds of conscience could be offered the option of noncombatant service with volunteer units such as the Friends Ambulance Unit. These units were administered by the Red Cross rather than directly by the War Office. Meyer, *An Equal Burden*, 70–1.

16. W. G. Macpherson, *History of the Great War Based on Official Documents,* Vol. 1: *Medical Services General History* (London: HMSO, 1921), 138.

17. Macpherson, *History of the Great War,* 1: 27.

18. Macpherson, *History of the Great War,* 50.

19. Mark Harrison, *The Medical War: British Military Medicine in the First World War* (Oxford: Oxford University Press, 2010), 26.

20. P. J. S. O'Grady, "The Organization and Uses of a Motor Ambulance Convoy," *Journal of the Royal Army Medical Corps* (69: 3 1937): 168.

21. Harrison, *The Medical War,* 124–142.

22. MacPherson, *History of the Great War,* 1:138.

23. G. H. Swindell, "In Arduis Fidelus: Being the Story of 4½ Years in the Royal Army Medical Corps," ms. memoir, n.d., 1, RAMC 421, Wellcome Library, London.

24. J. B. Bennett, "Memories of Gallipoli, August 1915–December 1915 at Suvla Bay and Anzac," ts. memoir, 1–2, Papers of J. B. Bennett, LIDDLE/WW1/GS/0119), Liddle Collection, University of Leeds.

25. Simkins gives the counterexample of Eric Wainright, a trainee pharmacist who attempted to enlist with the RAMC and was rejected as too short before enlisting with the 4th King's Own Yorkshire Light Infantry. This example, however, reflects more on the chaotic nature of enlistment in the early days of the war than on the specific requirements of RAMC recruitment policy. Simkins, *Kitchener's Army,* 180.

26. Macpherson, *History of the Great War,* 1:138.

27. Macpherson, *History of the Great War,* 1:138.

28. Winter, *The Great War and the British People,* 41.

29. MacPherson, *History of the Great War,* 1:139. An exception to this trend occurred in the summer of 1918, when 6,700 men from the highest national service group were posted to the RAMC.

30. MacPherson, *History of the Great War,* 1:138.

31. Edward Madigan, *Faith under Fire: Anglican Army Chaplains and the Great War* (Basingstoke: Palgrave Macmillan, 2011), 45–46, 48. Madigan points out that only a small percentage of the 600 Church of England clergymen who applied for commissions as military chaplains in the first three months of the war were successful, leaving many to seek noncombatant service elsewhere.

32. Macpherson, *History of the Great War,* 1:138.

33. MacPherson, *History of the Great War,* 1:140.

34. MacPherson, *History of the Great War,* 1: 140.

35. "Notes from Old Friends," *'Southern' Cross: The Monthly Journal of the 1ˢᵗ Southern General Hospital, Birmingham* 1 (June 1916): 148; "Obituary: Private Edward Guy," *'Southern' Cross* 2 (October 1917): 254; "Obituary: Private W. F. Prince," *'Southern' Cross* 3 1918): 44; "Obituary: Private C. T. Hillman," *'Southern' Cross* 3 (1918): 81; "Obituary: Private R. T. Astell," *'Southern' Cross* 3 (1918): 143; "Obituary: Private W. H. Jones," *'Southern' Cross* 3 (1918): 144.

36. "History of the 1st Southern General Hospital," *'Southern' Cross* 2 (July 1917): 166–67. The enlistment of women was also used as a strategy in relation to auxiliary

medical units such as mobile laboratories and base hospitals overseas. For further discussion of the significance of this strategy for the make-up of the RAMC, see Meyer, *An Equal Burden*, chap. 2.

37. Ward Muir, *Observations of an Orderly: Some Glimpses of Life and Work in an English War Hospital* (London: Simpkin, Marshall, Hamilton, Kent & Co., Ltd., 1917), 152.

38. Ana Carden-Coyne, *The Politics of Wounds: Military Patients and Medical Power in the First World War* (Oxford: Oxford University Press, 2014), 52–55.

39. Harrison, *The Medical War*, 63.

40. Jeffrey Reznick, *Healing the Nation: Soldiers and the Culture of Caregiving in Britain during the Great War* (Manchester: Manchester University Press, 2004), 99–112.

41. Harrison, *The Medical War*, 124.

42. Joanna Bourke, *Dismembering the Male: Men's Bodies, Britain and the Great War* (London: Reaktion Books, 1996), 89–94.

43. Wilfred Owen, *The Dead-Beat* (London: Chatto and Windus, 1917), 15–19.

44. Mark VII [Max Plowman], *A Subaltern on the Somme in 1916* (London: J. M. Dent & Sons, 1927), 52.

45. Whitehead, *Doctors in the Great War*, 156.

46. Ben Shephard, *A War of Nerves: Soldiers and Psychiatrists, 1914–1994* (London: Pimlico, 2002), 46–56.

47. Harrison, *The Medical War*, 295. See also Christine Hallett, *Containing Trauma: Nursing Work in the First World War* (Manchester: Manchester University Press, 2009), 53.

48. Susan Pedersen, *Family, Dependence and the Origins of the Welfare State: Britain and France, 1914–1945* (Cambridge: Cambridge University Press, 1993), 108–15. The most significant of the welfare benefits introduced to encourage enlistment was probably the separation allowance, which assured men that the state would continue to act as economic head of household during their period of service.

49. Helen Bettinson, "'Lost Souls in the House of Restoration'?: British Ex-Servicemen and War Disability Pensions, 1914–1930," (PhD dissertation, University of East Anglia, 2002), 83–92; Harrison, *The Medical War*, 301; Fiona Reid, *Medicine in First World War Europe: Soldiers, Medics, Pacifists* (London: Bloomsbury Academic, 2017), 191–98.

50. Peter Barham, *Forgotten Lunatics of the Great War* (New Haven, CT: Yale University Press, 2004), 211–21.

51. Bourke, *Dismembering the Male*, 67.

52. John Galsworthy, foreword to *The Inter-Allied Conference on the After-Care of Disabled Men (Second Annual Meeting, Held in London, May 20 to 25): Reports Presented to the Conference (by Various Authors)* (London: HMSO, 1918), 14–15, quoted in Reznick, *Healing the Nation*, 116.

53. Application for Alternative Retired Pay, 25 August 1921, PIN 26/21230, The National Archives (TNA); J. L. Campbell-White, letter to Ministry of Pensions, 2 November 1920, PIN 26/19930, TNA.

54. Reid, *Medicine in First World War Europe*, 198.

4. The Canadian Garrison Artillery Goes to War, 1914–1918

1. This chapter builds on Lee Windsor, Roger Sarty, and Marc Milner, *Loyal Gunners: 3rd Field Artillery Regiment (The Loyal Company) and the History of New Brunswick's*

Artillery, 1893–2012 (Waterloo, ON: Wilfrid Laurier University Press, 2016). I am indebted to Lee and Marc—as always.

2. G. W. L. Nicholson, *The Gunners of Canada: The History of the Royal Regiment of Canadian Artillery, Vol. 1, 1534–1919* (Toronto: McClelland and Stewart, 1967), provides the essential framework for this and all Canadian artillery history. For fuller treatment of the coastal artillery and references for the home defense parts of the present chapter, see, in addition to Windsor, Sarty, and Milner, *Loyal Gunners,* Roger Sarty, *The Maritime Defence of Canada* (Toronto: Canadian Institute for Strategic Studies, 1996); Brian Tennyson and Roger Sarty, *Guardian of the Gulf: Sydney, Cape Breton and the Atlantic Wars* (Toronto: University of Toronto Press, 2000); Barry Gough and Roger Sarty, "Sailors and Soldiers: The Royal Navy, the Canadian Forces, and the Defence of Atlantic Canada, 1890–1918," in *A Nation's Navy: In Quest of Canadian Naval Identity,* ed. Michael L. Hadley, Rob Huebert, and Fred W. Crickard (Montreal: McGill-Queen's University Press, 1996), 112–30.

3. General officer commanding (GOC) 6 Division to secretary of the militia council (SMC), 22 February 1915, militia headquarters confidential file (HQC) 843, reel C-5055, Record Group (RG) 24, Library and Archives Canada (LAC).

4. "1st Heavy Battery Historical Records," folder 33, file 13, box 4685, RG9 IIID, LAC.

5. Divisional Ammunition Column sailing list, accessed 7 November 2018, http://eco.canadiana/view/oochihm_9_09055.

6. "2nd Heavy Battery Historical Records," folder 33, file 16, box 4685, RG9 IIID1, LAC.

7. H. D. Clark, *Extracts from the War Diary and Official Records of the Second Canadian Ammunition Column* (Saint John, NB: J. and A. McMillan, 1921), 5–13; 2nd Divisional Ammunition Column sailing list, accessed 1 February 2019, http://www.eco.canadiana/view/oochihm_9_09056; "2nd Divisional Ammunition Col. Canadian Artillery Honours and Awards," folder 33, file 6, box 4685, RG9 IIID1, LAC.

8. "1st Heavy Battery Historical Records"; "2nd Heavy Battery Historical Records"; Martin Farndale, *History of the Royal Regiment of Artillery: Western Front 1914–18* (London: Royal Artillery Institution, 1986), 104–6.

9. Adjutant-General (AG) to GOC 6 Division, 3 June 1915, Military District (MD) 6 file 131-7-1, box 4555, RG 24, LAC; AG to 3 Division, 3 June 1915, HQ593-6-1, box 1372, RG 24, LAC; AG to officer commanding (OC) 4 Division, 3 June 1915, MD4 file 46-7-1, box 4483, RG 24, LAC.

10. OC 4 Division to SMC, 5 February 1915, Renouf to OC 4 Division, 5 June 1915, OC Montreal Heavy Brigade to assistant adjutant-general (AAG) in charge of administration, 4 Division, 7 June 1915, MD4 file 46-7-1, box 4483, RG 24, LAC. Minden Cole was a prominent figure in the artillery community. Born in 1859, he had joined the militia in 1876 and saw active service in the North-West Rebellion in 1885. A graduate of McGill University and a successful insurance broker, he commanded the Montreal heavy brigade in 1892–1901, led the Canadian team in the artillery competition at Shoeburyness, England, in 1896, and headed the Dominion Artillery Association in 1897–1898. See B. M. Greene, ed., *Who's Who and Why, 1919–20* (Toronto: International Press, n.d.), 782.

11. "Editor Guardian" and Nicholson to GOC 6 Division, 2 telegrams, 9 June 1915, MD 6 131-7-1, box 4555, RG 24, LAC.

12. AG to GOC 6 Division, 28 June 1915, MD 6 131-9-1, box 4555, RG 24, LAC.

13. Armstrong was another leading figure in local society, a lawyer with wide business interests who embodied the military patriotism to the British Empire that was such a prominent thread in Canadian nationalism. His father, John Russell Armstrong, also a prominent lawyer, had commanded the 3rd Regiment in 1885–1897, and Beverley, born in 1875, joined the regiment in 1891. In 1899 he volunteered for service in South Africa with the 1st Canadian Mounted Rifles and saw combat in 1900, during which he suffered a gunshot wound that led to the amputation of his lower right leg. He received the Queen's Medal with four clasps, and, as he noted in his entry in *Who's Who*, was "presented to Queen Victoria at Windsor Castle on the last occasion that she saw anyone outside of her family and household." He assumed command of the 3rd Regiment in 1912, volunteered for the CEF on the first day of the war, and personally lobbied Major-General Hughes for an overseas command, a dream that he never achieved. The success of the 3rd Regiment in recruiting for the CEF owed a great deal to Armstrong's leadership. B. M. Greene, ed., *Who's Who and Why, 1919–20*, 670.

14. Armstrong to AAG 6 Division, 21 June 1915, MD 6 131-1-4, box 4555, RG 24, LAC.

15. AG to GOC 6 Division, 30 June 1915, box 4555, RG 24, LAC.

16. War Office (WO) to Colonial Office, 30 July 1915, HQC 1716 pt. 1, box 6596, RG 24, LAC; Farndale, *History of the Royal Regiment of Artillery*, 116.

17. Deputy minister to military secretary to the governor-general, 6 August 1915, HQC 1716 pt. 1, box 6596, RG 24, LAC.

18. Chief of the imperial general staff (CIGS) to minister of Militia, Ottawa, received 6 September, HQC 1716 pt. 1, box 6596, RG 24, LAC.

19. AG to OC 4 Division, 15 September 1915, AAG in charge of administration 4 Division to Costigan, 16 September 1915, OC 4 Division to SMC, 17 September 1915, MD4 46-3-1, box 4483, RG 24, LAC.

20. Militia Ottawa to Troopers, cable, September 17, 1915, Troopers (CIGS) to Militia Ottawa, cable, received 20 September 1915, chief of the general staff (CGS) minute to AG, 21 September 1915, HQS 1716 pt. 1, vol. 6596, RG 24, LAC.

21. OC 3rd Regiment to AAG 6th Division, 29 September 1915, MD6 131-1-4, box 4555, RG 24, LAC.

22. Armstrong to Rutherford, 29 September 1915, box 4555, RG 24, LAC.

23. AG to GOC 6 Division, 9 October 1915, night letter, MD 6 131-8-1, box 4555, RG 24, LAC.

24. Thacker to Gwatkin, 27 September 1915, HQC 1716, pt. 1, box 6596, RG 24, LAC.

25. Quoted in Gwatkin to AG, 7 October 1915, HQC 1716, pt. 1, box 6596, RG 24, LAC.

26. Minden Cole to Gwatkin, 4 October 1915 and Gwaktin to AG, 7 October 1915 (quoted), HQC 1716 pt. 1, box 6596, RG 24, LAC.

27. CGS to AG, 23 October 1915 and captain, AAG to Mobilization, 16 November 1915, HQC 1716 pt. 1, box 6596, RG 24, LAC; Sailing list No. 2 Siege Battery, accessed 28 January 2019, http://data2.archives/e/e444/e101087845.

28. "No. 1 Can. Siege Battery Historical Records," folder 32, file 6, box 4685, RG9 IIID1, LAC; Sailing List No. 3 Battery, accessed 7 November 2018, http://eco.canadiana /view/oochihm9-09079.

29. WO to governor general for Militia, cable, April 6, 1916, HQC 1716 pt. 2, box 6596, "RG 24, LAC.

30. Gwynne for AG to CGS, April 11, 1916, HQC 1716 pt. 2, box 6596, RG 24, LAC; CGS to military secretary to governor-general, 12 April 1916, HQ 8679-3-4, box 2857, RG 24, LAC.

31. Peake took the new battery to the front, and commanded until he received a gunshot wound in the arm in June 1917. AG to GOC Military District (new designation for divisional areas; hereafter MD, 12 April 1916 (2 letters), Peake to deputy assistant adjutant and quarter master general (DAA&QMG) MD 6, 28 April 1916, MD 6 131-21-1, box 4556, RG 24, LAC; Major Arthur George Peake, digitized service file B7679-5025.pdf, box 7679-25, RG 150, accession 1992-93/166, LAC.

32. HQ 8679-3-4, box 2857, RG 24, LAC; Hugh MacLennan, ed., *McGill: The Story of a University* (London: George Allen and Unwin, 1960), 94.

33. GOC MD 6 to SMC, telegram, 13 April 1916, HQC 1716 pt. 2, box 6596, RG 24, LAC, quoted; AG to GOC MD 6, 14 April 1916, HQC 1716 pt. 2, box 6596, RG 24, LAC.

34. Allen to Armstrong, 29 July 1915, Correspondence Book 1915–1917, box 1, RG 9 IIJ6, LAC.

35. Born in Toronto in 1868, he had been an officer in that city's 10th Battalion for ten years and then joined the permanent force artillery in 1903. "9th Can. Siege Battery Historical Records," folder 33, file 5, box 4685, RG 9 IIID1, LAC.

36. GOC MD 6 to SMC, 27 March 1916, HQ 593-15-5, box 1458, RG 24, LAC; MD 6 131-23-1 and MD 6 131-24-1, box 4556, RG 24, LAC; "5th Divl. Amn. Column. Formerly 4th D.A.C. Historical Records," folder 34, file 10, box 4685, RG 9 IIID1, LAC; Sailing List 14th Brigade Canadian Field Artillery (CFA), accessed 20 January 2019, http://data2.archives/e/e444/e011087952.

37. "No. 1 Can. Siege Battery. Historical Records"; "No 2 Can. Siege Battery Historical Records," folder 32, file 9, box 4685, RG 9 IIID1, LAC; "3rd Can. Siege Battery Historical Records," folder 32, file 12, box 4685, RG 9 IIID1, LAC; "No 4 Can. Siege Battery Historical Records," folder 32, file 14, box 4685, RG 9 IIID1, LAC; war diary, 3rd Siege Battery, June–September 1916, digitized file fonandcol-2004796.pdf, box 4976, RG9 IIID3, LAC.

38. "5th Can. Siege Battery Historical Records," folder 32, file 17, box 4685, RG 9 IIID1, LAC; "No. 6 Battery Historical Records," folder 32, file 19, box 4685, RG 9 IIID1, LAC; war diary GOCRA Canadian Corps, 30 September and 5 October 1916, digitized file fonandcol-2004735.pdf, box 4957, RG 9 IIID3, LAC.

39. *Prominent People of the Maritime Provinces* (Montreal: Canadian Publicity Co., 1922), 18.

40. These on their arrival in England had been designated the 167th, 271st, 272nd and 273rd (Canadian) Siege Batteries, AAG, WO, to Field Marshal Commanding-in-Chief, British Armies in France, 2 January 1917, "7th Can. Siege Battery, Historical Records," folder 33, file 1, RG 9 IIID1, box 4685, LAC.

41. War diary 2nd Brigade, Canadian Garrison Artillery (CGA), 1 April 1917, digitized file fonandcol-2004792.pdf, box 4975, RG 9 IIID3, LAC; "1st Heavy Battery Historical Records," folder 33, file 13, box 4685, RG 9 IIID1, LAC.

42. War diary MD 7 9th Siege Battery [depot], digitized file fonandcol-205388.pdf, box 5065, RG 9 IIID3, a unique and detailed record of a home unit; "No. 10 Halifax

Siege Battery [History]," file GAQ8-15q, box 1832, RG 24, LAC; MD6 131-34-1, box 4557, RG 24, LAC.

43. CGS, Advanced Headquarters, to Second Army, 16 October 1917, folder 98, file 3, box 3864, RG 9 IIIC1, LAC.

44. "Organization McGill Siege Arty Bty," O-198-33, box 2897, RG 9 III, LAC; "10th Siege Battery Historical Records," folder 33, file 7, box 4685, RG9 IIID1, LAC; war diary 10th Canadian Siege Battery, digitized file fonandcol-2004803.pdf, box 4977, RG 9 IIID3, LAC.

45. "11th Siege Battery Historical Records,'" folder 33, file 9, box 4685, RG9 IIID1, LAC; war diary 11th Canadian Siege Battery, digitized file fonandcol-2004804.pdf, box 4977, RG 9 IIID3, LAC.

46. "12th Siege Battery Historical Records," folder 33, file 11, box 4685, RG9 IIID1, LAC; war diary 12th Canadian Siege Battery digitized file fonandcol-2004805, box 4977, RG 9 IIID3, LAC; Major Francis Arthur Robertson digitized service file B8354-S042, box 8354-42, RG 150, accession 1992–93/166, LAC.

47. "First Army No 1525 (G). O.B./2059," September 1917, folder 98, file 3, box 3864, RG 9 IIIC1, LAC.

48. War diaries 1st Brigade, CGA, digitized file fonandcol-2004791.pdf, 2nd Brigade, CGA, digitized file fonandcol-2004777.pdf, and 3rd Brigade, CGA fonandcol-2004793.pdf, all in box 4975, RG 9 IIID3, LAC.

5. "Returning Home to Fight"

The authors wish to thank the University of the West of England, Bristol, for grants in aid of research from their respective faculties to conduct the preliminary work for this chapter. They would also like to acknowledge the additional support from the Arts and Humanities Research Council (UK) when they were both involved as historical consultants and national advisors to the BBC's "World War One at Home" project between 2013 and 2016.

1. *Bristol and the War 1*, no. 3, 31 October 1914.

2. *Bristol and the War*, October 1914.

3. *Bristol Times and Mirror*, 19 October 1914.

4. *Bristol Times and Mirror*, 31 October 1914.

5. Charles Lucas, *The Empire at War* (London: Oxford University Press, 1921), 1:299.

6. E. A. Benians, *The Cambridge History of the British Empire*, vol. 3: *The Empire-Commonwealth 1870–1919*, ed. E. A. Benians, Sir James Butler, and C. E. Carrington (Cambridge: Cambridge University Press, 1959), 641–42; Robert Holland, "The British Empire and the Great War, 1914–1918," in *The Oxford History of the British Empire*, vol. 4: *The Twentieth Century*, ed. Judith M. Brown and Wm. Roger Louis (Oxford: Oxford University Press, 1999), 117. The figure for India, for which there were no less than seven expeditionary forces fighting on three continents, are equally impressive at 1.44 million combatants.

7. *The Union of South Africa and the Great War. Official History* (Pretoria: Government Printing and Stationary Office, 1924), 3.

8. Richard Holt, *Filling the Ranks: Manpower in the Canadian Expeditionary Force, 1914–1918* (Montreal: McGill-Queen's University Press, 2017), 43–44.

9. Kent Fedorowich, *Unfit for Heroes: Reconstruction and Soldier Settlement in the Empire between the Wars* (Manchester: Manchester University Press, 1995).

10. Kent Fedorowich, "The British Empire on the Move," in *The British Empire: Themes and Perspectives*, ed. Sarah Stockwell (Oxford: Blackwell Publishing, 2008), 64.

11. Richard White has led the way with "The Soldier as Tourist: The Australian Experience of the Great War," *War & Society* 5, no. 1 (1987): 63–77. See also Bart Ziino, "A Kind of Round Trip: Australian Soldiers and the Tourist Analogy, 1914–1918," *War & Society* 25, no. 2 (2006): 39–52; Felicity Barnes, "Dominion Soldiers on Leave in Europe (New Zealand) 1914–1918," in *International Encyclopaedia of the First World War*, ed. Ute Daniel, Peter Gatrell, Oliver Janz, Heather Jones, Jennifer D. Keene, Alan Kramer, and Bill Nasson (Berlin: Frei Universität Berlin, 2014). https://encyclopedia .1914-1918-online.net/project/about/#:~:text=International%20Encyclopedia%20 of%20the%20First%20World%20War%E2%80%9D%20is,More%20than%20 1%2C000%20articles%20will%20be%20gradually%20published.

12. Ulbe Bosma, "European Colonial Soldiers in the Nineteenth Century: Their Role in White Global Migration and Patterns of Colonial Settlement," *Journal of Global History* 4, no. 2 (2009): 317.

13. James Bennett, "'Massey's Sunday School Picnic Party': 'The Other Anzacs' or Honorary Australians?" *War & Society* 21, no. 2 (2003): 31–35; Barnes, "Dominion Soldiers on Leave," 4.

14. Michael McKernan, *The Australian People and the Great War* (Melbourne: Thomas Nelson, 1980), 116; E. M. Andrews, *The Anzac Illusion: Anglo-Australian Relations during World War I* (Melbourne: Cambridge University Press, 1993), 185. Roger Beckett, "The Australian Soldier in Britain," in *Australians in Britain: The Twentieth-Century Experience*, ed. Carl Bridge, Robert Crawford, and David Dunstan (Clayton, VIC: Monash University ePress, 2009), 6.1–6.17, challenges the negativity of both McKernan and Andrews.

15. Richard S. Grayson, "Military History from the Street: New Methods for Researching First World War Service in the British Military," *War in History* 21, no. 4 (2014): 465–95.

16. Tanja Bueltmann, David T. Gleeson, and Donald M. MacRaild, eds., *Locating the English Diaspora, 1500–2010* (Liverpool: Liverpool University Press, 2012).

17. Jonathan F. Vance, *Maple Leaf Empire: Canada, Britain, and the Two World Wars* (Oxford: Oxford University Press, 2012), 3–4.

18. Vance, *Maple Leaf Empire*, 3–4.

19. Recent scholarship reinforces these points: John C. Mitcham, *Race and Imperial Defence in the British World, 1870–1914* (Cambridge: Cambridge University Press, 2016); Steve Marti, *For Home and Empire: Voluntary Mobilization in Australia, Canada and New Zealand during the First World War* (Vancouver: University of British Columbia Press, 2019).

20. Carl Bridge and Kent Fedorowich, "Mapping the British World," *Journal of Imperial and Commonwealth History* 31, no. 2 (2003): 3.

21. Stephen Constantine, ed., *Emigrants and Empire: British Settlement in the Dominions between the Wars* (Manchester: Manchester University Press, 1990), 2; Eric Richards, *Britannia's Children: Emigration from England, Scotland, Wales and Ireland since 1600* (London: Hambledon, 2004), 225.

22. Fedorowich, "British Empire on the Move," 89.

23. Marjory Harper and Stephen Constantine, *Migration and Empire*, companion series, *Oxford History of the British Empire* (Oxford: Oxford University Press, 2010), 87; W. D. Borrie, *Immigration to New Zealand, 1854–1938* (Canberra: Australian National University Press, 1991), 152.

24. F. K. Crowley, *Australia's Western Third: A History of Western Australia from the First Settlement to Modern Times* (Melbourne: Heinemann, 1970), 157–58.

25. A. F. Duguid, *Official History of the Canadian Forces in the Great War 1914–1919*, General Series, vol. 1: *Chronology, Appendices and Maps* (Ottawa: J. O. Patenaude, 1938), appendix 132, 112–13. Passenger list for Spoors, Library and Archives Canada. http://www.bac-lac.gc.ca/eng/discover/immigration/immigration-records/passenger-lists/passenger-lists-1865-1922/Pages/item.aspx?IdNumber=12415&.

26. Robert Craig Brown and Ramsay Cook, *Canada 1896–1921: A Nation Transformed* (Toronto: McClelland and Stewart, 1976), 60.

27. Harper and Constantine, *Migration and Empire*, 297.

28. A. F. Duguid, *Official History of the Canadian Forces in the Great War 1914–1919: August 1914 to September 1915* (Ottawa: J. O. Patenaude, 1938), 138; Harold R. Peat, *Private Peat* (Middlesex: Echo Library, 2008), 12; *Bristol Times and Mirror*, 7 November 1914; war diary, notes, and battalion orders for 7th Battalion (November 1914) Victor Odlum papers, Manuscript Group (MG) 30, E300, Odlum papers, vol. 15, Library and Archives Canada (LAC).

29. Eugene Byrne and Clive Burlton, *Bravo, Bristol! The City at War, 1914–1918* (Bristol: Redcliffe Press, 2014), 44; service file for Thomas G. Spoors, accession 1992–93/166, Box 9201–34, Record Group (RG) 150, LAC; John Herd Thompson, *The Harvests of War: The Prairie West, 1914–1918* (Toronto: McClelland and Stewart, 1983), 24, gives the unit strength as 1,124 with 874, or 78 percent, born in the British Isles.

30. To date, the authors have identified the following number of Bristolians serving in the dominion forces: Canada 954; Australia 121; New Zealand 31; and South and East Africa 31. Only a handful were conscripted, and these were by the Canadian authorities after August 1917.

31. Desmond Morton, *When Your Number's Up: The Canadian Soldier in the First World War* (Toronto: Random House, 1993), 9, 278; Terry Copp, "The Military Effort, 1914–1918," in *Canada and the First World War: Essays in Honour of Robert Craig Brown*, ed. David Mackenzie (Toronto: University of Toronto Press, 2005), 37–38, 59, fn.32; *Canadian Annual Review 1914*, 188; Charles Lucas, *The Empire at War* (London: Oxford University Press, 1923), 2:17.

32. Morton, *When Your Number's Up*, 278; Duguid, *Official History, General Series*, appendix 86, 58.

33. Paul Baker, *King and Country Call: New Zealanders, Conscription and the Great War* (Auckland: Auckland University Press, 1988), 11, 15, 17. Steven Loveridge, *Calls to Arms: New Zealand Society and Commitment to the Great War* (Wellington: Victoria University Press, 2014), chap. 2, explores what it meant to be "British" in New Zealand at this time.

34. Ian McGibbon, "The Shaping of New Zealand's War Effort, August–October 1914," in *New Zealand's Great War: New Zealand, The Allies & The First World War*, ed. John Crawford and Ian McGibbon (Auckland: Exisle Publishing, 2007), 51.

35. Robert Stevenson, *To Win the Battle: The 1st Australian Division in the Great War* (Cambridge: Cambridge University Press, 2012); Peter Dennis and Jeff Grey, "New Zealanders in the AIF: An Introduction to the AIF Database Project," in *New Zealand's Great War: New Zealand, The Allies & The First World War*, ed. John Crawford and Ian McGibbon (Auckland: Exisle Publishing, 2007), 399, on UK enlistments in the AIF; Jean Bou and Peter Dennis, *The Centenary History of Australia and the Great War*, vol. 5 *The Australian Imperial Force* (Melbourne: Oxford University Press, 2016), 71–99.

36. C. E. W. Bean, *Anzac to Amiens* (Canberra: Australian War Memorial, 1961), 41.

37. Joan Beaumont, *Broken Nation: Australians in the Great War* (Sydney: Allen & Unwin, 2013), 14; L. L. Robson, *The First AIF: A Study of Its Recruitment, 1914–1918* (Melbourne: Melbourne University Press, 1982), 14–17.

38. Graham McInnes, *The Road to Gundagai* (London: Hamish Hamilton, 1965), 281–82.

39. Stevenson, *To Win the Battle*, 23.

40. Eric Wren, *Randwick to Hargicourt: History of the 3rd Battalion, AIF* (Sydney: Ronald G. McDonald, 1935), 15–18.

41. Walter C. Belford, *"Legs Eleven." Being the Story of the 11th Battalion (AIF) in the Great War of 1914–1918* (Perth, WA: Imperial Printing, 1940), 4, 6–7; James Hurst, *Game to the Last: The 11th Australian Infantry Battalion at Gallipoli*, 2nd ed. (Newport, NSW: Big Sky Publishing, 2011), 3–4; Suzanne Welborn, *Lords of Death* (Fremantle, WA: Freemantle Arts Centre Press, 1982).

42. Munro-Ferguson to General Sir Ian Hamilton, Commander-in-Chief, Home Army, 25 December 1914Sir Ronald Munro-Ferguson papers, box 5, fols. 3667–70, MS 696, National Library of Australia.

43. Ernest Scott, *Official History of Australia in the War of 1914–1918*, vol. 11 *Australia during the War* (Sydney: Angus & Robertson, 1941), 213.

44. Harold Baldwin, *"Holding the Line"* (Chicago: A. C. McClurg, 1918), 4.

45. Connaught to Harcourt, 5 October 1914, Sir Lewis Harcourt papers, dep 476, fols. 175–9, Bodleian Library (Oxford).

46. Recent scholarship has shown that there was strong support for the war even among Irish Catholics. See Mark G. McGowan, *The Imperial Irish: Canada's Irish Catholics Fight the Great War, 1914–1918* (Montreal: McGill-Queen's University Press, 2017).

47. Daniel G. Dancocks, *Gallant Canadians: The Story of the 10th Infantry Battalion, 1914–1919* (Calgary: Calgary Highlanders Regimental Fund Trust, 1990), 6.

48. R. C. Featherstonhaugh, *The 13th Battalion Royal Highlanders of Canada, 1914–1919* (Montreal: The 13th Battalion Royal Highlanders of Canada, 1925), 6.

49. J. King Gordon, ed., *Postscript to Adventure: The Autobiography of Ralph Connor (Charles W. Gordon)* (London: Hodder and Stoughton, 1938), 196.

50. Mark Zuehlke, *Brave Battalion: The Remarkable Saga of the 16th Battalion (Canadian Scottish) in the First World War* (Mississauga, ON: Wiley, 2008), 13.

51. Kenneth Radley, *We Lead, Others Follow: First Canadian Division, 1914–1918* (St. Catharines, ON: Vanwell Publishing, 2007), 46; Hugh M. Urquhart, *The History of the 16th Battalion (The Canadian Scottish Regiment)* (Toronto: Macmillan, 1932), appendix 6, 415.

52. Information obtained from the family headstone at Avonview cemetery provides further information of his wounding at La Bassée and his attachment to the 16th Canadian Scottish; service file for F. G. Flook, accession 1992–93/166, Box 3156–43, RG 150, LAC.

53. Jonathan Hyslop, "Cape Town Highlanders, Transvaal Scottish: Military 'Scottishness' and Social Power in Nineteenth and Twentieth Century South Africa," *South African Historical Journal* 47 (2002): 96–114, See Bill Nasson, *Springboks on the Somme: South Africa in the Great War, 1914–1918* (London: Penguin, 2007), 205–18, for John Buchan's role in constructing the "Celtic credibility" of the South African Brigade.

54. John Buchan, *The History of the South African Forces in France* (London: Thomas Nelson, 1920), 16–17, 21. There were 638 British-born and 595 South African–born; but if you add the 49 from the other unspecified nationals to the latter figure, the total is 644.

55. Morton, *When Your Number's Up*, 279.

56. Service file for Sergeant Frederick J. Harcombe, accession 1992–93/166, Box 4036–47, RG 150, LAC; passenger list for Harcombe, Library and Archives Canada, accessed 1 August 2019, https://www.bac-lac.gc.ca/eng/discover/immigration/immigration-records/passenger-lists/passenger-lists-1865-1922/Pages/item.aspx?IdNumber=12415&; service file for Company Sergeant-Major (CSM) Henry W. Hooper, accession 1992-93/166, Box 4483–39, RG 150, LAC. ibid.; passenger list for Hooper, Library and Archives Canada, accessed 1 August 2019, https://www.bac-lac.gc.ca/eng/discover/immigration/immigration-records/passenger-lists/passenger-lists-1865-1922/Pages/item.aspx?IdNumber=5897&.

57. Buchan, *South African Forces*, 17.

58. Service file for C. G. Stiff, accession 1992–93/166, Box 9331–37, RG 150, LAC.

59. *Feilding Star*, 5 October 1916.

60. *Sydney Morning Herald*, 31 July 1872, announcement of his marriage to Constance Woolley, fourth daughter of John Woolley DCL, University of Sydney; *Sydney Morning Herald*, 22 December 1877, birth of Lance; *Sydney Morning Herald*, Bacchus senior's death notice, 2 August 1878.

61. "Club Members 1872–1945. B," Clifton Rugby Football Club History, accessed 4 October 2015, http://www.cliftonrfchistory.co.uk/members/membersB.htm.

62. Ian McGibbon, ed., *The Oxford Companion to New Zealand Military History* (Auckland: Oxford University Press, 2000), 602.

63. *Manawatu Standard*, 7 November 1916; *Wanganui Chronicle*, 6 October 1916.

64. Pring's personnel file, Admiralty papers, ADM 188/422, The National Archives, London (TNA).

65. Pring, H. J. (aka William Clarke), AIF Personnel files, B2455, National Archives of Australia; *Sydney Sun*, 22 November 1921.

66. *The Education Department's Record of War Service, 1914–1919 Victoria* (Melbourne: Government Printer, 1921), 29–31. He is also honored on the following website which records a number of casualties from the Bristol Diocese: 2 October 2015. http://bristol-cathedral.co.uk/we-have-our-lives/person/roy-bailey. Bailey's personnel file while in the Royal Marine Light Infantry (RMLI), ADM 196/98/12, TNA; war diary, 1st Battalion, RMLI, May 1916–November 1918, ADM 137/3065, fols. 365–6.

6. Martial Race Theory and Recruitment in the Indian Army during Two World Wars

1. Kaushik Roy, "The Beginning of 'People's War' in India," *Economic and Political Weekly* 42, no. 19 (2007): 1724.

2. Kaushik Roy, "Managing the Environment: Disease, Sanitation and the Army in British-India, 1859–1913," in *Situating Environment History*, ed. R. Chakrabarti (New Delhi: Manohar, 2007), 187–219.

3. Kaushik Roy, "Coercion through Leniency: British Manipulation of the Courts-Martial System in the Post-Mutiny Indian Army, 1859–1913," *Journal of Military History* 65, no. 4 (2001): 957.

4. DeWitt Ellinwood, "Ethnicity in a Colonial Asian Army: British Policy, War, and the Indian Army, 1914–18," in *Ethnicity and the Military in Asia*, ed. Ellinwood and Cynthia H. Enloe (New Brunswick: Transaction Books, 1981), 97; *Proceedings of the Army in India Committee 1912* (Simla: Government Central Branch Press, 1913), 3:649; National Archives of India (NAI), New Delhi.

5. S. D. Pradhan, "Indian Army and the First World War," in *India and World War I*, ed. DeWitt Ellinwood and S. D. Pradhan (New Delhi: Manohar, 1978), 60. See also George MacMunn, *The Martial Races of India* (London: Sampson, Low, Marsten & Co., 1933).

6. Seema Alavi, *The Sepoys and the Company: Tradition and Transition in Northern India, 1770–1830* (New Delhi: Oxford University Press, 1995).

7. Heather Streets, *Martial Races: The Military, Race, and Masculinity in British Imperial Culture, 1857–1914* (Manchester: Manchester University Press, 2004), 1–2, 4–5, 7.

8. Lionel Caplan, "'Bravest of the Brave': Representations of 'The Gurkha' in British Military Writings," *Modern Asian Studies* 25, no. 3 (1991): 571–73.

9. Lionel Caplan, "Martial Gurkhas: The Persistence of a British Military Discourse on 'Race,'" in *The Concept of Race in South Asia*, ed. Peter Robb (New Delhi: Oxford University Press, 1995), 261, 264.

10. Brian Robson, ed., *Roberts in India: The Military Papers of Field-Marshal Lord Roberts, 1876–93* (Stroud: Alan Sutton, 1993), 258–59, 264–66, 310.

11. Kaushik Roy, *Brown Warriors of the Raj: Recruitment and the Mechanics of Command in the Sepoy Army, 1859–1913* (New Delhi: Manohar, 2008), 41, 109.

12. Michael O'Dwyer, *India as I Knew It* ([n.d.], repr. New Delhi: Mittal Publications, 2004), 215.

13. DeWitt C. Ellinwood, "An Historical Study of the Punjabi Soldier in World War I," in *Punjab Past and Present: Essays in Honour of Dr. Ganda Singh*, ed. Harbans Singh and N. Gerald Barrier (Patiala: Punjab University Press, 1976), 343.

14. S. D. Pradhan, "The Sikh Soldier in the First World War," in *India and World War I*, ed. DeWitt Ellinwood and S. D. Pradhan (New Delhi: Manohar, 1978), 216–17.

15. W. J. M. Spaight, "The History of Gurkha Recruitment," *Journal of the United Service Institution of India* 70, no. 299 (1940): 187.

16. Lionel Caplan, *Warrior Gentleman: "Gurkhas" in the Western Imagination* (Oxford: Berghahn Books, 1995), 22.

17. Santanu Das, "India and the First World War," in *A Part of History: Aspects of the British Experience of the First World War* (London: Continuum, 2008), 66.

18. Andrew Tait Jarboe, ed., *War News in India: The Punjabi Press during World War I* (London: I. B. Tauris, 2016), 20.

19. Algernon Rumbold, *Watershed in India: 1914–1922* (London: Athlone Press, 1979), 3.

20. The Ghadar volunteers (about 50 percent of whom were ex-soldiers of the Raj) had infiltrated into India with a view to bringing about a revolt, especially in the Indian Army. British intelligence learned of Ghadarite plans, which allowed authorities to crush the revolt before it even started. See A. C. Bose, "Indian Revolutionaries during the First World War—A Study of Their Aims and Weaknesses," in *India and World War I*, ed. DeWitt Ellinwood and S. D. Pradhan (New Delhi: Manohar, 1978), 111; Tan Tai Yong, *The Garrison State: The Military, Government and Society in Colonial Punjab, 1849–1947* (New Delhi: SAGE, 2005), 112.

21. N. Gerald Barrier, "Ruling India: Coercion and Propaganda in British India during the First World War," in *India and World War I*, ed. DeWitt Ellinwood and S. D. Pradhan (New Delhi: Manohar, 1978), 82.

22. Judith M. Brown, "War and the Colonial Relationship: Britain, India and the War of 1914–18," in *India and World War I*, ed. DeWitt Ellinwood and S. D. Pradhan (New Delhi: Manohar, 1978), 30–31.

23. Lal Baha, "The North-West Frontier in the First World War," in *World War I*, ed. Michael Neiberg (Aldershot: Ashgate, 2005), 481.

24. T. R. Moreman, "The Arms Trade and the North-West Frontier Pathan Tribes, 1890–1914," *Journal of Imperial and Commonwealth History* 22, no. 2 (1994): 201–2. The British political officers had to tour these areas and provide a written report that the men from these localities were politically reliable and could be recruited. Occasionally, serving Indian soldiers also provided a written guarantee that certain clans and tribes from their localities were loyal and martial—hence, worth recruiting in the Indian Army.

25. Kaushik Roy, *Indian Army and the First World War: 1914–18* (New Delhi: Oxford University Press, 2018), 39–40.

26. David Omissi, *The Sepoy and the Raj: The Indian Army, 1860–1940* (Houndmills: Macmillan, 1994), 148–49.

27. Military Department (MD), Censor Indian Mail (CIM) 1915–16, pt. 2, FF 169–340, week ending 5 February 1916, from Santo Chawan, Marathi, Lady Hardinge Hospital, Brockenhurst, to Narain Nawle, Deccan, 26 January 1916, L/MIL/5/826, India Records Office (IOR), British Library (BL), London.

28. Military Department (MD), Censor Indian Mail (CIM) 1915–16, pt. 2, FF 169–340, week ending 13 February 1916, Captain, Chief Censor, Indian Mails, Boulogne, 18 February 1916.

29. Santanu Das, *India, Empire, and First World War Culture: Writings, Images, and Songs* (Cambridge: Cambridge University Press, 2018).

30. O'Dwyer, *India as I Knew It*, 216, 232.

31. Tahir Mahmood, "Collaboration and British Military Recruitment: Fresh Perspectives from Colonial Punjab, 1914–1918," *Modern Asian Studies* 50, no. 5 (2016): 1474–1500.

32. David Omissi, "Europe through Indian Eyes: Indian Soldiers Encounter England and France, 1914–1918," *English Historical Review* 122, no. 496 (2007): 381.

33. DeWitt C. Ellinwood., *Between Two Worlds: A Rajput Officer in the Indian Army, 1905–21, Based on the Diary of Amar Singh of Jaipur* (Lanham: Hamilton Books, 2005), 356.

34. Recruiting in India before and during the War of 1914–18, 20, L/MIL/17/5/2152, IOR, BL, London.

35. Recruiting in India before and during the War of 1914–18, 21–22.

36. Recruiting in India before and during the War of 1914–18, appendix 19, 19–20, 87; Omissi, *The Sepoy and the Raj*, 54.

37. Statistical Abstract of Information regarding the Armies at Home and Abroad 1914–1920, 785, L/MIL/17/5/2382, IOR, BL, London. See also Douglas E. Delaney, *The Imperial Army Project: Britain and the Land Forces of the Dominions and India* (Oxford: Oxford University Press, 2017), 239 and appendix 2.

38. DeWitt C. Ellinwood, "The Indian Soldier, the Indian Army, and Change, 1914–1918," in *India and World War I*, ed. DeWitt Ellinwood and S. D. Pradhan (New Delhi: Manohar, 1978), 183.

39. Statistical Abstract of Information regarding the Armies at Home and Abroad 1914–1920, 161, 786.

40. Roger D. Long, "Introduction: India and the Great War, A Centennial Assessment," in *India and World War I: A Centennial Assessment*, ed. Roger D. Long and Ian Talbot, 1–42 (London: Routledge, 2018).

41. Notes for the Information of British Other Ranks Proceeding to India for Training at an Officer's Training School, published in 1942 and reprinted in 1943, 5, L/MIL/17/5/2288, IOR, BL, London.

42. Committee Communications, L/MIL/5/886, IOR, BL, London.

43. Gautam Sharma, *Nationalization of the Indian Army: 1885–1947* (New Delhi: Allied, 1996), 174.

44. P. Marsden, Enclosure, 29 September 1939, L/WS/1/136, IOR, BL, London.

45. *Rifleman to Colonel: Memoirs of Major Gajendra Malla 9th Gorkha Rifles*, comp. Tony Mains and Elizabeth Talbot Rice (New Delhi: Reliance Publishing House, 1999), 2, 29.

46. Note by Leo Amery, 1 January 1941, L/WS/1/456, IOR, BL.

47. *Rifleman to Colonel*, xviii, 20; Caplan, *Warrior Gentleman*, 22, 31–33.

48. Quoted from Recruitment in India, appendix 19, Note by General Molesworth on Indian Army Recruitment, July 21, 1943, L/WS/1/136, IOR, BL, London.

49. Steven I. Wilkinson, *Army and Nation: The Military and Indian Democracy since Independence* (Ranikhet: Permanent Black, 2015), 69.

50. Recruitment in the Indian Army from 3 September 1939 to 1 July 1945, L/MIL/17/5/2153, IOR, BL, London.

51. Kaushik Roy, "Axis Satellite Armies of World War II: A Case Study of the Azad Hind Fauj, 1942–45," *Indian Historical Review* 35, no. 1 (2008): 147–52.

52. Kaushik Roy, *India and World War II: War, Armed Forces, and Society, 1939–45* (New Delhi: Oxford University Press, 2016), 142–43; Kaushik Roy, "Military Loyalty in the Colonial Context: A Case Study of the Indian Army during World War II," *Journal of Military History* 73, no. 2 (2009): 527–27.

53. Kaushik Roy, "Discipline and Morale of the African, British and Indian Army Units in Burma and India during World War II: July 1943 to August 1945," *Modern Asian Studies* 44, no. 6 (2010): 1265, 1280–81.

54. Kaushik Roy, *Military Manpower, Armies and Warfare in South Asia* (London: Pickering & Chatto, 2013), 116.

55. Chandar S. Sundaram, *Indianization, the Officer Corps, and the Indian Army: The Forgotten Debate, 1817–1917* (Lanham, Maryland: Lexington, 2019), 211–37.

7. Manpower, Training, and the Battlefield Leadership of British Army Officers in the Era of the Two World Wars

1. George Orwell, "The Lion and the Unicorn," in *The Collected Essays, Journalism and Letters of George Orwell*, II, ed. Sonia Orwell and Ian Angus (Harmondsworth: Penguin, 1970), 83, 87–88. By "England", Orwell actually meant "Britain" *Ibid.*, 83.

2. David Cannadine, *Class in Britain* (London: Penguin, 2002 [1998]), 22; G. R. Searle, *A New England? Peace and War, 1886–1918* (Oxford: Oxford University Press, 2004), 100; for a stimulating critique of the use of class by historians, see Jon Lawrence, "The British sense of class," *Journal of Contemporary History* 35, no. 2 (2000): 307–18.

3. Kenyon to parents, 4 April 1926, L. F. R. Kenyon papers, Imperial War Museum (IWM) 84/8/2.

4. Jimmy Perry, *A Stupid Boy* (London: Century, 2002), 103.

5. David Cannadine, *The Decline and Fall of the British Aristocracy* (London: Penguin, 2005 [1990]), 264, 274, 277.

6. Ross McKibben, *Classes and Cultures: England 1918–1951* (Oxford: University Press, 1998), 237; minute by chief of the imperial general staff (CIGS), The National Archives, Kew (TNA), WO32/8386.

7. K. W. Mitchinson, *The Territorial Force at War, 1914–1916* (Basingstoke: Palgrave Macmillan, 2014), 30–31; Cannadine, *Decline and Fall*, 277.

8. *Interim Report of The War Office Committee on the Provision of Officers (a) for service with the Regular Army in war, and (b) for the Auxiliary Forces*, Parliamentary Papers (PP), Command (Cd) 3294, 1907, 4, 6.

9. Quoted in M. A. Wingfield, "The Supply and Training of Officers for the Army," *Journal of the Royal Services Institution* 69, no. 475 (1924): 433; Hamilton's comments in WO 163/15, TNA.

10. "Report of the Committee on Supply of Officers on Mobilization, 21 October 1909," Precis No. 453, and 122nd Meeting of Army Council, 21 March 1910, both in WO 163/364, TNA; Edward M. Spiers, *Haldane: An Army Reformer* (Edinburgh: Edinburgh University Press, 1980), 141–42.

11. For the next three paragraphs, see HL Deb., 17 September 1914, *Hansard* vol. 17, cc735–40; Peter Simkins, *Kitchener's Army: The Raising of the New Armies, 1914–1916* (Manchester: Manchester University Press, 1988), xiv, 212–25; Charles Messenger, *Call to Arms: The British Army 1914–18* (London: Weidenfeld and Nicolson, 2004), 289–93, 297–99, 313–14; G. D. Sheffield, *Leadership in the Trenches: Officer-Man Relations, Morale and Discipline in the British Army in the Era of the First World War* (Basingstoke: Macmillan, 2000), 30–32, 37–38, 54–60.

12. Excerpt from Annual Inspection Report, 1910, MR./17/113/3/4, Manchester Regiment Archives, Tameside Local Studies and Archives Centre; William Marshall, *Memories of Four Fronts* (London: Benn, 1929), 77–79.

13. Peter Hodgkinson, *British Infantry Battalion Commanders in the First World War* (Farnham: Ashgate, 2015), 211.

14. Haldane report, 12, WO 32/4353, TNA; Sheffield, *Leadership*, 175.

15. Haldane report, 3, 12, and note by CIGS, 9 August 1923, both in WO 32/4353, TNA. The report wished to improve the intellectual quality of officer candidates, by recruiting more from universities: it assumed that most cadets at Sandhurst and Woolwich "have not been conspicuously successful in school work" (18).

16. Brian Bond, *British Military Policy Between the Wars* (Oxford: Clarendon Press, 1980), 64–71.

17. Peter Cochrane, *Charlie Company: In Service with C Company 2nd Queen's Own Cameron Highlanders 1940–44* (Stroud: Spellmount, 2007 [1977]), 16–17.

18. Note by C. L. Baynes, 8 December 1937, note by Lt.-Gen. Sir Reginald May (quarter-master general [QMG]), 18 January 1938, "Report of the Committee on the Supply of Army Officers (Willingdon Report)," 10. note by Lt.-Gen. Sir Walter Kirke, all in WO32/4461, TNA.

19. Precis No. 1152, 3, WO 32/4353, TNA.

20. Note by W. Douglas, 16 February 1939, "Report of Committee on Commissions from the Ranks," WO32/4544, TNA; Note by Kirke, WO32/4461, TNA.

21. Jeremy A. Crang, *The British Army and the People's War* (Manchester: Manchester University Press, 2000), 22.

22. Crang, *British Army*, 22–24.

23. David French, *Raising Churchill's Army: The British Army and the War against Germany, 1919–1945* (Oxford: Oxford University Press, 2001), 129; Terry Crowdy, ed., *Donald Dean VC: The Memoirs of a Volunteer & Territorial from Two World Wars* (Barnsley: Pen & Sword, 2010), Kindle ed., chap. 7, paras. 32, 37.

24. Edward Smalley, *The British Expeditionary Force, 1939–40* (Basingstoke: Palgrave, 2015), 51–52, 71–74.

25. John Terraine, *The Right of the Line: The Royal Air Force in the European War, 1939–1945* (London: Sceptre, 1988 [1985]), 682.

26. Alex Danchev, "The Army and the Home Front, 1939–45," in *The Oxford History of the British Army*, ed. David Chandler and Ian Beckett (Oxford: Oxford University Press, 1996 [1994]), 312–14.

27. Crang, *British Army*, 24–25; Roger Broad, *The Radical General: Sir Ronald Adam and Britain's New Model Army, 1941–46* (Stroud: Spellmount, 2013), 105–20.

28. Crang, *British Army*, 25–38.

29. Montgomery to Alexander, telegram, 3 November 1943, WO 214/25, TNA; L. F. Ellis, *Victory in the West*, vol. 1, *The Battle of Normandy* (London: HMSO, 1962), 536.

30. Kenneth Trinder, unpublished memoir, 13, 16, Personal Narratives file, Oxfordshire and Buckinghamshire Light Infantry Archives, Soldiers of Oxfordshire Museum.

31. Wilfred I. Smith, *Code Word CANLOAN* (Toronto: Dundurn, 1992). For interoperability of imperial armies, see Douglas E. Delaney, *The Imperial Army Project: Britain and the Land Forces of the Dominions and India, 1902–1945* (Oxford: Oxford University Press, 2018).

32. Frank Coutts, *One Blue Bonnet: A Scottish Soldier Looks Back* (Edinburgh: Black and White Publishing, 1991), 52; Staniforth to parents, 6 November 1914, in *At War with the 16th (Irish) Division, 1914–1918: The Staniforth Letters*, ed. Richard S. Grayson (Barnsley: Pen & Sword, 2012), 20.

33. For the next three paragraphs see Sheffield, *Leadership*.

34. R. F. E. Laidlaw, ms. account, GALL 53/1, 11–12, Liddle Collection, University of Leeds. I It proved impossible to trace the owner of copyright of the Laidlaw papers, and both the author and the Liddle Collection would welcome information on this matter.

35. French, *Raising Churchill's Army*, 125; Coutts, *Blue Bonnet*, 62.

36. Cannadine, *Class*, 127; Geoffrey Field, "'Civilians in Uniform': Class and Politics in the British Armed Forces, 1939–1945," *International Labor and Working Class History* 80 (Fall 2011): 123; French, *Raising Churchill's Army*, 126; Jonathan Fennell, *Fighting the People's War: The British and Commonwealth Armies and the Second World War* (Cambridge: Cambridge University Press, 2019), 239–40, 629–46, 682.

37. Printed circular letter No. 3, March 1943, 3, ADAM 3/4/3, Adam papers, Liddell Hart Centre for Military Archives (LHCMA); printed circular letter No. 4, June 1943, 3, ADAM 3/4/4, Adam papers, LHCMA.

38. *The Times*, 16 January 1941, 5.

39. "Boomerang" [Alan Wood], *Bless 'Em All: An Analysis of the Morale, Efficiency and Leadership of the British Army* (London: Secker and Warburg, 1942), 52; "Socialist Subaltern," quoted in Crang, *British Army*, 62.

40. Middle East Censorship summaries, 10–12 September 1942, 3, WAII/46, Archives New Zealand (ANZ).

41. Crang, *British Army*, 64–68, 70.

42. John Gorman, *The Times of My Life: An Autobiography* (Barnsley: Pen & Sword, 2002 [n.d.]), Kindle ed., chap. 2, final para.; Douglas Rennie, "Middle East OCTU," in *Aim* (Magazine of Middle East Command), July 1944, 7.

43. Printed circular letter No. 3, March 1943, 4, ADAM 3/4/3, Adam papers, LHCMA; Crang, *British Army*, 68. For Adam's views on the importance of winning over COs, see unpaginated ms., Adam 3/10,

44. Unpaginated introduction, Adam 3–13, Adam papers, LHCMA.

45. Middle East censorship summaries, 10–16 September 1942, 3, WAII 1 462, ANZ.

46. 21 Army Group Censorship report, 15–30 June 1944, 2, 4, RG 24, vol. 10547, Library and Archives Canada (LAC).

47. 21 Army Group Censorship report, 16–31 March 1945, RG 24, vol. 10547, LAC.

48. Paul Cheall, ed., *Fighting Through from Dunkirk to Hamburg—A Green Howard's Wartime Memoir* (Barnsley: Pen & Sword, 2011), Kindle ed., chap. 4, para. 15, chap. 4, para. 3; French, *Churchill's Army*, 128–29.

49. Middle East censorship summaries, 30 September–6 October 1942, WAII/462, 6, ANZ.

50. Middle East censorship summaries, 10–16 September 1942, 3, 18–25 August 1942, 1, both in WAII/462, ANZ.

51. Jack Merewood, *To War with the Bays* (Cardiff: Queen's Dragoon Guards, 1996), 139, 155–56.

52. See N. F. Burrell, ts account, 2, LEEWW/2004–2680, Second World War Experience Centre.

53. P. R. (Patrick) Devlin ts account, 1, 3, 4–5, (new pagination) 3, 89/13/1, IWM. it proved impossible to trace the owner of copyright of the Devlin papers, and both the author and the Imperial War Museum would welcome information on this matter.

54. See Tim Travers, *The Killing Ground: The British Army, the Western Front and the Emergence of Modern Warfare 1900–1918* (London: Allen & Unwin, 1987); Max Hastings, *Overlord: D-Day and the Battle for Normandy, 1944* (London: Michael Joseph, 1984).

55. See Gary Sheffield, *Forgotten Victory: The First World War—Myths and Realities* (London: Headline, 2001); John Buckley, *Monty's Men: The British Army and the Liberation of Europe* (New Haven and London: Yale University Press, 2013).

56. Mark Connelly, *Steady the Buffs! A Regiment, a Region, and the Great War* (Oxford: Oxford University Press, 2006), 193, 208; Peter Hodgkinson, *British Infantry Battalion Commanders*, 200–7, 212–13; French, *Raising Churchill's Army*, 76–77, 80; Daniel Marston, *Phoenix from the Ashes: The Indian Army in the Burma Campaign* (Westport, CT: Praeger, 2003), 203, 228, 238. For Indian officers, see also Kaushik Roy's chapter in this book.

57. "Lessons from the Italian Campaign," December 1944, 77–78, WO 231/8, TNA.

8. Legitimacy, Consent, and the Mobilization of the British and Commonwealth Armies during the Second World War

1. Jonathan Fennell, *Fighting the People's War: The British and Commonwealth Armies and the Second World War* (Cambridge: Cambridge University Press, 2019), 678.

2. Fennell, *Fighting the People's War*, 91.

3. Margaret Gowing, "The Organisation of Manpower in Britain during the Second World War," *Journal of Contemporary History* 7, nos. 1–2 (1972): 148.

4. John Horne, "Introduction: Mobilizing for 'Total War,' 1914–1918," in *State, Society and Mobilization in Europe during the First World War*, ed. John Horne, (Cambridge: Cambridge University Press, 1997), 12.

5. Fennell, *Fighting the People's War*, 679–80; John Darwin, *The Empire Project: The Rise and Fall of the British World-System, 1830–1970* (New York: Cambridge University Press, 2009), 497.

6. Fennell, *Fighting the People's War*, 679–80; Darwin, *The Empire Project*, 497.

7. Fennell, *Fighting the People's War*, 88.

8. Fennell, *Fighting the People's War*, 88; I H-11a Report of the National Service Department, *Appendices to the Journals of the House of Representatives* (AJHR) 1943, 32; I H-11a Report of the National Service Department, *AJHR*, 1945, 21, 66; Report of the National Service Department, 1946, 21–33, 120, New Zealand Defence HQ Library. It must be noted that New Zealand kept much more robust statistics, and it is not outside the realms of possibility that these high figures could have been replicated across the Commonwealth.

9. Jonathan Fennell, "Soldiers and Social Change: The Forces Vote in the Second World War and New Zealand's Great Experiment in Social Citizenship," *English Historical Review* 132, no. 554 (2017), 86.

10. Fennell, *Fighting the People's War*, 680.

11. Fennell, *Fighting the People's War*, 680.

12. Fennell, *Fighting the People's War*, 680. Even if the total strength of the Royal Australian Air Force (RAAF) (about 60,000) and the new enlistments in the Navy (about 10,000) are added to the total of volunteers, recruitment was still below the First World War figure.

13. Fennell, *Fighting the People's War*, 680.

14. Fennell, *Fighting the People's War*, 680;

15. Fennell, *Fighting the People's War*, 66–77.

16. Fennell, *Fighting the People's War*, 681.

17. Fennell, *Fighting the People's War*, chap. 2; Horne, "Introduction," 2–14.

18. Jose Harris, *William Beveridge: A Biography* (Oxford: Clarendon Press: 1997), 416.

19. Harris, *William Beveridge*, 416.

20. Geoffrey G. Field, *Blood, Sweat, and Toil: Remaking the British Working Class, 1939–1945* (Oxford: Oxford University Press, 2011), 336.

21. Appreciation and Censorship Report No. 8, 19–25 February 1943, 6–7, War Office (WO) 204/10381 First Army Mail, The National Archives (TNA).

22. Appreciation and Censorship Report No. 14, April 2 to 8, 1943, 6, WO 204/10381 British North African Force (BNAF), TNA.

23. Appreciation and Censorship Report No. 19, 9 to 15 May, 6–7, WO 204/10381 First Army Mail, TNA.

24. Report on the Morale of British, Indian and African Troops in India Command and S.E.A. Command, February to April 1944, Appendix A, Post-War Prospects: A Note on British Forces Opinions as Seen in Censorship, L/WS/1/939, India Office Records (IOR), British Library (BL).

25. Stephen A. Hart, *Colossal Cracks: Montgomery's 21st Army Group in Northwest Europe, 1944–45* (Mechanicsburg, PA: Stackpole, 2007 [2000]), 44.

26. I. S. O. Playfair and C. J. C. Molony, *The Mediterranean and Middle East*, vol. 4, *The Destruction of the Axis Forces in Africa* (Uckfield, England: Naval & Military Press, 2004 [1966]), 460.

27. Carlo D'Este, *Bitter Victory: The Battle for Sicily 1943* (London: Aurum Press, 2008), 552, 597; Medical History of the Campaign in Sicily, July to August 1943, 1–2, Union War Histories (UWH) Box 346, South African National Defence Force Documentation Centre (SANDF, DOC).

28. S. Woodburn Kirby, *The War against Japan*, vol. 3, *The Decisive Battles* (London: HMSO, 1962), 372, 526–27; Timothy Moreman, *The Jungle, the Japanese and the British Commonwealth Armies at War, 1941–45: Fighting Methods, Doctrine and Training for Jungle Warfare* (London: Frank Cass, 2005), 144; Christopher Bayly and Tim Harper, *Forgotten Armies: Britain's Asian Empire & the War with Japan* (London: Penguin, 2005 [2004]), 390; Raymond Callahan, *Burma, 1942–1945* (London: Davis Poynter, 1978), 137.

29. C. P. Stacey, *The Victory Campaign: The Operations in North-West Europe, 1944–1945*, *Official History of the Canadian Army in the Second World War*, vol. 3 (Ottawa: Queen's Printer, 1966), 270.

30. Christine Ann Bielecki, "British Infantry Morale during the Italian Campaign, 1943–1945" (PhD dissertation, University College London, 2006),130.

31. Fennell, *Fighting the People's War*, 567–68.

32. Jonathan Fennell, "Reevaluating Combat Cohesion: The British Second Army in the Northwest Europe Campaign of the Second World War," in *Frontline: Combat and Cohesion in the Twenty-First Century*, ed. Anthony King (Oxford University Press, 2015), 141.

33. Fennell, "Reevaluating Combat Cohesion," 141.

34. Fennell, "Reevaluating Combat Cohesion," 142.

35. For an analysis of the multidimensional nature of morale, see Jonathan Fennell, "In Search of the 'X' Factor: Morale and the Study of Strategy," *Journal of Strategic Studies* 37, nos. 6–7 (2014), 799–828.

36. Report on the Morale of British, Indian, and Colonial Troops of Allied Land Forces, South East Asia, November 1944 to January 1945, 1, WO 203/4538, TNA.

37. Fennell, *Fighting the People's War*, 568–74. The quotation is from Alan Allport, *Browned Off and Bloody-Minded: The British Soldier Goes to War 1939–1945* (New Haven, CT: Yale University Press, 2015), 159.

38. Fennell, *Fighting the People's War*, 568–74.

39. Raymond Callahan, *Churchill and His Generals* (Lawrence: University Press of Kansas, 2007), 227; Callahan, *Burma*, 147.

40. Callahan, *Churchill and His Generals*, 227.

41. See Fennell, *Fighting the People's War*, chaps. 10 and 16.

42. Fennell, *Fighting the People's War*, 367–69.

43. Fennell, *Fighting the People's War*, 379–83.

44. F. L. W. Wood, *Political and External Affairs* (Wellington: Historical Publications Branch, 1958), 269.

45. Fennell, *Fighting the People's War*, 370.

46. Fennell, *Fighting the People's War*, 371–2.

47. Leonard Smith, "The French High Command and the Mutinies of Spring 1917," in *Facing Armageddon, The First World War Experienced*, ed. Hugh Cecil and Peter H. Liddle (London: Leo Cooper, 1996), 87.

48. Fennell, *Fighting the People's War*, 413.

49. Shelford Bidwell and Dominick Graham, *The Tug of War: The Battle for Italy, 1943–45* (London: Hodder & Stoughton, 1986), 185.

50. Middle East Military Censorship Fortnightly Summary (MEMCFS) No. 81, 12–25 January 1944, WAII/1/DA508/1 Vol. III, Archives New Zealand (ANZ); 2 New Zealand Field Censorship Section Weekly Report (2 NZ FCSWR), 12 December 1943, WAII/1/DA508/3, ANZ.

51. Defender to Main NZ Corps, 7 February 1944, WAII/8/70, ANZ.

52. MEMCFS No. 77, 17–30 November 1943, WAII/1/DA508/1 Vol. III, ANZ.

53. 2 NZ FCSWR, 26 February 1944, WAII/1/DA508/3, ANZ.

54. Fennell, *Fighting the People's War*, 415.

55. Defender to Main 2 NZ Div., 13 January 1944, WAII/8/70, ANZ. The second section of the 11th Reinforcement sailed at the end of March, the beginning of April 1944.

56. HQ 2 NZ Div. to Premier Wellington, 14 December 1943, WAII/8/70, ANZ; Brig. Stevens to Commander, 18 December 18 1943, WAII/8/70, ANZ; MEMCFS No. 75, 20 October–2 November 2, 1943, WAII/1/DA508/1 Vol. III, ANZ; 2 NZ FCSWR, 5 December 1943, WAII/1/DA508/3, ANZ.

57. Fennell, *Fighting the People's War*, 405–21. For a short assessment of the decline in the combat effectiveness of 2 New Zealand Division, see Gen. Freyberg to the Prime Minister, 7 June 1944, WAII/8/53, ANZ.

58. Fennell, *Fighting the People's War*, 211.

59. Fennell, *Fighting the People's War*, 419.

60. Fennell, *Fighting the People's War*, 419.

61. 2 NZ Div. to Defender Wellington, 3 July 1944, WAII/8/71, ANZ.

62. Gen. Freyberg to the Prime Minister, 7 June 1944.

63. Notes on Conference Held at Divisional HQ, 20 May 1944, WAII/8/52, ANZ.

64. Fennell, *Fighting the People's War*, 390.

65. Fennell, *Fighting the People's War*, 392.

66. Fennell, *Fighting the People's War*, 390–96.

67. Fennell, *Fighting the People's War*, 390–96.

68. Durban Military Censorship Summary No. 85, June 1944, Army Intelligence (AI) Gp Box 42/I/37/B, SANDF, DOC.

69. South African Military Censorship, Special Report No. 2, Memorandum on Intended Move North of Armoured Car Regiments, 25 November–9 December 1942, AI Gp 1 Box 81/I/71/B, SANDF, DOC.

70. C. P. Stacey, *The Victory Campaign*, 271.

71. Stacey, *The Victory Campaign*, 424; G. W. L. Nicholson, *The Canadians in Italy, 1943–1945* (Ottawa: Queen's Printer, 1966), 562.

72. Second Army, Quarterly Medical Report for period 1 April 1945 to 25 June 1945, 24–25, WO 177/322, TNA.

73. Fennell, *Fighting the People's War*, 568–73.

74. This was in spite of the fact that Mackenzie King had won a plebiscite allowing him to send conscripts overseas.

75. J. L. Granatstein, *Conscription in the Second World War* (Toronto: McGraw-Hill Ryerson, 1969), 57–64; Daniel Byers, *Zombie Army: The Canadian Army and Conscription in the Second World War* (Toronto: University of British Columbia Press, 2016), 227.

76. Granatstein, *Conscription in the Second World War*, 57–64. As Dan Byers has pointed out in *Zombie Army* (6), the origin of the use of the term "zombie" to describe Canadian conscripts is unknown.

77. Fennell, *Fighting the People's War*, 575–76.

78. Fennell, *Fighting the People's War*, 575–76.

79. Peter A. Russell, "BC's 1944 'Zombie' Protests Against Overseas Conscription," *BC Studies* 122 (Summer 1999): 67.

80. Russell, "BC's 1944 'Zombie' Protests," 70.

81. Byers, *Zombie Army*, 234–38, 69.

82. Horne, "Introduction," 2.

83. Horne, "Introduction," 4–5, 7, 12, 17.

84. S. P. MacKenzie, *Politics and Military Morale: Current-Affairs and Citizenship Education in the British Army, 1914–1950* (Oxford: Clarendon Press, 1992), 75.

9. "Enemy Aliens" and the Formation of Australia's 8th Employment Company

1. One excellent account among many is James Holland, *The Battle of Britain: Five Months That Changed History, May–October 1940* (New York: St. Martin's Press, 2011).

2. A good general survey of British measures regarding enemy aliens in wartime can be found in Richard Dove, ed. *"Totally un-English?" Britain's Internment of "Enemy*

Aliens" in Two World Wars (Amsterdam: Editions Rodopi BV, 2005). In an otherwise large literature, see also Ronald Stent, *A Bespattered Page? The Internment of "His Majesty's Most Loyal Enemy Aliens"* (London: William Collins, 1980).

3. A comprehensive account of this process is to be found in Peter and Leni Gillman, *"Collar the Lot!" How Britain Interned and Expelled Its Wartime Refugees* (London: Quartet, 1980).

4. On Canada's agreement to accept the internees and their subsequent reception, see Paula Draper, "The Accidental Immigrants: Canada and the Interned Refugees," parts 1 and 2, *Canadian Jewish Historical Society Journal* 2, nos. 1 and 2 (1979): 1–38, 80–112.

5. The story of the *Dunera*'s voyage to Australia has been recounted numerous times in a variety of formats. For the most definitive accounts, see Benzion Patkin, *The Dunera Internees* (Sydney: Cassell, 1979); Cyril Pearl, *The Dunera Scandal: Deported by Mistake* (Sydney: Angus and Robertson, 1983); Paul R. Bartrop, with Gabrielle Eisen, eds., *The Dunera Affair: A Documentary Resource Book* (Melbourne: Schwartz and Wilkinson/Jewish Museum of Australia, 1990); and Ken Inglis, Seumas Spark, and Jay Winter, eds. *Dunera Lives: A Visual History* (Clayton, Victoria: Monash University Publishing, 2018).

6. See, for example, the personal accounts in Bartrop and Eisen, eds., *Dunera Affair*, 151–90; Inglis, Spark and Winter, *Dunera Lives*, 65–107.

7. Handwritten minute by Sir George Pearce for Prime Minister J. A. Lyons, 2 June 1933, A434, file 49/3/7034, National Archives of Australia (NAA).

8. Paul R. Bartrop, *Australia and the Holocaust, 1933–1945* (Kew, Victoria: Australian Scholarly Publishing, 1994), 121–24.

9. The notion of "Good Jews" and "Bad Jews" with regard to immigration is explored in Paul R. Bartrop, "'Good Jews' and 'Bad Jews': Australian Perceptions of Jewish Migrants and Refugees, 1919–39," in *Jews in the Sixth Continent*, ed. W. D. Rubinstein (Sydney: Allen and Unwin, 1987), 169–84.

10. "Refugees (Jewish and Others)—General Policy File," Interior memorandum for Cabinet (*Immigration*) prepared by V. C. Thompson, 17 August 1938 (emphasis added), file 43/2/46, A433, NAA.

11. Prime Minister's Department to the High Commissioner's Office, "Immigration Policy Pt. 4 (1938–1944)," London, 6 September 1939, file A349/1/2 Pt. 4, A 461, NAA.

12. Home Office, London, *White Paper on Categories of Persons Eligible for Release from Internment*, October 1940, file A20/1/3 Pt. 1, A1608/1, NAA.

13. J. S. Duncan, Australia House (London) to the Secretary, Prime Minister's Department (Canberra), 20 November 1940, file A20/1/3 Pt. 1, A1608/1, NAA.

14. Teleprinter message to Secretary, Prime Minister's Department from Secretary, Department of the Army, 10 January 1941, file A20/1/3 Pt. 1, A1608/1, NAA.

15. Kurt Lewinski, "19 Wasted Months" (previously unpublished manuscript), in *The Dunera Affair: A Documentary Resource Book*, ed. Paul R. Bartrop, with Gabrielle Eisen (Melbourne: Schwartz and Wilkinson/Jewish Museum of Australia, 1990), 269–70.

16. The most comprehensive study of the *Queen Mary* internees is Paul R. Bartrop, "Incompatible with Security: Enemy Alien Internees from Singapore in Australia,

1940–45," *Journal of the Australian Jewish Historical Society* 6, part 1 (November 1993): 149–69.

17. Draft Press Statement, Department of the Army, Melbourne, 20 November 1941, file 63/401/335, MP729/6, NAA. The exact figure is unknown, but it was probably fewer than 100 given the context of the period.

18. Interview with Julian Layton, accession no. 004382/03, Department of Sound Records, Imperial War Museum (London).

19. "Diary of Mike Sondheim" (previously unpublished manuscript), in *The Dunera Affair: A Documentary Resource Book*, ed. Paul R. Bartrop, with Gabrielle Eisen (Melbourne: Schwartz and Wilkinson/Jewish Museum of Australia, 1990), 331.

20. "Letter from a Fruitpicker," *The Boomerang* (mimeographed camp newspaper), no. 36 (15–22 February 1942), in *The Dunera Affair: A Documentary Resource Book*, ed. Paul R. Bartrop, with Gabrielle Eisen (Melbourne: Schwartz and Wilkinson/Jewish Museum of Australia, 1990), 333.

21. "Letter from a Fruitpicker."

22. "Letter from a Fruitpicker."

23. June Factor, "Forgotten Soldiers: Aliens in the Australian Army's Employment Companies during World War II," accessed 30 January 2019, http://www.yosselbirstein.org/pdf/eng/other/Forgotten_Soldiers.pdf.

24. Lewinski, "19 Wasted Months," 337.

25. Lewinski, "19 Wasted Months," 337.

26. A useful summary of Broughton's life can be found in Inglis, Spark and Winter, *Dunera Lives*, 337.

27. Australian War Memorial (AWM), file 22/1/17, AWM 52.

28. Paul R. Bartrop, "Enemy Aliens or Stateless Persons? The Legal Status of Refugees from Germany in Wartime Australia," *Journal of the Australian Jewish Historical Society* 10, part 4 (November 1988): 270–80.

29. The author has heard this anecdote on numerous occasions from ex-*Dunera* internees over several decades; it might be apocryphal, but on the balance of probabilities, given those involved, it is likely to be accurate.

30. Scrapbook of Harry Jay (ex-8th Employment Company), extract from *Salt* 6, no. 4 (26 April 1943), in *The Dunera Affair: A Documentary Resource Book*, ed. Paul R. Bartrop, with Gabrielle Eisen (Melbourne: Schwartz and Wilkinson/Jewish Museum of Australia, 1990), 365. *Salt* was the magazine of the Australian Army Education Service during the war.

31. Scrapbook of Harry Jay, 365.

32. Bartrop and Eisen, *Dunera Affair*, 380–81.

33. "Letter from Ex-Internee in 8th Employment Company," *The Boomerang* (mimeographed camp newspaper), no. 48 (31 May 1942), in *The Dunera Affair: A Documentary Resource Book*, ed. Paul R. Bartrop, with Gabrielle Eisen (Melbourne: Schwartz and Wilkinson/Jewish Museum of Australia, 1990), 362–63.

34. "Letter from Ex-Internee in 8th Employment Company," 364.

35. Margaret Holmes, "Note on a Piece of Work with Refugee Students and Graduates who Came to Australia on the Transport 'Dunera,' (previously unpublished manuscript), in *The Dunera Affair: A Documentary Resource Book*, ed. Paul R. Bartrop, with Gabrielle Eisen (Melbourne: Schwartz and Wilkinson/Jewish Museum of Australia, 1990), 320–25.

36. F. M. Forde (Minister for the Army) to Ministers for Defence, Immigration and Information, and Labor and National Service, 20 November 1945, file 255/14/228, MP742/1, NAA.

37. See Inglis, Spark and Winter, *Dunera Lives*, 388–451, for a comprehensive coverage of the subsequent lives and achievements of many of those who had come to Australia as internees on the *Dunera*.

38. Scrapbook of Harry Jay, 368.

39. Walter Fletcher (Fleisch), previously unpublished 1990 reminiscence, in *The Dunera Affair: A Documentary Resource Book*, ed. Paul R. Bartrop, with Gabrielle Eisen (Melbourne: Schwartz and Wilkinson/Jewish Museum of Australia, 1990), 371.

40. Extract from minutes of Full Cabinet, Agendum 623, 14 March 1944, file A20/1/3 Pt. 2, A1608, NAA; War Cabinet minute (Cabinet Agendum 131/1944), 20 March 1944, file 712/1/20, A1308,NAA.

41. F. M. Forde (Minister for the Army) to Ministers for Defence, Immigration and Information, and Labor and National Service, 20 November 1945, file 255/14/228, MP742/1, NAA.

42. E. J. Holloway (Minister for Labor and National Service) to F. M. Forde (Minister for the Army), 24 November 1945, file 255/14/228, MP742/1, NAA.

10. The Body and Becoming a Soldier in Britain during the Second World War

1. Alan Badman interview, June 2002, accession 23227, reel 2, Imperial War Museum (IWM).

2. Army and A.T.S., 1939–46, appendix C, 80, WO277/12, The National Archives (TNA), Kew.

3. Ministry of Labour and National Service, *Manpower: The Story of Britain's Mobilisation for War* (London: HMSO, 1944), 11.

4. Jeremy Crang, *The British Army and the People's War, 1939–1945* (Manchester: Manchester University Press, 2000); David Fraser, *And We Shall Shock Them: The British Army in the Second World War* (London: Cassell Military, 1983); David French, *Raising Churchill's Army: The British Army and the War against Germany, 1919–1945* (Oxford: Oxford University Press, 2000).

5. Accounts of military training appear within popular histories of battalions and biographies of individual soldiers. However, there has been no in-depth academic study of the experience of British Army training during the Second World War.

6. Michel Foucault, *Discipline and Punish: The Birth of the Prison* (London: Penguin, 1979); Arthur Frank, "For a Sociology of the Body: An Analytical Review," in *The Body: Social Processes and Cultural Theory*, ed. Michel Featherstone, Michael Hepworth, and Bryan Turner (London: Sage, 1991), 36–102; David Morgan, "You Too Can Have a Body like Mine: Reflections on the Male Body and Masculinities," in *Body Matters: Essays on the Sociology of the Body*, ed. Sarah Scott and David Morgan (London: Falmer, 1993), 69–88.

7. Notable exceptions are: Joanna Bourke, *Dismembering the Male: Men's Bodies, Britain and the Great War* (London: Reaktion, 1999); Paul Higate, "The Body Resists: Everyday Clerking and Unmilitary Practice," in *The Body in Everyday Life*, ed. S. Nettleton and J. Watson (London: Routledge, 1998), 180–98.

8. Mark Harrison, *Medicine and Victory: British Military Medicine in the Second World War* (Oxford: Oxford University Press, 2004); Julie Anderson, *War, Disability and Rehabilitation in Britain: 'Soul of a Nation'* (Manchester: Manchester University Press, 2011).

9. James D. Campbell, *The Army Isn't All Work: Physical Culture and the Evolution of the British Army, 1860–1920* (London: Routledge, 2017), 104.

10. *Mass Observation* was a social research project designed to capture the everyday experiences of life in Britain between 1937 and 1948. During the Second World War several "observers" reported on day-to-day life in the armed forces. See Lucy Noakes, *War and the British: Gender, Memory and National Identity* (London: I. B. Tauris, 1998), 75.

11. Great Britain, House of Commons Parliamentary Papers, *Strength and Casualties of the Armed Forces and Auxiliary Services of the United Kingdom, 1939–1945*, Command Papers (Cmd.) 6832 (London: HMSO, 1946), 2.

12. See for example, Sidone Smith and Julia Watson, *Reading Autobiography* (Minneapolis: University of Minnesota Press, 2001), 37; Nigel de Lee, "Oral history and British soldiers' Experience," in *Time to Kill: The Soldier's Experience of War in the West*, ed. Paul Addison and Angus Calder (London: Pimlico, 1997), 365.

13. See for example Richard Vinen, *National Service: Conscription in Britain 1945–1963* (London: Penguin, 2014).

14. French, *Raising Churchill's Army*, 68.

15. Albert Edward Hunter interview, 1994, accession 34732, reel 1, IWM.

16. Diary for December 1942, 2, D 5134, *Mass Observation* Archive (MOA).

17. James Wyndham interview, October 2000, accession 20793, reel 4, IWM.

18. Diary for November 1940, D 5165, MOA.

19. See Sonya O. Rose, *Which People's War? National Identity and Citizenship in Wartime Britain, 1939–1945* (Oxford: Oxford University Press, 2003), 179.

20. Peter Holyhead interview, November 2000, accession 2099, reel 1, IWM.

21. Leslie Gray interview, January 2002, accession 22595, reel 1, IWM.

22. Great Britain, War Office (WO), *Army Training Memorandum No. 36 "War,"* (London: HMSO, September1940), 8.

23. John Dray interview, February 2004, accession 27053, reel 4, IWM.

24. William Dilworth interview, July 1998, accession 18435, reel 2, IWM.

25. Campbell, *The Army Isn't All Work*, 81.

26. Great Britain, WO, *Physical and Recreational Training* (London: HMSO, 1941), 4.

27. Great Britain, WO, *Basic and Battle Physical Training: Part I, General Principles of Basic and Battle Physical Training and Methods of Instruction* (London: HMSO, 1944), 21.

28. See for example, James Vernon, *Hunger: A Modern History* (Cambridge, MA: Harvard University Press, 2007), 96–104; Ina Zweiniger-Bargielowska, *Managing the Body: Beauty, Health and Fitness in Britain, 1880–1939* (Oxford: Oxford University Press, 2010), 137–39.

29. "Quality and Variety of Army's Meals," *Manchester Guardian*, 17 December 1940, 6.

30. WO, *Basic and Battle Physical Training: Part I*, 25–27.

31. James Wyndham interview, reel 4.

32. Private papers of David Evans, Documents 2028, 8, IWM.

33. Robert Ellison interview, 1999, accession 18743, reel 6, IWM.

34. Walter Chalmers interview, 1999, accession 19805, reel 2, IWM.

35. Roy Bolton interview, May 2002, accession 23195, reel 2, IWM.

36. John Gray interview, March 2000, accession 20202, reel 3, IWM.

37. John Dray interview, reel 4.

38. James Wyndham interview, reel 5.

39. William Dilworth interview, reel 2.

40. James Wyndham interview, reel 5.

41. Bert Scrivens interview, February 2007, accession 29536, reel 2, IWM.

42. Roy Bolton interview, reel 3.

43. Leslie Gray interview, reel 2.

44. James Wyndham interview, reel 5.

45. Neville Wildgust interview, 2002, accession 23848, reel 10, IWM.

46. Diary for January 1941, 6, D. 5061.1, MOA.

47. Russell King, interview, September 1998, accession 18512, reel 5, IWM.

48. Paul Ferris, *Sex and the British: A Twentieth-Century History* (London: Penguin, 1993), 43.

49. William Dilworth interview, reel 2.

50. Morris, Life in a Depot, January 1941, 4, TC29: Men in the Forces 1939–1956, 2/D, MOA.

51. Leonard England, Morale Report, June 1941, 3, TC29: Men in the Forces 1939–1956, 2/B, MOA.

52. In the army homosexual acts were classified under the offence of "indecency." An ordinary soldier found guilty of this crime faced up to two years' imprisonment, while an officer risked being cashiered (dismissed). WO, *Manual of Military Law* (London: HMSO, 1940), 115.

53. Private papers of R. H. Lloyd-Jones, Document 125, IWM.

54. Life in a Depot, 3, TC29, Forces: Men in the Forces 1939–1956, 2/E, MOA.

55. Recent estimates suggest that around 250,000 homosexual men served in the British armed forces between 1939 and 1945, but that up to 1,300,000 of the 6,508,000 men and women who served might have identified as "queer." See Emma Vickers, *Queen and Country: Same-Sex Desire in the British Armed Forces, 1939–45* (Manchester: Manchester University Press, 2013), 3–4.

56. Campbell, *The Army Isn't All Work*, 25–30.

57. WO, *Basic and Battle Physical Training: Part II, Basic Physical Training Tables and Basic Physical Efficiency Tests* (London: HMSO, 1944), 4–6.

58. WO, *Basic and Battle Physical Training: Part II*, 15–16.

59. Campbell, *The Army Isn't All Work*, 25–30.

60. WO, *Physical and Recreational Training*, 3.

61. WO, *Basic and Battle Physical Training: Part I*, 3.

62. See G. Dawson, *Soldier Heroes: British Adventure and the Imagining of Masculinities* (London: Routledge, 1994), 1.

63. Campbell, *The Army Isn't All Work*, 104.

64. WO, *Army Training Memorandum no. 36*, (London: HMSO, September 1940), 6.

65. WO, *Army Training Memorandum no. 42*, 1942, 24.

66. Robert Ellison interview, reel 3.

67. Roy Bolton interview, reel 2.

68. John Dray interview, reel 6.

69. Robert Ellison interview, reel 5.

70. Hew Strachan, "Training, Morale and Modern War," *Journal of Contemporary History* 41, no. 2 (2006): 223–24.

71. Vic Emery interview, January 2003, accession 24731, reel 3, IWM.

72. Kenneth Johnstone interview, 1986, accession 9185, reel 2, IWM.

73. Day to day life in the army, August 1940, 1, TC29, Forces: Men in the Forces 1939–1956, 2/E, MOA.

74. Bert Blackall interview, June 2003, accession 23347, reel 2, IWM.

75. Roy Bolton interview, reel 2.

76. Ian Sinclair interview, 1991, accession 11468, reel 3, IWM.

77. Robert Ellison interview, reel 4.

78. Francis A. Crew, *The Army Medical Services, Administration, Volume 1* (London: HMSO, 1953), 352–53.

79. S. Lyle Cummins, "Physical Development Centres," *Journal of the Royal Army Medical Corps* 18, no. 3 (1943): 184.

80. Ernest Harvey interview, n.d., accession 14977, reel 3, IWM.

81. Anthony Bashford interview, November 1992, accession 12907, reel 1, n.d.

82. Crew, *Army Medical Services, Volume 1*, 380.

83. Diary for January 1941, 6, D 5061.1, MOA.

84. "WW2 People's War Archive, A3331577," Percy Bowpitt for BBC, 26 November 2004, http://www.bbc.co.uk/ww2peopleswar/stories/77/a3331577.shtml.

85. Strachan, "Training, morale and modern war," 216.

86. WO, *Physical and Recreational Training*, 9.

87. WO, *Basic and Battle Physical Training, Part 1*, 8.

88. Tony Mason and Eliza Riedi, *Sport and the Military: The British Armed Forces, 1880–1960* (Cambridge: Cambridge University Press, 2010).

89. Morale report 2, 15 December 1940, 4, TC29, Forces: Men in the Forces 1939–1956, 2/D,, MOA.

90. W. A. Elliot, *Esprit de Corps: A Scots Guards Officer on Active Service, 1943–1945* (Wimborne: Michael Russell, 1996), 105.

91. WO, *Physical and Recreational Training*, 3.

92. John Gray interview, reel 3.

93. Ron Gray interview, reel 2.

94. James Wyndham interview, reel 5.

95. Kenneth New interview, September 2000, accession 20948, reel 1, IWM.

96. Roy Bolton interview, reel 2.

97. Crang, *The British Army*, 65.

11. Canada and the Mobilization of Manpower during the Second World War

1. For the most recent summary of these issues, which also provides an overview of the other relevant literature, see Daniel Byers, *Zombie Army: The Canadian Army and Conscription in the Second World War* (Toronto: University of British Columbia Press, 2016), esp. 13–34.

2. Byers, *Zombie Army*, 94; C. P. Stacey, *Arms, Men and Governments: The War Policies of Canada, 1939–1945* (Ottawa: Queen's Printer, 1970), 51; J. de N. Kennedy, *History of the Department of Munitions and Supply*, Vol. 2, *Controls, Service and Finance Branches, and Units Associated with the Department* (Ottawa: King's Printer, 1950), 355–56.

3. E. L. M. Burns, *Manpower in the Canadian Army, 1939–1945* (Toronto: Clarke, Irwin, 1956).

4. R. MacGregor Dawson, *The Conscription Crisis of 1944* (Toronto: University of Toronto Press, 1961), esp. 17, 29–33.

5. J. L. Granatstein, and J. M. Hitsman, *Broken Promises: A History of Conscription in Canada* (Toronto: Oxford University Press, 1977), esp. 158. See also J. L. Granatstein, *Canada's War: The Politics of the Mackenzie King Government, 1939–1945* (Toronto: Oxford University Press, 1975), esp. 216.

6. Michael D. Stevenson, *Canada's Greatest Wartime Muddle: National Selective Service and the Mobilization of Human Resources during World War II* (Montreal: McGill-Queen's University Press, 2001), 12 (emphasis added). For another, similar view, see David Allan Wilson, "Close and Continuous Attention: Human Resources Management in Canada during the Second World War" (PhD dissertation thesis, University of New Brunswick, 1997).

7. Richard J. Walker, "The Revolt of the Canadian Generals, 1944: The Case for the Prosecution," in *The Insubordinate and the Noncompliant: Case Studies of Canadian Mutiny and Disobedience, 1920 to Present*, ed. Howard G. Coombs (Kingston: Canadian Defence Academy Press, 2007), 55–100.

8. King's diaries were donated to Library and Archives Canada (LAC) as part of his larger collection of private papers following his death. They were first published in edited form in J. W. Pickersgill, ed., *The Mackenzie King Record*, 4 vols. (Toronto: University of Toronto Press, 1960–1970), then fully on microfilm for the 1930s–1940s as *The Mackenzie King Diaries, 1932–1949* (Toronto: University of Toronto Press, 1980), and today are fully accessible through the LAC website at http://www.bac-lac.gc.ca /eng/discover/politics-government/prime-ministers/william-lyon-mackenzie-king /Pages/search.aspx.

9. Stacey, *Arms, Men, and Governments*, 2, 8–9; Granatstein, *Canada's War*, 42–43; Douglas E. Delaney, *The Imperial Army Project: Britain and the Land Forces of the Dominions and India, 1902–1945* (Oxford: Oxford University Press, 2017), 203–8.

10. Stacey, *Arms, Men, and Governments*, 12–15; Granatstein, *Canada's War*, 24–25; Stacey, *Official History of the Canadian Army in the Second World War*, vol. 1, *Six Years of War: The Army in Canada, Britain, and the Pacific* (Ottawa: Queen's Printer, 1955), 34–64.

11. Stacey, *Arms, Men, and Governments*, 12–13, 15–16; Gilbert Norman Tucker, *The Naval Service of Canada: Its Official History*, vol. 2, *Activities on Shore during the Second World War* (Ottawa: King's Printer, 1952), 5–45, 269; W. A. B. Douglas et al., *No Higher Purpose: The Official Operational History of the Royal Canadian Navy in the Second World War*, vol. 2, part 1 (St. Catharines: Vanwell Publishing/Department of National Defence, 2002), 27–90.

12. Stacey, *Arms, Men, and Governments*, 30–31; Granatstein, *Canada's War*, 59–66.

13. Stacey, *Arms, Men, and Governments*, 17–30; Granatstein, *Canada's War*, 43–59; F. J. Hatch, *Aerodrome of Democracy: Canada and the British Commonwealth Air Training*

Plan, 1939–1945 (Ottawa: Supply and Services Canada, 1983), 1–26, 33; W. A. B. Douglas, *The Creation of a National Air Force: The Official History of the Royal Canadian Air Force* (Toronto: Supply and Services Canada/University of Toronto Press, 1986), 2:191–230, 343–47. Also King Diaries, September 27–28, 1939.

14. On the developments discussed here, in the rest of this paragraph, and the following three, see Stacey, *Six Years of War*, 72–85, 179, 181; Stacey, *Arms, Men, and Governments*, 31–36, 44–45, 48; Granatstein, *Canada's War*, 81, 93–103.

15. Hatch, *Aerodrome of Democracy*, 48–59, 101–12; Douglas, *The Creation of a National Air Force*, 231–39, 250–56.

16. Tucker, *The Naval Service of Canada*, 2:45–63, 274; Douglas et al., *No Higher Purpose*, 91–95, 130–45.

17. Stacey, *Arms, Men, and Governments*, 167.

18. Michael A. Hennessey, "The Industrial Front: The Scale and Scope of Canadian Industrial Mobilization during the Second World War," in *Forging a Nation: Perspectives on the Canadian Military Experience*, ed. Bernd Horn (St. Catharines: Vanwell, 2002), 143–44, 151; Jeffrey A. Keshen, *Saints, Sinners, and Soldiers: Canada's Second World War* (Vancouver: University of British Columbia Press, 2004), 42–46, 65–66; Stacey, *Arms, Men, and Governments*, 167.

19. Hennessey, "The Industrial Front," 143. For other excellent summaries of industrial mobilization during the war, see Stacey, *Arms, Men, and Governments*, 485–514; Robert Bothwell, "'Who's Paying for Anything These Days?' War Production in Canada, 1939–1945," in *Mobilization for Total War*, ed. N. F. Dreisziger (Waterloo: Wilfrid Laurier University Press, 1981), 57–69; Robert Bothwell and William Kilbourn, *C. D. Howe: A Biography* (Toronto: McClelland and Stewart, 1979), 123–79.

20. "The National Resources Mobilization Act, 1940," 4 George VI, chap. 13, *Acts of the Parliament of the Dominion of Canada*, 1939–1940 (Ottawa: King's Printer, 1940), 43. Also reproduced in full in Byers, *Zombie Army*, 245–46.

21. Developments related to conscription during the war are covered most fully in Stacey, *Arms, Men, and Governments*, 397–484; Granatstein and Hitsman, *Broken Promises*, 133–244; Byers, *Zombie Army* (and esp. 48–76 on the early ones described in this paragraph).

22. On Crerar, see in particular J. L. Granatstein, *The Generals: The Canadian Army's Senior Commanders in the Second World War* (Toronto: Stoddart, 1993), 83–115; Paul Douglas Dickson, *A Thoroughly Canadian General: A Biography of General H. D. G. Crerar.* (Toronto: University of Toronto Press, 2007).

23. Stacey, *Arms, Men, and Governments*, appendix T, 599–602; Byers, *Zombie Army*, 3, 5–6, 37–39, 71–72, 76–80, 82–88, 187–88.

24. Crerar, CGS (Chief of the General Staff), to Minister (of defense, J. L. Ralston), 14 July 1941, and typed notes by Ralston titled "General, Re[.]—Manpower—Re[.]—Needs," both in "Manpower Sixth Division, re[.] manpower. [*sic*]—with index, July 1941" (hereafter "Manpower Sixth Division"), vol. 117, MG27-III-B11 (Ralston Papers), LAC. Also unattributed British "Memorandum" attached to documents forwarded by Under Secretary of State for External Affairs (Canada), to Ralston, 13 January 1943, and notes by Ralston on its implications, both in "Manpower, Gen[eral]. (Secret), Vol. 2," vol. 52, Ralston Papers; Dickson, *A Thoroughly Canadian General*, 142–43; Delaney, *The Imperial Army Project*, 231.

25. On the creation of the final army program during 1941–1942, as well as Canada's commitments under the PJBD, see Byers, *Zombie Army*, 88–105.

26. A discussion of the implications of the army's commitments to Newfoundland can be found in Kenneth Stuart, Vice CGS, to Minister, 29 July 1941, "Manpower Sixth Division," vol. 117, Ralston Papers. On developments for all three services, see also Stacey, *Arms, Men, and Governments*, 134–36.

27. Byers, *Zombie Army*, 36–37, 72–76, 98–99, 102–5.

28. Memorandum of 28 February 1942, in *Ottawa at War: The Grant Dexter Memoranda, 1939–1945*, ed. Frederick W. Gibson and Barbara Robertson (Winnipeg: Manitoba Record Society, 1994), 282.

29. On the developments described throughout this paragraph, see in particular Byers, *Zombie Army*, 105–14. For various perspectives on the political events related to what is known as the "first conscription crisis" in 1942, see also Stacey, *Arms, Men, and Governments*, 399–402; Granatstein, *Canada's War*, 212–43; Granatstein and Hitsman, *Broken Promises*, 158–80; André Laurendeau, "The Conscription Crisis, 1942," in *André Laurendeau: Witness for Quebec*, ed. and transl. Philip Stratford, (Toronto: Macmillan, 1973), 1–121.

30. Developments related to NSS are summarized somewhat more fully in Byers, *Zombie Army*, 114–15. On labor relations, see Keshen, *Saints, Sinners, and Soldiers*, 55–64; Laurel Sefton MacDowell, "The Formation of the Canadian Industrial Relations System during World War Two," *Labour/Le Travailleur* 3 (1978): 175–96; Jeremy Webber, "The Malaise of Compulsory Conciliation: Strike Prevention in Canada during World War II, " *Labour/Le Travail* 15 (Spring 1985): 57–88.

31. Byers, *Zombie Army*, 115–16; Stacey, *Arms, Men, and Governments*, 416–17. See also Ruth Roach Pierson, *"They're Still Women After All": The Second World War and Canadian Womanhood* (Toronto: McClelland and Stewart, 1986); Jennifer A. Stephen, *Pick One Intelligent Girl: Employability, Domesticity, and the Gendering of Canada's Welfare State, 1939–1947* (Toronto: University of Toronto Press, 2007).

32. For example, see comments by D[onald] Gordon, Deputy Governor, Bank of Canada, to J. L. Ralston, 22 July 1941, "Manpower Sixth Division," vol. 117, Ralston Papers.

33. Transcript of interview with Major General Harry Letson (hereafter Letson interview), 27 May 1981, "BIOG FILE—L., Letson, Harry Farnham German," 9–10, Directorate of History and Heritage, Department of National Defence, Ottawa, Ontario.

34. "Memorandum on Man-Power Requirements and Supply in Canada," prepared by H. Carl Goldenberg and F. St. L. Daly, 11 June 1941, , "Compulsory Training, 1942: 4 months Training. Order of Call. N.R.M.A. May-June 1941, May 1942," vol. 68, Ralston Papers.

35. Granatstein and Hitsman, *Broken Promises*, 185–97 (esp. 194).

36. Allan D. English, *The Cream of the Crop: Canadian Aircrew, 1939–1945* (Montreal: McGill-Queen's University Press, 1996), 137–44.

37. On Ralston's reorganizations during 1942–1943, see Daniel Byers, "J. L. Ralston as Minister of National Defence during the Second World War: A Reassessment," *Canadian Army Journal* 16, no. 1 (2015): 82. On Browne's replacement, see Letson interview, 3; Geoffrey Hayes, *Crerar's Lieutenants: Inventing the Canadian Junior Army Officer, 1939–45* (Vancouver: University of British Columbia Press, 2017), 49.

38. Stevenson, *Canada's Greatest Wartime Muddle.*

39. Memorandum of 18 February 1942, *Ottawa at War*, 281–82; Dawson, *The Conscription Crisis of 1944*, 29–31; Granatstein and Hitsman, *Broken Promises*, 170, 188, 198–200; Bothwell, *C. D Howe*, 167–68, 172–73; J. E. Rea, "What Really Happened? A New Look at the Conscription Crisis, " *The Beaver* 74, no. 2 (1994): 12–17; Stevenson, *Canada's Greatest Wartime Muddle*, 5–6, 8; Walker, "The Revolt of the Canadian Generals, 1944, " 60–66, 70.

40. On the issues discussed up to now in this paragraph, see Byers, *Zombie Army*, 188–89.

41. See especially "Overseas Trip Nov.–Dec. 1943, Forestry Corps," vol. 59; "Overseas Trip Nov.–Dec. 1943, Order of Battle—3rd Canadian Infantry Division," vol. 61; "English Trip July–Aug. 1943, Forestry—(Return of Forestry Corps to Canada), (No. 7)—C.M.H.Q. Meeting," vol. 65; "Forestry Corps 1944, Summary of Rates of Pay, Leave Regulations, Personnel, Regulations, Application, Civilian Work, Jan[.]–March," vol. 79—all in Ralston Papers. See also Stacey, *Arms, Men, and Governments*, 411.

42. Stacey, *Arms, Men, and Governments*, 430–31. On these issues generally, see also Byers, *Zombie Army*, 126, 180–85, 190–97.

43. Howe to Ralston, copied to Thorson and Mitchell, 11 July 1942, "Military Manpower vs[.] Manpower for War Production . . . 1940–42," vol. 113, Ralston Papers.

44. Howe to A. D. P. Heeney, Secretary, Cabinet War Committee, 22 September 1942, "Manpower, vol. 2, Hon. J. L. Ralston," vol. 114, Ralston Papers.

45. On the various ways Canadians did resist assumptions that they should accept greater government direction during the war, see Keshen, *Saints, Sinners, and Soldiers.*

12. South African Manpower and the Second World War

1. On the South African neutrality crisis, see Andrew Stewart, "The British Government and the South African Neutrality Crisis, 1938–1939," *English Historical Review* 123, no. 503 (2008): 947–72.

2. E. P. Hartshorn, *Avenge Tobruk* (Cape Town: Purnell, 1960), 1.

3. Pierre van Ryneveld, South African Preparedness for War, September 1939, 1, Box 369, Union War History (UWH) Narratives, South African National Defence Force Archives (SANDFA).

4. Letter from Smuts to J. Martin, 30 November 1939, in W. K. Hancock and J. van der Poel, eds., *Selections from the Smuts Papers: Vol VI* (Cambridge: Cambridge University Press, 1966), 200–201.

5. The South African population was classified according to race and ethnicity. "European" denoted white, while "Non-European" included people classified as black, coloured, or Asian. The Non-European Army Service (NEAS) comprised the Native Military Corps (NMC), the Cape Corps (CC), and the Indian and Malay Corps (IMC).

6. The European male population between the ages of eighteen and sixty-five was as follows: eighteen to forty-four (452,369), forty-five to sixty (160,604), sixty-one to sixty-five (37,557).

7. Included in this figure were personnel for the armoured fighting vehicle (AFV) battalions (4,221), a Mines Engineering Brigade (5,320), and Lines of Communications MT Drivers for 10 Motor Transport companies (2,100) being replaced by "Non-European"

personnel. Statistics in Memorandum on Manpower, ca. late 1940, file 24/2, box 86, Chief of the General Staff (CGS) War, SANDF Documentation Centre, Pretoria.

8. Neil Orpen, *The Dukes* (Galvin: Cape Town, 1956), 95.

9. Manpower Wastage in the UDF, Memorandum on Manpower in the Union (European), August 1940, file 24/2, box 86, Chief of the General Staff (CGS) War, SANDF Documentation Centre.

10. H. J. Martin and N. D. Orpen, *South Africa at War: Military and Industrial Organisation and Operations in Connection with the Conduct of the War, 1939–1945* (Cape Town: Purnell, 1979), 44.

11. A South African infantry division totaled no fewer than 37,593 men, of whom 33,070 were to be European. Neil Orpen, *East African and Abyssinian Campaigns* (Cape Town: Purnell, 1968), 9, 85.

12. Manpower Wastage in the UDF.

13. Orpen, *East African and Abyssinian Campaigns*, 226–27.

14. Letter from CGS to General Manager SAR&H, 28 August 1940, Manpower Wastage in the UDF, file 24/2, box 86, CGS War, SANDF Documentation Centre. The term "coloured" was commonly used in South Africa to identify individuals of mixed race. It is used throughout this chapter to capture with historical accuracy how this part of the South African population was identified during the Second World War.

15. Anon., *We Fought the Miles: The History of the South African Railways at War, 1939–1945* (Johannesburg: SA Railways, c.1946), 105.

16. Some 1,076 miners were then already in uniform; Manpower Wastage in the UDF.

17. F. W. Cooper, *The Police Brigade: 6 S.A. Infantry Brigade, 1939–45* (Cape Town: Constantia, 1972).

18. Deborah Shackleton, "South Africa and the High Commission Territories during the Second World War: Politics and Policies Affecting War Mobilization," *Scientia Militaria* 30, no. 2 (2000): 240.

19. Letter from Brig. Gen. H. S. Wakefield to adjutant-general (AG), 6 November 1940, Manpower Wastage in the UDF, file 24/2, box 86, CGS War, SANDF Documentation Centre; Orpen, *East African and Abyssinian Campaigns*, 53, 87.

20. Orpen, *East African and Abyssinian Campaigns*, 53. Gwen Hewitt, *Womanhood at War: The Story of the SAWAS* (Johannesburg: private, n.d.).

21. J. F. Macdonald, *The War History of Southern Rhodesia* (Salisbury: Government of Southern Rhodesia, 1950), 2:474–77.

22. Letter from Lt. Col. G. C. G. Werdmuller Deputy Adjutant General (DAG) to AG, September 1940, Manpower Wastage in the UDF, file 24/2, box 86, CGS War, SANDF Documentation Centre.

23. Letter from Brig. Gen. F. H. Theron to CGS, 9 September 1940, Manpower Wastage in the UDF, file 24/2, box 86, CGS War.

24. Albert Grundlingh, "The King's Afrikaners? Enlistment and Ethnic Identity in the Union of South Africa's Defence Force during the Second World War, 1939–45," *Journal of African History* 40, no. 3 (1999): 354–55.

25. F. L. Monama, "Wartime Propaganda in the Union of South Africa, 1939–1945," (PhD dissertation, Stellenbosch University, 2014), chap. 4.

26. Thelma Gutsche, *The History and Social Significance of Motion Pictures in South Africa, 1895–1940* (Cape Town: Howard Timmins, 1972), 270, 328–29, 353, 371.

27. Memorandum on Manpower, ca. 1945, file Manpower, 1–8, 10–11, box 22, Civil, UWH, SANDF Documentation Centre. War Measure 6/41.

28. Douglas E. Delaney, *The Imperial Army Project: Britain and the Land Forces of the Dominions and India, 1902–1945* (Oxford: Oxford University Press, 2017), 254–55.

29. Extracts from conference between CGS and Members of the Legislative Assembly (MLAs), June 12, 1942, Manpower Wastage in the UDF, file 24/2, box 86, CGS War, SANDF Documentation Centre.

30. Carey Heydenrych, *Heck! What a Life! A Story about an Ordinary Fellow and His Extraordinary Wartime Experiences* (Cape Town: Salty Print, 1995), 11.

31. Extract from staff conference, 12 August 942, Manpower Wastage in the UDF, file 24/2, box 86, CGS War, SANDF Documentation Centre.

32. Extract from staff conference, 19 August 1942 and 16 August 1944, Manpower Wastage in the UDF, file 24/2, box 86, CGS War, SANDF Documentation Centre.

33. Extract from staff conference, 2 December 1942, and letter from Maj-Gen Frank Theron to Maj-Gen Evered Poole, 6 August 1944, Manpower Wastage in the UDF, file 24/2, box 86, CGS War, SANDF Documentation Centre.

34. Letter from CGS to AG, 31 August 1942, Manpower Wastage in the UDF, file 24/2, box 86, CGS War, SANDF Documentation Centre.

35. This figure for white male full-time volunteers (186,218) includes those who served in the Land Forces (132,194), the SAAF (44,569) and the SANF (9,455). This accords in round terms with the number (190,000) given in *The Official Yearbook of the Union of South Africa* (Pretoria: Government Printer, 1946), 20. Adding those who served in part-time units (63,341) brings the grand total of white male volunteers to 249,559.

36. Grundlingh, "The King's Afrikaners?"; Louis Grundlingh, "The Military, Race, and Resistance: The Conundrums of Recruiting Black South African Men during the Second World War," in *Africa and World War II*, ed. Judith A. Byfield, Carolyn A. Brown, Timothy Parson, and Ahmad Alawad Sikainga (New York: Cambridge University Press, 2015), 86–88.

37. Neil Roos, *Ordinary Springboks: White Servicemen and Social Justice in South Africa, 1939–1961* (Burlington, VT: Ashgate, 2005).

38. Letter from AG to Dechief, 5 February 1946, file AG(3)154/X/1235/7, box 139, AG3, SANDF Documentation Centre.

39. Grundlingh, "The Military, Race, and Resistance," 86–88.

40. Roos, *Ordinary Springboks*, 30.

41. Richard Holmes, *Acts of War: The Behaviour of Men in Battle* (London: Weidenfeld & Nicholson, 2003), 271–73.

42. James Ambrose Brown, *Retreat to Victory: A Springbok's Diary in North Africa: Gazala to El Alamein, 1942* (Rivonia, Johannesburg: Ashanti, 1991), 1.

43. Albert Grundlingh, "The King's Afrikaners?," 359.

44. As quoted in Ronald W. Tungay, *The Fighting Third* (Cape Town: Unie-Volkspers, 1947), 2.

45. Mike Sadler, *The War Story of Soldier 124280* (Pinetown, Durban: 30° South, 2014), 20.

46. J. F. Reitz, *Memoirs of a Somehow Soldier* (Caledon, Western Cape: private, n.d.), 79.

47. Letter from CGS to AG, 31 August 1942, Manpower Wastage in the UDF, file 24/2, box 86, CGS War, SANDF Documentation Centre.

48. Albert Grundlingh, "The King's Afrikaners?," 362.

49. S. G. Wolhuter, *The Melancholy State: The Story of a South African Prisoner-of-War* (Cape Town: Howard Timmins, 1983), 3.

50. Sampie de Wet, *Shifty in Italy* (N.p.: The Modern Printers, 1945), 2.

51. Letter from Mrs. Henderson to Lt. Charles Henderson, 19 March 1941, Senator Charles Henderson Papers, Natal Carbineers Archives, Pietermaritzburg.

52. Blamey, *A Company Commander Remembers*, 1.

53. Smuts quoted in Brown, *Retreat to Victory*, 21.

54. Gustav Bentz, "In for a Hell of a Time: The Wartime Experiences of Two South African Soldiers in the North African Desert,"5th War and Society in Africa Conference, Saldanha, Western Cape, 2006.

55. Cape Fortress Intelligence Summary No. 6, 5 November 1942, file Cape Fortress Air Defence (CFAD) 24/6/10 Intelligence Cape Fortress Summary, box 12, CFAD, SANDF Documentation Centre.

56. Reitz, *Memoirs of a Somehow Soldier*, 5–6.

57. Lennox van Onselen, *A Rhapsody in Blue* (Cape Town: Howard Timmins, 1960), 120.

58. David Brokensha, *Brokie's Way: An Anthropologist's Story: Love and Work in Three Continents* (Fish Hoek, Cape Town: Amani Press, 2007), 53.

59. K. W. Grundy, *Soldiers without Politics: Blacks in the South African Armed Forces* (Berkeley: University of California Press, 1983), 28–29.

13. Manpower Mobilization and Rehabilitation in New Zealand's Second World War

1. F. L. W. Wood, *The New Zealand People at War, Political and External Affairs* (Wellington: War History Branch, Department of Internal Affairs [DIA], 1958), 11.

2. "Report of the National Service Department," 1 June 1943, *Appendices to the Journals of the House of Representatives (AJHR)*, 1943, H-11A, 10.

3. Nancy M. Taylor, *The New Zealand People at War, The Home Front*, 2 vols. (Wellington: Historical Publications Branch, DIA, 1986), 1: 68.

4. Taylor, *The New Zealand People at War*, 1:79.

5. M. B. McGlynn, "History of the National Service Department, Manpower September 1939 to July 1940" (unpublished narrative, April 1948), 1–2, War Archives (WA) 121/31, Archives New Zealand (ANZ).

6. McGlynn, "History of the National Service Department," 3.

7. McGlynn, "History of the National Service Department," 3.

8. Organisation for National Security (ONS)141, "Reserved Occupations," 21 August 1939, External Affairs Records (EA) 1, 81/6/2 (4), ANZ. See also M. B. McGlynn, "Manpower for Industry 1939–1943" (unpublished narrative, June 1950), 2, WA 121/33, ANZ.

9. McGlynn, "Manpower for Industry 1939–1943," 3, 7.

10. McGlynn, "Manpower for Industry 1939–1943," 6.

11. McGlynn, "Manpower for Industry 1939–1943," 8–9.

12. McGlynn, "Manpower for Industry 1939–1943," 9. See also "Report of the National Service Department," 3. For a later version of the schedule see "Schedule of Important Occupations,"17 January 1941, 1, NS-DN4, ANZ.

13. "New Zealand Acts as Enacted," New Zealand Legal Information Institute (NZLII), accessed 20 December 2018, http://www.nzlii.org/nz/legis/hist_act/eraa 19404gv1940n1397/.

14. Wood, *The New Zealand People at War*, 141–42.

15. Quoted in John E. Martin, "The National Service Department and New Zealand's Manpower crisis of 1942," in *Kia Kaha, New Zealand and the Second World War*, ed. John Crawford (Auckland: Oxford University Press, 2000), 221.

16. "Report on the Mobilisation Branch for Period Sept 1939 to Sept 1945," 2, DA401.1-1, WAII, ANZ.

17. Taylor, *Home Front*, 1:110. Of the 65,000 volunteers 17,000 were found to be medically unfit, and 3,000 were held back on public interest grounds. "Report of the National Service Department," 9.

18. Director of National Service (DNS) to Minister of National Service, 2 February 1942, 83/3/11, EA1, ANZ. There were 16,200 males aged 19–45.

19. "Report on the Mobilisation Branch," 3. Some Maori who were wrongly called up in ballots opted to serve anyway and joined other 2 NZEF units.

20. "Report on the Mobilisation Branch," 2.

21. "Report of the National Service Department," 5.

22. DNS, "Amendment No. 12—National Service Emergency Regulations 1940," 20 June 1942, 1, NS-DN4, ANZ. See also "Report on the Mobilisation Branch," 2.

23. "Report of the National Service Department on Activities under the National Service Emergency Regulations 1940 and the Industrial Man-Power Emergency Regulations 1944," 28 June 1946, *AJHR*, 1946, H–11A, 21. The number of appeal boards declined to sixteen by February 1944.

24. "Report of the National Service Department," 6.

25. Taylor, *Home Front*, 1:247.

26. "Report of the National Service Department," 7.

27. "Report of the National Service Department," 10.

28. "Report of the National Service Department," 7.

29. "Report of the National Service Department," 33.

30. J. V. T. Baker, *The New Zealand People at War, War Economy* (Wellington: Historical Publications Branch, Department of Internal Affairs, 1965), 81.

31. Baker, *War Economy*, 97; "Report of the National Service Department on Activities," 134.

32. "Report of the National Service Department," 11.

33. Ibid.

34. Ian McGibbon, *New Zealand and the Second World War: The People, the Battles and the Legacy* (Auckland: Hodder Moa Beckett, 2003), 104–5. A third Australian division returned home after the battle of Alamein, October–November 1942.

35. McGibbon, *New Zealand and the Second World War*, 104–5.

36. "Report on the Mobilisation Branch," 11.

37. Peter Cooke and John Crawford, *The Territorials: The History of the Territorials and Volunteer Forces of New Zealand* (Auckland: Random House New Zealand, 2011), 238–39.

38. "Report of the National Service Department," 11.

39. "Report of the National Service Department," 11.

40. "Report of the National Service Department on Activities," 17.

41. Baker, *War Economy*, 81–82.

42. "Report of the National Service Department," 12.

43. "Report of the National Service Department," 12–13.

44. "Report on the Mobilisation Branch," 2.

45. "Report on the Mobilisation Branch," 99.

46. Taylor, *Home Front*, 2:1113.

47. Deborah Montgomerie, *Women's War, New Zealand Women 1939–45* (Auckland: Auckland University Press, 2001), 86.

48. Montgomerie, *Women's War*, 86; Baker, *War Economy*, 100.

49. Taylor, *Home Front*, 2:1074.

50. McGibbon, *New Zealand and the Second War*, 139.

51. McGibbon, *New Zealand and the Second War*, 134–35, 140–41.

52. "Report of the National Service Department," 21.

53. McGlynn, "History of the National Service Department," 122.

54. McGlynn, "History of the National Service Department," 128.

55. McGlynn, "History of the National Service Department," 140.

56. McGlynn, "History of the National Service Department," 13.

57. "Report on the Mobilisation Branch," 10; Wood, *The New Zealand People at War*, 267–69; McGibbon, *New Zealand and the Second World War*, 161.

58. "Report of the National Service Department on Activities," 6.

59. Coralie Clarkson, "The Reality of Return: Exploring the Experiences of World War One Soldiers after Their Return to New Zealand" (MA thesis, Victoria University of Wellington, 2011), 138.

60. Quoted in Jane Thomson, "The Policy of Land Sales Control: Sharing the Sacrifice," *New Zealand Journal of History* 25, no. 1 (1991): 3.

61. Thomson, "The Policy of Land Sales Control," 3.

62. "Rehabilitation Board, Report for Year Ended 31st March, 1944," *AJHR*, 1944, H–18, 4.

63. "Report of the National Service Department on Activities," 1946, 8.

64. "Rehabilitation Board, Report," 6, 8.

65. "Rehabilitation Board, Report," 26; Montgomerie, *Women's War*, 179–80.

66. Thomson, "The Policy of Land Sales Control," 9.

67. Thomson, "The Policy of Land Sales Control," 9.

68. Thomson, "The Policy of Land Sales Control," 8.

69. "Rehabilitation Board, Report," 18.

70. Thomson, "The Policy of Land Sales Control," 9.

71. Baker, *War Economy*, 517.

14. Caring for British Commonwealth Soldiers in the Aftermath of the Second World War

1. Rex Pope, "British Demobilization after the Second World War," *Journal of Contemporary History* 30, no. 1 (1995): 67; Peter Neary, Introduction, in *The Veterans Charter and Post–World War II Canada*, ed. Peter Neary and J. L. Granatstein (Montreal: Mc-Gill

Queen's University Press, 1998), 6; Graeme Powell and Stuart Macintyre, "Land of Opportunity: Australia's Post-War Reconstruction," National Archives of Australia, accessed August 2018, http://guides.naa.gov.au/land-of-opportunity/.

2. Jeff Keshen, "Getting It Right the Second Time Around: The Reintegration of Canadian Veterans of World War II." In *The Veterans Charter and Post–World War II Canada*, ed. Peter Neary and J. L. Granatstein (Montreal: Mc-Gill Queen's University Press, 1998), 69; After Victory in Europe, May 1945, A21.009 (D68), file 215, vol. 10508, Canadian Department of National Defence; news release, n.d., 7, vol. 272, Canadian Department of Veterans Affairs; Pope, "British Demobilization after the Second World War," 67–68; Graeme Powell and Stuart Macintyre, "Land of Opportunity: Australia's Post-War Reconstruction," National Archives of Australia, accessed August 2018, http://guides.naa.gov.au/land-of-opportunity/.

3. Powell and Macintyre, "Land of Opportunity," 67.

4. Desmond Morton, "'Kicking and Complaining': Demobilization Riots in the Canadian Expeditionary Force, 1918–1919," *Canadian Historical Review* 61, no. 3 (1980): 335.

5. Morton, "'Kicking and Complaining,'" 335.

6. Morton, "'Kicking and Complaining,'" 338.

7. "First World War: Western Front 1918," 20 June 2012, https://teara.govt.nz.en/first-world-war/page-7; Morton, "'Kicking and Complaining,'" 351.

8. Stephen Garton, "Demobilization and Empire: Empire Nationalism and Soldier Citizenship in Australia after the First World War—in Dominion Context," *Journal of Contemporary History* 50, no. 1 (2015): 136.

9. Pope, "British Demobilization," 66, 75; Keshen, "Getting It Right the Second Time Around," 70; Neary, Introduction, 10; Alex Cousley, Peter M. Siminski, and Simon Ville, "The Effects of World War II Military Service: Evidence from Australia," *Journal of Economic History* 77, no. 3 (2017): 838–65; Powell and Macintyre, *Land of Opportunity*; A. D. Macleod, "Psychiatric Casualties of World War II," *New Zealand Medical Journal* 113, July (2000): 248.

10. Eric Thornton, "Men in Morotai Protest at Shipping Delay," *Argus*, 11 December 1945: 1; Pope, "British Demobilization," 76.

11. Lloyd George, as quoted in "Ministry Men," University of Oxford World War I Centenary Continuations and Beginnings, accessed 1 September 2018, http://ww1centenary.oucs.ox.ac.uk/body-and-mind/lloyd-georges-ministry-men/.

12. Lloyd George, as quoted in "Ministry Men."

13. Garton, "Demobilization and Empire," 135; Neary, Introduction, 28; Nancy Taylor, *Official History of New Zealand in the Second World War, 1939–1945: Home Front Volume II* (Wellington: Historical Publications Branch, 1986), 1270; Deborah Cohen, *War Come Home: Disabled Veterans in Britain and Germany, 1914–1939* (Berkeley: University of California Press, 1999), 16.

14. Cohen, *War Come Home*, 16.

15. Coralie Clarkson, "Reality of Return: Exploring the Experiences of World War One Soldiers after Their Return to New Zealand," (MA Thesis: Victoria University of Wellington, 2011), 139–40.

16. Taylor, *Official History, II*: 1270.

17. Alice Aiken and Amy Buitenhuis, *Supporting Canadian Veterans with Disabilities* (Kingston: Defence Management Studies Program, School of Public Policy, Queen's

University, 2011), 6; Stephen Garton, *The Cost of War: Australians Return* (Melbourne: Oxford University Press, 1996), 80–81.

18. Canadian Department of Veterans Affairs (DVA), *Back to Civil Life* (Ottawa: DVA, 1946).

19. Ministry of Post-War Reconstruction, *Return to Civil Life* (Canberra: Commonwealth of Australia, 1945).

20. Walter S. Woods, *Rehabilitation (A Combined Operation)* (Ottawa: Queen's Printer, 1953), 16.

21. Relevant legislation includes, for the United Kingdom: War Pensions Act (1921), Pensions—Navy, Army, Air Force and Mercantile Marine Act (1939), Disabled Persons Employment Act (1944), Federated Superannuation System for Universities (War Service) Regulations (1949); for Canada: Pension Act (1941), Veteran's Land Act (1942), War Service Grants Act (1944), Veterans Rehabilitation Act (1945), Veterans' Business and Professional Loans Act (1946); for Australia: War Pensions Act (1916), Australian Soldier's Repatriation Act (1943), Re-Establishment and Employment Act (1945), War Gratuity Act (1945), Commonwealth Public Service Act (1947), Interim Forces Benefits Act (1947), Defence Forces Retirement Act (1948); and for New Zealand: Rehabilitation Act (1941), War Pensions Act (1943), Servicemen's Settlement and Land Sale Act (1943), Land Act (1948), Servicemen's Settlement Act (1950), War Pensions Act (1954). Veronica Hopner, *Home from War* (MA Thesis: Massey University, 2014), 71; H. J. Plunkett, *Land Developments by Government 1945–1969*, Technical Paper 14 (Lincoln College, 1971); Ashley Gould, *Proof of Gratitude? Soldier Land Settlement in New Zealand after World War I* (PhD dissertation, Massey University, 1992); Philip Payton, *Repat: A Concise History of Repatriation in Australia* (Canberra: DVA, 2018); Neary and Granatstein, *Veterans Charter*; and "UK Public General Acts," National Archives. Accessed 1 June 2018. https://www.legislation.gov.uk./ukpga.

22. The law entitled female veterans to the same rights as men. But it is questionable whether they benefited as much from these provisions. As Peter Neary points out, officials designed the system primarily to facilitate the return of male breadwinners to the civilian marketplace. It is also vital to note that Commonwealth governments generally extended the benefits afforded to veterans of the armed services to those men and women who served in auxiliary services. However, there is an important caveat. They were entitled to the same benefits, particularly those surrounding disability, only in the event that they served overseas in an active theater of war. Neary, Introduction, 10. Canadian Forces Advisory Council, *Origins and Evolution of Veterans Benefits in Canada* (Ottawa: Veterans Affairs Canada, 2004), 15; UK Ministry of Defence, "Guidance: War Pension Scheme: What You Need to Know" (London: HM Government. Last updated 16 August 2019. https://www.gov.uk/guidance/war-pension-scheme-wps ; and Canadian DVA, "Comparison with Allied Nations: Program Design," (Ottawa: Government of Canada, 2004).

23. Neary, Introduction, 8; Powell and Macintyre, *Land of Opportunity*; Taylor, *Home Front*, 1271–72; Canadian DVA, *Back to Civil Life*; and World Veterans Federation, *Social Affairs Rehabilitation, Comparative Report: Legislation Affecting Disabled Veterans and Other War Victims* WVF-DOC/830 (Paris: World Veterans Federation, September 1955), 4–49.

24. Taylor, *Official History, II*: 1278.

25. Taylor, *Official History, II*: 1279.

26. World Veterans Federation, *Social Affairs Rehabilitation*, 39–40; Keshen, "Getting It Right the Second Time Around," 72, 77; Powell and Macintyre, *Land of Opportunity*; Schedule A: Scale of Pensions for Disabilities, Percentage of Disabilities—Class and Annual Rate of Pensions, 1957–1958, PIN 15/3069, The National Archives (TNA).

27. Keshen, "Getting It Right the Second Time Around," 72, 77.

28. G. J. Downs, "Australia," *Journal of International and Comparative Social Welfare* 10.1 (1994): 20; World Veterans Federation, *Social Affairs Rehabilitation*, 47–49.

29. Neary, Introduction, 8–9; and Keshen, "Getting It Right the Second Time Around," 66.

30. Powell and Macintyre, *Land of Opportunity*.

31. Taylor, *Official History, II*: 1278–81.

32. Powell and Macintyre, *Land of Opportunity*.

33. World Veterans Federation, *Social Affairs Rehabilitation*, 40.

34. World Veterans Federation, *Social Affairs Rehabilitation*, 40; Veterans Affairs Canada—Canadian Forces Advisory Council, *Origins and Evolution of Veterans Benefits in Canada* (Ottawa: Veterans Affairs Canada, 2004; and Meghan Fitzpatrick, *Invisible Scars: Mental Trauma and the Korean War* (Vancouver and Toronto: University of British Columbia Press, 2017), pp. 85–86.

35. World Veterans Federation, Social Affairs Rehabilitation, 40–41; Sir Wilfred Kent Hughes, speech to the Commonwealth of Australia House of Representatives, Australian Universities Commission Bill 1959, Second Reading, 22 April 1959. https://historichansard.net/hofreps/1959/19590422_reps_23_hor23/.

36. Garton, *Cost of War*, 98.

37. Taylor, *Official History, II*: 1271–72.

38. Taylor, *Official History, II*: 1282.

39. Powell and Macintyre, *Land of Opportunity*.

40. The British were most indebted to their American ally, from whom they borrowed close to $4.3 billion USD in 1945 alone. Susan Howson, "Origins of Cheaper Money, 1945–1947," *Economic History Review*, n.s., 40, no. 3 (1987): 433.

41. Alan Allport, *Demobbed: Coming Home after the Second World War* (New Haven, CT: Yale University Press, 2009), 30.

42. Ben Shephard, *War of Nerves: Soldiers and Psychiatrists in the Twentieth Century* (Cambridge, MA: Harvard University Press, 2001), 327–28.

43. Shephard, *War of Nerves*, 327.

44. In contrast to Britain, American postwar veterans' legislation was exceedingly generous. Passed in 1944, the US Servicemen's Readjustment Bill, or GI Bill of Rights, closely mirrors laws passed and policies enacted across the Commonwealth. As in those nations, American lawmakers worked to ensure that returning service personnel could access everything from unemployment benefits to favorable business and home loans. However, the unprecedented growth of the US economy facilitated far more lavish provisions, particularly to finance education. This included benefits to cover tuition and living expenses for the veteran and associated dependents. Moreover, there was no limitation on the length of study. As a result, nearly 2.2 million attended university and another 5.6 million took vocational training. This represented 51 percent of US veterans and is widely credited for helping transform the American middle class. Suzanne Mettler, "How the GI Bill Built the Middle Class and Enhanced

Democracy," *Scholars Strategy Network Key Findings* (January 2012), 1; US Department of Veterans Affairs, "Born of Controversy: The GI Bill of Rights," accessed December 2019, https://www.va.gov/opa/publications/celebrate/gi-bill.pdf.

45. Pension and Rehabilitation Schemes of Dominions, Colonies and Other Countries (New War) CANADA, 1950s, PIN 15/3069, TNA; Commonwealth of Australia, House of Representatives, 26 September 1956 (Mr. Bryant Gordon), accessed 14 May 2018, https://historichansard.net/hofreps/1956/19560926_reps_22_hor12/; and Commonwealth of Australia, Senate, 16 September 1959 (Sir Walter Cooper), accessed 14 May 2018, https://historichansard.net/hofreps/1959/19590916_reps_23_hor24/.

46. Pension and Rehabilitation Schemes of Dominions, Colonies and Other Countries.

47. Pension and Rehabilitation Schemes of Dominions, Colonies and Other Countries; and Meghan Fitzpatrick, *Invisible Scars: Mental Trauma and the Korean War* (Vancouver and Toronto: University of British Columbia Press, 2017), 85–86.

48. UK Ministry of Pensions and National Insurance, Allowance for Lowered Standard of Occupation: Memo for the Information of Members of War Pensions Committees, 1964, PIN 59/84, TNA; Notes on War Pension Schemes of Great Britain, Canada, Australia, New Zealand and South Africa, September 1945, PIN 15/3069, TNA; Report on British War Pensioners for 1964, July 1965, PIN 18/500, TNA; Cousley, Siminski and Ville, "The Effects of World War II Military Service: Evidence from Australia"; Downs, "Australia," 18. The amount of financial compensation associated with the percentage disabled varied from country to country. Nonetheless, the UK system provides a fairly representative example. For instance, in the early 1960s a British veteran in receipt of a pension for 100 percent disablement would receive £6 15s a week (£118.92 in today's currency). Report on British War Pensioners for 1964; British National Archives Currency Converter, accessed 3 April 2018, http://www.nationalarchives.gov.uk/currency-converter/#currency-result.

49. There were some exceptions to the rules. For example, veterans received compensation in one lump sum payment if the disability was deemed "minor." However, countries varied in how they defined this term. In the United Kingdom, this included all ex-servicemen assessed as 20 percent disabled or less, but the Canadian government considered only cases fewer than 5 percent. World Veterans Federation, *Social Affairs Rehabilitation*, 32–33.

50. Notes on War Pension Schemes of Great Britain, Canada, Australia, New Zealand and South Africa; Downs, "Australia," 7, 10; and World Veterans Federation, *Social Affairs Rehabilitation*, 22–23.

51. Legislation provided prisoners of war (POWs) with the same pension rights as other ex-service members. In 1971, Canada became the only Commonwealth country to award a specific POW pension by agreeing to award former detainees of the Japanese military a "minimum disability of 50 per cent of the full disability pension . . . who had an assessed disability and had been imprisoned for a year or more." The Canadian government granted these veterans an additional 30 percent pension several years later in the 1976 Former Prisoners of War Act. It awarded disability pensions to all other POWs at "10 per cent for those who had been in captivity between 3 and 18 months; 15 per cent for . . . 18 and 30 months; and 20 per cent for anyone detained more than 30 months." Peter Yeend, *Compensation (Japanese Internment Bill)*, Bills Digest No. 6 (Can-

berra: Commonwealth of Australia, 2001), 7; Jonathan Vance, *Objects of Concern: Canadian Prisoners of War through the Twentieth Century* (Vancouver: University of British Columbia Press, 1994), 217–234; Aiken and Buitenhuis, *Supporting Canadian Veterans with Disabilities*, 4; Les Peate, Korean Veterans Association of Canada, email to author, 16 June 2012; and World Veterans Federation, *Social Affairs Rehabilitation*, 32.

52. Government departments responsible for pensions included: Ministry of Pensions and National Insurance (UK); Department of Veterans Affairs (Canada; presently Veterans Affairs Canada); Department of Repatriation (Australia; presently Department of Veterans Affairs); Department of Veterans Affairs (New Zealand). Report on War Pensioners for 1955, 1956, PIN 19/277, Ministry of Pensions and National Insurance, TNA (; Downs, "Australia"; World Veterans Federation, *Social Affairs Rehabilitation*, 4–6.

53. Pension and Rehabilitation Schemes of Dominions, Colonies and Other Countries; Government of New Zealand, War Pensions Act, 1954; Stephen Uttley, "New Zealand," *Journal of International and Comparative Social Welfare* 10, no.1 (1994): 46; Commonwealth of Australia, Senate, 16 September 1959 (Sir Walter Cooper).

54. Uttley, "New Zealand," 46.

55. Cousley, Siminski and Ville, "Effects of World War II Military Service"; Kim Beazley, Speech to Commonwealth of Australia House of Representatives, Repatriation Bill 1955, Second Reading, 13 October 1955, https://historichansard.net/hofreps/1955/19551013_reps_21_hor8/#subdebate-17-0; Law Commission, *A New Support Scheme for Veterans: A Report on the Review of The War Pensions Act 1954* (Wellington, New Zealand, May 2010), 78; and Fitzpatrick, *Invisible Scars*, 87.

56. A. E. W. Ward to Mr. Dennys, Royal Warrant—Onus of Proof, 3 July 1956, PIN 59/2, TNA; and World Veterans Federation, *Social Affairs Rehabilitation*; and Fitzpatrick, *Invisible Scars*, 87.

57. "Care for the Wounded and Ill—Canada's Treatment and Pension Policy," *Globe and Mail*, 21 November 1944; Report on British War Pensioners for 1964; and Committee Examining Ministry of Defence/National Health Service Collaboration, Use of Service Hospitals for War Pensioners, 15 September 1978, PIN 59/483, TNA; Powell and Macintyre, *Land of Opportunity*; Uttley, "New Zealand," 50.

58. World Veterans Federation, *Social Affairs Rehabilitation*, 44–45.

59. World Veterans Federation, *Social Affairs Rehabilitation*, 44–45.

60. Keshen, "Getting It Right the Second Time Around," 77.

61. Keshen, "Getting It Right the Second Time Around," 72, 77; Canadian DVA, *Back to Civil Life*; Mary Tremblay, "Going Back to Main Street: Development and Impact of Casualty Rehabilitation for Veterans with Disabilities, 1945–1948," in *The Veterans Charter and Post–World War II Canada*, ed. Peter Neary and J. L. Granatstein (Montreal: Mc-Gill Queen's University Press, 1998), 161–62, 165–67.

62. Julie Anderson, "'Turned into Taxpayers': Paraplegia, Rehabilitation and Sport at Stoke Mandeville, 1944–1956," *Journal of Contemporary History* 38, no. 3 (2003): 461–475.

63. Tremblay, "Going Back to Main Street," 165.

64. Senator Walter Cooper, Minister for Repatriation, Speech to the Commonwealth of Australia Senate, Appropriation Bill No. 2 (1949–1950), 22 June 1950. https://historichansard.net/senate/1950/19500622_senate_19_208/#subdebate-21-0.

65. Earle Brown and Michael F. Klassen, "War, Facial Surgery and Itinerant Kiwis: New Zealand Plastic Surgery Story," *Australasian Journal of Plastic Surgery* 1, no. 1 (2018): 58–74.

66. Terry Copp, "From Neurasthenia to Post-Traumatic Stress Disorder: Canadian Veterans and the Problem of Persistent Emotional Disabilities," in *The Veterans Charter and Post–World War II Canada*, ed. Peter Neary and J. L. Granatstein (Montreal: Mc-Gill Queen's University Press, 1998), 150–151; R. H. Ahrenfeldt, "Army Psychiatric Service," in *Medical Services in the War, Principal Medical Lessons of the Second World War*, ed. Salisbury McNalty and W. Franklin Mellor (London: HMSO, 1968), 108.

67. Kristy Muir, "The Predisposition Theory, Human Rights and Australian Psychiatric Casualties of War," *Australian Journal of Human Rights* 13, no. 1 (2007): 200–201.

68. Edgar Jones, Ian Palmer, and Simon Wessely, "War Pensions (1900–1945): Changing Models of Psychological Understanding," *British Journal of Psychiatry* 180 no. 4 (2002): 377.

69. Garton, *Cost of War*, 109–10.

70. Anon to Secretary, Mental Hospital Management Committee, 9 January 1951, PIN 59/216, TNA.

71. Garton, *Cost of War*, 109–110; and Fitzpatrick, *Invisible Scars*, 87.

72. Muir, "The Predisposition Theory," 199–200, 204.

73. Travis E. Dancey, "The Interaction of the Welfare State and the Disabled," *Canadian Medical Association Journal* 103 (August 1970): 274–77; Travis E. Dancey, "Treatment in the Absence of Pensioning for Psychoneurotic Veterans," *American Psychiatric Journal* 107, no. 5 (1950): 347; Harold Palmer, "The Problem of Neurosis in Ex-Soldiers," *New Zealand Medical Journal* (1949): 129.

74. Dancey, "Treatment in the Absence," 347.

75. Pension and Rehabilitation Schemes of Dominions, Colonies and Other Countries.

76. UK, House of Commons, *Debates*, 14 March 1960, *Hansard*, series 5, vol. 619, cc. 923–24; Pension and Rehabilitation Schemes of Dominions, Colonies and Other Countries; Uttley, "New Zealand," 46; World Veterans Federation, *Social Affairs Rehabilitation*, 15–20.

77. Thomas to Mr. Trew, 20 December 1957, PIN 2894, TNA; and Fitzpatrick, *Invisible Scars*, 88.

78. Atkinson, Memorandum—Decentralisation of Action—Other Rank Pensioners Receiving Psychiatric Treatment, PIN 59/216, TNA; Garton, *The Cost of War*, 167–69; F. J. Marcham, Norcross Awards: Report on the Service Patient Scheme for Mental Cases, April 1959, PIN 15/4084, TNA; Commonwealth of Australia, Senate, 22 June 1950 (Sir Walter Cooper). https://historichansard.net/senate/1950/19500622 _senate_19_208/#subdebate-21-0.

79. Bill Rawling, *Myriad Challenges of Peace: Canadian Forces Medical Practitioners Since the Second World War* (Ottawa: Canadian Government Publishing, 2004), 122–23, 247–49, 259; Colonel for Vice-Adjutant General to Secretary, Medical Services Coordinating Committee, 30 October 1958, PIN 14/44, TNA; Committee Examining Ministry of Defence/National Health Service Collaboration, Use of Service Hospitals for Pensioners, 15 September 1978, PIN 59/483, TNA; World Veterans Federation, *Social Affairs Rehabilitation*, 7–10; Dancey, "Interaction of the Welfare State and the Disabled," 275–77.

80. Muir, "The Predisposition Theory," 205.

81. Muir, "The Predisposition Theory," 205.

82. Anon to Mr. Birtles, 17 October 1957, PIN 15/4084, TNA; Anon to Secretary, Mental Hospital Management Committee, 9 January 1951, PIN 59/216, TNA; Garton,

The Cost of War, 167–69; Dancey, "Interaction of the Welfare State and the Disabled," 275–77; Dancey, "Treatment in the Absence of Pensioning," 348–49; Commonwealth of Australia, Senate, 22 June 1950 (Sir Walter Cooper); and Fitzpatrick, *Invisible Scars*, 89.

83. Paragraphs on War Pensions Proposed by the Mental Welfare Commission for Scotland for Inclusion the Forthcoming Report, April 1971, PIN 18/616, TNA; and Fitzpatrick, *Invisible Scars*, 92.

84. Anon to Mr. Birtles, 17 October 1957, PIN 15/4084, TNA; Report on British War Pensioners for the Year 1955, 1956, PIN 19/277, TNA; Anon to Secretary, Mental Hospital Management Committee; Marcham, Norcross Awards.

85. Note of a Meeting to Consider the Position of War Pensioners in Hospital, 13 July 1971, PIN 18/616, TNA; L. Errington to Miss Riddelsdell, War Pensioners in Hospital, 28 July 1971, PIN 35/416, TNA; R. G. Cope to Mr. Pagdin, 8 July 1971, PIN 18/616, TNA.

86. R. Windsor to Mr. Overend and Mr. Errington, War Pensions and Industrial Injuries, 2 July 1971, PIN 18/616, TNA; and Fitzpatrick, *Invisible Scars*, 93.

87. Norcross to Mr. Beavan, 17 November 1955, PIN 15/3144, TNA.

88. Norcross to Mr. Beavan; and Fitzpatrick, *Invisible Scars*, 90.

89. The authors of a 2002 British study estimate that the United Kingdom has awarded 30,000 pensions for psychoneurosis to Second World War veterans. In a recent study, Kristy Muir concludes that Australia has recognized approximately 31,503 ex-service members as psychiatric casualties from the First World War to Vietnam. New Zealand has granted around 10,070 pensions for mental health to veterans who served from 1939 to 1945. However, there are no accurate statistics available for Canada. Roughly 21 percent of all Canadian veterans currently in receipt of a disability pension receive benefits for a psychiatric diagnosis. Jones, Palmer, and Wessely, "War Pensions (1900–1945)," 377; Mr. Keith Cameron Wilson, Speech to the Commonwealth of Australia House of Representatives, Repatriation Bill 1958, Second Reading, 25 September 1958, https://historichansard.net/hofreps/1958/19580925_reps_22_hor21/#subdebate-33-0; Garton, *Cost of War*, 84, 115; Muir, "The Predisposition Theory," 196; Uttley, "New Zealand," 47; Alison Parr, *Silent Casualties: New Zealand's Unspoken Legacy of the Second World War* (North Shore: Tandem Press, 1995), 14–15; and Veterans Affairs Canada, "Mental Health," Government of Canada, accessed 12 September 2018, http://www.veterans.gc.ca/eng/about-us/statistics/8–0.

90. "Charles William Miller," Veterans Stories, Memory Project, accessed August 2018, http://www.thememoryproject.com/stories/1574:charles-william-miller/.

91. Kristy Muir, "Public Peace, Private Wars: The Psychological Effects of War on Australian Veterans," *War & Society* 26, no. 1 (2007): 68.

92. Muir, "Public Peace, Private Wars," 73.

93. "Conrad Landry, Army," Veterans Stories, Memory Project, accessed August 2018, http://www.thememoryproject.com/stories/1690:conrad-landry/.

94. Parr, *Silent Casualties*, 146.

95. Muir, "The Predisposition Theory," 196.

96. Neary, *On to Civvy Street*, 275.

97. R. Scott Sheffield, "Veterans' Benefits and Indigenous Veterans of the Second World War in Australia, Canada, New Zealand and the United States," *Wicazo SA Review* 32, no. 1 (Spring 2017): 64.

Conclusion: The Many Dimensions of Mobilizing Military Manpower

1. National Resources Mobilization Act, 1940, *Acts of the Parliament of Canada, 1939–1940* (Ottawa: King's Printer, 1940), 43.

2. Timothy Winegard, *Indigenous Peoples of the Dominions and the First World War* (Cambridge: Cambridge University Press, 2012); R. Scott Sheffield and Noah Riseman, *Indigenous Peoples and the Second World War: The Politics, Experiences, and Legacies of War in the US, Canada, Australia, and New Zealand* (Cambridge: Cambridge University Press, 2018).

3. War Office, *Statistics of the Military Effort of the British Empire During the Great War, 1914–1920* (London: HMSO, 1922), 29–30, 739–79.

4. See John C. Mitcham, *Race and Imperial Defence in the British World, 1870–1914* (Cambridge: Cambridge University Press, 2016); Jesse Tumblin, *The Quest for Security: Sovereignty, Race, and the Defense of the British Empire, 1898–1931* (Cambridge: Cambridge University Press, 2019).

Select Bibliography

The following works deal in whole or in part with the issue of military manpower for the British Empire and Commonwealth in the era of the two world wars.

Allport, Alan. *Browned Off and Bloody-Minded: The British Soldier Goes to War, 1939–1945*. New Haven, CT: Yale University Press, 2015.

Anderson, Julie. *War, Disability and Rehabilitation in Britain: "Soul of a Nation."* Manchester: Manchester University Press, 2011.

Baker, J. V. T. *The New Zealand People at War, War Economy*. Wellington: Historical Publications Branch, Department of Internal Affairs, 1965.

Baker, Paul. *King and Country Call: New Zealanders, Conscription, and the Great War*. Auckland: Auckland University Press, 1988.

Bartlett, Thomas, and Keith Jeffery. "An Irish Military Tradition?" In *A Military History of Ireland*, edited by Thomas Bartlett and Keith Jeffery. Cambridge: Cambridge University Press, 1996, 1–25.

Bartrop, Paul R., and Gabrielle Eisen, eds. *The Dunera Affair: A Documentary Resource Book*. Melbourne: Schwartz and Wilkinson / Jewish Museum of Australia, 1990.

Bean, Charles. *Official History of Australia in the War of 1914–1918*, vol. 3, *The Australian Imperial Force in France, 1916*. Sydney: Angus and Robertson, 1941.

Beaumont, Joan. *Broken Nation*. Crows Nest, NSW: Allen and Unwin, 2013.

Beckett, Ian F. W., and Keith Simpson, eds., *A Nation in Arms: The British Army and the First World War*. Barnsley South Yorkshire: Pen & Sword, 2014.

Bou, Jean, and Peter Dennis. *The Centenary History of Australia and the Great War*, vol. 5, *The Australian Imperial Force*. South Melbourne: Oxford University Press, 2016.

Bowman, Timothy. *Carson's Army: The Ulster Volunteer Force, 1910–22*. Manchester: Manchester University Press, 2007.

Broad, Roger. *Volunteers and Pressed Men: How Britain and Its Empire Raised Its Forces in Two World Wars*. Croydon: Fonthill, 2016.

Byers, Daniel. *Zombie Army: The Canadian Army and Conscription in the Second World War*. Vancouver: University of British Columbia Press, 2016.

Campbell, James D. *The Army Isn't All Work: Physical Culture and the Evolution of the British Army, 1860–1920*. London: Routledge, 2017.

Cannadine, David. *The Decline and Fall of the British Aristocracy*. London: Penguin, 2005 [1990].

Caplan, Lionel. *Warrior Gentleman: "Gurkhas" in the Western Imagination*. Oxford: Berghahn Books, 1995.

Churchill, Winston S. "The Few." Speech to the House of Commons, 20 August 1940. The International Churchill Society. Accessed 8 December 2020. https://winstonchurchill.org/resources/speeches/1940-the-finest-hour/the-few/.

Cohen, Deborah. *The War Come Home: Disabled Veterans in Great Britain and Germany, 1914–1939*. Berkeley: University of California Press, 2001.

Constantine, Stephen, and Marjory Harper. *Migration and Empire*, companion series, *Oxford History of the British Empire*. Oxford: Oxford University Press, 2010.

Copp, Terry, and Mark Osborne Humphries, eds. *Combat Stress in the 20th Century: The Commonwealth Perspective*. Kingston, ON: Canadian Defence Academy Press, 2010.

Crang, Jeremy A. *The British Army and the People's War*. Manchester: Manchester University Press, 2000.

Crawford, John. "'The Willing Horse Is Being Worked to Death': New Zealand's Manpower Problems and Policies in 1917." In *Turning Point 1917: The British Empire at War*, edited by Douglas E. Delaney and Nikolas Gardner. Vancouver: University of British Columbia Press, 2017, 114–38.

Crawford, John, and Ian McGibbon, eds. *New Zealand's Great War: New Zealand, The Allies & The First World War*. Auckland: Exisle Publishing, 2007.

Crew, Francis A. *The Army Medical Services, Administration, Volume I*. London: HMSO, 1953.

Das, Santanu. *India, Empire, and First World War Culture: Writings, Images, and Songs*. Cambridge: Cambridge University Press, 2018.

Delaney, Douglas E. *The Imperial Army Project: Britain and the Land Forces of the Dominions and India, 1902–1945*. Oxford: Oxford University Press, 2017.

Delaney, Douglas E., and Nikolas Gardner, eds. *Turning Point 1917: The British Empire at War*. Vancouver: University of British Columbia Press, 2017.

Denman, Terence. "The Catholic Irish Soldier in the First World War: The 'Racial Environment,'" *Irish Historical Studies* 27, no. 108 (1991): 352–65.

Durflinger, Serge Marc. *Veterans with a Vision: Canada's War Blinded in Peace and War*. Vancouver: University of British Columbia Press, 2010.

Ellinwood, DeWitt C., and S. D. Pradhan, eds. *India and World War I*. New Delhi: Manohar, 1978.

Fedorowich, Kent. "The British Empire on the Move." In *The British Empire: Themes and Perspectives*, edited by Sarah Stockwell. Oxford: Blackwell Publishing, 2008.

Fitzpatrick, David. "The Logic of Collective Sacrifice: Ireland and the British Army, 1914–1918." *Historical Journal* 38, no. 4 (1995): 1017–30.

——. "Militarism in Ireland, 1900–1922." In *A Military History of Ireland*, edited by Thomas Bartlett and Keith Jeffery. Cambridge: Cambridge University Press, 1996, 380–401.

Garton, Stephen. *The Cost of War: Australians Return*. Melbourne: Oxford University Press, 1996.

Granatstein, J. L. *Canada's War: The Politics of the Mackenzie King Government, 1939–1945*. Toronto: Oxford University Press, 1975.

Granatstein, J. L., and J. M. Hitsman. *Broken Promises: A History of Conscription in Canada*. Toronto: Oxford University Press, 1977.

Granatstein, J. L., and Peter Neary, eds. *The Veterans Charter and Post–World War II Canada*. Montreal: McGill-Queen's University Press, 1998.

Grayson, Richard S. *Belfast Boys: How Unionists and Nationalists Fought and Died Together in the First World War*. London: Continuum, 2009.

Greene, B. M, ed. *Who's Who and Why, 1919–20*. Toronto: International Press, n.d.

Grey, Jeffrey. *The Australian Army*. Melbourne: Oxford University Press, 2001.

Grieves, Keith. *The Politics of Manpower, 1914–1918*. Manchester: Manchester University Press, 1988.

Grundlingh, Albert. "The King's Afrikaners? Enlistment and Ethnic Identity in the Union of South Africa's Defence Force during the Second World War, 1939–45." *Journal of African History* 40, no. 3 (1999): 351–65.

Grundlingh, Louis. "The Military, Race, and Resistance: The Conundrums of Recruiting Black South African Men during the Second World War." In *Africa and World War II*, edited by Judith A. Byfield et al. Judith A. Byfield, Carolyn A. Brown, Timothy Parson, and Ahmad Alawad Sikainga, New York:, Cambridge University Press, 2015, 86–88.

Harris, Stephen. *Canadian Brass: the Making of a Professional Army, 1860–1939*. Toronto: University of Toronto Press, 1988.

Harrison, Mark. *The Medical War: British Military Medicine in the First World War*. Oxford: Oxford University Press, 2010.

Holt, Richard. *Filling the Ranks: Manpower in the Canadian Expeditionary Force, 1914–1918*. Montreal: McGill-Queen's University Press, 2017.

Humphries, Mark Osborne. *A Weary Road: Shell Shock in the Canadian Expeditionary Force, 1914–1918*. Toronto: University of Toronto Press, 2018.

Inglis, Ken, Seumas Spark, and Jay Winter, eds. *Dunera Lives: A Visual History*. Clayton, Victoria: Monash University Publishing, 2018.

Jones, Edgar, and Simon Wessely. *Shell Shock to PTSD: Military Psychiatry from 1900 to the Gulf War*. New York: Psychology Press, 2005.

Keshen, Jeff. "Getting It Right the Second Time Around: The Reintegration of Canadian Veterans of World War II." In *The Veterans Charter and Post–World War II Canada*, edited by Peter Neary and J. L. Granatstein. Montreal: McGill-Queen's University Press, 1998.

Larsson, Marina. *Shattered Anzacs: Living with the Scars of War*. Sydney: University of New South Wales Press, 2009.

Macintyre, Stuart, and Graeme Powell. "Land of Opportunity: Australia's Post-War Reconstruction." National Archives of Australia. Accessed August 2018. http://guides.naa.gov.au/land-of-opportunity/.

Macpherson, W. G. *History of the Great War Based on Official Documents*, Vol. 1, *Medical Services General History*. London: HMSO, 1921.

Marston, D. P. *Phoenix from the Ashes: The Indian Army in the Burma Campaign*. Westport, CT: Praeger Publishers, 2003.

Marti, Steve. *For Home and Empire: Voluntary Mobilization in Australia, Canada, and New Zealand during the First World War*. Vancouver: University of British Columbia Press, 2019.

Marti, Steve, and William John Pratt, eds. *Fighting with the Empire: Canada, Britain, and Global Conflict, 1867–1947*. Vancouver: University of British Columbia Press, 2019.

Martin, H. J., and N. D. Orpen. *South Africa at War: Military and Industrial Organization and Operations in Connection with the Conduct of the War, 1939–1945*. Cape Town: Purnell, 1979.

McGlynn, M. B. "History of the National Service Department, Manpower September 1939 to July 1940," unpublished narrative, April 1948, 1–2. Archives New Zealand, War Archives 121/31.

Meyer, Jessica. *Men of War: Masculinity and the First World War in Britain*. London: Palgrave Macmillan, 2009.

Mitcham, John C. *Race and Imperial Defence in the British World, 1870–1914*. Cambridge: Cambridge University Press, 2016.

Morton, Desmond. *When Your Number's Up: The Canadian Soldier in the First World War*. Toronto: Random House, 1993.

Morton-Jack, George. *The Indian Empire at War: From Jihad to Victory, the Untold Story of the Indian Army in the First World War*. London: Little, Brown, 2018.

Neary, Peter. Introduction. In *The Veterans Charter and Post–World War II Canada*, edited by Peter Neary and J. L. Granatstein. Montreal: McGill-Queen's University Press, 1998.

O'Dwyer, Michael. *India as I Knew It*. N.d. Reprint, New Delhi: Mittal Publications, 2004.

Omissi, David. *The Sepoy and the Raj: The Indian Army, 1860–1940*. London: MacMillan, 1994.

Palazzo, Albert. *The Australian Army: A History of Its Organization, 1901–2001*. Melbourne: Oxford University Press, 2001.

Parker, H. M. D. *Manpower*. London: HMSO, 1957.

Parr, Alison. *Silent Casualties: New Zealand's Unspoken Legacy of the Second World War*. North Shore, New Zealand: Tandem Press, 1995.

Perry, F. W. *The Commonwealth Armies: Manpower and Organisation in Two World Wars*. Manchester: Manchester University Press, 1988.

Piggott, A. J. K. *Manpower Problems*. London: HMSO, 1949.

Pope, Rex. "British Demobilization after the Second World War." *Journal of Contemporary History* 30, no. 1 (January 1995).

Prasad, S. N. *Expansion of the Armed Forces and Defence Organization, 1939–45*. Calcutta: Combined Inter-Services Historical Section, 1956.

Reitz, J. F. *Memoirs of a Somehow Soldier*. Private: Caledon, Western Cape, n.d.

"Report of the National Service Department." June 1, 1943. *Appendices to the Journals of the House of Representatives (AJHR)*, 1943, H-11A.

"Report on the Mobilisation Branch for period Sept 1939 to Sept 1945." 2, ANZ, WAII, DA401.

Reznick, Jeffrey S. *Healing the Nation: Soldiers and the Culture of Caregiving in Britain during the Great War*. Cultural History of War series. Manchester: Manchester University Press, 2011.

Roy, Kaushik. *India and World War II: War, Armed Forces, and Society, 1939–45*. New Delhi: Oxford University Press, 2016.

Roy, Kaushik, ed. *The Indian Army in the Two World Wars*. Leiden: Brill, 2012.

Sandford, Stephen. *Neither Unionist nor Nationalist: The 10th (Irish) Division in the Great War*. Dublin: Irish Academic Press, 2015.

Sheffield, Gary. *Leadership in the Trenches: Officer-Man Relations, Morale and Discipline in the British Army in the Era of the First World War*. Basingstoke: Macmillan, 2000.

Sheffield, R. Scott, and Noah Riseman. *Indigenous Peoples and the Second World War: The Politics, Experiences, and Legacies of War in the US, Canada, Australia, and New Zealand*. Cambridge: Cambridge University Press, 2018.

Simkins, Peter. *Kitchener's Army: The Raising of the New Armies, 1914–1916*. Barnsley, South Yorkshire: Pen & Sword, 2007.

Stacey, C. P. *Arms, Men and Governments: The War Policies of Canada, 1939–1945*. Ottawa: Queen's Printer, 1970.

Stapleton, Tim. "The Africanization of British Imperial Forces in the East African Campaign." In *Turning Point 1917: The British Empire at War*, edited by Douglas E. Delaney and Nikolas Gardner. Vancouver: University of British Columbia Press, 2017, 139–59.

Stevens, W. G. *Official History of New Zealand in the Second World War, 1939–1945: Problems of 2 NZEF*. Wellington: War History Branch, 1958.

Stevenson, Michael D. *Canada's Greatest Wartime Muddle: National Selective Service and the Mobilization of Human Resources during World War II*. Montreal: McGill-Queen's University Press, 2001.

Sundaram, Chandar S. *Indianization, the Officer Corps, and the Indian Army: The Forgotten Debate, 1817–1917*. Lanham, Maryland: Lexington Books, 2019.

Taylor, Nancy M. *The New Zealand People at War, The Home Front*, 2 vols. Wellington: Historical Publications Branch, Department of Internal Affairs, 1986.

Tumblin, Jesse. *The Quest for Security: Sovereignty, Race, and the Defense of the British Empire, 1898–1931*. Cambridge: Cambridge University Press, 2020.

van der Waag, Ian. *A Military History of Modern South Africa*. Johannesburg: Jonathan Ball, 2015.

War Office, *Statistics of the Military Effort of the British Empire during the Great War, 1914–1920*. London: HMSO, 1922.

——. *Physical and Recreational Training*. London: HMSO, 1941.

——. *Basic and Battle Physical Training: Part I, General Principles of Basic and Battle Physical Training and Methods of Instruction*. London: HMSO, 1944.

Winegard, Timothy. *Indigenous Peoples of the Dominions and the First World War*. Cambridge: Cambridge University Press, 2012.

Winter, J. M. *The Great War and the British People*. Basingstoke: Macmillan, 1985.

Woods, James. *Militia Myths: Ideas of the Canadian Citizen Soldier, 1896–1921*. Vancouver: University of British Columbia Press, 2010.

Yong, Tan Tai. *The Garrison State: The Military, Government and Society in Colonial Punjab, 1849–1947*. New Delhi: SAGE, 2005.

Notes on Contributors

Paul R. Bartrop is Visiting Professorial Fellow at the University of New South Wales (Australian Defence Force Academy), Canberra. He was formerly Professor of History at Florida Gulf Coast University, Fort Myers, Florida. His research interests include the Holocaust, modern Jewish history, genocide in the modern world, the two world wars, and Europe in the twentieth century. His recent publications include *Children of the Holocaust* (2020), and (ed.), *The Routledge History of the Second World War* (2021), *Heroines of Vichy France: Rescuing French Jews during the Holocaust* (2019), *Perpetrating the Holocaust: Leaders, Enablers, and Collaborators* (2019), *The Evian Conference of 1938 and the Jewish Refugee Crisis* (2018). He is coeditor of the four-volume *The Holocaust: An Encyclopedia and Document Collection* (2017), which won the Society for Military History Distinguished Book Award for 2018 (Reference).

Charles Booth is associate professor in Strategy and Organisation at the University of the West of England, Bristol. He was one of the founding editors of the academic journal *Management & Organizational History*. His current research interests include issues of public memory and commemoration, counterfactual and other modal narratives in organizational history and future studies, and critical management and organizational history more generally. Among his publications are *Boundary work in theory and practice: Past, present and future* (2014), "Термен не мрет: A fractional biography of failure" (2013, *Management & Organizational History*), "Post-modernity and the exceptionalism of the present in dark tourism" (2012, *Unconventional Parks, Tourism and Recreation Research*, with Rebecca Casbeard), and "Social remembering and organizational memory" (2010, *Organization Studies*, with Michael Rowlinson, Peter Clark, Agnes Delahaye, and Stephen Procter).

Jean Bou is senior lecturer in the Strategic and Defence Studies Centre at the Australian National University. He also lectures at the Australian Command and Staff College. In 2006 he joined the SDSC as a researcher for the Official History of Australian Peacekeeping, Humanitarian, and Post-Cold War

Operations and is the coauthor of the forthcoming fourth volume. He has also been a historian in the Military Section of the Australian War Memorial. He is the author or coeditor of several books on Australian military history. He has a particular interest in Australian military history from before federation to today, with an emphasis on aspects of late-colonial/early federation defense, and the First and Second World Wars.

ANDREW L. BROWN is a serving officer in the Canadian Army and currently teaches in the history department at the Royal Military College of Canada. He is a graduate of the Canadian Army Command and Staff College and the Joint Command and Staff Programme at the Canadian Forces College. His research interests include the Canadian Army in the world wars, officer and NCO training in the Canadian Army, and the role of intelligence in military operations.

DANIEL BYERS is associate professor of History at Laurentian University. A leading expert on Canada in the Second World War, he is the author of *Zombie Army: The Canadian Army and Conscription in the Second World War* (2016), published as part of the award-winning Studies in Canadian Military History series at the University of British Columbia Press. He is also the author of numerous articles on Canada in the period of the two world wars.

DOUGLAS E. DELANEY holds the Canada Research Chair (CRC) in War Studies at the Royal Military College of Canada. He is the author of *The Soldiers' General: Bert Hoffmeister at War* (2005), which won the 2007 C. P. Stacey Prize for Canadian Military History, *Corps Commanders: Five British and Canadian Generals at War, 1939–1945* (2011), and *The Imperial Army Project: Britain and the Land Forces of the Dominions and India, 1902–1945* (2018). He is also coeditor of *Turning Point 1917: The British Empire at War* (2017) and *Capturing Hill 70: Canada's Forgotten Battle of the First World War* (2016).

KENT FEDOROWICH is a specialist in Anglo-dominion relations and a reader in British Imperial and Commonwealth history at the University of the West of England (Bristol). His areas of expertise and interest include the prisoner of war experience, empire migration, and the British World. He has published widely on these subjects in learned journals and scholarly collections of essays. Among his publications are (with Bob Moore) *The British Empire and its Italian Prisoners of War, 1940–1947* (2002); edited with Andrew S. Thompson, *Empire, migration and identity in the British World* (2013); and edited with Jayne Gifford, *Sir Earle Page's British War Cabinet Diary, 1941–1942* (2021). In September 2020, he was appointed as a Research Fellow in the Department of Military History, School for Security and Africa, Faculty of Military Science, at Stellenbosch University (South Africa).

JONATHAN FENNELL is Reader in Modern History in the Department of Defence Studies, King's College London, and codirector of the Sir Michael Howard Centre for the History of War. His research focuses on the political, sociocultural, and institutional factors affecting the conduct of war and experience of soldiers on the battlefield. He has written extensively about British and Commonwealth forces during the Second World War. His recent book, *Fighting the People's War: The British and Commonwealth Armies and the Second World War* (2019), won the Royal United Services Institute (RUSI) Duke of Wellington Medal for Military History 2020, and the Society for Army Historical Research Templer Medal for the History of the British Army 2020.

MEGHAN FITZPATRICK specializes in the history of operational stress injuries and military health. Her work has been published in various journals, including Oxford's *Social History of Medicine*. Her book, *Invisible Scars* (2017), offers the first extended exploration of British Commonwealth psychiatric practices during the Korean War (1950–1953) and provides an intimate look at the history of military psychological trauma in the twentieth century.

MARK FROST is the postdoctoral research fellow in war studies at the Royal Military College of Canada. He received his PhD from King's College London and has taught as a graduate teaching assistant in the Defence Studies Department of King's College, based at the Joint Services Command and Staff College, Shrivenham, UK. He is also a member of the King's Second World War Research Group. His chapter on "The British and Indian Army Staff Colleges in the Interwar Years" appeared in *Military Education and the British Empire, 1815–1949*, edited by D. E. Delaney, R. C. Engen and M. Fitzpatrick (2018).

RICHARD S. GRAYSON is one of the foremost authorities on both Ireland in the First World War and the history of Irish identity. A professor of twentieth century history, and Head of History at Goldsmiths, University of London, he is also the chair of the Imperial War Museum's Academic Advisory Group and a member of the Northern Ireland World War I Centenary Project. He is coeditor of the British Journal for Military History and has authored, coauthored, or edited seven books and published more than twenty articles and book chapters. He is currently working on *Dublin's Great Wars: Home Rule, The First World War, the Easter Rising and Ireland's Fight for Independence, 1912–1923*.

Ian McGibbon is a historian with the New Zealand Ministry for Culture and Heritage. One of the preeminent experts in his field, he is a specialist in New Zealand diplomatic and military history focusing in particular on New Zealand's involvement in twentieth century wars. He has published the two-volume official history of New Zealand's involvement in the Korean War, *New Zealand and the Korean War, Volume 1, Politics and Diplomacy* (1992) and *New Zealand and the Korean War, Volume II, Combat Operations* (1996), a history of New Zealand's involvement in the Second World War, *New Zealand and the Second World War, The People, the battles and the legacy* (2004), *New Zealand's Vietnam War, A history of combat, commitment and controversy* (2010), and the *Oxford Companion to New Zealand Military History* (2000). In 1997 he was made an Officer of the New Zealand Order of Merit for services to historical research.

Jessica Meyer is Associate Professor of Modern British History at the University of Leeds. Her research interests include the histories of gender, particularly masculinity, medicine and warfare. She has published extensively about masculine identity and the medical history of war. She is the author of two major monographs in her field: *Men of War: Masculinity and the First World War in Britain* (2009) and *An Equal Burden: The Men of the Royal Army Medical Corps in the First World War* (2019). She is currently undertaking a research project on the history of post–First World War civil reintegration and disability pensions in Britain.

Emma Newlands is a lecturer in modern British history at the University of Strathclyde, Glasgow. Her research interests focus on war, medicine, and military culture. She is the author of *Civilians into Soldiers: War, the Body and British Army Recruits, 1939–1945* (2014). She is currently working on a project on health in the British Armed Forces in the postwar era, which involves conducting oral history interviews with ex-service personnel to understand how they have engaged with and resisted military healthcare regimes.

Kaushik Roy is Guru Nanak Chair Professor in the Department of History, Jadavpur University, Kolkata, India, and Global Fellow at the Peace Research Institute, Oslo, Norway. He is one of the world's leading historians on the Indian Army in both world wars. He has authored, coauthored, or edited more than twenty books and has written more than fifty articles for edited volumes and peer-reviewed journals.

Roger Sarty teaches in the Department of History, Wilfrid Laurier University. He was historian at the Department of National Defence, contributed to the official history of the Royal Canadian Air Force, and led the Royal Canadian Navy official history team. He was head of the Exhibition Development and Historical Research Division at the Canadian War Museum and then deputy director of the museum. He is currently working on a documents volume on the origins and early development of the Canadian navy, 1867–1923, and a biographical and historiographical study of the first Canadian academic military historians, 1936–1967.

GARY SHEFFIELD is professor of War Studies at the University of Wolverhampton. He began his academic career in the Department of War Studies, Royal Military Academy Sandhurst, before joining the Defence Studies Department of King's College London, based at the Joint Services Command and Staff College, where he was Land Warfare Historian on the Higher Command and Staff Course. He was chair of War Studies at the University of Birmingham before moving to Wolverhampton in 2013. An internationally recognized expert on the First World War, especially the role of the British Army, he is the author or editor of over twenty books, including *The Chief: Douglas Haig and the British Army* (2011), *The Somme* (2004), and *Forgotten Victory: The First World War—Myths and Realities* (2001), and the author or coauthor of numerous articles and book chapters. He is currently writing *Civilian Armies: The Experience of British and Dominion Soldiers in the Two World Wars*.

IAN VAN DER WAAG is professor and head of the Department of Military History at the University of Stellenbosch, as well as a Fellow of the Modern War Institute, at the United States Military Academy, West Point. A leading authority in his field, he is the author of *A Military History of Modern South Africa* (2015). The first book of its kind, it provides an overview of the South African experience of war from 1899 to 2000. He is the author, coauthor, or editor of seven books and has published more than thirty articles and chapters in peer-reviewed journals and collections.

Index

Figures and tables are indicated by f and t following the page number.